Depressive Rumination

NATURE, THEORY AND TREATMENT

Depressive Rumination

NATURE, THEORY AND TREATMENT

Edited by

COSTAS PAPAGEORGIOU

University of Lancaster, UK

ADRIAN WELLS

University of Manchester, UK

WILEY

AP 5 '07

This publication is designed to provide accurate and authoritative information in regard to
the subject matter covered. It is sold on the understanding that the Publisher is not engaged
in rendering professional services. If professional advice or other expert assistance is
required, the services of a competent professional should be sought.

Other Wiley Editorial Offices

John Wiley & Sons Inc., 111 River Street, Hoboken, NJ 07030, USA

Jossey-Bass, 989 Market Street, San Francisco, CA 94103-1741, USA

Wiley-VCH Verlag GmbH, Boschstr. 12, D-69469 Weinheim, Germany

John Wiley & Sons Australia Ltd, 33 Park Road, Milton, Queensland 4064, Australia

John Wiley & Sons (Asia) Pte Ltd, 2 Clementi Loop #02-01, Jin Xing Distripark, Singapore 129809

John Wiley & Sons Canada Ltd, 22 Worcester Road, Etobicoke, Ontario, Canada M9W 1L1

Wiley also publishes its books in a variety of electronic formats. Some content that appears in print
may not be available in electronic books.

Library of Congress Cataloging-in-Publicaton Data

Depressive rumination : nature, theory, and treatment / edited by
  Costas Papageorgiou, Adrian Wells.
    p. cm.
Includes bibliographical references and index.
ISBN 0-471-48692-2 (cloth : alk. paper) – ISBN 0-471-48693-0 (pbk. : alk paper)
    1. Depression, Mental.   2. Emotions and cognition.
I. Papageorgiou, Costas.   II. Wells, Adrian.
RC537.D457 2004
616.85'27 – dc21   2003008385

British Library Cataloguing in Publication Data

A catalogue record for this book is available from the British Library

ISBN 0-471-48692-2 (hbk)
ISBN 0-471-48693-0 (pbk)

Project management by Originator, Gt Yarmouth, Norfolk (typeset in 10/12pt Times)
Printed and bound in Great Britain by TJ International Ltd, Padstow, Cornwall
This book is printed on acid-free paper responsibly manufactured from sustainable forestry
in which at least two trees are planted for each one used for paper production.

Contents

About the Editors

Costas Papageorgiou is Senior Lecturer at Lancaster University and was Deputy Director of the Specialist Service for Affective (Mood) Disorders in Manchester. He obtained a BSc from the University of Buckingham and an MA and a Doctorate in Clinical Psychology from the University of Liverpool. Dr Papageorgiou has expertise in the assessment and treatment of depression. He has been extensively involved in investigating rumination and depression and has co-authored the first empirical studies examining the link between rumination, depression, and metacognition. Dr Papageorgiou has presented papers in numerous national and international conferences and published peer-reviewed articles on cognitive and metacognitive theory and therapy of emotional disorders, particulary depression. He has guest-edited two special issues on the Persistence of Depressive and Anxious Thinking (*Behavior Therapy*) and Rumination and Depression (*Cognitive Therapy and Research*).

Adrian Wells is Reader in Clinical Psychology at the University of Manchester and Professor at the Norwegian University of Science and Technology, Trondheim. He is recognized for his contribution to the development of cognitive theory and therapy of emotional disorders. He has published widely in peer-review journals and has authored/co-authored several ground-breaking books in the field. These works include: *Cognitive Therapy of Anxiety Disorders: A Practice Manual and Conceptual Guide* (John Wiley & Sons); *Emotional Disorders and Metacognition: Innovative Cognitive Therapy* (John Wiley & Sons); and *Attention and Emotion: A Clinical Perspective* (Lawrence Erlbaum). Professor Wells' research interests are in the areas of cognitive–attentional processes in emotional disorder, metacognition and cognitive therapy, and specific disorders including social phobia, generalized anxiety, PTSD, and obsessional problems. He is a pioneer of "metacognitive therapy" for emotional disorders.

Contributors

Lyn Y. Abramson, Department of Psychology, University of Wisconsin-Madison, 1202 West Johnson Street, Madison, WI 53706-1696, USA

Lauren B. Alloy, Departmet of Psychology, Temple University, 1701 North 13th Street, Philadelphia, PA 19122, USA

Melissa A. Brotman, Department of Psychology, University of Pennsylvania, 3815 Walnut Street, Philadelphia, PA 19104-6196, USA

Robert J. DeRubeis, Department of Psychology, University of Pennsylvania, 3815 Walnut Street, Philadelphia, PA 19104-6196, USA

Peter Fisher, Academic Division of Clinical Psychology, University of Manchester, Rawnsley Building, Manchester Royal Infirmary, Oxford Road, Manchester M13 9WL, UK

Olivier Luminet, Research Unit for Emotion, Cognition, and Health, Department of Psychology, University of Louvain at Louvain-la-Neuve, 10 Place Cardinal Mercier, B-1348 Louvain-la-Neuve, Belgium

Sonja Lyubomirsky, Department of Psychology, University of California, Riverside, CA 92521, USA

Donal MacCoon, Department of Psychology, University of Wisconsin-Madison, 1202 West Johnson Street, Madison, WI 53706-1696, USA

Leonard L. Martin, Department of Psychology, University of Georgia, Athens, GA 30602-3013, USA

Gerald Matthews, Department of Psychology, University of Cincinnati, Cincinnati, OH 45221-0376, USA

Dean McMillan, Academic Division of Clinical Psychology, University of Manchester, Rawnsley Building, Manchester Royal Infirmary, Oxford Road, Manchester M13 9WL, UK

Susan Nolen-Hoeksema, Department of Psychology, University of Michigan, 525 East University Avenue, Ann Arbor, MI 48109-1109, USA

Costas Papageorgiou, Doctoral Programme in Clinical Psychology, Institute for Health Research, University of Lancaster, Lancaster LA1 4YT, UK

Christine Purdon, Department of Psychology, University of Waterloo, Waterloo, Ontario N2L 3G1, Canada

Matthew S. Robinson, Massachusetts Mental Health Center, 74 Fenwood Road, Boston, MA 02155, USA

Ilan Shrira, Department of Psychology, University of Georgia, Athens, GA 30602-3013, USA

Greg J. Siegle, Western Psychiatric Institute and Clinic, University of Pittsburgh School of Medicine, 3811 O'Hara Street, Pittsburgh, PA 15213, USA

Jelena Spasojević, Department of Psychology, Temple University, 1701 North 13th Street, Philadelphia, PA 19122, USA

Helen M. Startup, Department of Psychology, Henry Wellcome Building P077, Institute of Psychiatry, De Crespigny Park, Denmark Hill, London SE3 8AF, UK

Julian F. Thayer, Gerontology Research Center, National Institute on Aging, 5600 Nathan Shock Drive, Baltimore, MD 21224-6825, USA

Chris Tkach, Department of Psychology, University of California, Riverside, CA 92521, USA

Adrian Wells, Academic Division of Clinical Psychology, University of Manchester, Rawnsley Building, Manchester Royal Infirmary, Oxford Road, Manchester M13 9WL, UK

Richard M. Wenzlaff, Department of Psychology, College of Liberal and Fine Arts, The University of Texas at San Antonio, 6900 North Loop 1604 West, San Antonio, TX 78249-0652, USA

Preface

Depression is the most common psychological disorder incurring significant personal, social, and economic costs. Cognitive approaches have been highly influential in the conceptualization and treatment of depression. Several cognitive processes have been implicated in the development, maintenance, and recurrence/relapse of depression. In the past 15 years, persistent, recyclic, negative thinking, in the form of rumination, has attracted increasing theoretical and empirical attention as an important factor.

This book brings together leading theorists, researchers, and clinicians working in the field of rumination and depression. The aim of the book is to provide a comprehensive analysis of the nature, effects, measurement, and treatment of rumination. This volume is divided into three parts.

In Part I, five chapters describe the nature and consequences of rumination. In Chapter 1, Papageorgiou and Wells examine concepts of rumination and compare this construct with other related cognitive processes, such as worry. The chapter discusses possible functions of rumination and the relationships between rumination, depression, and metacognitive beliefs. Lyubomirsky and Tkach (Chapter 2) describe in detail a ruminative style of responding to depressed mood and review experimental and correlational research documenting its many adverse consequences. In Chapter 3, Spasojevic, Alloy, Abramson, MacCoon, and Robinson describe their research focusing on reactive rumination, which they view as a response to negative mood, negative life events, or both. Wenzlaff (Chapter 4) examines rumination in the context of mental control in which cognitive biases and thought suppression can intensify negative thinking. The deleterious impact of depressed mood on mental control is also considered as contributing to rumination. In Chapter 5, Siegle and Thayer review the physiological correlates of depressive rumination as a way of measuring and understanding its nature and underlying mechanisms. An important advantage of physiological assessments is that they may provide a more objective index of rumination.

In Part II, three leading theories of rumination are described. Nolen-Hoeksema (Chapter 6) presents her response styles theory, in which rumination is a process whereby individuals focus on the causes and consequences of depression. This, in turn, is thought to contribute to the perpetuation and exacerbation of depressive symptoms. In Chapter 7, Matthews and Wells present their information processing model of emotional disorders to account for the causes and consequences of depressive rumination. In this multilevel model, rumination is seen as a maladaptive coping strategy closely linked to individuals' metacognitive beliefs. Martin, Shrira, and Startup (Chapter 8) review the goal progress theory of rumination and consider rumination as a function of goal progress, stop rules, and cerebral lateralization. Part II of the book concludes with a comparison and appraisal of these theories of rumination. Here Brotman and DeRubeis (Chapter 9) analyse the similarities and differences between theories and suggest areas of synthesis.

In Part III, the measurement and treatment of rumination is considered. Luminet (Chapter 10) describes specific self-report measures of rumination and related constructs and discusses their psychometric properties. In Chapter 11, Purdon presents a comprehensive review of existing psychological treatments for rumination across disorders. This chapter considers the applicability of these treatments to rumination in depression. McMillan and Fisher (Chapter 12) provide a description of common techniques used to treat depressive thinking in the course of cognitive therapy. These techniques draw on traditional strategies aimed at modifying the content of negative thoughts and beliefs in depression. In the final chapter, Wells and Papageorgiou (Chapter 13) present a new treatment approach that is specifically targeted at the depressive ruminative style of thinking. The chapter describes an array of metacognitive treatment strategies derived from an information processing model.

We have attempted to produce a book that as a body of work will help readers to identify rumination, distinguish it from related processes, understand its antecedents and consequences, and guide clinicians in their assessment and choice of treatment strategies. We hope that this volume will serve to stimulate future research on the link between rumination and depression.

Costas Papageorgiou
Adrian Wells

Acknowledgements

Costas Papageorgiou is grateful to his colleagues at the Doctoral Programme in Clinical Psychology, Lancaster University and the Department of Clinical Psychology, North Manchester General Hospital, for their support during the preparation of the manuscript. Adrian Wells is grateful to Joyce Russell for her secretarial assistance. We are also grateful to Andy O'Hare for his assistance in the graphical production of versions of the book cover. Finally, we would like to thank the team at Wiley, especially Vivien Ward and Lesley Valerio, for their encouragement.

I Nature and Consequences of Rumination

1 Nature, Functions, and Beliefs about Depressive Rumination

COSTAS PAPAGEORGIOU
Institute for Health Research, University of Lancaster, UK

ADRIAN WELLS
Academic Division of Clinical Psychology, University of Manchester, UK

Consider the following questions: What is rumination? How does rumination overlap with, and differ from, other cognitive processes and products? What is the role of rumination in depression? What factors are responsible for initiating and maintaining rumination, and how is rumination linked to depression? In this chapter, we address each of these questions by exploring the phenomenology of depressive rumination. The chapter begins by examining definitions of rumination. The second section reviews studies comparing depressive rumination with other forms of repetitive negative thinking. The next section considers the functions of rumination in depression. The final section explores the relationships between rumination, depression, and metacognitive beliefs.

DEFINITIONS OF RUMINATION

Rumination, crudely defined as persistent, recyclic, depressive thinking, is a relatively common response to negative moods (Rippere, 1977) and a salient cognitive feature of dysphoria and major depressive disorder. Examples of ruminative thoughts include: "why am I such a loser?", "my mood is so bad," "why do I react so negatively?", "I just can't cope with anything," and "why don't I feel like doing anything?" A chain of ruminative thoughts may be symptomatic of dysphoria or clinical depression, but it may also be perceived as serving a function. In view of the potential to advance our knowledge of the mechanisms of depressive onset, maintenance, and recurrence, rumination has attracted increasing theoretical and empirical interest in the past 15 years.

Depressive Rumination: Nature, Theory and Treatment
Edited by Costas Papageorgiou and Adrian Wells. © 2004 John Wiley & Sons Ltd

An important starting point in the process of understanding ruminative thinking and its link to depression is to examine notions of the concept of rumination. A number of definitions have been proposed from various psychological perspectives. According to Martin and Tesser (1989, 1996) rumination is a generic term that refers to several varieties of recurrent thinking. That is, rumination refers to the entire class of thought that has a tendency to recur. Martin and Tesser (1996, p. 7) proposed the following definition of rumination:

> Rumination is a class of conscious thoughts that revolve around a common instrumental theme and that recur in the absence of immediate environmental demands requiring the thoughts. Although the occurrence of these thoughts does not depend on direct cueing by the external environment, indirect cueing by the environment is likely given the high accessibility of goal-related concepts. Although the external environment may maintain any thought through repeated cueing, the maintenance of ruminative thoughts is not dependent upon such cueing.

Nolen-Hoeksema and colleagues have been instrumental in advancing our knowledge of ruminative thinking in depression. The response styles theory of depression (Nolen-Hoeksema, 1991) conceptualizes rumination as repetitive and passive thinking about symptoms of depression and the possible causes and consequences of these symptoms. According to this perspective, rumination involves "repetitively focusing on the fact that one is depressed; on one's symptoms of depression; and on the causes, meanings, and consequences of depressive symptoms" (Nolen-Hoeksema, 1991, p. 569).

More recent definitions of rumination have been proposed by investigating rumination on current feelings of sadness or "rumination on sadness" (Conway, Csank, Holm, & Blake, 2000) and rumination about negative inferences following stressful life events or "stress-reactive rumination" (Alloy et al., 2000; Robinson & Alloy, 2003). In Conway et al.'s (2000) definition, rumination "consists of repetitive thoughts concerning one's present distress and the circumstances surrounding the sadness" (p. 404). According to this definition, the ruminative thoughts (1) relate to the antecedents or nature of negative mood, (2) are not goal-directed and do not motivate individuals to make plans for remedial action, and (3) are not socially shared while individuals are engaged in rumination.

Grounded on the hopelessness theory of depression (Abramson, Metalsky, & Alloy, 1989) and Beck's (1967) cognitive theory of depression, Alloy and colleagues (Alloy et al., 2000; Robinson & Alloy, 2003) proposed a conceptual extension of Nolen-Hoeksema's (1991) response styles theory (see also Zullow & Seligman, 1990 for a similar extension). In this extension, Alloy and colleagues developed the concept of stress-reactive rumination to refer to the tendency to ruminate on negative inferences following stressful life events. Here stress-reactive rumination is thought to occur prior to the onset of depressed mood, whereas emotion-focused rumination, as suggested by

Nolen-Hoeksema (1991), is thought to occur in response to depressed mood. Data from the Temple-Wisconsin Cognitive Vulnerability to Depression Project (Alloy & Abramson, 1999) suggest that stress-reactive rumination plays a crucial role in the aetiology of depression. Alloy et al. (2000) demonstrated that the interaction between negative cognitive styles and stress-reactive rumination predicted the retrospective lifetime rate of major depressive episodes as well as hopelessness depressive episodes. In a subsequent study, Robinson and Alloy (2003) found that the same interaction predicted the prospective onset, number, and duration of major depressive and hopelessness depressive episodes (for further details, see Chapter 3).

The review of definitions of rumination indicates that, although there are similarities between the various definitions proposed, different theorists define rumination somewhat differently. As noted by Siegle (2000), this problem is clearly reflected in existing measures of rumination. Siegle (2000) investigated the extent to which different measures of rumination represented a single construct in a factor analytic study. The results suggested that there were several separate constructs represented in the measures (for further details, see Chapter 5). Therefore, there appears to be a range of subcomponents of rumination, and it is conceivable that their contribution to dysphoria or depression may differ. Future research on rumination should clearly operationalize the type as well as components of rumination being examined.

COMPARISONS OF DEPRESSIVE RUMINATION WITH OTHER COGNITIVE PROCESSES AND PRODUCTS

Given the above conceptualizations of rumination, there are apparent similarities and differences between this process and other related cognitive processes and products (namely, negative automatic thoughts, self-focused attention or private self-consciousness, and worry). An examination of the overlap and differences between rumination and other cognitive constructs may assist in refining the concept of rumination. However, to date little is known about the similarities and differences between rumination and other cognitive constructs, or whether the similarities or differences are important contributors to psychopathology. This section reviews the literature on the overlapping and distinct features of rumination and other related or similar constructs.

RUMINATION VS. NEGATIVE AUTOMATIC THOUGHTS

Rumination may be distinguished from the negative automatic thoughts that are typical of depression. According to Beck's (1967, 1976) content specificity hypothesis, depression is characterized by thoughts containing themes of past personal loss or failure. Papageorgiou and Wells (2001a) have argued that, although negative automatic thoughts are relatively brief shorthand appraisals of loss and failure in depression, rumination consists of longer chains of repetitive, recyclic, negative, and self-focused thinking that may well occur as a response to initial negative thoughts. Studies have also demonstrated that ruminative thinking predicts depression over and above its shared variance with several types of negative cognitions (e.g., Nolen-Hoeksema, Parker, & Larson, 1994; Spasojevic & Alloy, 2001).

RUMINATION VS. SELF-FOCUSED ATTENTION AND PRIVATE SELF-CONSCIOUSNESS

A conceptual distinction can be made between ruminative thinking and the depressive self-focusing style (Pyszczynski & Greenberg, 1987). Although the focus of the depressive style is on reducing discrepancies between ideal and real states following failure (Pyszczynski, Greenberg, Hamilton, & Nix, 1991), the focus of rumination is more specific and has been hypothesized to involve coping in the form of problem-solving, which does not necessarily occur following failure (Wells & Matthews, 1994). Rumination may also be differentiated from private self-consciousness (Fenigstein, Scheier, & Buss, 1975), a disposition to chronically self-focus and self-analyse regardless of mood. Nolen-Hoeksema and Morrow (1993) demonstrated that, although rumination remained a significant predictor of depressed mood after statistically controlling for private self-consciousness, private self-consciousness was not a significant predictor of depression after controlling for rumination. In addition to these distinctions, Papageorgiou and Wells (2001a) suggested that, while rumination in depression is likely to involve self-relevant chains of negative thoughts, not all forms of ruminative thinking are necessarily self-relevant. For instance, individuals may ruminate about the humanitarian effects of recent warfare. We believe that depressive rumination specifically encompasses self-focused thinking and negative appraisals of the self, emotions, behaviours, situations, life stressors, and coping. Thus, self-focus is a component of rumination that links to some, but not all, aspects of the content or form that rumination takes.

RUMINATION VS. WORRY

Rumination appears to be closely related to worry. Although worry is a common cognitive feature of anxiety disorders and a cardinal feature of generalized anxiety disorder, it has been reported to be elevated in individuals with depression (Starcevic, 1995). Worry has been defined as "a chain of thoughts and images, negatively affect-laden and relatively uncontrollable; it represents an attempt to engage in mental problem-solving on an issue whose outcome is uncertain but contains the possibility of one or more negative outcomes" (Borkovec, Robinson, Pruzinsky, & DePree, 1983, p. 10). Earlier research exploring the nature of depressive and anxious thinking showed that these types of cognitions were clearly distinct phenomena (Clark & de Silva, 1985; Clark & Hemsley, 1985). The content of chains of anxious (worrisome) thoughts is likely to differ from depressive (ruminative) thoughts in that the former may be particularly characterized by themes of anticipated threat or danger in the future (Beck, 1967, 1976; Borkovec et al., 1983), while rumination may involve themes of past personal loss or failure (Beck, 1967, 1976). In a content analysis of naturally occurring worrisome thoughts, Szabo and Lovibond (2002) found that 48% of worrisome thoughts could be characterized as reflecting a problem-solving process, 17% as anticipation of future negative outcomes, 11% "rumination", and 5% as reflecting "palliative" thoughts and "self-blame". In another study, worrisome thinking was characterized by more statements implying catastrophic interpretations of future events than dysphoric ruminative thinking (Molina, Borkovec, Peasley, & Person, 1998). These studies suggest that there are content differences between rumination and worry.

Earlier approaches to understanding the nature of different styles of thinking had focused predominantly on the thematic content of thought in depression and anxiety. More recent theoretical and empirical evidence suggests that other dimensions of thinking, apart from content, are involved in vulnerability to, and maintenance of, psychopathology. Wells and Matthews (1994) argue that it is not only the content of perseverative negative thinking that may be relevant to understanding psychopathology but also the nature, flexibility, and beliefs about thinking that have consequences for information processing and self-regulation. According to Wells and Matthews (1994), two components of thinking styles should be considered in this context: (1) process dimensions (e.g., attentional involvement, dismissability, distraction, etc.), and (2) metacognitive dimensions (e.g., beliefs or appraisals about thinking and ability to monitor, objectify, and regulate thinking). Therefore, the study of dimensions of thinking styles may allow us to systematically construct a profile of the constituents of thinking processes that contribute to specific and/or general manifestations of psychological disturbance. To date, two studies have explored the process and metacognitive dimensions of rumination and worry (Papageorgiou & Wells, 1999a, b).

In a preliminary study, Papageorgiou and Wells (1999a) compared the process and metacognitive dimensions of naturally occurring depressive (ruminative) thoughts and anxious (worrisome) thoughts in a non-clinical sample. Participants were provided with a diary for recording and rating the content of their first and second depressive and anxious thoughts occurring during a two-week period. The results revealed that, although ruminative and worrisome thinking shared a number of similarities, they also differed on several dimensions. Figure 1.1 illustrates the differences between rumination and worry on the dimensions assessed. In comparison with rumination, worry was found to be significantly greater in verbal content, associated with more compulsion to

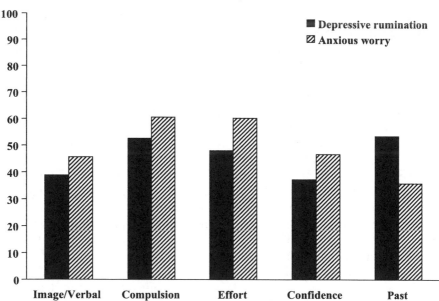

Figure 1.1. Process and metacognitive differences between depressive rumination and anxious worry in a non-clinical sample.

act, and more effort and confidence in problem-solving. Rumination was significantly more past-oriented than worry. Following adjustments for multiple comparisons, the only remaining significant differences were those concerned with dimensions of effort to problem-solve and past orientation. Relationships between dimensions of thinking and affective responses for each style of thinking were also explored in this study. This was achieved by partialling out anxiety when examining correlates of depression intensity and partialling out depression when examining correlates of anxiety intensity. Greater depression was significantly correlated with lower confidence in problem-solving ability and greater past orientation of the ruminative thoughts. In relation to the worrisome thoughts, greater anxiety was significantly correlated with less dismissibility of worry, greater distraction by worry, metaworry (i.e., worry about worry: Wells, 1994), compulsion to act on worry, and more attentional focus on worries. Therefore, these preliminary data appear to be consistent with the notion that different components of thinking style are associated with emotional disturbance (Wells & Matthews, 1994). However, the generalizability of these findings is limited by the non-clinical sample recruited.

In a subsequent study, we set out to extend these findings in clinical samples (Papageorgiou & Wells, 1999b). For this purpose, individuals whose predominant style of thinking is characterized by depressive rumination (e.g., individuals with major depressive disorder) and anxious worry (e.g., individuals with panic disorder) were recruited into the study. To reduce the overlap of

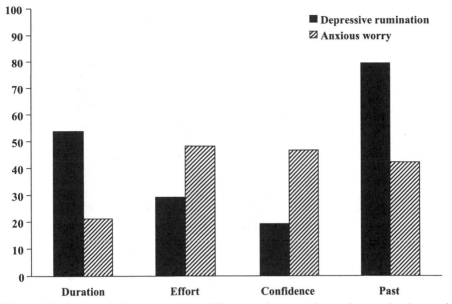

Figure 1.2. Process and metacognitive differences between depressive rumination and anxious worry in individuals with major depressive disorder.

rumination and worry, it was ensured that there was no diagnostic overlap between the two clinical samples. A non-clinical group was included in order to control for "pathological" status. We assumed that a non-clinical group would show non-pathological varieties of rumination and worry, thus enabling us to identify differences between normal and abnormal thinking styles. In this study, we aimed to address three fundamental questions. In the first question, we set out to determine whether process and metacognitive dimensions distinguish between the rumination and worry of individuals with major depressive disorder. The data showed that, in comparison with worry, the rumination of the depressed group was rated as significantly longer in duration, lower in effort to problem-solve, lower in confidence in problem-solving, and greater in past orientation. These data are presented in Figure 1.2. Following adjustments for multiple comparisons, the only remaining significant differences were those concerned with dimensions of confidence in problem-solving and past orientation.

In the second question, the objective was to establish similarities and differences between the predominant styles of pathological thinking in each disorder (i.e., rumination in major depressive disorder vs. worry in panic disorder). In comparison with the worry of the panic disorder group, the rumination of the depressed group was rated as significantly longer in duration, less controllable, less dismissible, and associated with lower effort to problem-solve, lower confidence in problem-solving, and a greater past orientation. These data are

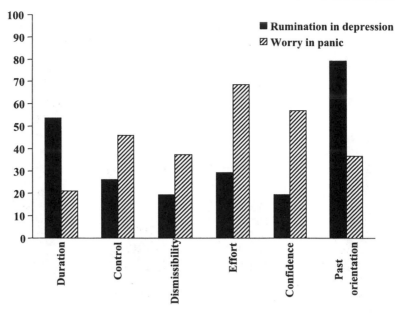

Figure 1.3. Process and metacognitive differences between rumination in patients with depression and worry in patients with panic disorder.

illustrated in Figure 1.3. Nonetheless, after adjustments for multiple comparisons, the only remaining significant differences were those concerned with dimensions of effort to problem-solve, confidence in problem-solving, and past orientation.

Finally, we addressed the question of whether dimensions of rumination differ across disorders (i.e., is pathological rumination in depression different from that in panic disorder patients and non-clinical samples whose rumination is less problematic?). The analyses demonstrated that, in comparison with the rumination of panic patients and non-clinical participants, that of the depressed group was rated as more intrusive, comprising greater metaworry, and associated with lower effort and less confidence in problem-solving, and a greater past orientation. The duration of rumination in both the depressed and panic disorder groups was significantly longer than that in the non-clinical sample. Moreover, the depressed group paid significantly more attention to their ruminative thinking than did the non-clinical sample. These data are shown in Figure 1.4. Following statistical adjustments, only the duration of rumination in the depressed group remained significantly longer than that in non-clinical participants. Thus, empirical evidence suggests that although rumination and worry share a number of similarities, they also differ on several dimensions (Papageorgiou & Wells, 1999a, b). The most reliable differences found between these two styles of thinking are effort and confidence in

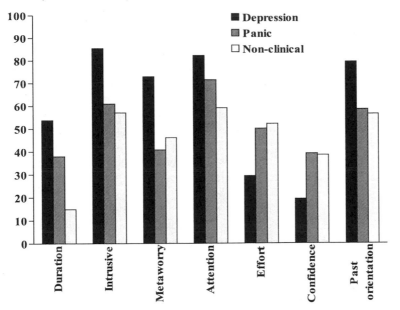

Figure 1.4. Process and metacognitive differences in rumination between patients with depression, patients with panic disorder, and non-clinical participants.

problem-solving and past orientation. It appears that pathological rumination and worry differ in terms of their motivational characteristics and metacognitive judgements of problem-solving confidence. This may be important since both rumination and worry have been conceptualized as coping strategies (Wells & Matthews, 1994), and yet the characteristics of rumination seem ill-suited to problem-solving or coping when compared with worry. These data also shed light on the differences between abnormal (depressive) and normal (non-clinical) varieties of rumination. Clearly, further research is required to explore the process and metacognitive dimensions of rumination and worry.

In addition to the above studies investigating the relationships between rumination, worry, depression, and anxiety, other studies have relied on self-report measures of both rumination and worry to further explore the overlap and differences between these constructs (Fresco, Frankel, Mennin, Turk, & Heimberg, 2002; Segerstrom, Tsao, Alden, & Craske, 2000). In these studies, rumination has been assessed in the way conceptualized by Nolen-Hoeksema (1991), using the Ruminative Responses Scale (RRS: Nolen-Hoeksema & Morrow, 1991), while worry has been measured using the Penn State Worry Questionnaire (PSWQ: Meyer, Miller, Metzger, & Borkovec, 1990). Segerstrom et al. (2000) found strong correlations between rumination and worry, suggesting an overlap of 16–21%, in both non-clinical and clinical samples. Moreover, using structural equation modelling, they reported that a latent variable (described as "repetitive thought") involving manifest variables of rumination and worry was significantly correlated with depression and anxiety. These data led the authors to conclude that goal interruption, failures of emotional processing, and information processing may result in repetitive thought that increases negative mood states, such as depression and anxiety. In the study by Fresco et al. (2002), the items from the RRS and PSWQ were subjected to factor analysis. This revealed a four-factor solution consisting of two rumination factors labelled "dwelling on the negative" and "active cognitive appraisal", and two worry factors labelled "worry engagement" and "absence of worry". The "dwelling on the negative" and "worry engagement" factors emerged as distilled measures of rumination and worry, respectively. Fresco et al. (2002) also reported that scores on these factors were highly correlated with each other and demonstrated equally strong relationships to depression and anxiety. Therefore, consistent with naturalistic studies of the dimensions of rumination and worry (Papageorgiou & Wells, 1999a, b), research using questionnaire measures of rumination and worry indicates that, although rumination and worry have a number of overlapping features, they also represent distinct cognitive processes that are closely related to depression and anxiety, respectively.

FUNCTIONS OF RUMINATION

Laboratory, cross-sectional, and prospective studies have shown that rumination in response to experimentally induced or naturally occurring depressed mood is associated with several deleterious outcomes. In a review of these negative consequences, Lyubomirsky and Tkach (for further details, see Chapter 2) list the following: prolonged and more severe negative affect and depressive symptoms, negatively biased thinking, poor problem-solving, impaired motivation and inhibition of instrumental behaviour, impaired concentration and cognition, and increased stress/problems. In addition to these consequences, rumination has been found to delay recovery from major depression in cognitive-behavioural therapy (Siegle, Sagrati, & Crawford, 1999). Despite these consequences of rumination, it is puzzling to understand why people choose to ruminate. However, a number of theoretical accounts have been proposed.

In their generic conceptualization, Martin and Tesser (1989, 1996) view rumination as a function of goal progress. They propose that rumination is instrumental to the attainment of higher-order goals (i.e., rumination serves the function of discrepancy reduction). By this definition, however, Martin and Tesser do not imply that rumination is always beneficial. According to these authors, although rumination does not always lead individuals to progress toward their desired goals, that is its function. In Nolen-Hoeksema's (1991) response styles theory, it is suggested that rumination helps individuals to focus inwardly and evaluate their feelings and their problematic situation in order to gain insight. In an experimental study, Lyubomirsky and Nolen-Hoeksema (1993) found that dysphoric participants induced to ruminate believed that they were gaining insight about themselves and their problems, even though they were producing relatively poor solutions to these problems.

BELIEFS ABOUT RUMINATION

Identification of beliefs about rumination may contribute to understanding the functions of rumination within the context of information processing models. An information processing model that appears promising in achieving this goal is the Self-Regulatory Executive Function (S-REF) model of emotional disorders (Wells & Matthews, 1994). In the S-REF model, perseverative negative thinking, in the form of rumination or worry, is conceptualized as one of several ubiquitous factors involved in disorder vulnerability and maintenance. Rumination and worry are viewed as coping strategies. The model accounts for the information processing mechanisms that are involved in initiating and maintaining perseverative negative thinking of this kind. More specifically, Wells and Matthews proposed that the knowledge base (beliefs) of emotionally vulnerable individuals is responsible for predisposing them to select and engage in rumination (i.e., perseverative negative thinking is thought to be associated with, and directed by, underlying metacognitive beliefs concerning its functions and consequences). Emerging empirical evidence supports this notion.

In a preliminary study, Papageorgiou and Wells (2001b) used a semi-structured interview to explore the presence and content of metacognitive beliefs about rumination in patients with *DSM-IV* (American Psychiatric Association [APA], 1994) recurrent major depressive disorder without concurrent Axis I disorders. The results showed that all of the patients held both positive and negative metacognitive beliefs about rumination. The content of positive metacognitive beliefs reflected themes concerning rumination as a coping strategy (e.g., "I need to ruminate about my problems to find answers to my depression," "ruminating about my depression helps me to understand past mistakes and failures"). Negative metacognitive beliefs about rumination reflected themes concerning the uncontrollability and harm of rumination (e.g., "ruminating about my problems is uncontrollable," "ruminating could make me harm myself") and the interpersonal and social consequences of rumination (e.g., "people will reject me if I ruminate," "everyone would desert me if they knew how much I ruminate about myself"). Additional examples of positive and negative metacognitive beliefs about rumination are presented in Table 1.1. The results are consistent with the notion that positive and negative metacognitive beliefs about rumination may be related to ruminative thinking in individuals with depression. The meta-cognitive beliefs elicited in this study were subsequently utilized to develop measures of positive and negative metacognitive beliefs about rumination to

Table 1.1. Examples of positive and negative metacognitive beliefs about rumination

Positive beliefs about rumination	Negative beliefs about rumination
In order to understand my feelings of depression, I need to ruminate about my problems	Ruminating makes me physically ill
I need to ruminate about the bad things that have happened in the past to make sense of them	When I ruminate, I can't do anything else
I need to ruminate about my problems to find the causes of my depression	Ruminating means I'm out of control
Ruminating about my problems helps me to focus on the most important things	Ruminating will turn me into a failure
Ruminating about the past helps me to prevent future mistakes and failures	Ruminating means I'm a bad person
Ruminating about my feelings helps me to recognize the triggers for my depression	It is impossible not to ruminate about the bad things that have happened in the past
Ruminating about the past helps me to work out how things could have been done better	Only weak people ruminate

Source: Papageorgiou & Wells, 2001a, 2001b; Papageorgiou et al., in preparation

examine relationships between rumination, depression, and metacognition. These relationships are discussed in the next section.

RELATIONSHIPS BETWEEN RUMINATION, DEPRESSION, AND METACOGNITIVE BELIEFS

To date, cross-sectional and prospective studies from our research programme have supported the link between rumination, depression, and specific metacognitive beliefs. These studies have relied on instruments that were constructed using the pool of items derived from the positive and negative metacognitive beliefs reported by individuals with depression in the study by Papageorgiou and Wells (2001b). These instruments include the Positive Beliefs about Rumination Scale (PBRS: Papageorgiou & Wells, 2001a) and the Negative Beliefs about Rumination Scale (NBRS: Papageorgiou, Wells, & Meina, in preparation). The PBRS and NBRS have been shown to have good psychometric properties of reliability and validity (for further details, see Chapter 10).

Empirical evidence has demonstrated that positive metacognitive beliefs about rumination, as measured by the PBRS, are significantly and positively associated with rumination and depression in non-clinical samples (Papageorgiou & Wells, 2001a, Study 4; 2001c; 2003, Study 2) and individuals with clinical depression (Papageorgiou & Wells, 2003, Study 1; Papageorgiou et al., in preparation). Similarly, both subtypes of negative metacognitive beliefs about rumination (i.e., beliefs concerning uncontrollability and harm and the interpersonal and social consequences of rumination), as measured by NBRS1 and NBRS2, respectively, have been found to be significantly and positively correlated with rumination and depression in non-clinical samples (Papageorgiou & Wells, 2001c; 2003, Study 2) as well as samples of clinically depressed individuals (Papageorgiou & Wells, 2003, Study 1; Papageorgiou et al., in preparation). Research has also demonstrated that both positive and negative metacognitive beliefs about rumination significantly distinguish patients with recurrent major depression from patients with panic disorder and agoraphobia, and patients with social phobia (Papageorgiou & Wells, 2001a, Study 5; Papageorgiou et al., in preparation).

On the basis of Wells and Matthews' (1994) S-REF model of emotional disorders and empirical evidence supporting the relationships between rumination, depression, and metacognition, we recently constructed a clinical metacognitive model of rumination and depression (Papageorgiou & Wells, 2003). This model is illustrated in Figure 1.5. According to this model, positive beliefs about the benefits and advantages of rumination are likely to motivate individuals to engage in sustained rumination. Once rumination is activated, individuals then appraise this process as both uncontrollable and harmful (negative beliefs 1) and likely to produce detrimental interpersonal and social consequences (negative beliefs 2). The activation of negative beliefs and appraisals about rumination then contributes to the experience of depression. Therefore, a number of vicious cycles of rumination, depression, and specific metacognitive beliefs may be responsible for the maintenance of the depressive

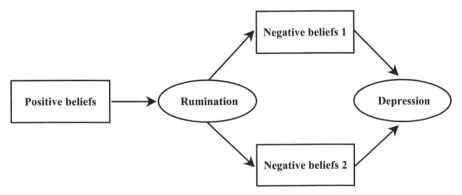

Figure 1.5. Basic components and structure of a clinical metacognitive model of rumination and depression

experience. The statistical fit of this clinical metacognitive model of rumination and depression has been tested in clinical and non-clinical samples. In the study on depressed participants, a good model fit was obtained consistent with S-REF predictions (Papageorgiou & Wells, 2003, Study 1). In the study on non-clinical participants, the data supported the existence of a somewhat structurally different metacognitive model of rumination and depression (Papageorgiou & Wells, 2003, Study 2). One difference in the models appears to be the nature of the relationships between rumination, negative metacognitive beliefs, and depression. Clearly, future studies should aim to conduct further model comparisons in order to formalize mediation relationships. However, the data concerning depressed participants suggest that positive beliefs about rumination are closely linked to a tendency to ruminate in response to depressed mood. Moreover, negative beliefs about rumination seem to serve a key function in mediating the relationship between rumination and depressive symptoms. These relationships as well as the statistical fit of the clinical metacognitive model of rumination and depression have also been supported in a prospective study of metacognitive vulnerability to depression conducted in a non-clinical sample (Papageorgiou & Wells, 2001c).

The above findings have important clinical implications. They suggest that cognitive therapy of depression could focus on strategies specifically designed to modify positive and negative metacognitive beliefs about rumination. Such strategies form an important part of cognitive therapy of generalized anxiety disorder (Wells, 1997). More specifically, cost–benefit analyses of positive beliefs about rumination and verbal reattribution of negative beliefs about rumination, especially those concerned with uncontrollability and harm of rumination, may be effective in the treatment of rumination and clinical depression. Moreover, Wells and Matthews (1994) argue that treatment may focus on increasing metacognitive control or flexibility, which may be achieved through the practice of attention training treatment (ATT: Wells, 1990, 2000). Indeed, in a preliminary study, Papageorgiou and Wells (2000) evaluated the effectiveness of ATT in a single-case series of patients with recurrent major depressive disorder. Following ATT, all patients showed clinically significant reductions across measures of depression, rumination, and metacognition. These gains were maintained at the 12-month follow-up assessments. Therefore, ATT appears to be a promising technique in modifying actual rumination and maladaptive metacognitive beliefs about rumination in individuals with recurrent major depression. It seems to be worthwhile to conduct further studies evaluating the effectiveness of specific strategies designed to modify positive and negative metacognitive beliefs about rumination in depression.

The empirical evidence reviewed in this chapter supports the need to develop specific rumination-focused interventions that target the process, rather than just content, of ruminative thinking in depression. Such interventions are currently being evaluated as part of our research programme.

SUMMARY AND CONCLUSIONS

In this chapter, we began by reviewing a number of definitions of rumination. These definitions have ranged from generic to specific conceptualizations of ruminative thinking in depression. Even specific definitions appear to differ in content and focus, which is reflected in the existing measures of rumination. Further advances in the field are likely to follow from a more detailed and specific definition of depressive rumination and its components. We also examined similarities and differences between rumination and other closely related cognitive constructs. It appears that the content of rumination is not the only feature that distinguishes rumination from worry, and pathological from normal rumination. Moreover, process and metacognitive dimensions appear to correlate with depression. Whether the similarities or differences between rumination and other constructs are critical contributors to psychopathology remains to be determined in future investigations. The hypothesized functions of rumination were also reviewed and empirical support was found for the role of metacognitive beliefs about rumination in depression. Finally, the relationships between rumination, depression and metacognition were examined. Accumulating evidence demonstrates that metacognitive beliefs are associated with depressive rumination, and preliminary data suggest that negative beliefs about rumination may mediate the relationship between rumination and depression.

REFERENCES

Abramson, L. Y., Metalsky, G. I., & Alloy, L. B. (1989). Hopelessness depression: A theory-based subtype of depression. *Psychological Review*, **96**, 358–372.

Alloy, L. B. & Abramson, L. Y. (1999). The Temple-Wisconsin Cognitive Vulnerability to Depression (CVD) project: Conceptual background, design and methods. *Journal of Cognitive Psychotherapy: An International Quarterly*, **13**, 227–262.

Alloy, L. B., Abramson, L. Y., Hogan, M. E., Whitehouse, W. G., Rose, D. T., Robinson, M. S. et al. (2000). The Temple-Wisconsin Cognitive Vulnerability to Depression (CVD) project: Lifetime history of Axis I psychopathology in individuals at high and low cognitive vulnerability to depression. *Journal of Abnormal Psychology*, **109**, 403–418.

American Psychiatric Association (1994). Diagnostic and Statistical Manual of Mental Disorders (4th edn). Washington, DC: American Psychiatric Association.

Beck, A. T. (1967). *Depression: Clinical, Experimental, and Theoretical Aspects*. New York: Harper & Row.

Beck, A. T. (1976). *Cognitive Therapy and the Emotional Disorders*. New York: International Universities Press.

Borkovec, T. D., Robinson, E., Pruzinsky, T., & DePree, J. A. (1983). Preliminary exploration of worry: Some characteristics and processes. *Behaviour Research and Therapy*, **21**, 9–16.

Clark, D. A. & de Silva, P. (1985). The nature of depressive and anxious, intrusive thoughts: Distinct or uniform phenomena? *Behaviour Research and Therapy*, **23**, 383–393.

Clark, D. A. & Hemsley, D. R. (1985). Individual differences in the experience of depressive and anxious, intrusive thoughts. *Behaviour Research and Therapy*, **23**, 625–633.

Conway, M., Csank, P. A. R., Holm, S. L., & Blake, C. K. (2000). On assessing individual differences in rumination on sadness. *Journal of Personality Assessment*, **75**, 404–425.

Fenigstein, A., Scheier, M., & Buss, A. H. (1975). Public and private self-consciousness: Assessment and theory. *Journal of Consulting and Clinical Psychology*, **43**, 522–527.

Fresco, D. M., Frankel, A. N., Mennin, D. S., Turk, C. L., & Heimberg, R. G. (2002). Distinct and overlapping features of rumination and worry: The relationship of cognitive production to negative affective states. *Cognitive Therapy and Research*, **26**, 179–188.

Lyubomirsky, S. & Nolen-Hoeksema, S. (1993). Self-perpetuating properties of dysphoric rumination. *Journal of Personality and Social Psychology*, **65**, 339–349.

Martin, L. L. & Tesser, A. (1989). Toward a motivational and structural theory of ruminative thought. In: J. S. Uleman & J. A. Bargh (eds), *Unintended Thought* (pp. 306–326). New York: Guilford Press.

Martin, L. L. & Tesser, A. (1996). Some ruminative thoughts. In: R. S. Wyer (ed.), *Advances in Social Cognition* (Vol. 9, pp. 1–47). Mahwah, NJ: Lawrence Erlbaum.

Meyer, T. J., Miller, M. L., Metzger, R. L., & Borkovec, T. D. (1990). Development and validation of the Penn State Worry Questionnaire. *Behaviour Research and Therapy*, **28**, 487–495.

Molina, S., Borkovec, T. D., Peasley, C., & Person, D. (1998). Content analysis of worrisome streams of consciousness in anxious and dysphoric participants. *Cognitive Therapy and Research*, **22**, 109–123.

Nolen-Hoeksema, S. (1991). Responses to depression and their effects on the duration of depressive episodes. *Journal of Abnormal Psychology*, **100**, 569–582.

Nolen-Hoeksema, S. & Morrow, J. (1991). A prospective study of depression and posttraumatic stress symptoms after a natural disaster: The 1989 Loma Prieta earthquake. *Journal of Personality and Social Psychology*, **61**, 115–121.

Nolen-Hoeksema, S. & Morrow, J. (1993). Effects of rumination and distraction on naturally occurring depressed mood. *Cognition and Emotion*, **7**, 561–570.

Nolen-Hoeksema, S., Parker, L. E., & Larson, J. (1994). Ruminative coping with depressed mood following loss. *Journal of Personality and Social Psychology*, **67**, 92–104.

Papageorgiou, C. & Wells, A. (1999a). Process and metacognitive dimensions of depressive and anxious thoughts and relationships with emotional intensity. *Clinical Psychology and Psychotherapy*, **6**, 156–162.

Papageorgiou, C. & Wells, A. (1999b). Dimensions of depressive rumination and anxious worry: A comparative study. Paper presented at the *33rd Annual Convention of the Association for Advancement of Behavior Therapy*, Toronto.

Papageorgiou, C. & Wells, A. (2000). Treatment of recurrent major depression with attention training. *Cognitive and Behavioral Practice*, **7**, 407–413.

Papageorgiou, C. & Wells, A. (2001a). Positive beliefs about depressive rumination: Development and preliminary validation of a self-report scale. *Behavior Therapy*, **32**, 13–26.

Papageorgiou, C. & Wells, A. (2001b). Metacognitive beliefs about rumination in recurrent major depression. *Cognitive and Behavioral Practice*, **8**, 160–164.

Papageorgiou, C. & Wells, A. (2001c). Metacognitive vulnerability to depression: A prospective study. Paper presented at the *35th Annual Convention of the Association for Advancement of Behavior Therapy, Philadelphia*.

Papageorgiou, C. & Wells, A. (2003). An empirical test of a clinical metacognitive model of rumination and depression. *Cognitive Therapy and Research*, **27**, 261–273.

Papageorgiou, C., Wells, A., & Meina, L. J. Development and preliminary validation of the Negative Beliefs about Rumination Scale. Manuscript in preparation.

Pyszczynski, T. & Greenberg, J. (1987). Self-regulatory perseveration and the depressive self-focusing style: A self-awareness theory of reactive depression. *Psychological Bulletin*, **102**, 122–138.

Pyszczynski, T., Greenberg, J., Hamilton, J. H., & Nix, G. (1991). On the relationship between self-focused attention and psychological disorder: A critical reappraisal. *Psychological Bulletin*, **110**, 538–543.

Rippere, V. (1977). "What's the thing to do when you're feeling depressed?": A pilot study. *Behaviour Research and Therapy*, **15**, 185–191.

Robinson, S. M. & Alloy, L. B. (2003). Negative cognitive styles and stress-reactive rumination interact to predict depression: A prospective study. *Cognitive Therapy and Research*, **27**, 275–291.

Segerstrom, S. C., Tsao, J. C. I., Alden, L. E., & Craske, M. G. (2000). Worry and rumination: Repetitive thought as a concomitant and predictor of negative mood. *Cognitive Therapy and Research*, **24**, 671–688.

Siegle, G. J. (2000). Convergence and divergence in measures of rumination. Paper presented at the *34th Annual Convention of the Association for Advancement of Behavior Therapy, New Orleans*.

Siegle, G. J., Sagrati, S., & Crawford, C. E. (1999). Effects of rumination and initial severity on response to cognitive therapy for depression. Paper presented at the *33rd Annual Convention of the Association for the Advancement of Behavior Therapy, Toronto*.

Spasojevic, J. & Alloy, L. B. (2001). Rumination as a common mechanism relating depressive risk factors to depression. *Emotion*, **1**, 25–37.

Starcevic, V. (1995). Pathological worry in major depression: A preliminary report. *Behaviour Research and Therapy*, **33**, 55–56.

Szabo, M. & Lovibond, P. F. (2002). The cognitive content of naturally occurring worry episodes. *Cognitive Therapy and Research*, **26**, 167–177.

Wells, A. (1990). Panic disorder in association with relaxation induced anxiety: An attentional training approach to treatment. *Behavior Therapy*, **21**, 273–280.

Wells, A. (1994). Attention and the control of worry. In: G. C. L. Davey & F. Tallis (eds), *Worrying: Perspectives on Theory, Assessment, and Treatment*. Chichester, UK: John Wiley & Sons.

Wells, A. (1997). *Cognitive Therapy of Anxiety Disorders: A Practice Manual and Conceptual Guide*. Chichester, UK: John Wiley & Sons.

Wells, A. (2000). *Emotional Disorders and Metacognition: Innovative Cognitive Therapy*. Chichester, UK: John Wiley & Sons.

Wells, A. & Matthews, G. (1994). *Attention and Emotion: A Clinical Perspective*. Hove, UK: Lawrence Erlbaum.

Zullow, H. M. & Seligman, M. E. P. (1990). Pessimistic rumination predicts defeat of presidential candidates, 1900 to 1984. *Psychological Inquiry*, **1**, 52–61.

2 The Consequences of Dysphoric Rumination

SONJA LYUBOMIRSKY AND CHRIS TKACH

University of California, Riverside, USA

Many people believe that when they become depressed or dysphoric they should try to focus inwardly and evaluate their feelings and their situation in order to gain self-insight and find solutions that might ultimately resolve their problems and relieve their depressive symptoms (Lyubomirsky & Nolen-Hoeksema, 1993; Papageorgiou & Wells, 2001a, b; Watkins & Baracaia, 2001). Challenging this assumption, numerous studies over the past two decades have shown that repetitive rumination about the implications of one's depressive symptoms actually maintains those symptoms, impairs one's ability to solve problems, and ushers in a host of negative consequences (see Nolen-Hoeksema, 1991, 1996, for reviews). In this chapter, we describe in detail a ruminative style of responding to depressed mood and review both experimental and correlational research documenting its many adverse consequences.

RUMINATIVE RESPONSES TO NEGATIVE MOOD

Ruminative responses to negative mood and other depressive symptoms are thoughts and behaviors that repetitively focus the individual's attention on his or her negative feelings and the nature and implications of those feelings (Nolen-Hoeksema, 1991). For example, when feeling depressed or dysphoric, some people isolate themselves to brood about the problems at the root of their distress (e.g., "my children are too much for me to handle") without taking action to solve those problems, or dwell about the causes and consequences of their depressive symptoms (e.g., "why haven't I been able to just snap out of this?") without doing anything constructive to relieve those symptoms (Lyubomirsky, Tucker, Caldwell, & Berg, 1999; Nolen-Hoeksema, 1996). Other examples include thinking about how alone, unmotivated, lethargic,

Depressive Rumination: Nature, Theory and Treatment
Edited by Costas Papageorgiou and Adrian Wells. © 2004 John Wiley & Sons Ltd

and hopeless one feels (e.g., "I just can't get going") and worrying about the implications of one's state of mind (e.g., "what if I can't muster the energy to go to work tomorrow?"). Although such thoughts may naturally arise for anyone who experiences a depressed mood, some people persist in ruminating on the meanings, causes, and consequences of their feelings and symptoms without taking action to address their situation or to distract themselves. Indeed, the tendency to engage in rumination in response to negative moods appears to be both a relatively common (Rippere, 1977) and stable coping style (Nolen-Hoeksema, Morrow, & Fredrickson, 1993; Nolen-Hoeksema, Parker, & Larson, 1994). For example, in one study, 83% of students who recorded their daily moods for 30 consecutive days showed consistent styles of responding to their negative moods (e.g., by ruminating or not ruminating) within the same day and across all days (Nolen-Hoeksema et al., 1993).

Although dysphoric individuals may be hoping that their ruminations will help them solve their problems or relieve their symptoms, correlational studies have shown that people who engage in passive rumination are actually less likely to use active, planful problem solving to cope with problems or negative life events (Nolen-Hoeksema & Morrow, 1991; see also Carver, Scheier, & Weintraub, 1989). An adaptive and instrumental alternative that we have investigated is to use pleasant or neutral distractions to lift one's mood and relieve one's depressive symptoms; and only then, if necessary, to undertake problem solving. Distracting responses are thoughts and behaviors that help divert one's attention away from one's depressed mood and its consequences and turn it to pleasant or benign thoughts and activities that are absorbing, engaging, and capable of providing positive reinforcement (Nolen-Hoeksema, 1991; cf. Csikszentmihalyi, 1990)—for example, going for a run or a bike ride, seeing a movie with friends, or concentrating on a project at work. Effective distractions do not include inherently dangerous or self-destructive activities, such as reckless driving, heavy drinking, drug abuse, or aggressive behavior, which may be distracting in the short term, but harmful in the long run. Indeed, engaging in such behaviors has been found to be significantly correlated with using ruminative, not distracting, responses to cope with depressed mood (Nolen-Hoeksema & Morrow, 1991). Distracting oneself with negative thoughts while depressed is also unlikely to be successful (Wenzlaff, Wegner, & Roper, 1988).

Having described what dysphoric ruminative responses are, we now turn our attention to what they are *not*. Although recent interest in ruminative thinking (e.g., Wyer, 1996) has prompted a number of reconceptualizations of rumination—for example, as reflecting a broad class of instrumentally oriented recurring thoughts in response to goal discrepancies (Martin & Tesser, 1996)—we conceptualize ruminative responses to dysphoria as generally not adaptive or instrumental and as frequently occurring in the absence of goal discrepancy reduction (cf. Nolen-Hoeksema, 1996; Nolen-Hoeksema & Morrow, 1991; see also Erber & Wegner, 1996; Linville, 1996; Waenke & Schmid, 1996). For example, ruminative responses differ from structured problem-solving in that they involve thinking about one's depressive symptoms and their meanings without actively doing anything to alleviate those symptoms or making any decisions or concrete plans of action. Although ruminations are often problem-focused (Lyubomirsky et al., 1999, Study 2), correlational studies have shown that people who engage in passive emotion-focused and self-focused rumination are actually less likely to endorse the use of active, structured problem-solving to cope with problems or stressful circumstances (Nolen-Hoeksema & Morrow, 1991; see also Carver et al., 1989).

Ruminative responses also differ, both theoretically and empirically, from the depressive self-focusing style (Pyszczynski & Greenberg, 1987) and from private self-consciousness (Fenigstein, Scheier, & Buss, 1975). Pyszczynski, Greenberg, and colleagues emphasize that the defining feature of their depressive style is the focus on insurmountable discrepancies between ideal and real self-images following failure (cf. Pyszczynski, Greenberg, Hamilton, & Nix, 1991, p. 540). This focus on self-discrepancies, they argue, can maintain depression. In contrast, ruminative responses are simply thoughts and behaviors that maintain one's attention on one's existing distress or depressive symptoms and need not involve concerns about personal failures. Similarly, whereas private self-consciousness is defined as a general tendency to chronically self-analyze regardless of one's mood (Fenigstein et al., 1975), we define rumination specifically as a response to an existing negative mood. Finally, dysphoric ruminative thought should be distinguished from worry, which primarily consists of negative thoughts and expectations about perceived future threats; from traumatic ruminations, which are intrusive thoughts about a specific trauma; and from emotion-focused coping, which includes a mixed collection of responses to a negative life event, including participation in distracting activities, wishful thinking, and suppression or denial.

THE CONSEQUENCES OF RUMINATION

Although many people feel compelled to ruminate about themselves and their problems when experiencing dysphoria or depression, converging empirical evidence suggests that such a coping style is associated with numerous deleterious outcomes. The most powerful evidence for the adverse effects of rumination comes from experimental studies that have recruited naturally dysphoric participants and induced them to ruminate in the laboratory (i.e., by instructing them to focus on their feelings, physical symptoms, and personal characteristics) and then assessed these participants' moods, cognitions, or behavior immediately after they have ruminated (e.g., Lyubomirsky, Caldwell, & Nolen-Hoeksema, 1998; Lyubomirsky & Nolen-Hoeksema, 1993, 1995; Lyubomirsky et al., 1999; Nolen-Hoeksema & Morrow, 1993; see also

Morrow & Nolen-Hoeksema, 1990, which used an induction of sad mood). Alternatively, in other investigations, researchers have assessed individual differences in ruminative style using the Response Styles Questionnaire (RSQ: e.g., Nolen-Hoeksema & Morrow, 1991; Nolen-Hoeksema et al., 1993, 1994), a measure of chronic responses to negative moods, and have related scores on the RSQ to other variables of interest using cross-sectional or longitudinal designs (e.g., Nolen-Hoeksema, McBride, & Larson, 1997; Nolen-Hoeksema et al., 1994). Although the correlational nature of the latter studies does not permit inferences regarding causal direction, these investigations are valuable in bolstering the evidence from the induction studies, as well as for allowing researchers to generalize the experimental laboratory findings to individuals with a history of dysphoric rumination in naturalistic settings.

NEGATIVE AFFECT AND DEPRESSIVE SYMPTOMS

The most widely studied consequence of dysphoric rumination is undoubtedly negative mood. To date, numerous studies have shown that people who engage in ruminative responses to dysphoria experience longer and more severe periods of depressed mood than those who use distracting responses. For example, laboratory manipulations of rumination or self-focus (e.g., "think about the kind of person you are") maintain or enhance depressed mood in dysphoric or clinically depressed participants, whereas distraction or external focus manipulations (e.g., "think about the size of the Statue of Liberty") produce significant relief from depressed mood (Gibbons et al., 1985; Lyubomirsky et al., 1998, 1999; Morrow & Nolen-Hoeksema, 1990; Nolen-Hoeksema & Morrow, 1993; Papageorgiou & Wells, 2000; Trask & Sigmon, 1999; Watkins & Teasdale, 2001; Wells, 1990). Importantly, manipulations of rumination have been found not to induce depressed mood in nondysphoric individuals (e.g., Lyubomirsky et al., 1998; Lyubomirsky & Nolen-Hoeksema, 1993, 1995; Lyubomirsky et al., 1999; Morrow & Nolen-Hoeksema, 1990; Nolen-Hoeksema & Morrow, 1993), suggesting that it is the *combination* of dysphoria and rumination that maintains depressed mood.

Studies of naturally occurring dysphoria (e.g., due to stress or traumatic life events) have further shown that people who habitually respond to their negative moods with passive, repetitive rumination report longer and more severe periods of dysphoria than those who manage their mood with pleasant, distracting activities (Nolen-Hoeksema & Davis, 1999; Nolen-Hoeksema & Larson, 1999; Nolen-Hoeksema, Larson, & Grayson, 1999; Nolen-Hoeksema & Morrow, 1991; Nolen-Hoeksema et al., 1993, 1994, 1997; Roberts, Gilboa, & Gotlib, 1998; Schwartz & Koenig, 1996; Segerstrom, Tsao, Alden, & Craske, 2000; Wood, Saltzberg, Neale, Stone, & Rachmiel, 1990). For example, Nolen-Hoeksema and colleagues have conducted several longitudinal studies of the response styles of bereaved individuals. In one such study, caretaking relatives of terminally ill patients who showed a more ruminative style (as assessed by the RSQ) were more depressed six months after their loved one had died, even after controlling for initial depression levels, social support, and concurrent stressors (Nolen-Hoeksema et al., 1994; see Bodnar & Kiecolt-Glaser, 1994, for similar results). Similarly, men whose partners had recently died of AIDS were at a greater risk for psychological distress both one month and twelve months after the loss if they evidenced negative ruminative thoughts during free response interviews (Nolen-Hoeksema et al., 1997).

Other investigations have examined people's chronic responses to traumatic events, as well as to everyday stress and strain. For example, in one study, Stanford University students who reported a tendency to ruminate in an assessment conducted two weeks before the 1989 San Francisco area earthquake were more dysphoric ten days and seven weeks after the earthquake than students who did not have ruminative tendencies, even after their levels of depressed mood before the earthquake were statistically controlled (Nolen-Hoeksema & Morrow, 1991). Furthermore, a study of community-dwelling adults revealed a significant association between ruminative response styles and protracted periods of depressive symptoms (Nolen-Hoeksema, 2000; Nolen-Hoeksema et al., 1999). And, in a daily diary study, the more frequently students reported engaging in ruminative responses to their naturally occurring negative moods the longer their periods of depressed mood, even after taking into account the initial severity of the mood (Nolen-Hoeksema et al., 1993).

Although the majority of research on the relationship between rumination and negative mood has been focused on dysphoric or depressed affect, similar findings have been reported for other negative moods, such as anxiety (Fritz, 1999; Schwartz & Koenig, 1996; Segerstrom et al., 2000) and anger (Rusting & Nolen-Hoeksema, 1998, Studies 1 and 3). Ruminative responses have also been found to be associated with clinically significant psychiatric symptoms, including suicidal ideation (Eshun, 2000) and signs of post-traumatic stress (Nolen-Hoeksema & Morrow, 1991).

Unlike earlier research on dysphoric rumination, recent studies have increasingly assessed major depression in participants to determine whether rumination has similar effects for clinical levels of depressive symptoms. For example, prospective longitudinal studies have found that initially nondepressed individuals who have a ruminative style of responding to negative mood are more likely to experience a major depressive episode (American Psychiatric Association [APA], 1987, 1994) from one to 2.5 years later (Just & Alloy, 1997; Nolen-Hoeksema, 2000; Nolen-Hoeksema et al., 1999; Spasojevic & Alloy, 2001) and more inclined to have severe depressive symptoms (Just & Alloy, 1997; Nolen-Hoeksema, 2000) than individuals without such a style. Furthermore, a large longitudinal study of over 1,100 community-based adults showed that those who evidenced both clinical depression *and* a ruminative style at the initial assessment had relatively more severe and longer lasting depressive symptoms one year later, were less likely to show remission of their depression, and more likely to have symptoms of anxiety (Nolen-Hoeksema, 2000; Nolen-Hoeksema et al., 1999). Similarly, a study of unipolar depressed inpatients found that those who showed a ruminative style after being discharged had higher levels of depression and were more inclined to still show signs of a major depressive episode after four months (Kuehner & Weber, 1999). These studies suggest that rumination may have a deteriorating effect on the course of depressive episodes in clinically depressed patients.

NEGATIVELY BIASED THINKING

Many investigations to date have provided evidence that dysphoric rumination negatively biases people's thinking. For example, in laboratory studies, dysphoric participants induced to ruminate, relative to nondysphorics or those induced to distract, have been found to give more pessimistic attributions for interpersonal problems and upsetting experiences (e.g., "I always seem to fail") and to choose more negatively biased and distorted interpretations of hypothetical life events (e.g., minimizing their successes and overgeneralizing from their failures) (Lyubomirsky & Nolen-Hoeksema, 1995, Study 1; Lyubomirsky et al., 1999, Study 2; see also Greenberg, Pyszczynski, Burling, & Tibbs, 1992), as well as to make more negative self-evaluations (e.g., "I'm unattractive" or "my problems are unsolvable") and to feel less control over their lives (Lyubomirsky et al., 1999). In other experimental studies, as compared with distraction, rumination in the presence of a depressed mood led students to spontaneously retrieve more negative memories from their recent past (e.g., "my girl cheated on me in Santa Barbara") and to recall negative events (such as "my parents punished me unfairly") as having occurred more frequently in their lives (Lyubomirsky et al., 1998; see also McFarland & Buehler, 1998, Study 2; Pyszczynski, Hamilton, Herring, & Greenberg, 1989). Dysphoric ruminators also have been shown to make relatively more gloomy predictions about positive events in their future (e.g., "I won't have many friends after I graduate": Lyubomirsky & Nolen-Hoeksema, 1995, Study 2; see also Pyszczynski, Holt, & Greenberg, 1987, Studies 2 and 3) and to have low expectations for the likelihood of solving their problems (Lyubomirsky et al., 1999, Studies 1 and 3) and engaging in fun activities (Lyubomirsky & Nolen-Hoeksema, 1993, Study 1). In all of these studies, dysphoric participants instructed to distract for eight minutes have proven to be no more pessimistic or negative in their thinking than nondysphorics (see also Pyszczynski et al., 1987, 1989).

A revealing set of results come from a study in which students' actual ruminative thoughts, as spoken into an audiotape recorder, were coded by judges (Lyubomirsky et al., 1999, Study 2). Rumination led dysphoric students to mull over their most troubling problems, such as declining school performance, financial woes, and conflicts with family members. At the same time, those who engaged in rumination while depressed were inclined to be negative, self-critical, and likely to blame themselves for these problems (e.g., thinking "I'm lazy" or "I've always had trouble keeping my friends"); in addition, they showed reduced self-confidence and optimism (e.g., "I'll never pass Biology"), and diminished feelings of control ("I'm lost when it comes to my parents"). By contrast, the ruminative thoughts of nondysphorics were rated as significantly more positive, optimistic, and less problem-focused. Corroborating evidence was provided in another study, in which students prepared written "thought samples" after either being instructed to ruminate or to distract (Lyubomirsky, Kasri, & Zehm, in press, Study 1). Dysphoric ruminators displayed relatively more negatively biased thoughts in general (e.g., "college is too hard") and about themselves (e.g., "I feel all alone") throughout the study session.

Although correlational studies documenting a link between a tendency to ruminate and depressogenic, pessimistic thinking can offer only tentative conclusions regarding the direction of influence, such studies provide insights into the thoughts of "natural" ruminators, permitting greater external validity and bolstering the already rich experimental evidence. For example, in a study of 137 students, scores for ruminative style were significantly correlated with a pessimistic attributional style (e.g., stable, global, and internal explanations of negative events), maladaptive attitudes (e.g., pessimism, low expectations of control, and perfectionism), and self-criticism (e.g., "if I fail to live up to expectations, I feel unworthy": Spasojevic & Alloy, 2001). In investigations of community-dwelling adults, ruminative style has been found to be associated with a pessimistic outlook (Nolen-Hoeksema et al., 1994) and a reduced sense of mastery over one's life (Nolen-Hoeksema & Jackson, 2001; Nolen-Hoeksema et al., 1999; see also Waenke & Schmid, 1996). Corroborating the results from the rumination induction studies, individuals with a tendency to ruminate have also been found to express negatively biased thoughts in free associations, to evaluate both themselves (Ward, Lyubomirsky, Sousa, & Nolen-Hoeksema, 2003) and their families (Aymanns, Filipp, & Klauer, 1995) in an unfavorable way, to recall negatively biased memories (McFarland & Buehler, 1998, Studies 3, 4, and 5), and to show low self-confidence in their plans (Ward et al., 2003).

POOR PROBLEM-SOLVING

In addition to enhancing negatively biased thinking, rumination in the context of a depressed mood has been shown to impair people's problem-solving skills. Specifically, dysphoric rumination appears to interfere with one or more of the "stages" of the problem-solving process—that is, (1) definition or appraisal of the problem, (2) generation and selection of alternative solutions, and (3) solution implementation (e.g., D'Zurilla & Goldfried, 1971). Studies have provided evidence that ruminative focusing leads dysphoric individuals to appraise their problems as overwhelming and unsolvable (stage 1: Lyubomirsky et al., 1999, Studies 1 and 3), to fail to come up with effective problem solutions (stage 2: Lyubomirsky et al., 1999, Study 3; Lyubomirsky & Nolen-Hoeksema, 1995, Study 3), and to be reluctant to implement them (stage 3: Lyubomirsky et al., 1999, Studies 1 and 3; see also Lyubomirsky & Nolen-Hoeksema, 1993; Ward et al., 2003).

To date, the strongest evidence for the thesis that rumination impairs problem solving comes from an experiment in which, after engaging in either a ruminative or distracting task, students were instructed to imagine themselves experiencing several interpersonal and achievement problems (e.g., "a friend seems to be avoiding you": cf. Platt & Spivack, 1975) and then to write detailed descriptions of the steps they would take to resolve each problem (Lyubomirsky & Nolen-Hoeksema, 1995, Study 1; for a replication, see Lyubomirsky et al., 1999, Study 3). Dysphoric students who ruminated generated less effective solutions to the hypothetical problems than dysphorics who distracted or nondysphoric participants who ruminated or distracted (see also Brockner, 1979; Brockner & Hulton, 1978; Kuhl, 1981; Strack, Blaney, Ganellen, & Coyne, 1985).

Formulating an effective solution to one's personal problems is clearly an important step of the problem-solving process. However, even once a promising plan has been conceived, an equally important step is to actually go ahead and carry it out. Unfortunately, this part appears to be difficult for dysphoric ruminators. For example, in one laboratory study, dysphoric students who ruminated about themselves came up with perfectly good solutions to their most pressing current problems (e.g., "study harder" or "spend less money"), but showed a reduced likelihood of actually implementing those solutions (Lyubomirsky et al., 1999, Studies 1 and 3; see also Lyubomirsky & Nolen-Hoeksema, 1993, Study 1).

Naturalistic, correlational studies further reinforce the laboratory evidence. People with ruminative tendencies report being relatively less inclined to engage in active problem-solving during stressful times (Nolen-Hoeksema & Morrow, 1991), tend to show maladaptive and even dangerous responses to interpersonal offenses (e.g., "I'll make him pay": McCullough, Bellah, Kilpatrick, & Johnson, 2001; McCullough et al., 1998), and express reduced satisfaction and commitment to their solutions and plans (Ward et al., 2003).

IMPAIRED MOTIVATION AND INHIBITION OF INSTRUMENTAL BEHAVIOR

One of the ways that ruminative responses to depressed mood can interfere with effective problem-solving is by sapping people's motivation and initiative. Rumination maintains one's focus on one's depressive symptoms, which may persuade dysphorics that they lack the efficacy and wherewithal to engage in constructive behavior (e.g., to carry out solutions to problems or to participate in mood-alleviating activities). Indeed, the results of several studies suggest that people who focus on themselves and their feelings in the context of a negative mood show reduced motivation to initiate instrumental behavior. For example, Lyubomirsky and colleagues (1999) asked students to generate their three biggest problems and then to come up with possible solutions to these problems. Rumination led dysphoric respondents to come up with solutions to their problems that they believed to be effective, but at the same time it lowered the likelihood that they would actually take action to solve these problems. Supporting these findings, a previous study revealed that, although dysphoric ruminators recognized that pleasant, distracting activities would lift their mood, they were unwilling to do them (Lyubomirsky & Nolen-Hoeksema, 1993, Study 1; see also Wenzlaff et al., 1988).

The consequences of ruminative thinking for the inhibition of instrumental action can be troublesome or inconvenient at best, and serious and dangerous at worst. In the domain of health, laboratory and field studies suggest that women with chronic ruminative styles suffer heightened distress upon discovering potential health symptoms (e.g., a breast lump) and, consequently, delay seeking a diagnosis (Lyubomirsky, Kasri, & Chang, 2003). For example, a recent naturalistic investigation showed that women with breast cancer with a tendency to ruminate reported having delayed the presentation of their initial cancer symptoms to a physician more than two months longer than did nonruminators (Study 2). Notably, the relation between rumination and delay was not mediated by anxiety or cancer-related fears. In another set of studies, undergraduate ruminators engaged in community problem solving (i.e., formulating a plan to overhaul their university's housing system or to improve the course curriculum) were found to be more reluctant than non-ruminators to put into effect the plans that they devised (Ward et al., 2003). In sum, ruminators' motivational deficits may inhibit them from enacting solutions to problems or taking appropriate action in various situations.

IMPAIRED CONCENTRATION AND COGNITION

Rumination in the context of dysphoria has also been found to interfere with concentration and to impair performance on cognitive tasks. In a series of three experimental laboratory studies, dysphoric students who ruminated about their feelings and personal characteristics reported diminished concentration on academic tasks, needed additional time during reading and test-taking, and displayed impaired work strategies and performance (Lyubomirsky, Kasri, & Zehm, in press; see also Kuhl, 1981; Strack et al., 1985). For example, in one study, as compared with dysphoric distractors, dysphoric ruminators who were instructed to read a passage from a graduate school entrance exam reported more difficulty concentrating and more frequent interfering, off-task thoughts (e.g., "I thought about the difficulty of the task"), were slower in reading the passage, and more likely to return to previously read material. In yet another study, dysphoric ruminators were less proficient at catching spelling and grammatical mistakes on a page of written prose than dysphoric distractors or nondysphoric students. Again, rumination alone in the absence of a depressed mood was not associated with impaired concentration in these studies.

Investigations using cognitive laboratory tasks highlight possible cognitive deficits associated with rumination. For example, depressed or dysphoric participants who engaged in ruminative thinking were more likely to show evidence of a type of "overgeneral" (i.e., categoric) autobiographical memory implicated in the maintenance of depression (Watkins & Teasdale, 2001; Watkins, Teasdale, & Williams, 2000), as well as to exhibit memory impairments in a controlled retrieval task (Hertel, 1998), than participants who did not focus or ruminate about themselves. Furthermore, a recent study found that individuals with a ruminative style made more perseverative errors on the Wisconsin Card Sorting Test, a task that requires cognitive flexibility and set shifting, and took more time on a measure of psychomotor speed than did nonruminators (R. N. Davis & Nolen-Hoeksema, 2000). Finally, dysphoric students induced to focus on themselves or on their feelings have been found to perform relatively worse on cognitive discrimination (Kuhl, 1981) and anagram-solving tasks (Strack et al., 1985). Although the precise implications of the cognitive impairments demonstrated in these studies are not yet clear, individuals with a ruminative style may be at risk for performance decrements in educational and occupational domains.

INCREASED STRESS AND PROBLEMS

The array of adverse consequences associated with dysphoric rumination can conspire to produce additional negative effects, including those for people's health, relationships, and levels of stress and emotional adjustment. It is worth noting, however, that research evidence for these effects comes solely from correlational investigations.

Threats to physical health

For example, as described above, relative to nonruminators, women with a ruminative style have been shown to delay help-seeking for a serious physical symptom—a breast lump (Lyubomirsky, Kasri, & Chang, 2003). The results of this work are significant in light of research findings that the longer a woman waits to seek a diagnosis after discovering a breast symptom the more advanced her cancer will be and the lower likelihood of her survival (e.g., Neave, Mason, & Kay, 1990). Although research in the health domain is scarce, other correlational studies have also found associations between rumination and health risks. For example, a tendency toward rumination was related to low compliance with one's medical regimen among a diverse set of cancer patients in Germany (Aymanns et al., 1995), and emotion-focused rumination predicted rehospitalization four months after a coronary event, such as a heart attack, among first-time patients (Fritz, 1999).

Impaired social relationships

The interpersonal relationships of dysphoric ruminators also clearly suffer. Although to date only cross-sectional research has been conducted to investigate this issue, the results are quite consistent. First, chronic ruminators appear to behave in ways that are counterproductive to their relationships with family, friends, and even strangers. For example, several studies have found an association between rumination and the desire for revenge after an interpersonal transgression or slight (e.g., "I want to see her hurt and miserable": McCullough et al., 1998, 2001), as well as increased aggression following a provocation (Collins & Bell, 1997). Other investigations have provided evidence that ruminators, as compared with non-ruminators, suffer from "unmitigated communion" (i.e., the tendency to assume undue responsibility for the well-being of others: Nolen-Hoeksema & Jackson, 2001), dependency (e.g., "I often think about the danger of losing someone who is close to me"), and neediness (e.g., "I urgently need things that only other people can provide": Spasojevic & Alloy, 2001). Thus, it is not surprising that people who ruminate in response to depressed moods are perceived unfavorably by others (Schwartz & McCombs Thomas, 1995). These socially maladaptive tendencies may also account in part for the greater social friction that chronic ruminators experience following a trauma (Nolen-Hoeksema & Davis, 1999; Nolen-Hoeksema et al., 1994), as well as for their reports of receiving inadequate social support (Nolen-Hoeksema & Davis, 1999; Nolen-Hoeksema et al., 1994) and lower quality instrumental family support, in particular (Aymanns et al., 1995). For example, in the study by Aymanns and colleagues, the families of cancer patients with a ruminative style were more likely to avoid communicating with them about the disease and less inclined to urge the patients to take personal initiative.

Stress and emotional adjustment

Although many people ruminate because they believe that it will help solve their problems, ironically, ruminative responses to distress have been associated with ever-greater problems and stress. Nolen-Hoeksema and colleagues have documented that over a year-long period ruminators report more increases in stressful events in their lives (Nolen-Hoeksema et al., 1999) and more social friction and social isolation (Nolen-Hoeksema & Davis, 1999) than do nonruminators (see also Nolen-Hoeksema et al., 1994). In another study, caregivers of relatives with progressive dementia reported greater stress and fewer social roles and social contacts after their loved one's death if they had a tendency to ruminate (Bodnar & Kiecolt-Glaser, 1994). Not surprisingly, dysphoric rumination also appears to be associated with low morale and poor emotional adjustment. For example, following a traumatic event—such as a natural disaster, the diagnosis of a serious illness, or the death of a partner or close relative—individuals with a chronic ruminative style, as compared with non-ruminators, have been found to express less positive mood and fewer positive states of mind (Nolen-Hoeksema et al., 1997), to show poorer coping and worse emotional adjustment (Fritz, 1999), to experience intrusive and avoidant thoughts (Nolen-Hoeksema et al., 1997), as well as other symptoms of post-traumatic stress disorder (Nolen-Hoeksema & Morrow, 1991), and to exhibit maladaptive attitudes (Spasojevic & Alloy, 2001).

A VICIOUS CYCLE

The research reviewed above paints a fairly grim portrait of the many adverse outcomes likely to characterize an individual with a tendency to ruminate in response to his or her depressive symptoms. Although the empirical evidence for each of these negative consequences is oftentimes drawn from separate research investigations, it is important to note that the various outcomes are likely to have reciprocal influences on one another and thus cannot be truly disentangled. We suggest that the combination of rumination and dysphoria activates a vicious cycle among negative affect and depressive symptoms, negatively-biased thinking, poor problem solving, impaired motivation and inhibited instrumental behavior, impaired concentration and cognition, and increased stress and problems (see Figure 2.1). Furthermore, each part (or parts) of this vicious cycle may influence and "feed back" onto another part (or parts), and the sequence of relationships may follow a variety of paths.

As an illustration of one possible sequence of relationships, rumination in the context of a depressed mood may amplify the effects of the negative mood on thinking by selectively priming mood-relevant information and activating networks of negative memories, beliefs, expectations, and schemas (e.g., Bower, 1991; Forgas, 1991; Teasdale, 1983). In turn, the resulting negatively-biased judgments and interpretations may maintain, or even enhance, depressed mood, nourishing the vicious cycle between depressed mood and thinking. Depressed mood plus rumination may similarly enhance the effects of negative mood on problem solving and motivation (e.g., by heightening self-doubts about one's ability to tackle problems or by depressing the motivation and resourcefulness to do so) and instrumental behavior (e.g., by impairing one's concentration or cognitive agility). For example, when a chronic ruminator is feeling depressed, her personal problems and stresses can become overwhelming and even take on threatening proportions. Consequently, she may allow her overly pessimistic expectations to inhibit herself from taking appropriate risks. Alternatively, her negative thoughts may promote self-fulfilling prophecies in which she acts on her negative conclusions and expectations in ways that create trouble (e.g., by confronting her spouse about nonexistent marital problems or by passing up a perfectly good job).

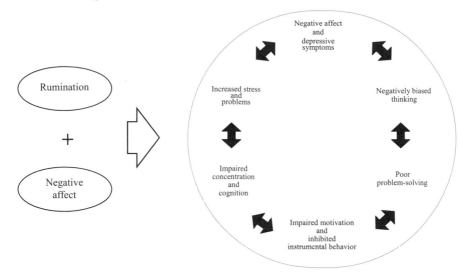

Figure 2.1. A vicious cycle between rumination, negative affect, and multiple adverse consequences

Furthermore, dysphoric ruminators may interpret their circumstances in a distorted and pessimistic manner and retrieve unpleasant memories from their past to support their negative conclusions. Consequently, they may take too long to think about how to resolve their problems; they may generate poor solutions; or, alternatively, they may come up with good solutions, but, given their reduced energy and motivation, be reluctant to initiate action to go through with them. The final result is that the problems do not disappear, or worse, are aggravated, thus maintaining or further exacerbating negative mood and adding more firewood to feed the vicious cycle (see Figure 2.1).

As an illustration of yet another possible sequence of relationships, deficits in concentration, motivation and instrumental behavior may reduce people's effectiveness at work and their facility in social situations, leading to strained relationships and lost business opportunities, and in turn contributing to ever-greater problems and distress. For example, dysphoric ruminators appear to have generally low expectations of control and to believe that they lack the energy, resources, or ability to respond appropriately to their life situations. As a result, they may fail to take constructive action or to enact appropriate solutions to problems. Furthermore, their ruminative thoughts, which are often absorbing, compelling, and self-perpetuating, are likely to intrude during both trivial and important everyday activities and chores, thereby interfering with concentration and performance. For example, engaging in dysphoric rumination could lead people to neglect important social cues during a conversation with their boss, to miss an opportunity to present their views during a business meeting, or to be inattentive to their child or spouse. In sum, by triggering a host of cognitive, motivational, and behavioral deficits, dysphoric ruminators may unwittingly end up exacerbating their problems and elevating their levels of stress, thus, further reinforcing their depressive symptoms (see Figure 2.1). Indeed, the ultimate negative consequence of dysphoric rumination may be continued dysphoric rumination.

FUTURE DIRECTIONS AND IMPLICATIONS

The results from numerous experimental and correlational investigations converge on the conclusion that dysphoric rumination is associated with negative, and sometimes even dangerous, outcomes. The research reviewed in this chapter highlights the consequences of ruminative responses to depressed mood for negative affect and clinical depressive symptoms, for negative, pessimistic thinking and ineffective problem solving, for impaired motivation, concentration, and cognition, for the inhibition of instrumental action, and, finally, for increased stress and problems. Undoubtedly, more research is needed to establish the robustness and breadth of these effects, especially with more routine use of experimental designs to allow for stronger causal inferences. For example, the domains of health and interpersonal relationships have received relatively little empirical attention. Future investigators could study the actual behavior of dysphoric individuals in social situations immediately after they have ruminated, as well as determine how ruminators are perceived by significant others, peers, and strangers. Furthermore, the health habits and health outcomes of people induced to engage in rumination or who have a history of ruminative tendencies could be examined.

Ideally, future researchers should use more sophisticated methodologies to bolster the findings of the extant studies, which have almost exclusively relied on self-reports. Behavioral and "real-time" measures, such as codings of videotaped behavior, informant records of activities, or experience sampling methods (Csikszentmihalyi & Larson, 1987), could tap what dysphoric ruminators "actually" do, rather than what they report doing or what they intend to do—for example, in implementing solutions to problems (Lyubomirsky et al., 1999; Ward et al., 2003) or in delaying help seeking for health symptoms (Lyubomirsky, Kasri, & Chang, 2003). Reaction time and physiological measures (e.g., assessments of cardiovascular and immune parameters) could also be used to assess the effects of rumination on physical states and on various aspects of cognition, as well on the "signatures" of the basic emotions (Frijda, 1986; Lazarus, 1991). Furthermore, a challenge for future investigators would be to develop innovative ways to measure more directly such constructs as insight (Lyubomirsky & Nolen-Hoeksema, 1993), motivation (Lyubomirsky et al., 1999), and concentration (Lyubomirsky, Kasri, & Zehm, in press).

Another direction for future research would be to extend and improve current measures of ruminative style (i.e., the RSQ), as well as the procedures for inducing rumination in the laboratory. For example, following recent research suggesting that ruminative responses may be multidimensional in nature (Fritz, 1999; Roberts et al., 1998), researchers may wish to consider developing separate measures of distinct components of rumination. Furthermore, because tendencies to ruminate, as well as most of the outcome measures used in the research in this area, are customarily measured via self-report, we must be vigilant of inherent difficulties with this method. Participants may show systematic bias in their responses or be simply unaware of their cognitive and affective experiences and thus unable to accurately report them. For example, if ruminators are more attuned to their internal states than non-ruminators, they may report greater intensity or variability in their emotions and physical symptoms. Nevertheless, we believe that the participants themselves are our best resources for information about their own internal, subjective states. However, further research may benefit from combining self-report assessments with more "objective" evaluations, such as informant reports and behavioral observations.

Rumination inductions also suffer from their own special problems. For example, because rumination occurs "in people's heads," researchers cannot verify whether participants are actually doing what they are asked to do. Thus, despite the challenge, it is important to develop effective and appropriate manipulation checks. Promising research directions also lie in investigating the precise mechanisms by which rumination produces its deleterious effects. For example, whether the critical feature of ruminative thoughts is their repetitive, disorganized, image-based, or chaotic nature remains a question for the future. Finally, it is essential to test the viability of the hypothesized ensuing vicious cycle. Alternative technologies might be developed to capture the reciprocal and self-perpetuating influences displayed in Figure 2.1 (e.g., by separately manipulating each variable involved in the vicious cycle or by using simultaneous online or reaction time assessments of these variables).

Future research also promises to determine whether the findings of the work described here generalize to other populations within and outside of the United States and Western Europe. Unfortunately, virtually all of the experimental studies of dysphoric rumination have used undergraduate student samples, whereas many of the cross-sectional and longitudinal studies have included diverse groups of community-dwelling adults. Furthermore, given the existence of distinct cultural norms and expectations for desirable and appropriate ways to respond to depressed mood and depressive symptoms, it is likely that the rates, phenomenology, and effects of ruminative thought differ across cultural, national, and ethnic boundaries. For example, in cultures that place a lower value on self-analysis and self-understanding or ones that encourage or necessitate distraction (e.g., through work and subsistence activity), episodes of dysphoric rumination may be short-circuited easily and frequently, thus reducing the likelihood of them contaminating the ruminator's subsequent affect, cognition, and behavior.

Finally, and perhaps most important, applied research should test interventions to teach individuals prone to ruminate alternative emotion regulation strategies in response to negative feelings and stressful or traumatic life events. To break the vicious cycle, mood management strategies, such as the types of cognitive control (Alford & Beck, 1997), attention training (Papageorgiou & Wells, 2000; Wells, 1990), and behavioral (Lewinsohn, Munoz, Youngren, & Zeiss, 1986) techniques taught by cognitive-behavioral therapists, can help alleviate depressive symptoms and counter ruminative thoughts. Diminished levels of stress, problems, and negatively biased thinking, as well as increased motivation, concentration, initiative, and problem-solving skills, will inevitably follow.

When asked "what's the thing to do when you're feeling depressed?" fully one-third of survey participants, ages 9 to 68, spontaneously mentioned reflecting on the reasons for their dysphoric mood (Rippere, 1977). Women, in particular, have been observed to ruminate in even greater numbers (Nolen-Hoeksema, 1996; Nolen-Hoeksema et al., 1999). Furthermore, in two recent studies, 80% of self-identified ruminators (Watkins & Baracaia, 2001) and 100% of individuals with major depression (Papageorgiou & Wells, 2001a) reported various benefits to rumination, such as increased control over one's feelings and deeper self-understanding and insight into current problems. Indeed, contemporary Western culture appears to embrace the notion that contemplating one's feelings in the face of personal problems and negative moods is valuable and adaptive. Our hope is that the force of the accumulating research evidence will eventually erode this belief, so that millions of people can avoid suffering the negative consequences of dysphoric rumination described herein.

ACKNOWLEDGMENTS

This research was supported in part by a faculty intramural grant from the University of California Academic Senate. Correspondence concerning this chapter should be addressed to Sonja Lyubomirsky, Department of Psychology, University of California, Riverside, CA 92521 (email: sonja@ citrus.ucr.edu).

REFERENCES

Alford, B. A. & Beck, A. T. (1997). *The Integrative Power of Cognitive Therapy*. New York: Guilford Press.

American Psychiatric Association (1987). *Diagnostic and Statistical Manual of Mental Disorders* (3rd edn, revised). Washington, DC: American Psychiatric Association.

American Psychiatric Association (1994). *Diagnostic and Statistical Manual of Mental Disorders* (4th edn). Washington, DC: American Psychiatric Association.

Aymanns, P., Filipp, S-H., & Klauer, T. (1995). Family support and coping with cancer: Some determinants and adaptive correlates. *British Journal of Social Psychology*, **34**, 107–124.

Bodnar, J. C. & Kiecolt-Glaser, J. K. (1994). Caregiver depression after bereavement: Chronic stress isn't over when it's over. *Psychology and Aging*, **9**, 372–380.

Bower, G. H. (1991). Mood congruity of social judgments. In: J.P. Forgas (ed.), *Emotion and Social Judgments* (pp. 31–53). Oxford, UK: Pergamon Press.

Brockner, J. (1979). The effects of self-esteem, success, failure, and self-consciousness on task performance. *Journal of Personality and Social Psychology*, **37**, 1732–1741.

Brockner, J. & Hulton, A. J. B. (1978). How to reverse the vicious cycle of low self-esteem: The importance of attentional focus. *Journal of Experimental Social Psychology*, **14**, 564–578.

Carver, D. S., Scheier, M. F., & Weintraub, J. K. (1989). Assessing coping strategies: A theoretically based approach. *Journal of Personality and Social Psychology*, **56**, 267–283.

Collins, K. & Bell, R. (1997). Personality and aggression: The Dissipation–Rumination Scale. *Personality and Individual Differences*, **22**, 751–755.

Csikszentmihalyi, M. (1990). *Flow: The Psychology of Optimal Experience*. New York: Harper & Row.

Csikszentmihalyi, M. & Larson, R. (1987). Validity and reliability of the experience-sampling method. *Journal of Nervous and Mental Disease*, **175**, 526–536.

Davis, R. N. & Nolen-Hoeksema, S. (2000). Cognitive inflexibility among ruminators and nonruminators. *Cognitive Therapy and Research*, **24**, 699–711.

D'Zurilla, T. J. & Goldfried, M. R. (1971). Problem solving and behavior modification. *Journal of Abnormal Psychology*, **78**, 107–126.

Erber, R. & Wegner, D. M. (1996). Ruminations on the rebound. In: R. S. Wyer, Jr (ed.), *Ruminative Thoughts* (pp. 73–79). Mahwah, NJ: Lawrence Erlbaum.

Eshun, S. (2000). Role of gender and rumination in suicide ideation: A comparison of college samples from Ghana and the United States. *Cross-Cultural Research: The Journal of Comparative Social Science*, **34**, 250–263.

Fenigstein, A., Scheier, M., & Buss, A. H. (1975). Public and private self-consciousness: Assessment and theory. *Journal of Consulting and Clinical Psychology*, **43**, 522–527.

Forgas, J. (1991). *Emotion and Social Judgments*. Elmsford, NY: Pergamon Press.

Frijda, N. H. (1986). *The Emotions*. Cambridge, UK: Cambridge University Press.

Fritz, H. L. (1999). The role of rumination in adjustment to a first coronary event. *Dissertation Abstracts International: Section B: The Sciences & Engineering*, **60** (1-B), 0410.

Gibbons, F. X., Smith, T. W., Ingram, R. E., Pearce, K., Brehm, S. S., & Schroeder, D. (1985). Self-awareness and self-confrontation: Effects of self-focused attention on members of a clinical population. *Journal of Personality and Social Psychology*, **48**, 662–675.

Greenberg, J., Pyszczynski, T., Burling, J., & Tibbs, K. (1992). Depression, self-focused attention, and the self-serving attributional bias. *Personality and Individual Differences*, **13**, 959–965.

Hertel, P. T. (1998). Relation between rumination and impaired memory in dysphoric moods. *Journal of Abnormal Psychology*, **107**, 166–172.

Just, N. & Alloy, L. B. (1997). The response styles theory of depression: Tests and an extension of the theory. *Journal of Abnormal Psychology*, **106**, 221–229.

Kuehner, C. & Weber, I. (1999). Responses to depression in unipolar depressed patients: An investigation of Nolen-Hoeksema's response styles theory. *Psychological Medicine*, **29**, 1323–1333.

Kuhl, J. (1981). Motivational and functional helplessness: The moderating effect of state versus action orientation. *Journal of Personality and Social Psychology*, **40**, 155–170.

Lazarus, R. S. (1991). *Emotion and Adaptation*. New York: Oxford University Press.

Lewinsohn, P. M., Munoz, R. F., Youngren, M. A., & Zeiss, A. M. (1986). *Control Your Depression*. New York: Prentice Hall.

Linville, P. (1996). Attention inhibition: Does it underlie ruminative thought? In: R. S. Wyer, Jr (ed.), *Ruminative Thoughts* (pp. 121–133). Mahwah, NJ: Lawrence Erlbaum.

Lyubomirsky, S., Caldwell, N. D., & Nolen-Hoeksema, S. (1998). Effects of ruminative and distracting responses to depressed mood on retrieval of autobiographical memories. *Journal of Personality and Social Psychology*, **75**, 166–177.

Lyubomirsky, S., Kasri, F., & Chang, O. (2003). *Ruminative Style and Delay of Presentation of Breast Cancer Symptoms*. Manuscript in preparation.

Lyubomirsky, S., Kasri, F., & Zehm, K. (in press). Dysphoric rumination impairs concentration on academic tasks. *Cognitive Therapy and Research*.

Lyubomirsky, S. & Nolen-Hoeksema, S. (1993). Self-perpetuating properties of dysphoric rumination. *Journal of Personality and Social Psychology*, **65**, 339–349.

Lyubomirsky, S. & Nolen-Hoeksema, S. (1995). Effects of self-focused rumination on negative thinking and interpersonal problem solving. *Journal of Personality and Social Psychology*, **69**, 176–190.

Lyubomirsky, S., Tucker, K. L., Caldwell, N. D., & Berg, K. (1999). Why ruminators are poor problem solvers: Clues from the phenomenology of dysphoric rumination. *Journal of Personality and Social Psychology*, **77**, 1041–1060.

Martin, L. L. & Tesser, A. (1996). Some ruminative thoughts. In: R. S. Wyer, Jr (ed.), *Ruminative Thoughts* (pp. 1–47). Mahwah, NJ: Lawrence Erlbaum.

McCullough, M. E., Bellah, C. G., Kilpatrick, S. D., & Johnson, J. L. (2001). Vengefulness: Relationships with forgiveness, rumination, well-being, and the Big Five. *Personality and Social Psychology Bulletin*, **27**, 601–610.

McCullough, M. E., Rachal, K. C., Sandage, S. J., Worthington, E. L., Jr, Brown, S. W., & Hight, T. L. (1998). Interpersonal forgiving in close relationships. II: Theoretical elaboration and measurement. *Journal of Personality and Social Psychology*, **75**, 1586–1603.

McFarland, C. & Buehler, R. (1998). The impact of negative affect on autobiographical memory: The role of self-focused attention to moods. *Journal of Personality and Social Psychology*, **75**, 1424–1440.

Morrow, J. & Nolen-Hoeksema, S. (1990). Effects of responses to depression on the remediation of depressive affect. *Journal of Personality and Social Psychology*, **58**, 519–527.

Neave, L. M., Mason, B. H., & Kay, R. G. (1990). Does delay in diagnosis of breast cancer affect survival? *Breast Cancer Research Treatment*, **15**, 103–108.

Nolen-Hoeksema, S. (1991). Responses to depression and their effects on the duration of depressive episodes. *Journal of Abnormal Psychology*, **100**, 569–582.

Nolen-Hoeksema, S. (1996). Chewing the cud and other ruminations. In: R. S. Wyer, Jr (ed.), *Ruminative Thoughts* (pp. 135–144). Mahwah, NJ: Lawrence Erlbaum.

Nolen-Hoeksema, S. (2000). The role of rumination in depressive disorders and mixed anxiety/depressive symptoms. *Journal of Abnormal Psychology*, **109**, 504–511.

Nolen-Hoeksema, S. & Davis, C. G. (1999). "Thanks for sharing that": Ruminators and their social support networks. *Journal of Personality and Social Psychology*, **77**, 801–814.

Nolen-Hoeksema, S. & Jackson, S. (2001). Mediators of the gender difference in rumination. *Psychology of Women Quarterly*, **25**, 37–47.

Nolen-Hoeksema, S. & Larson, J. (1999). *Coping with Loss*. Mahwah, NJ: Lawrence Erlbaum.

Nolen-Hoeksema, S., Larson, J., & Grayson, C. (1999). Explaining the gender difference in depressive symptoms. *Journal of Personality and Social Psychology*, **77**, 1061–1072.

Nolen-Hoeksema, S., McBride, A., & Larson, J. (1997). Rumination and psychological distress among bereaved partners. *Journal of Personality and Social Psychology*, **72**, 855–862.

Nolen-Hoeksema, S. & Morrow, J. (1991). A prospective study of depression and posttraumatic stress symptoms after a natural disaster: The 1989 Loma Prieta earthquake. *Journal of Personality and Social Psychology*, **61**, 115–121.

Nolen-Hoeksema, S. & Morrow, J. (1993). Effects of rumination and distraction on naturally occurring depressed mood. *Cognition and Emotion*, **7**, 561–570.

Nolen-Hoeksema, S., Morrow, J., & Fredrickson, B. L. (1993). Response styles and the duration of episodes of depressed mood. *Journal of Abnormal Psychology*, **102**, 20–28.

Nolen-Hoeksema, S., Parker, L., & Larson, J. (1994). Ruminative coping with depressed mood following loss. *Journal of Personality and Social Psychology*, **67**, 92–104.

Papageorgiou, C. & Wells, A. (2000). Treatment of recurrent major depression with attention training. *Cognitive and Behavioral Practice*, **7**, 407–413.

Papageorgiou, C. & Wells, A. (2001a). Metacognitive beliefs about rumination in recurrent major depression. *Cognitive and Behavioral Practice*, **8**, 160–164.

Papageorgiou, C. & Wells, A. (2001b). Positive beliefs about depressive rumination: Development and preliminary validation of a self-report scale. *Behavior Therapy*, **32**, 13–26.

Platt, J. J. & Spivack, G. (1975). *Manual for the Means-Ends Problem-Solving Procedure (MEPS): A Measure of Interpersonal Cognitive Problem-solving Skill*. Philadelphia: Hahneman Medical College and Hospital.

Pyszczynski, T. & Greenberg, J. (1987). Self-regulatory perseveration and the depressive self-focusing style: A self-awareness theory of reactive depression. *Psychological Bulletin*, **102**, 122–138.

Pyszczynski, T., Greenberg, J., Hamilton, J. H., & Nix, G. (1991). On the relationship between self-focused attention and psychological disorder: A critical reappraisal. *Psychological Bulletin*, **110**, 538–543.

Pyszczynski, T., Hamilton, J. C., Herring, F. H., & Greenberg, J. (1989). Depression, self-focused attention, and the negative memory bias. *Journal of Personality and Social Psychology*, **57**, 351–357.

Pyszczynski, T., Holt, K., & Greenberg, J. (1987). Depression, self-focused attention, and expectancies for positive and negative future life events for self and others. *Journal of Personality and Social Psychology*, **52**, 994–1001.

Rippere, V. (1977). "What's the thing to do when you're feeling depressed?"—A pilot study. *Behavior Research and Therapy*, **15**, 185–191.

Roberts, J. E., Gilboa, E., & Gotlib, I. H. (1998). Ruminative response style and vulnerability to episodes of dysphoria: Gender, neuroticism, and episode duration. *Cognitive Therapy and Research*, **22**, 401–423.

Rusting, C. L. & Nolen-Hoeksema, S. (1998). Regulating responses to anger: Effects of rumination and distraction on angry mood. *Journal of Personality and Social Psychology*, **74**, 790–803.

Schwartz, J. A. J. & Koenig, L. J. (1996). Response styles and negative affect among adolescents. *Cognitive Therapy and Research*, **20**, 13–36.

Schwartz, J. L. & McCombs Thomas, A. (1995). Perceptions of coping responses exhibited in depressed males and females. *Journal of Social Behavior and Personality*, **10**, 849–860.

Segerstrom, S. C., Tsao, J. C. I., Alden, L. E., & Craske, M. G. (2000). Worry and rumination: Repetitive thought as a concomitant and predictor of negative mood. *Cognitive Therapy and Research*, **24**, 671–688.

Spasojevic, J. & Alloy, L. B. (2001). Rumination as a common mechanism relating depressive risk to depression. *Emotion*, **1**, 25–37.

Strack, S., Blaney, P. H., Ganellen, R. J., & Coyne, J. C. (1985). Pessimistic self-preoccupation, performance deficits, and depression. *Journal of Personality and Social Psychology*, **49**, 1076–1085.

Teasdale, J. D. (1983). Negative thinking in depression: Cause, effect, or reciprocal relationship? *Advances in Behavior Research and Therapy*, **5**, 3–26.

Trask, P. C. & Sigmon, S. T. (1999). Ruminating and distracting: The effects of sequential tasks on depressed mood. *Cognitive Therapy and Research*, **23**, 231–246.

Waenke, M. & Schmid, J. (1996). Rumination: When all else fails. In: R. S. Wyer, Jr (ed.), *Ruminative Thoughts* (pp. 177–187). Mahwah, NJ: Lawrence Erlbaum.

Ward, A. H., Lyubomirsky, S., Sousa, L., & Nolen-Hoeksema, S. (2003). Can't quite commit: Rumination and uncertainty. *Personality and Social Psychology Bulletin*, **29**, 96–107.

Watkins, E. & Baracaia, S. (2001). Why do people ruminate in dysphoric moods? *Personality and Individual Differences*, **30**, 723–734.

Watkins, E. & Teasdale, J. D. (2001). Rumination and overgeneral memory in depression: Effects of self-focus and analytic thinking. *Journal of Abnormal Psychology*, **110**, 353–357.

Watkins, E., Teasdale, J. D., & Williams, R. M. (2000). Decentring and distraction reduce overgeneral autobiographical memory in depression. *Psychological Medicine*, **30**, 911–920.

Wells, A. (1990). Panic disorder in association with relaxation induced anxiety: An attention training approach to treatment. *Behavior Therapy*, **21**, 273–280.

Wenzlaff, R. M., Wegner, D. M., & Roper, D. W. (1988). Depression and mental control: The resurgence of unwanted negative thoughts. *Journal of Personality and Social Psychology*, **55**, 882–892.

Wood, J. V., Saltzberg, J. A., Neale, J. M., Stone, A. A., & Rachmiel, T. B. (1990). Self-focused attention, coping responses, and distressed mood in everyday life. *Journal of Personality and Social Psychology*, **58**, 1027–1036.

Wyer, Jr, R. S. (ed.) (1996). *Ruminative Thoughts*. Mahwah, NJ: Lawrence Erlbaum.

3 Reactive Rumination: Outcomes, Mechanisms, and Developmental Antecedents

JELENA SPASOJEVIĆ AND LAUREN B. ALLOY
Temple University, Philadelphia, USA

LYN Y. ABRAMSON AND DONAL MACCOON
University of Wisconsin-Madison, USA

MATTHEW S. ROBINSON
Massachusetts Mental Health Center, Boston and Harvard Medical School, USA

Depressive rumination, generally conceptualized as an emotion regulation strategy or a metaemotional cognitive process (Gross, 1999), has been a topic of increasing theoretical and empirical interest over the last two decades. Rumination can be defined crudely as a perseverative self-focus that is recursive and persistent in nature. Several theorists, each in a somewhat different way, have argued for the importance of this kind of self-focus in the etiology of depression (e.g., Carver & Scheier, 1981; Ingram, 1990; Pyszczynski & Greenberg, 1987; Teasdale, 1988). Response style theory, proposed by Nolen-Hoeksema (1987, 1991), followed in this tradition, but defined rumination in a more narrow way. Nolen-Hoeksema conceptualized depressive rumination as "repetitively focusing on the fact that one is depressed; on one's symptoms of depression; and on the causes, meanings, and consequences of depressive symptoms" (Nolen-Hoeksema, 1991, p. 569) and suggested that individuals who respond to mildly dysphoric or depressive mood by consistently engaging in rumination tend to have more persistent and severe depressive episodes than those who respond to negative affect by distracting themselves from it. Thus, Nolen-Hoeksema's ruminative response style represents a specific emotion- and self-focused coping style. In contrast to other prevailing cognitive theories of depression that emphasize the content of negative cognitions that arise in response to stressful life events (i.e.,

Depressive Rumination: Nature, Theory and Treatment
Edited by Costas Papageorgiou and Adrian Wells. © 2004 John Wiley & Sons Ltd

hopelessness theory: Abramson, Metalsky, & Alloy, 1989 and Beck's theory, 1967), response style theory focuses upon the cognitive and behavioral manner in which individuals react to their sad mood. According to Nolen-Hoeksema's theory, if people passively focus on their emotional states and get "stuck" in the ruminative cycle whenever they feel down, their depressed mood will likely persist and get worse.

This chapter will focus on reactive rumination, a term we are using to describe rumination that occurs in response to negative mood, negative life events, or both. We believe that many conclusions drawn from research on various forms of depressive rumination could be generalized to other affective states, as well.

RUMINATION LEADS TO DEPRESSION

The role of rumination in prolonging and intensifying depression has been empirically supported in both laboratory and field studies. For example, in a mood induction study in which responses to induced depressive mood were experimentally manipulated, remediation of depressive affect was smallest in the ruminative-passive group. Also, degree of rumination had a greater impact on the remediation of depressive mood than did level of activity (Morrow & Nolen-Hoeksema, 1990). In a naturalistic study of 79 individuals, Nolen-Hoeksema, Morrow, and Fredrikson (1993) found that people tended to be consistent in their responses to depressive mood, measured daily for 30 consecutive days. In addition, participants' level of rumination predicted the duration of depressive symptomatology.

The authors of three prospective field studies with different populations examined the relationship between initial rumination and subsequent depressive symptomatology. In a serendipitous study of 137 students who survived the 1989 Loma Prieta earthquake, pre-quake rumination levels significantly predicted depressive symptoms seven weeks after the earthquake (Nolen-Hoeksema & Morrow, 1991). Initial rumination also predicted depressive symptomatology six months later in a sample of 253 bereaved adults (Nolen-Hoeksema, Parker, & Larson, 1994). The result was maintained even after controlling for gender and the initial levels of depression, social support, stress, and pessimism. Finally, the tendency to ruminate was related to more persistent depression in a 12-month longitudinal study of recently bereaved men who lost their partners due to AIDS, even when controlling for initial depressive symptomatology (Nolen-Hoeksema, McBride, & Larson, 1997).

In summary, substantial empirical evidence has established rumination as a maintenance factor for depressive mood. The reviewed results also indicated that rumination leads to exacerbation of an existent sad mood. But can it lead to a clinically meaningful depressive episode? Findings from our labs suggested an affirmative answer. Just and Alloy (1997) examined the role of rumination in predicting onsets of depression among the 189 participants in the Temple-Wisconsin Cognitive Vulnerability to Depression (CVD) project (Alloy & Abramson, 1999). The CVD Project prospectively followed initially nondepressed freshmen who were at high vs. low cognitive risk for depression to test the etiological hypotheses of the cognitive vulnerability–stress models of depression (Abramson et al., 1989; Beck, 1967). The CVD project participants were selected by screening a large sample of Temple University (Philadelphia) and University of Wisconsin freshmen (about 5,500) with the Cognitive Style Questionnaire (CSQ: Alloy et al., 2000) and the Dysfunctional Attitudes Scale (DAS: Weissman & Beck, 1978). Individuals who scored in the highest (most negative) and in the lowest (most positive) quartile on both the CSQ and the DAS were designated at high (HR) and low (LR) cognitive risk for depression, respectively. In the second phase of the screening process, a modified Schedule for Affective Disorders and Schizophrenia-Lifetime (Mod-SADS-L: Endicott & Spitzer, 1978) interview was administered to a randomly selected subsample of the HR and LR individuals. Based on several exclusion criteria (current *DSM-III-R* [American Psychiatric Association, 1994] or Research Diagnostic Criteria (RDC) diagnosis of any episodic mood disorder or any other current Axis I psychiatric disorder, current serious medical illness, and past bipolar spectrum disorder), a final CVD project sample was identified. The CVD project participants at Temple University (TU) who completed the Response Styles Questionnaire (RSQ: Nolen-Hoeksema & Morrow, 1991) were included in Just and Alloy's study (only participants at the TU site completed the RSQ). Rumination was assessed using the Ruminative Responses subscale of the RSQ, which represents the most validated measure of the construct. An alternative instrument, Rumination on Sadness Scale (RSS: Conway, Csank, Holm, & Blake, 2000) has been used in only one study thus far. The RSQ asks individuals to indicate what they "generally do when feeling down, sad, or depressed," using four-point Likert scales. The Ruminative Responses subscale of the RSQ consists of 21 items assessing responses to depressed mood that are self-focused (e.g., "think about all your shortcomings, failings, faults, mistakes"), symptom-focused (e.g., "think about how hard it is to concentrate"), or focused on possible causes and consequences of the depressive mood (e.g., "think 'I won't be able to do my job/work because I feel so badly'").

Just and Alloy's (1997) results indicated that initial rumination scores predicted the onset of depressive episodes over the 18-month follow-up, even after controlling for the participants' cognitive risk status. Initial rumination scores were also related to the severity of prospective depressive episodes. In addition, individuals' reported tendency to ruminate in response to depressed mood was shown to be fairly consistent over one year, suggesting the dispositional nature of ruminative response style. The response style measured in the nondepressed state also predicted the responses participants reported they actually used when in a depressive episode. Thus, Nolen-Hoeksema's theory was supported and extended, promulgating the trait tendency to ruminate when sad as a valid and reasonably stable vulnerability factor for development of clinically meaningful depression.

The findings from Nolen-Hoeksema's (2000) recent study with a randomly selected community sample of 1,132 participants provided further support for ruminative response style as a depressogenic risk factor. Initial rumination scores predicted onset of major depressive episodes (diagnosed with a diagnostic interview) over a year in this sample, even when controlling for initial depressive symptomatology (Nolen-Hoeksema, 2000). In conclusion, the tendency to engage in ruminative coping in response to depressive mood seems to be a trait-like vulnerability factor for the development of longer, more intense depressive symptomatology as well as clinically significant depressive episodes. It should be emphasized that the accumulated longitudinal findings are not explained away by the concurrent relationship between initial rumination scores and depressive mood.

It is apparent that Nolen-Hoeksema's formulation of depressive rumination as perseverative focusing on one's emotions (as well as causes and conse- quences of one's emotional state) in response to depressed mood has been the most influential conceptualization of the role rumination plays in the etiology of depression. Nolen-Hoeksema (1991) emphasized that rumination may occur once the depressed mood is already present, assuming that all indi- viduals experience at least mildly depressed mood from time to time. Given the abundance of empirical evidence linking this kind of mood-focused rumination and depression, we wondered whether rumination contributes to the develop- ment of depression even before the initial onset of the depressed mood. Does rumination also exert detrimental effects at the early stage of encountering undesirable life events, in addition to the stage during which one starts to feel sad, down, or depressed? Robinson and Alloy (2003) proposed that rumi- nating on negative cognitions when encountering negative life events would lead to depressive mood and subsequently contribute to the initial development of depressive episodes.

The accumulating evidence from our labs suggests that people who have negative cognitive styles and thus tend to make maladaptive inferences when encountering stress are more likely to develop depression than people with more positive cognitive styles (Abramson, Alloy, & Metalsky, 1995; Alloy et al., 1999, 2003). Specifically, according to hopelessness theory (Abramson et al., 1989), individuals who typically attribute negative events in their lives to stable and global causes and infer negative consequences and negative self-characteristics following negative events are hypothesized to be more vulnerable to developing episodes of depression when they experience negative life events than individuals who do not exhibit these negative inferential styles. Similarly, in Beck's theory (1967), people who have negative self-schemata that contain dysfunctional attitudes (like believing that their self-worth depends on others' approval or on being perfect) are hypothesized to be more likely to experience depressive episodes when they confront "congruent" stressors.

Robinson and Alloy (2003) hypothesized that individuals who exhibit both negative cognitive styles and the tendency to ruminate on the negative inferences following stressful events would be most likely to experience depressive episodes. They termed this kind of rumination "stress-reactive rumination" and measured it with a scale that was fashioned after the RSQ. The participants were asked to indicate how often they experience each of the items (e.g., "think about how the stressful event was all your fault" and "think about how things like this always happen to you") after encountering a major negative event. Robinson and Alloy tested their hypotheses with data from the CVD project. Although stress-reactive rumination correlated highly with Nolen-Hoeksema's depressive rumination in this sample, the overlap was not complete. Both retrospective and prospective analyses indicated that the interaction between cognitive risk status and stress-reactive rumination was related to the occurrence of major depressive episodes (Alloy et al., 2000; Robinson & Alloy, 2003). Nondepressed participants who had a tendency to make negative inferences in response to stressors and to ruminate about these inferences both had higher lifetime prevalence of major depressive episodes and were more likely to experience major depressive episodes during the 2.5-year follow-up, compared with all other groups. The interaction of stress-reactive rumination with negative cognitive styles was a stronger predictor of major depressive episodes than was an interaction of Nolen-Hoeksema's depressive rumination with negative cognitive styles. Therefore, the results from our labs suggest that stress-reactive rumination plays an important role in the etiology of depression. The relationship between stress-reactive rumination, which occurs prior to the onset of depressed mood, and emotion-focused rumination (à la Nolen-Hoeksema), which occurs in response to depressed mood, should be further clarified in future studies. In so far as both kinds of rumination seem to be strongly implicated in depression, it is conceivable that a latent depressive rumination construct could capture a general tendency to ruminate at various stages of a depressogenic cycle.

INDIVIDUAL DIFFERENCES IN THE TENDENCY TO RUMINATE

In so far as individual differences exist in the way people regulate their emotions, some people seem to regularly engage in depressive rumination. However, rumination does not seem to be an adaptive emotion regulation strategy in so far as persistently focusing on negative cognitions and on one's depressive mood appears to worsen rather than alleviate it. Why then do certain individuals continue to ruminate in spite of the dire consequences? Papageorgiou and Wells (2001a, b) offered an explanation by examining positive metacognitive beliefs about rumination in people with recurrent major depression. Individuals espousing these beliefs reported that, in the context of dealing with the depression, rumination is a helpful strategy for gaining insight, identifying causes and triggers of depression, solving problems, preventing future mistakes and failures, and prioritizing important tasks. People holding these positive metacognitive beliefs tended to ruminate more than individuals without such beliefs. Moreover, rumination mediated the relationship between the positive beliefs and state and trait depression in this sample. Converging evidence for one type of positive belief about rumination comes from Lyubomirsky and Nolen-Hoeksema's (1993) study in which ruminators believed that they were gaining greater psychological insight.

Recent theoretical work from our labs, aimed at integrating hopelessness and Beck's theory with depressive rumination, suggests additional reasons for the recalcitrant nature of rumination. MacCoon, Abramson, Mezulis, Hankin, and Alloy (2003) propose that all individuals enter a self-regulatory cycle after experiencing a stressor, but cognitively vulnerable individuals have difficulty exiting this cycle. Basing their argument on Carver and Scheier's (1990) self-regulatory perspective, MacCoon et al. propose that when we encounter a negative life event, we tend to turn our attention inward, toward the evaluation of the problem situation. Focusing attention on the discrepancy between the current and desired state (termed "checking") normally leads to finding a solution for the problem, relinquishing goals, or distracting, all of which provide a way to productively exit the self-regulatory cycle. Cognitively vulnerable individuals, however, are likely to have difficulty with all three exits. First, stable and global attributions (e.g., "I am stupid") do not suggest solutions. Second, in so far as cognitively vulnerable people tend to link negative outcomes to more important, higher order goals (e.g., "if I'm stupid I won't get into medical school"), they are not likely to relinquish desire for the goal or distract themselves by focusing on less negative content. Thus, it becomes extremely difficult, if not impossible, for the cognitively vulnerable individual to disengage attention from the perceived discrepancy. This results in self-regulatory perseveration without satisfactory resolution, which can be conceptualized as rumination (see also Pyszczynski & Greenberg, 1987). Rumination in turn leads to ever more depressive mood by keeping depressogenic schemata active and by hindering more active and adaptive coping strategies. MacCoon et al. therefore provide an attentional mechanism through which negative cognitive styles coupled with a negative life event necessitate depressive rumination and consequently affect depression. This perspective also suggests a way of conceptualizing rumination that is both more general than Nolen-Hoeksema's theory (in that content need not be related to depression) and more specific (it defines rumination as a self-regulatory cycle and proposes specific mechanisms through which such a cycle can be initiated and maintained).

Rumination may represent a more general mechanism through which many different risk factors result in depression. Substantial empirical support exists showing that women ruminate more than men (Butler & Nolen-Hoeksema, 1994; Nolen-Hoeksema, 1987; Nolen-Hoeksema, Larson, & Grayson, 1999; Nolen-Hoeksema et al., 1993, 1994; Schwartz & Koenig, 1996). In addition, more concurrent depressive symptomatology, a larger number of stressors, less perceived social support, optimism, and neuroticism were all related to more rumination (Nolen-Hoeksema & Davis, 1999; Nolen-Hoeksema et al., 1994; Roberts, Gilboa, & Gotlib, 1998). More specifically, Roberts et al. (1998) showed that rumination mediated the relationship between neuroticism and the duration of students' retrospectively reported worst lifetime episode of dysphoria and Nolan, Roberts and Gotlib (1998) showed that rumination mediated the relationship between initial levels of neuroticism and depressive symptomatology eight to ten weeks later, controlling for the initial depressive symptoms. These two studies, however, are limited by their use of self-report scales to measure current and past episodes of dysphoria and depressive symptomatology. The findings should be replicated with clinical depressives, if we are to draw more definite conclusions about the role of rumination in the etiology of clinically meaningful depression. Still, the accumulated empirical evidence indicates that some very divergent vulnerability factors for depression, ranging from environmental to personality vulnerabilities, are associated with rumination.

Recent findings from our labs provided direct support for the contention that rumination might serve as a common proximal mechanism linking depressive risk factors and subsequent depression. Spasojevic and Alloy (2001) examined the role of ruminative response styles as mediators of the effects of several hypothesized risk factors on the subsequent development of *DSM-III-R* major depressive episodes (MDEs) in a 2.5-year prospective study with initially nondepressed individuals from the CVD project. Spasojevic and Alloy chose the risk factors that represent well three different theoretical approaches to studying depression: cognitive (negative cognitive styles and self-criticism), interpersonal (dependency and neediness), and epidemiological (history of past depression). Each of these variables has received empirical support as risk factors for depression (for a brief review, see Spasojevic & Alloy, 2001). Spasojevic and Alloy hypothesized that participants vulnerable to the development of depressive episodes, based on exhibiting various vulnerability factors, would consistently engage in rumination in response to their depressive affect. In turn, the ruminative response was hypothesized to directly influence the development of depressive episodes by prolonging and intensifying the depressive affect (Nolen-Hoeksema, 1991).

Spasojevic and Alloy (2001) found that all of the examined depressive risk factors (namely, negative cognitive styles, self-criticism, dependency, neediness, and history of past depressive episodes) were significantly related to rumination. These results were maintained even when controlling simultaneously for cognitive risk status and concurrent depressive symptomatology (only concurrent depressive symptoms were controlled in the case of negative cognitive styles, because they are redundant with cognitive risk status). Spasojevic and Alloy proceeded to test whether rumination mediated the relationships between the risk factors of interest and the number of prospective MDEs. Indeed, ruminative response style did mediate the predictive relationship between four hypothesized risk factors, negative cognitive styles, self-criticism, neediness, history of past MDEs, and number of prospective MDEs. Dependency was not related to the number of prospective MDEs in this sample.

In summary, our findings suggest that individuals who report higher levels of negative cognitive styles, self-criticism, dependency, neediness, and a history of past MDEs tend to ruminate more in response to depressive mood compared with individuals who do not have these depressogenic risk factors. In addition, these individuals have a higher likelihood of experiencing depressive episodes. Most importantly, all of the examined risk factors that predicted clinical depression over the 2.5-year follow-up in the CVD project did so through rumination. Therefore, we propose that the tendency to ruminate elucidates a process by which very diverse vulnerabilities lead to clinically meaningful depression. Rumination may represent a common expression of more global personality characteristics that influence the development of depressive episodes. Also relevant is MacCoon et al.'s (2003) proposed attentional mechanism that might be used to account for rumination as a general self-regulatory problem.

It is pertinent to emphasize another finding from Spasojevic and Alloy's (2001) study. In so far as rumination represents a special kind of self-focus, we proceeded to contrast it with a more general self-awareness construct (namely, private self-consciousness: Fenigstein, Scheier, & Buss, 1975). Nolen-Hoeksema et al. (1994) argued for the distinctiveness of the rumination construct, reporting a moderate significant association between private self-consciousness and rumination. We believe, however, that convincing support for the unique value of rumination can be obtained only by testing concepts like private self-consciousness alongside rumination, and comparing their predictive power. Therefore, Spasojevic and Alloy performed all of the same analyses with private self-consciousness as with rumination. Private self-consciousness did not mediate any of the relationships between the risk factors and number of subsequent MDEs, indicating that the role of rumination in the etiology of depression is not explained primarily by its overlap with general self-focus.

DEVELOPMENTAL ORIGINS OF RUMINATION

Given that the tendency to engage in ruminative coping seems to be a trait-like vulnerability for the development of clinical depression and that rumination mediates the effects of other risk factors on depression, we now turn to the following question: who becomes a ruminator? Although developmental antecedents of the ruminative response style have not been examined empirically, Nolen-Hoeksema (1998) proposed that children who fail to learn active coping strategies and those who feel little control over their environment might be especially prone to becoming ruminators. There is some evidence suggesting that intrusive and critical mothers tend to have children who become helpless and passive when upset (Nolen-Hoeksema, Wolfson, Mumme, & Guskin, 1995). Interestingly, the two parenting dimensions that also have been implicated in the development of depression are parental overprotection (also referred to as high psychological control or low autonomy) and lack of emotional warmth (also referred to as low positive involvement or high rejection). Depressed adolescents and adults consistently report having over-intrusive, overcontrolling, authoritarian, and rejecting parents (for review, see Barber, 1996; Burbach & Borduin, 1986; Gerlsma, Emmelkamp, & Arrindell, 1990).

Children who are abused often feel no control over their lives and might thus be likely to engage in anxious and depressive rumination. A number of studies have supported a link between childhood abuse and adult depression. Most studies to date have focused on sexual abuse (for reviews, see Beitchman et al., 1992; Browne & Finkelhor, 1986; Dhaliwal, Gauzas, Antonowicz, & Ross, 1996), whereas more recent research has examined the role of physical (e.g., Roosa, Reinholtz, & Angelini, 1999) and emotional abuse (e.g., Gibb et al., 2001). No published studies to date have directly investigated childhood abuse as a developmental antecedent of the adult tendency to ruminate.

Spasojevic and Alloy (2002) examined two potential developmental antecedents of rumination, history of childhood abuse and parenting styles, with the data from the CVD project. We hypothesized that psychologically overcontrolling and rejecting parenting and a childhood history of sexual, emotional, and physical abuse would be significantly related to rumination. We also predicted that rumination would mediate the relationships between these developmental factors and number of major depressive episodes over the 2.5-year follow-up. The history of childhood abuse was retrospectively measured using a self-report scale assessing a wide range of specific events by asking respondents to indicate whether they experienced the specific event, their age at onset and offset of the event, and frequency of occurrence (see Gibb et al., 2001). Parenting was also assessed retrospectively using the widely used and well-validated measure of mothers' and fathers' parenting behaviors, the Children's Report of Parental Behavior Inventory (CRPBI: Schaefer, 1965). The CRPBI yields three dimensions: acceptance/rejection (the extent to which the parent expresses care and affection for the child), autonomy/psychological control (the extent to which parents control their children through indirect psychological methods and denial of autonomy), and firm/lax control (the extent to which parents consistently enforce compliance by making rules or threatening punishment).

Spasojevic and Alloy's (2002) results indicated that people who report having psychologically overcontrolling parents (both mothers and fathers) tend to engage in rumination in response to depressed mood. Moreover, rumination mediated the relationship between the overcontrolling parenting and depression in the college-aged offspring. In contrast, rejecting parenting was not related to rumination in this study. Our findings support Nolen-Hoeksema's (1998) hypothesis suggesting that children whose parents act intrusively and fail to teach them active coping strategies might enter the ruminative cycle ending in depression. These autonomy-deprived children may have little chance to develop a sense of control over their environment. They may instead turn inward and, in futile attempts at regulating their emotions, become ruminators. Interestingly, a study that examined developmental antecedents of pathological worry, a process similar but not identical to rumination (regarding the relationship between rumination and worry, see Papageorgiou & Wells, 1999; Segerstrom, Tsao, Alden, & Craske, 2000), found that parental rejection and enmeshed or role-reversed relationships were more common in people with generalized anxiety disorder compared with controls (Cassidy, 1995). The divergent origins of worry vs. rumination may contribute to our incipient understanding of their distinct features as well as their obvious links. However, before much needed replication and extension of the developmental research with rumination and worry is conducted, one should be cautious not to overinterpret the emerging findings.

Spasojevic and Alloy (2002) also found that a history of reported childhood emotional abuse and, for women, a history of reported childhood sexual abuse was related to the tendency to ruminate. Among men, a history of reported sexual abuse was not related to rumination, possibly due to statistical constriction of range. Very few men reported instances of sexual abuse in our sample, leading us to refrain from speculating about the meaning of gender moderating the relationship between sexual abuse and rumination. In line with some previous research from our labs (Gibb et al., 2001), a reported history of childhood physical abuse was not related to depressive rumination. Further, our results indicated that rumination mediated the relationships of childhood emotional and sexual (for women only) abuse to episodes of major depression. Children who are sexually and/or emotionally maltreated may become especially despondent and feel like they have nobody to turn to but themselves. They are likely to experience intense helplessness and hopelessness, due to the complete lack of control over their circumstances. The resultant internal focusing in futile attempts to understand and control the negative emotions and the embrace of passive coping strategies like rumination (in contrast to experimenting with problem-solving, adaptive distraction, or reframing the situation) has a significant potential for setting in motion a rumination–depression vicious circle among the abused children. Due to the self-sustaining and self-perpetuating quality of this circle, which becomes more habitual and entrenched as the children mature, we are likely to witness a stubborn persistence of a ruminative coping style in adulthood.

INTERPERSONAL OUTCOMES OF RUMINATION

The emerging picture of depressive rumination suggests a process invariably tied with profoundly deleterious effects. These undesirable effects of rumination can be attributed to several factors. Findings from experimental studies indicate that rumination leads to more negative, biased interpretations of events (Lyubomirsky & Nolen-Hoeksema, 1995), facilitates recall of negative autobiographical memories and events (Lyubomirsky, Caldwell, & Nolen-Hoeksema, 1998), hinders interpersonal problem-solving (Lyubomirsky & Nolen-Hoeksema, 1995), and reduces willingness to participate in pleasant activities (Lyubomirsky & Nolen-Hoeksema, 1993). Thus, it seems that by keeping the attention focused on negative content, and by impeding more active and productive coping, rumination leads into deepening depression. Negative interpersonal consequences of rumination may provide another important mechanism linking rumination to depression. Considering the nature of depressive rumination, it is likely that high-trait ruminators routinely alienate their interpersonal environment, causing depletion of protective factors like social support and/or an increase in interpersonal stress, criticism, and abandonment. Among people who recently lost a loved one, high-trait ruminators indeed reported seeking more social support, but receiving less social support over approximately 18 months (Nolen-Hoeksema & Davis, 1999).

A recent study from our labs (Spasojevic & Alloy, 2003) examined the interpersonal effects of persistent rumination with the data from the CVD project. We used the Life Events Scale and Stress Interview (Alloy & Abramson, 1999) to assess negative interpersonal events/stress and the Social Support Inventory (SSI: Brown, Brady, Lent, Wolfert, & Hall, 1987) to measure perceived needed social support, received social support and fit between one's social support needs and resources, all across the 2.5-year follow-up. We found that individuals who initially exhibited a higher tendency to ruminate reported needing more social support, but having less of their social support needs met over the 2.5 years. We also found that ruminative response style predicted the cumulative number of negative interpersonal events over the same 2.5-year period, suggesting a stress generation effect of persistent rumination. Further analyses examining three subscales of the RSQ rumination scale identified in previous research (Roberts et al., 1998) revealed that *symptom-based rumination* and *self-isolation/introspection* were both related to the prospective interpersonal stress, whereas *self-blame* was not. In addition, the relationship between ruminating on depressive symptoms and interpersonal stress was mediated by the mean level of reported social support needs over the 2.5 years. All of the results were maintained after controlling for the number of past depressive episodes, cognitive risk status, and initial depressive symptomatology.

To explore whether this discrepancy in the reporting of negative life events was due to an actual stress generation effect or due to a reporting bias, the negative interpersonal events were categorized as either independent or dependent upon a person's behavior, consistent with previous research on stress generation in depression (Hammen, 1991). The tendency to ruminate significantly predicted the cumulative number of dependent interpersonal events, but not independent interpersonal events. Furthermore, the occurrence of life events reported in the self-report questionnaire by the subject, but disqualified subsequently by the interviewer, were examined as evidence of overreporting. Ruminative response did not predict the proportion of disqualified interpersonal events out of the cumulative number of interpersonal events over the 2.5-year follow-up. Both of these findings support the stress generation effect of persistent rumination. In conclusion, it seems that habitually engaging in depressive rumination leads to several undesirable interpersonal outcomes, including less social support and greater interpersonal stress. Thus, the inherently intrapersonal phenomenon of depressive rumination becomes embedded in the social context, as significant others, friends and relatives of high ruminators might become increasingly irritated with its recursive, maladaptive, isolating and pessimistic nature. Interpersonal stress and rejection in turn feed back into the depressive mood, all the while inflaming the rumination.

CONCLUSION

In this chapter, we reviewed the robust evidence linking rumination to depressive mood and clinical depression, as well as burgeoning findings pertaining to the observed individual differences in the tendency to ruminate. We explored the reasons behind the stubborn and self-perpetuating nature of depressive rumination, further suggesting that rumination might represent a common proximal expression of the more global factors that predispose people to depression. Finally, we presented data from two recent studies that began to elucidate developmental antecedents and interpersonal consequences of the tendency to habitually engage in depressive rumination. The emerging picture of depressive rumination is a complex one and we hope that this review adds to the increasing understanding of its many faces and roles in psychopathology.

REFERENCES

Abramson, L. Y., Alloy, L. B., & Metalsky, G. I. (1995). Hopelessness depression. In: G. M. Buchanan & M. E. P. Seligman (eds), *Explanatory Style* (pp. 113–134). Hillsdale, NJ: Lawrence Erlbaum.

Abramson, L. Y., Metalsky, G. I., & Alloy, L. B. (1989). Hopelessness depression: A theory-based subtype of depression. *Psychological Review*, **96**, 358–372.

Alloy, L. B. & Abramson, L. Y. (1999). The Temple-Wisconsin Cognitive Vulnerability to Depression (CVD) project: Conceptual background, design and methods. *Journal of Cognitive Psychotherapy: An International Quarterly*, **13**, 227–262.

Alloy, L. B., Abramson, L. Y., Hogan, M. E., Whitehouse, W. G., Rose, D. T., Robinson, M. S., Kim, R. S., & Lapkin, J. B. (2000). The Temple-Wisconsin Cognitive Vulnerability to Depression (CVD) project: Lifetime history of Axis I psychopathology in individuals at high and low cognitive vulnerability to depression. *Journal of Abnormal Psychology*, **109**, 403–418.

Alloy, L. B., Abramson, L. Y., Whitehouse, W. G., Hogan, M. E., Panzarella, C., & Rose, D. T. (2003). Prospective incidence of first onsets and recurrences of deppression in individuals at high and low cognitive risk for depression. Manuscript under editorial review.

Alloy, L. B., Abramson, L. Y., Whitehouse, W. G., Hogan, M. E., Tashman, N. A., Steinberg, D. L., Rose, D. T., & Donovan, P. (1999). Depressogenic cognitive styles: Predictive validity, information processing and personality characteristics, and developmental origins. *Behaviour Research and Therapy*, **37**, 503–531.

American Psychiatric Association (1994). *Diagnostic and Statistical Manual of Mental Disorders* (4th edn). Washington, DC: American Psychiatric Association.

Barber, B. K. (1996). Parental psychological control: Revisiting a neglected construct. *Child Development*, **67**, 3296–3319.

Beck, A. T. (1967). *Depression: Clinical, Experimental, and Theoretical Aspects*. New York: Harper & Row.

Beitchman, J. H., Zucker, K. J., Hood, J. E., daCosta, G. A., Arkman, D., & Cassavia, E. (1992). A review of the long-term effects of child sexual abuse. *Child Abuse and Neglect*, **16**, 101–117.

Brown, S. D., Brady, T., Lent, R. W., Wolfert, J., & Hall, S. (1987). Perceived social support among college students: Three studies of the psychometric characteristics and counseling uses of the social support inventory. *Journal of Counseling Psychology*, **34**, 337–354.

Browne, A. & Finkelhor, D. (1986). Impact of child sexual abuse: A review of the research. *Psychological Bulletin*, **99**, 66–77.

Burbach, D. J. & Borduin, C. M. (1986). Parent–child relations and the etiology of depression: A review of methods and findings. *Clinical Psychology Review*, **6**, 133–153.

Butler, L. D. & Nolen-Hoeksema, S. (1994). Gender differences in responses to depressed mood in a college sample. *Sex Roles*, **30**, 331–346.

Carver, C. S. & Scheier, M. F. (1981). *Attention and Self-regulation: A Control-theory Approach to Human Behavior*. New York: Springer-Verlag.

Carver, C. S. & Scheier, M. F. (1990). Origins and functions of positive and negative affect: A control-process view. *Psychological Review*, **97**, 19–35.

Cassidy, J. (1995). Attachment and generalized anxiety disorder. In: D. C. Cicchetti & S. Toth (eds), *Rochester Symposium on Developmental Psychopathology: Emotion, Cognition and Representation* (pp. 343–370). Rochester, NY: University of Rochester Press.

Conway, M., Csank, P. A. R., Holm, S. L., & Blake, C. K. (2000). On individual differences in rumination on sadness. *Journal of Personality Assessment*, **75**, 404–425.

Dhaliwal, G. K., Gauzas, L., Antonowicz, D. H., & Ross, R. R. (1996). Adult male survivors of childhood sexual maltreatment: Prevalence, sexual maltreatment characteristics, and long-term effects. *Clinical Psychology Review*, **16**, 619–639.

Endicott, J. & Spitzer, R. A. (1978). A diagnostic interview: The Schedule for Affective Disorders and Schizophrenia. *Archives of General Psychiatry*, **35**, 837–844.

Fenigstein, A., Scheier, M. E., & Buss, A. (1975). Public and private self-consciousness. *Journal of Consulting and Clinical Psychology*, **43**, 522–527.

Gerlsma, C., Emmelkamp, P. M. G., & Arrindell, W. A. (1990). Anxiety, depression, and perception of early parenting: A meta-analysis. *Clinical Psychology Review*, **10**, 251–277.

Gibb, B. E., Alloy, L. B., Abramson, L. Y., Rose, D. T., Whitehouse, W. G., Donovan, P., Hogan, M. E., Cronholm, J., & Tierney, S. (2001). History of childhood maltreatment, negative cognitive styles, and episodes of depression in adulthood. *Cognitive Therapy and Research*, **25**, 425–446.

Gross, J. J. (1999). Emotion regulation: Past, present, future. *Cognition and Emotion*, **13**, 551–573.

Hammen, C. (1991). Generation of stress in the course of unipolar depression. *Journal of Abnormal Psychology*, **100**, 555–561.

Ingram, R. (1990). Self-focused attention in clinical disorders: Review and a conceptual model. *Psychological Bulletin*, **107**, 156–176.

Just, N. & Alloy, L. B. (1997). The response styles theory of depression: Tests and an extension of the theory. *Journal of Abnormal Psychology*, **106**, 221–229.

Lyubomirsky, S., Caldwell, N. D., & Nolen-Hoeksema, S. (1998). Effects of ruminative and distracting responses to depressed mood on retrieval of autobiographical memories. *Journal of Personality and Social Psychology*, **75**, 166–177.

Lyubomirsky, S. & Nolen-Hoeksema, S. (1993). Self-perpetuating properties of dysphoric rumination. *Journal of Personality and Social Psychology*, **65**, 339–349.

Lyubomirsky, S. & Nolen-Hoeksema, S. (1995). Effects of self-focused rumination on negative thinking and interpersonal problem solving. *Journal of Personality and Social Psychology*, **69**, 176–190.

MacCoon, D., Abramson, L., Mezulis, A., Hankin, B., & Alloy, L. B. (2003). *The Role of Attention in Connecting Cognitive Vulnerability to Rumination: Insights from a Self-regulatory Perspective*. Manuscript under editorial review.

Morrow, J. & Nolen-Hoeksema, S. (1990). Effects of responses to depression on the remediation of depressive affect. *Journal of Personality and Social Psychology*, **58**, 519–527.

Nolan, S. A., Roberts, J. E., & Gotlib, I. H. (1998). Neuroticism and ruminative response style as predictors of change in depressive symptomatology. *Cognitive Therapy and Research*, **22**, 445–455.

Nolen-Hoeksema, S. (1987). Sex differences in unipolar depression: Evidence and theory. *Psychological Bulletin*, **101**, 259–282.

Nolen-Hoeksema, S. (1991). Responses to depression and their effects on the duration of depressive episodes. *Journal of Abnormal Psychology*, **100**, 569–582.

Nolen-Hoeksema, S. (1998). Ruminative coping with depression. In: J. Heckhausen & C. S. Dweck (eds), *Motivation and Self-regulation across the Life Span*. New York: Cambridge University Press.

Nolen-Hoeksema, S. (2000). The role of rumination in depressive disorders and mixed anxiety/depressive symptoms. *Journal of Abnormal Psychology*, **109**, 504–511.

Nolen-Hoeksema, S. & Davis, C. G. (1999). "Thanks for sharing that": Ruminators and their social support networks. *Journal of Personality and Social Psychology*, **77**, 801–814.

Nolen-Hoeksema, S., Larson, J., & Grayson, C. (1999). Explaining the gender difference in depressive symptoms. *Journal of Personality and Social Psychology*, **77**, 1061–1072.

Nolen-Hoeksema, S., McBride, A., & Larson, J. (1997). Rumination and psychological distress among bereaved partners. *Journal of Personality and Social Psychology*, **72**, 855–862.

Nolen-Hoeksema, S. & Morrow, J. (1991). A prospective study of depression and posttraumatic stress symptoms after a natural disaster: The 1989 Loma Prieta Earthquake. *Journal of Personality and Social Psychology*, **61**, 115–121.

Nolen-Hoeksema, S., Morrow, J., & Fredrickson, B. L. (1993). Response style and the duration of episodes of depressed mood. *Journal of Abnormal Psychology*, **102**, 20–28.

Nolen-Hoeksema, S., Parker, L. E., & Larson, J. (1994). Ruminative coping with depressed mood following loss. *Journal of Personality and Social Psychology*, **67**, 92–104.

Nolen-Hoeksema, S., Wolfson, A., Mumme, D., & Guskin, K. (1995). Helplessness in children of depressed and nondepressed mothers. *Developmental Psychology*, **31**, 377–387.

Papageorgiou, C. & Wells, A. (1999). Process and meta-cognitive dimensions of depressive and anxious thoughts and relationships with emotional intensity. *Clinical Psychology and Psychotherapy*, **6**, 156–162.

Papageorgiou, C. & Wells, A. (2001a). Metacognitive beliefs about rumination in recurrent major depression. *Cognitive and Behavioral Practice*, **8**, 160–164.

Papageorgiou, C. & Wells, A. (2001b). Positive beliefs about depressive rumination: Development and preliminary validation of a self-report scale. *Behavior Therapy*, **32**, 13–26.

Pyszczynski, T. & Greenberg, J. (1987). Self-regulatory perseveration and the depressive focusing style: A self-awareness theory of reactive depression. *Psychological Bulletin*, **102**, 122–138.

Roberts, J. E., Gilboa, E., & Gotlib, I. H. (1998). Ruminative response style and vulnerability to episodes of dysphoria: Gender, neuroticism, and episode duration. *Cognitive Therapy and Research*, **22**, 401–423.

Robinson, S. M. & Alloy, L. B. (2003). Negative inferential style and stress-reactive rumination: Interactive risk factors in the etiology of depression. *Cognitive Therapy and Research*, **27**, 275–291.

Roosa, M. W., Reinholtz, C., & Angelini, P. J. (1999). The relation of child sexual abuse and depression in young women: Comparisons across four ethnic groups. *Journal of Abnormal Child Psychology*, **27**, 65–76.

Schaefer, E. S. (1965). A configural analysis of children's reports of parent behavior. *Journal of Consulting Psychology*, **27**, 552–557.

Schwartz, J. A., & Koenig, L. J. (1996). Response styles and affect among adolescents. *Cognitive Therapy and Research*, **20**, 13–36.

Segerstrom, S. C., Tsao, J. C. I., Alden, L. E., & Craske, M. G. (2000). Worry and rumination: Repetitive thought as a concomitant and predictor of negative mood. *Cognitive Therapy and Research*, **24**, 671–688.

Spasojevic, J. & Alloy, L. B. (2001). Rumination as a common mechanism relating depressive risk factors to depression. *Emotion*, **1**, 25–37.

Spasojevic, J. & Alloy, L. B. (2003). *Interpersonal Consequences of a Ruminative Response Style.* Manuscript in preparation, Temple University.

Spasojevic, J. & Alloy, B. L. (2002). Who becomes a depressive ruminator?: Developmental antecedents of ruminative response style. *Journal of Cognitive Psychotherapy: An International Quarterly*, **16**, 405–419.

Teasdale, J. D. (1988). Cognitive vulnerability to persistent depression. *Cognition and Emotion*, **2**, 247–274.

Weissman, A. & Beck, A. T. (1978). Development and validation of the Dysfunctional Attitude Scale: A preliminary investigation. Paper presented at the *Meeting of the American Educational Research Association, Toronto.*

4 Mental Control and Depressive Rumination

RICHARD M. WENZLAFF

The University of Texas at San Antonio, USA

We are often of two minds when it comes to negative thoughts. On the one hand, it is unsettling to think about personal inadequacies, unrealized goals, interpersonal concerns, or other unpleasant matters that threaten emotional well-being. On the other hand, if we dismiss these thoughts, we risk losing potentially valuable information that can help us identify problems that need to be addressed. Fortunately, most people are reasonably adept at resolving this dilemma by constructively attending to the negative thoughts that warrant consideration, while discarding those they judge to be without merit. Some individuals, however, fail to achieve this type of mental control and lapse into a depressive cycle of thought suppression and rumination.

This chapter explores the factors that undermine depressed individuals' efforts to control persistent negative thoughts. It begins by examining the origins and nature of cognitive biases that lead depression-prone individuals to construe their worlds in ways that promote negative thinking. The second section explores cognitive precursors to depressive rumination and shows how thought suppression can mask and potentially intensify negative thoughts. The next two sections consider the deleterious impact of depressive moods on mental control and how it can lead to misguided rationalizations for rumination. The final section examines some promising ways of disrupting the self-perpetuating cycle of thought suppression and rumination.

It is worth noting at the outset that some of the studies reviewed here employed dysphoric college students who were identified on the basis of responses to standardized depression inventories. A number of investigators have suggested caution in generalizing results from such samples to clinically depressed patients (Gotlib, 1984; Hammen, 1980; Kendall, Hollon, Beck, Hammen, & Ingram, 1987). However, other investigators have argued that research with dysphoric groups can provide useful insights into clinical depression, noting empirical evidence that dysphoria and clinical depression are on a continuum (Enns, Cox, & Borger, 2001; Vredenburg, Flett, & Krames, 1993;

Depressive Rumination: Nature, Theory and Treatment
Edited by Costas Papageorgiou and Adrian Wells. © 2004 John Wiley & Sons Ltd

Weary, Edwards, & Jacobson, 1995). Indeed, comparable results with college and clinical samples have been obtained in depression research across a variety of domains, including self-verification processes (Giesler, Josephs, & Swann, 1996; Swann, Wenzlaff, Krull, & Pelham, 1992), attitudes (Eaves & Rush, 1984; Weissman, 1979), attentional biases (Gotlib & McCann, 1984; Klieger & Cordner, 1990), and thoughts (Hollon & Kendall, 1980; Krantz & Hammen, 1979). Thus, there is a substantial body of research that suggests a meaningful correspondence between the depression-related effects obtained with clinical and non-clinical samples. However, because the issue of generalizability remains unresolved, the present review uses the label "dysphoric" to identify non-clinical samples.

COGNITIVE BIASES: THE SEEDS OF RUMINATION

Depressed individuals seem to view their worlds through a mental prism that highlights negative aspects of their experiences while minimizing the positive facets of their lives. This type of negative bias may arise from learned patterns of thinking that guide perceptions and judgments (Bartlett, 1932; Beck, 1967). There is growing evidence that a depressive mindset develops early in life and can be fostered by a variety of factors including dysfunctional parenting (Blatt & Homann, 1992), social skills deficits (Cole, Jacquez, & Maschman, 2001), maltreatment (Cutler & Nolen-Hoeksema, 1991; Gibb, Alloy, & Tierney, 2001), and stressful life events (Compas, 1987; Compas, Grant, & Ey, 1994).

These difficult life experiences can foster negative expectations that in turn help promote a heightened state of awareness for negative material. Research has supported this idea by showing that depressive moods are associated with a tendency to preferentially focus on negative information. For example, in a study by Wenzlaff, Rude, Taylor, Stultz, and Sweatt (2001), dysphoric and non-dysphoric participants identified words that were hidden in a letter grid containing equal numbers of positive, negative, and neutral words. The task involved finding words by selecting adjacent letters running sequentially forward, backward, up, or down. Dysphoric participants identified more negative than positive words, whereas the non-dysphoric group found more positive items than negative ones. A subsequent study (Wenzlaff, 2002) using similar methodology found that dysphoric individuals typically identified negative words before the positive items, thereby providing further evidence of a negative attentional bias.

Research using a modified version of the Stroop color-naming task has also provided evidence of an attentional bias among depressed individuals (for a review, see Ingram, Miranda, & Segal, 1998). The Emotion-Stroop task requires participants to name the colors of tachistiscopically presented words that have depressive, neutral, or manic connotations. If depressed individuals possess a cognitive bias for depressive material, their attention should be drawn to depressed content words, thereby interfering with their ability to name the color of the words. Indeed, unlike non-depressed individuals, depressed participants are slower in naming the colors of depressed content words, compared with neutral or manic content words (Gotlib & McCann, 1984; Williams & Nutly, 1986).

Cognitive biases among depressed individuals have also been evidenced with respect to judgments and memory. For example, compared with non-depressed people, dysphoric and depressed individuals are more likely to magnify the importance of failures (Wenzlaff & Grozier, 1988), discount achievements (Sweeney, Anderson, & Bailey, 1986), and recall more negative information (Blaney, 1980). These negative tendencies could foster depressive ruminations by populating the mind with negative thoughts and doubts about self-worth.

Taken together, the evidence indicates that depressed individuals' cognitions are tainted by negativity in a variety of domains including attentional processes, judgments, and memory. Although the precise nature and function of the mechanisms underlying these biases are not well established (Matthews & Wells, 2000), it is clear that they represent a state of mind that could promote ruminative thinking. One of the important questions is whether this negative mental set contributes to the development of depression or is a byproduct of the mood disorder itself. To address this issue, recent research has searched for evidence of depressive biases among formerly depressed individuals who are at high risk for relapse.

COGNITIVE PRECURSORS TO DEPRESSION

The identification of cognitive precursors to depression is important because it would suggest that negative thinking plays a role in the development of the mood disorder and is not simply a concomitant of the emotional disturbance. Moreover, research on cognitive precursors to depression may shed light on the factors that contribute to the escalation of ruminative thinking, thereby offering potential insights for prevention and treatment.

In an attempt to identify cognitive antecedents to depression, investigators have typically studied the cognitions of formerly depressed individuals who have relapse rates as high as 80% (Judd, 1997). The presence of depressive patterns of thinking prior to relapse would offer compelling evidence of a cognitive vulnerability to depression. However, most of the early research in this area found that under normal circumstances formerly depressed individuals did not show elevated levels of negative thinking relative to never-depressed people. In a comprehensive review of this research, Ingram et al. (1998) state that, "An inescapable conclusion from the majority of these studies is that depressive cognition is largely [mood] state dependent" (p. 157). The possibility that depressive thinking is simply a byproduct of the mood disturbance has prompted an ongoing debate about the etiological role of cognitions in depression (Ingram et al., 1998).

MEASUREMENT SENSITIVITY

Research on cognitive vulnerability to depression has typically relied on standardized measures of depressive thinking that ask participants to indicate their endorsement of depression-relevant attitudes, thoughts, or appraisals. Examples include the Dysfunctional Attitudes Scale (DAS: Weissman & Beck, 1978), the Automatic Thoughts Questionnaire (Hollon & Kendall, 1980), and the Attributional Style Questionnaire (ASQ: Seligman, Abramson, Semmel, & von Baeyer, 1979). However, these methods of assessment may be unlikely to detect cognitive precursors to depression for two reasons. First, although the measures in question are able to detect the dysfunctional thoughts that accompany active depression, they may be insensitive to the more subtle forms of depressive thinking that precede the disorder. After all, cognitive models of depression suggest that if depressive thinking were manifestly negative the person would be in a state of depression, not remission. Thus, the cognitions that portend depression are likely to elude detection using standard, self-report measures.

Although a growing number of investigators acknowledge the need for more information-processing measures (Gotlib, Kurtzman, & Blehar, 1997; Hedlund & Rude, 1995; Rude, Covich, Jarrold, Hedlund, & Zentner, 2001; Segal & Dobson, 1992), improved measurement sensitivity alone may not be sufficient to detect cognitive antecedents to depression. Detection may also be difficult because the thoughts in question may be masked by mental control. This possibility is suggested by recent research that finds that formerly depressed individuals engage in high levels of chronic thought suppression. Moreover, several studies now indicate that, when these thought suppression efforts are disrupted, negative patterns of thinking emerge.

THE MASK OF SUPPRESSION

Compared with people who have never had an episode of depression, formerly depressed individuals report significantly higher levels of chronic thought suppression (Wenzlaff & Bates, 1998; Wenzlaff & Eisenberg, 2001; Wenzlaff, Meier, & Salas, 2002; Wenzlaff, et al. 2001; Wenzlaff, Rude, & West, 2002) and expend more effort trying to maintain a positive frame of mind (Coyne & Calarco, 1995). These findings suggest that, despite the absence of a depressive mood, formerly depressed individuals are struggling to suppress emotionally threatening thoughts. Although this struggle to exert mental control may normally keep unwanted thoughts at bay, it can backfire when mental control efforts are disrupted, leading to a surge in negative thoughts.

Ironic processes

Numerous studies indicate that, when thought suppression is disrupted unwanted thoughts enter awareness with greater intensity and frequency than would have occurred if mental control had never been attempted (for a review, see Wenzlaff & Wegner, 2000). For example, in a study by Wenzlaff and Bates (2000), participants unscrambled sentences that could form either a positive or a negative theme. Some participants were instructed to suppress negative thoughts, whereas others were told to form whatever statements first came to mind. Under normal conditions, the suppression group formed more positive sentences than did the control group. However, with the imposition of a cognitive load, the suppression group actually formed more negative statements than did the group that was not suppressing.

A close examination of the processes involved in suppression reveals how this form of mental control can ironically promote unwanted thoughts. Ironic processes theory (Wegner, 1994; Wegner & Wenzlaff, 1996) suggests that thought suppression involves two mechanisms: an intentional distraction process that diverts attention from unwanted thoughts; and a monitoring system that remains vigilant for intrusions that call for renewed distraction. Although the distraction process is effortful and consciously guided, the monitoring system is usually unconscious and less demanding of mental effort. Under normal circumstances, these two processes work in concert so that distraction diverts awareness from unwanted thoughts, while the monitoring system subtly prompts it to further action at the first sign of failure.

At one level, then, the distraction and monitoring processes are complementary, helping assure that unwanted thoughts are relegated to the fringes of consciousness. At another level, however, the monitoring system can undermine the goal of suppression by maintaining vigilance for the very thoughts that have been targeted for elimination. The unwanted thoughts supplied by the monitoring process are most apt to become problematic when distraction is disrupted. Because cognitive demands are more apt to interfere with controlled processes rather than automatic ones (Posner & Snyder, 1975; Shiffrin & Schneider, 1977), situations that tax cognitive resources should disrupt distraction, while leaving the monitoring process relatively unimpeded. The net result of this state of affairs is that unwanted thoughts would intrude awareness with greater frequency and potency than would have occurred if suppression had never been attempted.

Unmasking depressive thoughts

In the first study to test the possibility that suppression can mask depressive thinking, Wenzlaff and Bates (1998) found that the addition of a cognitive load caused a depressive shift in formerly depressed individuals' performance on an experimental task. The task involved unscrambling sentences that could form either a depressive or a positive theme. For example, by choosing five words, participants could unscramble "bright looks the very future dismal" into "the future looks very bright" or "the future looks very dismal." Under no-load conditions, the formerly depressed and never-depressed groups equally favored positive sentences. However, the imposition of a cognitive load (rehearsal of a series of numbers) caused formerly depressed individuals to shift toward negative statements, making their responses resemble those of the actively depressed participants. This load-induced shift in negative thinking was positively correlated with high levels of chronic thought suppression.

In a follow-up study, Wenzlaff et al. (2001) assessed formerly depressed individuals' performance on a novel measure of thought accessibility that involved detecting emotionally relevant words in a letter grid. The task (described earlier) involved finding words by selecting adjacent letters in a letter grid. The results indicated that under normal circumstances both the formerly depressed and never-depressed groups identified mostly positive words. However, under cognitive load the formerly depressed group identified more negative words, reaching levels equivalent to a currently dysphoric group. A similar pattern of results was obtained in a study where participants inter-preted homophones under varying time constraints (Wenzlaff & Eisenberg, 2001). Unlike never-depressed participants, formerly depressed individuals interpreted recorded homophones (e.g., dye/die, pane/pain) in a more negative fashion when they were under time pressure. In each of these studies, the load-related surge in negative thinking was significantly correlated with chronic thought suppression.

The findings from these load studies are consistent with ironic processes theory, which suggests that the disruption of the effortful distraction process allows the automatic monitoring process to exert greater influence, thereby ushering into awareness the very thoughts that had been targeted for elimina-tion. Further support for this possibility comes from longitudinal studies showing that thought suppression is associated with heightened levels of rumination and depressive affect (Rude, Wenzlaff, Gibbs, Vane, & Whitney, 2002; Wenzlaff & Bates, 1998). Of particular relevance is a recent study showing that over time higher levels of life stress interacted with chronic suppression to increase the risk of depressive rumination (Wenzlaff & Luxton, in press).

Added cognitive demands (e.g., life stress, load, time pressure) may be especially likely to foster negative thoughts among people who are at risk for depression because of the cognitive biases they possess. To the extent that these biases exert an automatic influence over attentional processes, cognitive demands would interfere with controlled processes (e.g., distraction) and allow the biases to exert greater influence, resulting in more negative thoughts. However, this possibility remains speculative. Research in this area has not examined the relative contribution of ironic effects and cognitive biases to the load-related surge in negative thinking among at-risk individuals. Moreover, it is unclear to what extent depression-related biases of attention are automatic or strategic (Matthews & Wells, 2000).

Notwithstanding questions about the relative contribution of cognitive biases and ironic effects, the research shows that at-risk individuals engage in high levels of thought suppression even though those efforts are likely to prove ineffective and potentially counterproductive when cognitive demands arise. The allure of thought suppression persists even after individuals have succumbed to depression. Numerous studies have found the depressed individuals score high on measures of chronic thought suppression (Rude et al., in press; Wegner & Zanakos, 1994; Wenzlaff & Bates, 1998; Wenzlaff & Eisenberg, 2001). Unfortunately, once the depressive mood has taken hold, it can aggravate the problems associated with thought suppression.

THE IMPACT OF DEPRESSIVE MOODS ON MENTAL CONTROL

The ability to exert mental control during depression is diminished by two mood-related factors. First, the mood itself can absorb cognitive resources, making it difficult to exert the effortful distraction required for effective thought suppression. Second, the depressive mood can undermine mental control by activating associations to emotionally relevant thoughts, while making mood-incongruent thoughts less accessible.

RESOURCE DEPLETION

Depressed individuals show deficits in recall, problem-solving, general learning, motor speed, and intellectual functioning (for a review, see Hartlage, Alloy, Vazquez, & Dykman, 1993). These deficits suggest that the depressed mood reduces cognitive capacity and interferes with effortful processes (Hasher & Zacks, 1979). Investigators have proposed a variety of explanations for the apparent resource-depleting effects of depression, including biological mechanisms (Roy-Byrne, Weingartner, Bierer, Thompson, & Post, 1986), stress-related factors (Brewin, 1989), and underarousal (Hartlage et al., 1993). Although the precise reasons for this type of cognitive impairment have not been firmly established, it has clear implications for mental control.

If the depressed mood itself depletes cognitive resources, then it would undermine suppression in the same way that a cognitive load does in the laboratory. Recall that suppression involves both an effortful distraction process and an automatic monitoring process that remains vigilant for unwanted thoughts that signal the need to renew distraction. Without adequate resources, the distraction process would be rendered ineffective, but the monitoring process would continue unabated, thereby ushering unwanted thoughts into consciousness. As these thoughts became more prominent, the depressed individual would likely renew suppression efforts, thus assuring that the monitoring process would continue to produce ironic effects. This situation is aggravated by the fact that the depressed mood also enhances the accessibility of mood-congruent thoughts.

MOOD-CONGRUENT THOUGHTS

Insufficient cognitive resources are not the only problem confronting depressed individuals who are trying to suppress unwanted thoughts. Depressed moods can also impair mental control by activating associations to negative thoughts, thereby making them more compelling and difficult to suppress. During depression, negative thoughts often come to mind spontaneously, whereas summoning pleasant thoughts requires a special degree of effort (Bower, 1981). The enhanced accessibility of negative thoughts caused by a depressive mood can pose special problems for thought suppression. In order to keep negative thoughts at bay, it is necessary to redirect attention to other thoughts. However, in depression the thoughts that are most accessible for distraction are also apt to be negatively toned, thereby prompting the return of the unwanted thought through a chain of association.

Ineffective distraction

Research by Wenzlaff, Wegner, and Roper (1988) examined the idea that depressed individuals' efforts to suppress negative thoughts are undermined by the selection of distracters that are emotionally related to the suppression target. In the study dysphoric and non-dysphoric participants read a passage that depicted either a very positive event or a very negative one. Afterward, half the participants were instructed to suppress thoughts about the passage; the other half received no suppression instructions. Participants then provided written reports of their stream of consciousness for the next nine minutes. Analysis of these thought reports indicated that during the first several minutes of the thought reporting period, participants in the suppression condition had fewer passage-related thoughts than did the no-suppression groups. Over time, however, dysphoric participants in the suppression condition experienced an increasing number of thoughts about the negative passage. Unlike their non-dysphoric counterparts, dysphoric individuals' efforts to suppress the negative passage ultimately failed and they eventually reported as many thoughts about the negative passage as did dysphoric participants who were not suppressing. In contrast, dysphoric individuals were highly successful in suppressing thoughts about the positive passage.

Consistent with predictions, dysphoric individuals chose distractors that helped redirect attention to the unwanted material. Analysis of the thought protocols indicated that, unlike non-dysphoric participants who distracted themselves from negative thoughts by diverting attention to relatively positive thoughts, dysphoric participants chose relatively negative thoughts as the focus of distraction. Although these negative distractors aided the suppression of the positive passage, they served as reminders of the negative passage, leading to a high rate of negative intrusions over time. Presumably, dysphoric individuals did not choose negative distractors by design, but instead gravitated to them by default. The enhanced accessibility of mood-congruent thoughts not only facilitated their selection as distractors, but also helped assure that those distractors would eventually serve as reminders of the unwanted thought.

When the inappropriate selection of a distractor cues associations to the unwanted thought, it prompts renewed distraction efforts. If the new distractor is also emotionally related to the unwanted thought, it will again lead to failure, thus creating a vicious cycle of mood-congruent distraction and intrusive thoughts. This repetitive interplay among the unwanted thoughts, the mood state, and distractors can strengthen the associative links that bind them. Wenzlaff, Wegner, and Klein (1991) tested this idea in two ways. First, the investigators examined the frequency of previously suppressed thoughts during mood states that were similar or different from the ones that existed during suppression. Second, they assessed whether the suppression-related mood state would return when the suppressed information was allowed to enter consciousness. The findings indicated that reinstating the original mood (using a mood manipulation) that existed during suppression facilitated the return of the previously suppressed thought. Conversely, participants who were induced to think about a previously suppressed topic experienced a reinstatement of the mood state that existed when they had originally engaged in suppression. These findings are particularly striking because, even though the suppression target was affectively neutral (i.e., a white bear), it became linked to whatever mood (positive or negative) was present during suppression.

Suppression-related binding of thought and mood has implications for understanding the relationship between depression and mental control. By trying to suppress unwanted thoughts, depressed individuals may unwittingly forge particularly strong associations between the unwanted material and the depressive mood. Thus, when the unwanted thoughts later re-emerge, they would help prompt a return of the depressive mood. Conversely, a reinstatement of the depressive mood that was present during suppression would help cue previously suppressed thoughts.

Mood priming

We have already seen that cognitive demands can disrupt formerly depressed individuals' suppression efforts, thereby enabling unwanted thoughts to emerge. The influence of suppressed thoughts during remission may also become more pronounced when formerly depressed individuals experience an emotional downturn that triggers associations to suppressed material. Indeed, correlational studies have found that formerly depressed individuals display more negative thinking during naturally occurring negative mood shifts (Miranda & Persons, 1988; Miranda, Persons, & Byers, 1990; Roberts & Kassel, 1996). Investigators have also used mood induction procedures as a more precise method for identifying the impact of mood on formerly depressed individuals' cognitions. With some notable exceptions (e.g., Dykman, 1997), most of these studies have shown that, during transient negative mood shifts, formerly depressed individuals experience more negative cognitions than do people who have never had a depressive episode (for a review, see Ingram et al., 1998). For example, Teasdale and Dent (1987) found that during normal mood states, formerly depressed participants did not differ from never-depressed individuals on measures of adjective recall. However, when a negative mood was induced, formerly depressed participants recalled more negative, self-relevant adjectives than did never-depressed participants.

Similar results have been obtained in studies assessing dysfunctional attitudes (Miranda, Gross, Persons, & Hahn, 1998; Miranda & Persons, 1988; Roberts & Kassel, 1996). In the absence of a negative mood state, formerly depressed and never-depressed individuals do not differ in their endorsement of dysfunctional attitudes. However, following a negative mood induction, formerly depressed individuals shift toward more dysfunctional attitudes, whereas never-depressed individuals are relatively unaffected (for an exception, see Brosse, Craighead, & Craighead, 1999). The experimental induction of negative moods in at-risk individuals has also revealed more subtle cognitive biases that involve depression-related shifts in attention (for a review, see Gotlib & Krasnoperova, 1998).

The results of the mood-priming studies are consistent with the idea that formerly depressed individuals' attempts to suppress negative thinking can be disrupted by negative mood states that prompt associations to the unwanted material. However, none of these priming studies specifically assessed the role of thought suppression. Most of this research is based on the idea that negative patterns of thinking simply become latent when the depressive mood lifts (Persons & Miranda, 1992). However, the high rate of thought suppression observed in formerly depressed individuals suggests that negative thoughts are more virulent than they are dormant. Moreover, there is a growing recognition that self-generated attempts to regulate moods are common and play a crucial role in determining the quality of emotional life (Erber, 1996; Gross, 1998; Josephson, Singer, & Salovey, 1996). Thus, it seems improbable that individuals who experience the emotional turmoil and mental anguish of depression simply wait passively for the pain to end without struggling to remedy their plight. Although the desire to gain control over unwanted thoughts can lead to thought suppression, it might also prompt a closer examination of the intrusive thoughts in order to achieve some understanding and resolution.

MOTIVATED RUMINATION?

Although thought suppression is a common practice during depression, there are some depressed individuals who report that they intentionally dwell on their negative thoughts (Nolen-Hoeksema & Morrow, 1991; Nolen-Hoeksema, Parker, & Larson, 1994; Papageorgiou & Wells, 2001). These individuals typically believe that ruminating about negative thoughts and feelings can provide insight and facilitate problem-solving. Unfortunately, this belief is based on false hope. A variety of studies show that deliberate rumination actually worsens depressive moods and reinforces maladaptive patterns of thinking (Nolen-Hoeksema, Larson, & Grayson, 1999; Nolen-Hoeksema, McBride, & Larson, 1997; Nolen-Hoeksema & Morrow, 1993; Nolen-Hoeksema et al., 1994; Wood, Saltzberg, Neale, Stone, & Rachmiel, 1990).

Although some depressed individuals see value in rumination, in actual practice they may vacillate between dwelling on negative material and trying to suppress unwanted thoughts. Recent research indicates that there is a strong, positive correlation between suppression (as measured by the White Bear Suppression Inventory: Wegner & Zanakos, 1994) and rumination (as measured by the short form of the Rumination Scale: Nolen-Hoeksema & Morrow, 1991). In a study involving 225 participants, the correlation between these two measures was 0.54 (Wenzlaff & Luxton, 2003). This finding suggests that depressed individuals often seek relief from the vagaries of intentional rumination by engaging in thought suppression. As we have already seen, however, suppression can aggravate the situation by ironically fueling intrusive thoughts. As suppression efforts backfire and return unwanted thoughts to consciousness with renewed potency, the depressed person may be compelled to consider them more carefully. Intentional rumination, however, is likely to worsen mood, further increasing the accessibility of negative thoughts and assuring that renewed suppression efforts will fail.

BREAKING THE CYCLE OF SUPPRESSION AND RUMINATION

Although other chapters in this book provide an excellent consideration of treatment methods, it is worth noting here some approaches that hold special promise for breaking the cycle of suppression and rumination.

GOAL FRAMING IN MENTAL CONTROL

Recent research suggests that a simple change in the goal of mental control may reduce or eliminate the ironic effects of thought suppression. According to ironic processes theory (Wegner, 1994), there is an important difference between trying *to* think positive thoughts (an approach-oriented goal) and trying *not* to think negative thoughts (an avoidance-oriented goal). When the goal of mental control is to think positive thoughts, the automatic monitoring process is alert for either neutral or negative thoughts that would signal failure. In contrast, the avoidance goal of suppressing negative thoughts invokes a monitoring process that is exclusively vigilant for negative thoughts. Thus, although both goals involve the effortful redirection of attention to positive material, the monitoring process associated with suppression is more likely to evoke negative thoughts.

Support for the superiority of approach-oriented strategies comes from a variety of sources, including recent personality research on individual differences in the conceptualization of personal goals. This work compares two types of people: those who emphasize moving toward desirable outcomes and those who focus on trying to avert unwanted outcomes. This research indicates that, compared with an approach orientation, an emphasis on avoidance is less advantageous and is associated with more undesirable outcomes (Elliot & Sheldon, 1997; Elliot, Sheldon, & Church, 1997). These results are consistent with research that has experimentally manipulated the emphasis on approach or avoidance goals (Elliot & Harackiewicz, 1996; Roney & Sorrentino, 1995).

Recent research has specifically examined the consequences of approach and avoidance forms of mental control. In a series of studies, Wenzlaff & Bates (2000) instructed participants to either think positive thoughts or suppress negative thoughts. The investigators examined the efficacy of these approaches when mental control was disabled (e.g., under cognitive load). The results indicated that, whereas suppression led to an ironic rebound of negative thoughts, the positive goal orientation did not. This finding helps explain why positive distraction—in the absence of suppression—often leads to mood improvement for depressed individuals (Barden, Garber, Leiman, Ford, & Masters, 1985; Fennell & Teasdale, 1984; Gibbons et al., 1985; Lyubomirsky & Nolen-Hoeksema, 1993; Morrow & Nolen-Hoeksema, 1990; Nolen-Hoeksema & Morrow, 1993). These emotional benefits may be especially likely to occur when positive distractors are made readily available (Wenzlaff et al., 1988).

ADAPTIVE EXPRESSION

As noted earlier, there is an important distinction between depressive rumination and the adaptive expression of negative thoughts and feelings. Depressive rumination involves the perpetual recycling of negative thoughts. The ostensible goals of depressive rumination involve gaining insight about troubling thoughts and feelings and achieving some resolution of the problems. However, the actual results of rumination are usually an intensification of negative thoughts and a worsening of mood. In contrast, adaptive expression initially involves the venting of negative thoughts and feelings without regard to achieving insight or resolution. This type of expression can take the form of verbalizing one's thoughts and feelings or simply writing them down (Pennebaker, 1995, 1997). Without the pressure to resolve troubling thoughts and emotions, the person is less likely to become mired in them. A variety of studies indicate that this type of expression has beneficial effects for both emotional and physical well-being (Pennebaker, 1988, 1997; Pennebaker, Colder, & Sharp, 1990).

Adaptive expression may yield emotional and cognitive benefits for a variety of reasons. First, it discourages unproductive rumination and avoids the ironic effects of thought suppression. In addition, whereas rumination and suppression may inflate the perceived importance of negative thoughts, adaptive expression is likely to diffuse negative thoughts by desensitizing the person to them. Finally, unlike intentional rumination that imposes undue pressure to find solutions, expression may allow for the gradual realization of new insights and a more integrated perspective of the self (Pennebaker, 1997).

Similar benefits may accrue as the result of meditation. This technique can enable a person to achieve a state of mind where thoughts—regardless of their desirability—are simply allowed to enter and leave consciousness without intent or deliberation. This type of passive mentation is associated with a variety of psychological and physical benefits (Kabat-Zinn, Lipworth, & Burney, 1985; Miller, Fletcher, & Kabat-Zinn, 1995). Under the rubric of "mindfulness meditation" or "attentional control therapy," theorists have advocated this technique as an adjunct to traditional cognitive therapy for depression (Beevers, Wenzlaff, Hayes, & Scott, 1999; Teasdale, Segal, & Williams, 1995). A related technique, although different in some important theoretical and practical ways, is attentional training (Wells, 1990). This treatment is designed to reduce self-focus and increase attentional and meta-cognitive control. Preliminary research indicates that it is a promising treatment for depression and reduces rumination, negative automatic thoughts, and self-focused attention (Papageorgiou & Wells, 2000).

SUMMARY

The mental lives of depressed individuals are tainted by cognitive biases that promote intrusive, negative thoughts. Attempts to suppress these unwanted thoughts can backfire, making them more intrusive and emotionally destructive. Once the depressive mood has taken hold, it makes negative thoughts more accessible and depletes the cognitive resources needed for mental control. Frustrated by their inability to suppress unwanted thoughts, depressed individuals may reluctantly embrace negative thoughts in a misguided effort to gain insight. Unfortunately, this mental maneuver is likely to perpetuate negative thinking and promote more unhappiness. The mental control problems associated with depression can potentially be alleviated with coping strategies that circumvent thought suppression by emphasizing positive goals while allowing for the adaptive expression of unwanted thoughts.

ACKNOWLEDGMENT

Research reported herein was supported by a National Institutes of Health Grant (GM 08194).

REFERENCES

Barden, R. C., Garber, J., Leiman, B., Ford, M. E., & Masters, J. C. (1985). Factors governing the effective remediation of negative affect and its cognitive and behavioral consequences. *Journal of Personality and Social Psychology*, **49**, 1040–1053.

Bartlett, F. C. (1932). *Remembering*. Cambridge, UK: Cambridge University Press.

Beck, A. T. (1967). *Depression: Clinical, Experimental, and Theoretical Aspects*. New York: Harper & Row.

Beevers, C. G., Wenzlaff, R. M., Hayes, A. M., & Scott, W. D. (1999). Depression and the ironic effects of thought suppression. *Clinical Psychology: Science and Practice*, **6**, 133–148.

Blaney, P. H. (1980). Affect and memory: A review. *Psychological Bulletin*, **99**, 229–246.

Blatt, S. H. J. & Homann, E. (1992). Parent–child interaction in the etiology of dependent and self-critical depression. *Clinical Psychology Review*, **12**, 47–91.

Bower, G. H. (1981). Mood and memory. *American Psychologist*, **36**, 129–148.

Brewin, C. R. (1989). Cognitive change processes in psychotherapy. *Psychological Review*, **96**, 379–394.

Brosse, A. L., Craighead, L. W., & Craighead, W. E. (1999). Testing the mood-state hypothesis among previously depressed and never-depressed individuals. *Behavior Therapy*, **30**, 97–115.

Cole, D. A., Jacquez, F. M., & Maschman, T. L. (2001). Social origins of depressive cognitions: A longitudinal study of self-perceived competence in children. *Cognitive Therapy and Research*, **25**, 377–396.

Compas, B. E. (1987). Stress and life events during childhood and adolescence. *Clinical Psychological Review*, **7**, 275–302.

Compas, B. E., Grant, K. E., & Ey, S. (1994). Psychosocial stress and child/adolescent depression: Can we be more specific? In: W. M. Reynolds & H. F. Johnston (eds), *Handbook of Depression in Children and Adolescents* (pp. 509–523). New York: Plenum Press.

Coyne, J. C. & Calarco, M. M. (1995). Effects of the experience of depression: Application of focus groups and survey methodologies. *Psychiatry*, **58**, 149–163.

Cutler, S. E. & Nolen-Hoeksema, S. (1991). Accounting for sex differences in depression through female victimization: Childhood sexual abuse. *Sex Roles*, **24**, 425–438.

Dykman, B. M. (1997). A test of whether negative emotional priming facilitates access to latent dysfunctional attitudes. *Cognition and Emotion*, **11**, 197–222.

Eaves, G. & Rush, A. J. (1984). Cognitive patterns in symptomatic and remitted unipolar major depression. *Journal of Abnormal Psychology*, **93**, 31–40.

Elliot, A. J. & Harackiewicz, J. (1996). Approach and avoidance achievement goals and intrinsic motivation: A mediational analysis. *Journal of Personality and Social Psychology*, **70**, 461–475.

Elliot, A. J. & Sheldon, K. M. (1997). Avoidance achievement motivation: A personal goals analysis. *Journal of Personality and Social Psychology*, **73**, 171–185.

Elliot, A. J., Sheldon, K. M., & Church, M. A. (1997). Avoidance personal goals and subjective well-being. *Personality and Social Psychology Bulletin*, **23**, 915–927.

Enns, M. W., Cox, B. J., & Borger, S. C. (2001). Correlates of analogue and clinical depression: A further test of the phenomenological continuity hypothesis. *Journal of Affective Disorders*, **66**, 175–183.

Erber, R. (1996). The self-regulation of moods. In: L. L. Martin & A. Tesser (eds), *Striving and Feeling: Interactions among Goals, Affect, and Self-regulation* (pp. 251–275). Mahwah, NJ: Lawrence Erlbaum.

Fennell, M. J. V. & Teasdale, J. D. (1984). Effects of distraction on thinking and affect in depressed patients. *British Journal of Clinical Psychology*, **23**, 65–66.

Gibb, B. E., Alloy, L. B., & Tierney, S. (2001). History of childhood maltreatment, negative cognitive styles, and episodes of depression in adulthood. *Cognitive Therapy and Research*, **25**, 425–446.

Gibbons, F. X., Smith, T. W., Ingram, R. E., Pearce, K., Brehm, S. S., & Schroeder, D. (1985). Self-awareness and self-confrontation: Effects of self-focused attention on members of a clinical population. *Journal of Personality and Social Psychology*, **48**, 662–675.

Giesler, R. B., Josephs, R. A., & Swann, W. B. (1996). Self-verification in clinical depression: The desire for negative evaluation. *Journal of Abnormal Psychology*, **105**, 358–368.

Gotlib, I. H. (1984). Depression and general psychopathology in university students. *Journal of Abnormal Psychology*, **93**, 19–30.

Gotlib, I. H. & Krasnoperova, E. (1998). Biased information processing as a vulnerability factor for depression. *Behavior Therapy*, **29**, 603–617.

Gotlib, I. H., Kurtzman, H. S., & Blehar, M. C. (1997). Cognition and depression: Issues and future directions. *Cognition and Emotion*, **11**, 663–673.

Gotlib, I. H. & McCann, C. D. (1984). Construct accessibility and clinical depression: A longitudinal investigation. *Journal of Abnormal Psychology*, **96**, 199–204.

Gross, J. J. (1998). The emerging field of emotion regulation: An integrative review. *Review of General Psychology*, **2**, 271–299.

Hammen, C. L. (1980). Depression in college students: Beyond the Beck Depression Inventory. *Journal of Consulting and Clinical Psychology*, **48**, 126–128.

Hartlage, S., Alloy, L. B., Vasquez, C., & Dykman, B. (1993). Automatic and effortful processing in depression. *Psychological Bulletin*, **113**, 247–278.

Hasher, L. & Zacks, R. T. (1979). Automatic and effortful processes in memory. *Journal of Experimental Psychology: General*, **108**, 356–389.

Hedlund, S. & Rude, S. S. (1995). Evidence of latent depressive schemas in formerly depressed individuals. *Journal of Abnormal Psychology*, **104**, 517–525.

Hollon, S. D. & Kendall, P. C. (1980). Cognitive self-statements in depression: Development of an automatic thoughts questionnaire. *Cognitive Therapy and Research*, **4**, 383–395.

Ingram, R. E., Miranda, J., & Segal, Z. V. (1998). *Cognitive Vulnerability to Depression*. New York: Guilford Press.

Josephson, B. R., Singer, J. A., & Salovey, P. (1996). Mood regulation and memory: Repairing sad moods with happy memories. *Cognition and Emotion*, **10**, 437–444.

Judd, L. L. (1997). The clinical course of unipolar major depressive disorders. *Archives of General Psychiatry*, **54**, 989–991.

Kabat-Zinn, J., Lipworth, L., & Burney, R. (1985). The clinical use of mindfulness meditation for the self-regulation of chronic pain. *Journal of Behavioral Medicine*, **149**, 936–943.

Kendall, P. C., Hollon, S. D., Beck, A. T., Hammen, C. L., & Ingram, R. E. (1987). Issues and recommendations regarding use of the Beck Depression Inventory. *Journal of Abnormal Psychology*, **11**, 289–299.

Klieger, D. M. & Cordner, M. D. (1990). The Stroop task as measure of construct accessibility in depression. *Personality and Individual Differences*, **11**, 19–27.

Krantz, S. & Hammen, C. (1979). Assessment of cognitive bias in depression. *Journal of Abnormal Psychology*, **88**, 611–619.

Lyubomirsky, S. & Nolen-Hoeksema, S. (1993). Self-perpetuating properties of dysphoric rumination. *Journal of Personality and Social Psychology*, **65**, 339–349.

Matthews, G. & Wells, A. (2000). Attention, automaticity, and affective disorder. *Behavior Modification*, **24**, 69–93.

Miller, J. J., Fletcher, K., & Kabat-Zinn, J. (1995). Three-year follow-up and clinical implications of a mindfulness meditation-based stress reduction intervention in the treatment of anxiety disorders. *General Hospital Psychiatry*, **17**, 192–200.

Miranda, J., Gross, J. J., Persons, J. B., & Hahn, J. (1998). Mood matters: Negative mood induction activates dysfunctional attitudes in women vulnerable to depression. *Cognitive Therapy and Research*, **22**, 363–376.

Miranda, J. & Persons, J. B. (1988). Dysfunctional attitudes are mood-state dependent. *Journal of Abnormal Psychology*, **97**, 76–79.

Miranda, J., Persons, J. B., & Byers, C. N. (1990). Endorsement of dysfunctional beliefs depends on current mood state. *Journal of Abnormal Psychology*, **99**, 237–241.

Morrow, J. & Nolen-Hoeksema, S. (1990). Effects of responses to depression on the remediation of depressive affect. *Journal of Personality and Social Psychology*, **58**, 519–527.

Nolen-Hoeksema, S., Larson, J., & Grayson, C. (1999). Explaining the gender difference in depressive symptoms. *Journal of Personality and Social Psychology*, **77**, 1061–1072.

Nolen-Hoeksema, S., McBride, A., & Larson, J. (1997). Rumination and psychological distress among bereaved partners. *Journal of Personality and Social Psychology*, **72**, 855–862.

Nolen-Hoeksema, S. & Morrow, J. (1991). A prospective study of depression and posttraumatic stress symptoms after a natural disaster: The 1989 Loma Prieta earthquake. *Journal of Personality and Social Psychology*, **61**, 115–121.

Nolen-Hoeksema, S. & Morrow, J. (1993). Effects of rumination and distraction on naturally occurring depressed mood. *Cognition and Emotion*, **7**, 561–570.

Nolen-Hoeksema, S., Parker, L., & Larson, J. (1994). Ruminative coping with depressed mood following loss. *Journal of Personality and Social Psychology*, **67**, 92–104.

Papageorgiou, C. & Wells, A. (2000). Treatment of recurrent major depression with attention training. *Cognitive and Behavioral Practice*, **7**, 407–413.

Papageorgiou, C. & Wells, A. (2001). Positive beliefs about depressive rumination: Development and preliminary validation of a self-report scale. *Behavior Therapy*, **32**, 13–26.

Pennebaker, J. W. (1988). Confession, inhibition, and disease. In: L. Berkowitz (ed.), *Advances in Experimental Social Psychology* (Vol. 22, pp. 211–244). Orlando, FL: Academic Press.

Pennebaker, J. W. (1995). Emotion, disclosure, and health: An overview. In: J. W. Pennebaker (ed.), *Emotion, Disclosure, and Health* (pp. 3–10). Washington, DC: American Psychological Association.

Pennebaker, J. W. (1997). Writing about emotional experiences as a therapeutic process. *Psychological Science*, **8**, 162–166.

Pennebaker, J. W., Colder, M., & Sharp, L. K. (1990). Accelerating the coping process. *Journal of Personality and Social Psychology*, **58**, 528–537.

Persons, J. B. & Miranda, J. (1992). Cognitive theories of vulnerability to depression: Reconciling negative evidence. *Cognitive Therapy and Research*, **16**, 485–502.

Posner, M. I. & Snyder, C. R. R. (1975). Attention and cognitive control. In: R. L. Solso (ed.), *Information Processing and Cognition: The Loyola Symposium* (pp. 55–85). Hillsdale, NJ: Lawrence Erlbaum.

Roberts, J. E. & Kassel, J. D. (1996). Mood-state dependence in cognitive vulnerability to depression: The roles of positive and negative affect. *Cognitive Therapy and Research*, **20**, 1–12.

Roney, C. & Sorrentino, R. (1995). Reducing self-discrepancies or maintaining self-congruence? Uncertainty orientation, self-regulation, and performance. *Journal of Personality and Social Psychology*, **68**, 485–497.

Roy-Byrne, P. P., Weingartner, H., Bierer, L. M., Thompson, K., & Post, R. M. (1986). Effortful and automatic cognitive processes in depression. *Archives of General Psychiatry*, **43**, 265–267.

Rude, S. S., Covich, J., Jarrold, W., Hedlund, S., & Zentner, M. (2001). Detecting depressive schemata in vulnerability individuals: Questionnaires vs. laboratory tasks. *Cognitive Therapy and Research*, **25**, 103–116.

Rude, S. S., Wenzlaff, R. M., Gibbs, B., Vane, J., & Whitney, T. (2002). Negative interpretative biases predict subsequent depressive symptoms. *Cognition and Emotion*, **16**, 423–440.

Segal, Z. V. & Dobson, K. S. (1992). Cognitive models of depression: Report from a consensus development conference. *Psychological Inquiry*, **3**, 219–224.

Seligman, M. E. P., Abramson, L., Semmel, A., & von Baeyer, C. (1979). Depressive attributional style. *Journal of Abnormal Psychology*, **88**, 242–248.

Shiffrin, R. M. & Schneider, W. (1977). Controlled and automatic human information processing. II: Perceptual learning, automatic attending, and a general theory. *Psychological Review*, **84**, 127–190.

Swann, W. B., Wenzlaff, R. M., Krull, D. S., & Pelham, B. W. (1992). Allure of negative feedback: Self-verification strivings among depressed persons. *Journal of Abnormal Psychology*, **101**, 293–306.

Sweeney, P. D., Anderson, K., & Bailey, S. (1986). Attributional style in depression: A meta-analytic review. *Journal of Personality and Social Psychology*, **50**, 974–991.

Teasdale, J. D. & Dent, J. (1987). Cognitive vulnerability to depression: An investigation of two hypotheses. *British Journal of Clinical Psychology*, **26**, 113–126.

Teasdale, J. D., Segal, Z., & Williams, M. G. (1995). How does cognitive therapy prevent depressive relapse and why should attentional control (mindfulness) training help? *Behaviour Research and Therapy*, **33**, 25–39.

Vredenburg, K., Flett, G. L., & Krames, L. (1993). Analogue versus clinical depression: A critical reappraisal. *Psychological Bulletin*, **113**, 327–344.

Weary, G., Edwards, J. A., & Jacobson, J. A. (1995). Depression research methodologies in the *Journal of Personality and Social Psychology*: A reply. *Journal of Personality and Social Psychology*, **68**, 885–891.

Wegner, D. M. (1994). Ironic processes of mental control. *Psychological Review*, **101**, 34–52.

Wegner, D. M. & Wenzlaff, R. M. (1996). Mental control. In: E. T. Higgins & A. W. Kruglanski (eds), *Social Psychology: Handbook of Basic Principles* (pp. 466–492). New York: Guilford Press.

Wegner, D. M. & Zanakos, S. (1994). Chronic thought suppression. *Journal of Personality*, **62**, 615–640.

Weissman, A. N. (1979). The Dysfunctional Attitude Scale: A validation study (Doctoral dissertation, University of Pennsylvania, 1978). *Dissertation Abstracts International*, **40**, 1389–1390B.

Weissman, A. N. & Beck, A. T. (1978). Development and validation of the Dysfunctional Attitude Scale: A preliminary investigation. Paper presented at the *Annual Meeting of the American Educational Research Association, Toronto, Ontario*.

Wells, A. (1990). Panic disorder in association with relaxation induced anxiety: An attentional training approach to treatment. *Behavior Therapy*, **21**, 273–280.

Wenzlaff, R. M. (2002). Attentional bias and vulnerability to depression. Manuscript in preparation.

Wenzlaff, R. M. & Bates, D. E. (1998). Unmasking a cognitive vulnerability to depression: How lapses in mental control reveal depressive thinking. *Journal of Personality and Social Psychology*, **75**, 1559–1571.

Wenzlaff, R. M. & Bates, D. E. (2000). The relative efficacy of concentration and suppression strategies of mental control. *Personality and Social Psychology Bulletin*, **26**, 1200–1212.

Wenzlaff, R. M. & Eisenberg, A. R. (2001). Mental control after dysphoria: Evidence of a suppressed, depressive bias. *Behavior Therapy*, **32**, 27–45.

Wenzlaff, R. M. & Grozier, S. A. (1988). Depression and the magnification of failure. *Journal of Abnormal Psychology*, **97**, 90–93.

Wenzlaff, R. M., & Luxton, D. D. (2003). The role of thought suppression in depressive rumination. *Cognitive Therapy and Research*, **27**, 293–308.

Wenzlaff, R. M., Meier, J., & Salas, D. M. (2002). Thought suppression and memory biases during and after depressive moods. *Cognition and Emotion*, **16**, 403–422.

Wenzlaff, R. M., Rude, S. S., Taylor, C. J., Stultz, C. H., & Sweatt, R. A. (2001). Beneath the veil of thought suppression: Attentional bias and depression risk. *Cognition and Emotion*, **15**, 435–452.

Wenzlaff, R. M., Rude, S. S., & West, L. M. (2002). Cognitive vulnerability to depression: The role of thought suppression and attitude certainty. *Cognition and Emotion*, **27**, 293–308.

Wenzlaff, R. M. & Wegner, D. M. (2000). Thought suppression. *Annual Review of Psychology*, **51**, 59–91.

Wenzlaff, R. M., Wegner, D. M., & Klein, S. B. (1991). The role of thought suppression in the bonding of thought and mood. *Journal of Personality and Social Psychology*, **60**, 500–508.

Wenzlaff, R. M., Wegner, D. M., & Roper, D. W. (1988). Depression and mental control: The resurgence of unwanted negative thoughts. *Journal of Personality and Social Psychology*, **55**, 882–892.

Williams, J. M. G. & Nutly, D. D. (1986). Construct accessibility, depression, and the emotional Stroop task: Transient mood or stable structure? *Personality and Individual Differences*, **7**, 485–491.

Wood, J. V., Saltzberg, J. A., Neale, J. M., Stone, A. A., & Rachmiel, T. B. (1990). Self-focused attention, coping responses, and distressed mood in everyday life. *Journal of Personality and Social Psychology*, **58**, 1027–1036.

5 Physiological Aspects of Depressive Rumination

GREG J. SIEGLE

Western Psychiatric Institute and Clinic, University of Pittsburgh, USA

JULIAN F. THAYER

Gerontology Research Center, National Institute of Aging, Baltimore, USA

Physiological assessment provides a window to brain and autonomic processes and thus may aid in understanding causal mechanisms underlying psychological phenomena. Though causal cognitive theories of rumination abound (e.g., Ingram, 1984; Martin & Tesser, 1989; Nolen-Hoeksema, 1987; Philippot & Rime, 1998; Wells, 2000), these theories have been only loosely related to underlying physiology. This chapter surveys potential physiological correlates of depressive rumination as a way of understanding its nature and underlying mechanisms. We focus on physiological processes associated with repetitive, intrusive, negative cognitions since they are central to most formulations of depressive rumination. While there is little published data explicitly linking physiological constructs to depressive rumination, we suggest that considering multiple assessment technologies from neuroimaging to monitoring vagal tone yields a picture of depression as involving sustained processing of emotional information and decreased ability to recover from emotional stimuli. Such sustained processing seconds or minutes after emotional stimuli may underlie aspects of depressive rumination that last for hours or days.

The promise of physiological assessment of rumination lies in its potential to go beyond what self-report measures provide alone. Self-report assessments of rumination may be subject to concerns regarding subject intent and subjective scoring. They may also assess dissimilar constructs. For example, self-report measures of rumination have nominally assessed a trait predisposition to think about depressive symptoms (Nolen-Hoeksema, Morrow, & Fredrickson, 1993), metacognitive features (Papageorgiou & Wells, 1999), distress over exposure to negative stimuli (Luminet, Rime, & Wagner, submitted), and searching for meaning in negative experiences (Fritz, 1999). In contrast, physiological measurement provides objective, less easily manipulable data.

In addition physiological measures provide direct links to underlying brain mechanisms and the ability to measure processes online, as they occur, both in the lab and increasingly in naturalistic environments via ambulatory monitoring techniques.

POTENTIAL PHYSIOLOGICAL MECHANISMS UNDERLYING DEPRESSIVE RUMINATION

To the extent that rumination involves sustained or repetitive negative thoughts, it is expected to result in sustained brain activity. Such sustained brain activity could result from positive feedback loops (i.e., processes that continuously reignite themselves) and from decreased activity in structures responsible for shutting off such loops. We will suggest that feedback between brain structures responsible for emotional processing (particularly, the amygdala system) and decreased cortical inhibition of these structures could be important to depressive rumination.

COGNITIVE-AFFECTIVE LOOPS AND THE AMYGDALA–HIPPOCAMPAL COMPLEX

Ingram (1984) suggests that if cognition is represented as a network in which activation spreads between nodes with semantic and affective content (e.g., Bower, 1981), depression could involve strongly activated connections between negative affective nodes and associated semantic nodes (e.g., representing a loss), creating feedback loops that propagate depressive affect and cognition. Teasdale (1988) similarly suggests that depressed mood could activate negative cognitions that reactivate the depressed mood, leading to sustained elaborative processing of negative information. Such sustained affective associational processes seem similar to depressive rumination, involving repeated involuntary emotional associations. To the extent that rumination involves repeated consideration of emotional aspects of information, brain structures responsible for processing affective information are expected to display sustained activity. The amygdala, in particular, has been implicated in recognizing emotional features of information and in generating negative emotions (e.g., LeDoux, 1996). The amygdala is highly and reciprocally connected to the hippocampus, a brain structure implicated in recollection of episodic associations with information (e.g., Tucker & Derryberry, 1992). Feedback between these systems could thus involve recognizing emotional features of information, being reminded of personally relevant events or information and leading to new emotional associations. Disruptions in both volume and activity of these structures have been noted in depressed individuals and implicated in the maintenance of depression (e.g., Abercrombie et al., 1998; Dougherty & Rauch, 1997; Drevets, 1999; Drevets et al., 1992; Hornig, Mozley, & Amsterdam, 1997; Sheline, Sanghavi, Mintun, & Gado, 1999).

DECREASED INHIBITION OF AFFECTIVE PROCESSING—THE ROLE OF THE PREFRONTAL CORTEX

Sustained or repetitive emotional thoughts and feelings could also occur if brain structures responsible for processing emotional information are not inhibited, or "shut off" properly. The frontal lobes, in particular, have reciprocal neural connections with the amygdala and hippocampal systems. Davidson (e.g., 1994, 2000) suggests the dorsolateral prefrontal cortex (DLPFC) may be specifically involved in inhibition of the amygdala. Decreased prefrontal regional cerebral blood flow has commonly been observed in depressed individuals (e.g., Baxter et al., 1989; Bench, Friston, Brown, Frankowiak, & Dolan, 1993) along with decreased DLPFC activity at rest (e.g., Davidson, 1994) and during information processing tasks associated with frontal activity (e.g., Butters, Zmuda, Varhola, Reynolds, & Becker, 2000). Similarly, multiple studies have shown that non-depressed individuals have decreased DLPFC activity during induced sad moods (e.g., Baker, Frith, & Dolan, 1997; Gemar, Kapur, Segal, Brown, & Houle, 1996; Liotti et al., 2000).

Other, more medial frontal structures have been hypothesized to perform similar functions. Research implicates the insula in maintaining emotional information and the orbitofrontal cortex in its inhibition; this literature has shown decreased orbitofrontal activation in depression (Drevets & Raichle, 1998; Mayberg, 1997; Mayberg et al., 1997, 1999). Drevets (1999) suggests an observed inverse relationship of orbitofrontal activation and amygdalar activation represents a modulation of the amygdala by the orbitofrontal cortex; direct projections exist between the structures (Ray & Price, 1993). Rolls (2000) also implicates the orbitofrontal cortex in storing affective aspects of information, such as how rewarding it is. Connections from the orbitofrontal cortex to the amygdala, via the insula, link these systems (Rolls, 2000). Preliminary research further suggests that the same depressed individuals show decreased orbitofrontal activation and increased negative cognitions (Drevets, pers. commun.). Skinner (1985) has further suggested that an intact frontal cortex may tonically inhibit subcortical (amygdala) activity. Direct and indirect pathways by which the frontal cortex modulates parasympathetic activity via subcortical inputs have also been identified, and these mechanisms have been related to post myocardial infarction depression and the related increased risk of reinfarction and death (Ter Horst, 1999; Ter Horst & Postema, 1997).

Depressive rumination often takes the form of intense conflict (e.g., manifested by worry, self-doubt, and cognitive interference) (Sarason, 1960; Schwartzer, 1996). A host of research implicates the anterior cingulate in monitoring conflict among competing responses to a stimulus (e.g., Botvinik, Nystrom, Fissell, Carter, & Cohen, 1999; Carter et al., 2000) and, more generally, in processing emotional information (e.g., Whalen et al., 1998). To the extent that response conflict can be generalized to the types of intrapsychic conflict common in depressed individuals the anterior cingulate may also be important to understanding depressive rumination. Disruptions in anterior cingulate activity have indeed been commonly reported in depression (e.g., Drevets et al., 1997; Mayberg et al., 1999). Davidson (2000) therefore suggests that the anterior cingulate may be involved in conflict associated with emotional processing (e.g., the inappropriateness of showing emotion in certain situations) and could thus represent emotional conflict.

A COMPUTATIONAL MODEL OF THE PROPOSED INTERACTIONS—THE NEED FOR ENVIRONMENTAL PRECURSORS

We have implicated a number of brain areas in rumination; their interactions are shown schematically in the top half of Figure 5.1. A computational neural network model incorporating some of these structures has been used to simulate emotion identification (bottom half of Figure 5.1: Siegle, 1999; Siegle & Hasselmo, 2002; Siegle & Ingram, 1997; Siegle, Steinhauer, Stenger, Thase, & Carter, 2002a). In neural networks, activation propagates between computational units that represent populations of neurons. In this model, environmental inputs feed to affective feature identification units (an analog of aspects of the amygdala system) and non-affective feature recognition units (potentially, an analog of the hippocampal system), and feedback occurs between them. Activation feeds forward to decision units (an analog of prefrontal areas) that inhibit the affective feature recognition units. When feedback is increased between the affective and non-affective feature detection units or inhibition from output units is decreased, the model exhibits sustained processing of *all* emotional stimuli (Siegle & Hasselmo, 2002). To exhibit sustained processing of just negative information, the model's representations of these stimuli could also be strengthened, as an analog of "overlearning" or thinking about a negative event to excess. Thus, as increased feedback or decreased cortical inhibition may represent vulnerability factors for rumination, a well-learned diatheses or stressor may also be required to set this process in motion. These three disruptions (overlearning, increased feedback, decreased inhibition) interact non-linearly to produce the depicted time series in which introducing an analog of depression leads to sustained activity in affective and non-affective identification features; particularly, a feature corresponding to non-presented personally relevant negative information becomes and remains active in the analog of depression. Other cognitive models of rumination (e.g., Wells & Matthews, 1994) are consistent with similar physiological formulations.

METHODS FOR DETECTING PHYSIOLOGICAL MANIFESTATIONS OF RUMINATION

A number of designs can be employed to assess brain mechanisms involved in rumination. If rumination involves sustained brain processes, assessment could involve measuring a sustained physiological signal in response to some emotional stimulus. The most direct designs involve inducing rumination, for example, by manipulating self-focus or stress. Physiological activity can be measured directly after the induction or during a "recovery" period, as an index of sustained processing. Alternatively, emotional information can be presented to subjects followed by some delay, and physiological variables can be measured during the delay period to assess sustained activity. A weaker design involves looking for tonic or baseline differences in physiological measurements thought to be related to rumination; a great deal of the literature treats depressive rumination as a trait variable (e.g., Nolen-Hoeksema et al., 1993), rather than as a phenomenon that occurs in the presence of a particular affective challenge. This treatment is consistent with the ideas we have discussed in this chapter (e.g., that depression is characterized by generally decreased inhibition of the amygdala system by the cortex). Construct validity of these methods can be increased by correlating physiological indices with self-reported rumination.

NEUROIMAGING OF RELATIONSHIPS BETWEEN BRAIN ACTIVITY AND RUMINATION

SUSTAINED PROCESSING FOLLOWING EMOTIONAL STIMULI

There have been few attempts to directly index sustained activity in the amygdala, hippocampus, and anterior cingulate, or sustained decreased pre-frontal cortex activity in ruminators, and fewer studies that examined these phenomena in the context of rumination. Davidson and colleagues have consistently found that negative affect varies with amygdala metabolism (e.g., Davidson, 2000) and, recently, have also found that amygdala activity is strongly correlated with an index of behavioral inhibition (Irwin, Davidson, Kalin, Sorenson, & Turski, 1998). Siegle, Steinhauer et al. (2002) subjected depressed and never-depressed controls to alternating 15-second emotion iden-tification trials and 18-second working memory trials (to invoke the prefrontal cortex). Using functional magnetic resonance imaging (fMRI), they found that bilateral amygdala activity in depressed individuals increased throughout both the emotion identification and subsequent Sternberg trial, up to 30 seconds after presentation of negative words, but not for neutral or positive words. This pattern was not apparent for controls. The difference in late amygdala activity to positive and negative words was correlated with a number of self-report

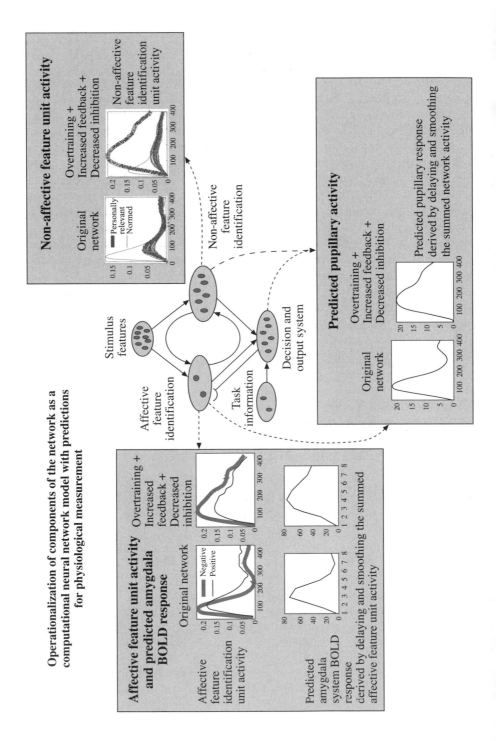

Operationalization of components of the network as a computational neural network model with predictions for physiological measurement

Non-affective feature unit activity

Original network

Overtraining + Increased feedback + Decreased inhibition

Non-affective feature identification unit activity

— Personally relevant
Normed

Non-affective feature identification

Predicted pupillary activity

Original network

Overtraining + Increased feedback + Decreased inhibition

Predicted pupillary response derived by delaying and smoothing the summed network activity

Stimulus features

Affective feature identification

Task information

Decision and output system

Affective feature unit activity and predicted amygdala BOLD response

Original network

Overtraining + Increased feedback + Decreased inhibition

Affective feature identification unit activity

— Negative
Positive

Predicted amygdala system BOLD response derived by delaying and smoothing the summed affective feature unit activity

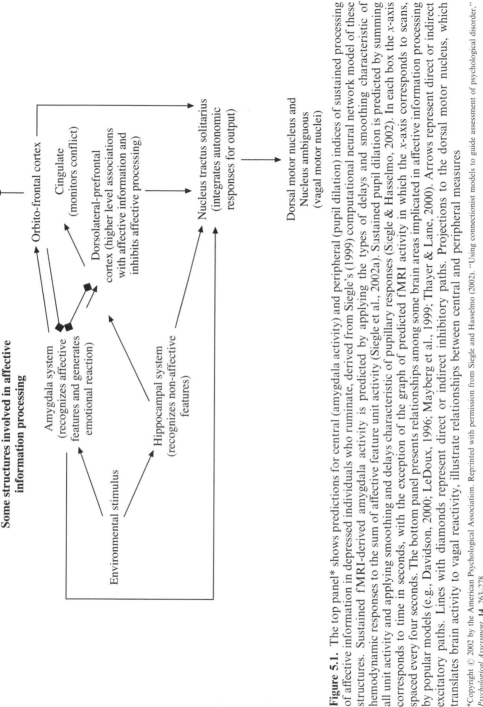

Some structures involved in affective information processing

Orbito-frontal cortex

Cingulate (monitors conflict)

Amygdala system (recognizes affective features and generates emotional reaction)

Dorsolateral-prefrontal cortex (higher level associations with affective information and inhibits affective processing)

Hippocampal system (recognizes non-affective features)

Nucleus tractus solitarius (integrates autonomic responses for output)

Environmental stimulus

Dorsal motor nucleus and Nucleus ambiguous (vagal motor nuclei)

Figure 5.1. The top panel* shows predictions for central (amygdala activity) and peripheral (pupil dilation) indices of sustained processing of affective information in depressed individuals who ruminate, derived from Siegle's (1999) computational neural network model of these structures. Sustained fMRI-derived amygdala activity is predicted by applying the types of delays and smoothing characteristic of hemodynamic responses to the sum of affective feature unit activity (Siegle et al., 2002a). Sustained pupil dilation is predicted by summing all unit activity and applying smoothing and delays characteristic of pupillary responses (Siegle & Hasselmo, 2002). In each box the x-axis corresponds to time in seconds, with the exception of the graph of predicted fMRI activity in which the x-axis corresponds to scans, spaced every four seconds. The bottom panel presents relationships among some brain areas implicated in affective information processing by popular models (e.g., Davidson, 2000; LeDoux, 1996; Mayberg et al., 1999; Thayer & Lane, 2000). Arrows represent direct or indirect excitatory paths. Lines with diamonds represent direct or indirect inhibitory paths. Projections to the dorsal motor nucleus, which translates brain activity to vagal reactivity, illustrate relationships between central and peripheral measures

measures of rumination ($r > 0.4$), including Fritz's (1999) multidimensional rumination measure, Nolen-Hoeksema's Response Styles Questionnaire (Nolen-Hoeksema et al., 1993), and the Revised Impact of Life Events scale (Horowitz, Wilner, & Alvarez, 1979), as well as factor analytically derived total scores from Luminet et al.'s (submitted) measure of rumination on a negative thought and Papageorgiou and Wells's diary-based measure of rumination (Papageorgiou & Wells, 1999).

INCREASED TONIC AMYGDALA AND HIPPOCAMPUS METABOLISM, DECREASED PREFRONTAL ACTIVITY

As described previously, tonic amygdala hyperactivity has been demonstrated using PET (position emission tomography) and fMRI in depressed individuals (e.g., Abercrombie et al., 1998; Drevets, 1999), along with decreased (primarily left) dorsolateral prefrontal activity (e.g., Baxter et al., 1989; Bench et al., 1993; Heinriques & Davidson, 1991) and decreased orbitofrontal activity (Drevets & Raichle, 1998; Mayberg, 1997; Mayberg et al., 1997, 1999). While these disruptions could reflect an increased tendency to ruminate, their specificity is unclear given that such disruptions are also present in animal models of depression (e.g., Zangen, Overstreet, & Yadid, 1999).

DECREASED HIPPOCAMPAL AND AMYGDALA VOLUMES IN DEPRESSION

Depressed individuals have repeatedly been observed to be hypercortisolemic. This state is suggested to facilitate excitotoxic effects of the neurotransmitter glutamate (e.g., Drevets, 2000). As projections from amygdala to hippocampus, and vice-versa, are primarily glutamatergic, prolonged feedback between these structures could be associated with decreased amygdala volume. Indeed, depressed individuals have been observed to have smaller hippocampal and core amygdala nuclei than controls (Drevets, 2000; Sheline, Mokhtar, & Price 1998, Sheline et al., 1999; Siegle, Konecky, Thase, & Carter, 2003). Preliminary data further suggest that sustained amygdala activity to negative information is particularly associated with decreased amygdala volume in depressed individuals (Siegle, Konecky et al., 2003).

PERIPHERAL PHYSIOLOGICAL DETECTION OF RUMINATION

Though central indicators of sustained brain processes in response to emotional information may be ideal, these mechanisms are difficult and expensive to assess and can only be done in a laboratory. In addition, central mechanisms have not been directly related to health consequences. In contrast, peripheral physiological mechanisms that potentially reflect central processes of interest, including, for example, blood pressure, heart rate, heart rate variability, and pupil dilation, may be of more general utility and have been linked to health outcomes. Connections of central to peripheral mechanisms are also fairly well specified; many of these are schematically illustrated in the top half of Figure 5.1. The following sections describe paths from central mechanisms hypothesized to drive depressive rumination to peripheral measures and supportive data suggesting relationships between the peripheral measures and rumination.

DISRUPTED VAGAL CONTROL

Theoretical considerations

When frontal structures are disinhibited, there are autonomically induced changes, such as increased heart rate and blood pressure. Disrupted autonomic activity could therefore also be considered a potentially sensitive, if not specific, physiological correlate of rumination. In particular, a disruption in autonomically mediated heart rate variability (HRV) may be expected. Vagal activity has negative chronotropic [heartbeat-influencing] and dromotropic [affecting the conductivity of cardiac muscle] effects that promote efficient cardiac functioning through the restraint of rate and conduction velocity, which is necessary for cardiac stability, responsiveness, and flexibility (Levy, 1990). The interplay of sympathetic and parasympathetic outputs of the central nervous system at the sinoatrial node produces the complex beat-to-beat variability that is characteristic of a healthy, adaptive organism (Saul, 1990). Decreased HRV thus signifies disruption in an organism's self-regulatory ability, leading to diminished ability to respond effectively to environmental stimuli. In particular, orbitofrontal cortex and insula activity have been associated with HRV (Lane, Reiman, Ahern, & Thayer, 2000).

Empirical data—reductions in heart rate variability in depression

Diminished tonic HRV and the associated reduction of vagally mediated cardiovascular control have been associated with a variety of pathological states and dispositions (for reviews, see Friedman & Thayer, 1998b; Stein & Kleiger, 1999), including depression (Thayer, Smith, Rossy, Sollers, & Friedman, 1998). Depression has also been linked with cardiovascular disease, which is associated with decreased HRV (Brosschot & Thayer, 1998). Reduced vagally mediated HRV is consistent with other symptoms of depression that could be associated with rumination, including poor attentional control, ineffective emotional regulation, and behavioral inflexibility (Friedman & Thayer, 1998a, b).

Empirical data—stimulus-related changes in heat rate variability

Though little evidence has directly examined relationships between rumination and vagal tone, there is a great deal of suggestive evidence regarding similar constructs, such as worry and perseveration. Worry has particularly been associated with coronary heart disease (Kubzansky et al., 1997) and decreased vagal activity (Thayer, Friedman, & Borkovec, 1996). For example, numerous studies have found decreased vagally mediated HRV during experimentally induced worry (Lyonfields, Borkovec, & Thayer, 1995; Thayer, Friedman, & Borkovec, 1996). Lyonfields et al. (1995) had anxious and non-anxious subjects identify an area of current concern. They were then instructed to imagine this situation and to worry about this situation. For the non-anxious participants HRV decreased significantly from baseline levels for both the imagery and worry conditions. However, the decrease was greater during the worry condition compared with the imagery condition. For the anxious participants HRV levels were lower during all conditions, including baselines, compared with the non-anxious participants. This group showed little condition-specific modulation of HRV, suggesting that these individuals (the chronic worriers) were less responsive to the task demands. Thayer et al. (1996) asked patients with generalized anxiety disorder (GAD) and matched non-anxious participants to relax and to "worry as you normally do." Patients with GAD had lower HRV across all conditions compared with matched non-anxious participants. Also, HRV decreased in both groups when they were asked to worry. Taken together these studies suggest that worry is associated with decreased vagally mediated HRV.

In a recent experiment, Johnsen et al. (2002) examined inhibitory responses in an emotional Stroop paradigm. Dental phobics were first exposed to recorded scenes of dental procedures and then administered the emotional Stroop test. In addition to the traditional color-congruent and color-incongruent words, they also were asked to respond to neutral words and dental-related words, such as drill and cavity, which were threatening to these patients. All subjects exhibited longer reaction times to the incongruent color words and the dental-related threat words and, thus, displayed a difficulty in inhibiting pre-potent responses. However, greater HRV was associated with faster reaction times to these words, consistent with the link among vagally mediated HRV, inhibitory ability, and frontal lobe function. These results support the idea that vagally mediated HRV is associated with attentional regulation and ability to inhibit pre-potent but inappropriate responses. To the extent that these data generalize to depressive rumination, vagal tone may thus be a useful indicator of physiological aspects of rumination.

Simulation—stimulus-related changes in heart rate variability (HRV)

We have recently used the model shown in Figure 5.1b to stimulate the effects of increased exposure to negative information and decreased prefrontal activity on HRV (Thayer & Siegle, 2002). These simulations suggested that exactly the same mechanisms that we have suggested lead to increased and sustained amygdala activity in depression would also lead to decreased HRV. Decreased prefrontal inhibition of the amygdala system alone is predicted to lead to decreased HRV in response to both positive and negative information. Decreased prefrontal inhibition coupled with overexposure to negative information is predicted to lead specifically to decreased HRV for negative information. Thus we predict that rumination on negative information will be specifically associated with increased HRV to negative stimuli.

INCREASED DIFFUSE AUTONOMIC NERVOUS SYSTEM ACTIVITY

Theoretical considerations

Another potentially sensitive, though not specific, physiological correlate of rumination involves diffusely increased autonomic nervous system activity. Investigators have identified broad functional networks within the central nervous system that support goal-directed behavior and adaptability. These systems involve many of the structures we have implicated; sustained, stimulus-related disruption in these systems may thus reflect rumination and are detectable using peripheral physiological measurement.

For example, the central autonomic network (CAN: Benarroch, 1993, 1997) receives and integrates visceral, humoral, and environmental information, and coordinates autonomic, endocrine, and behavioral responses to environmental challenges. The CAN includes, among other structures, the anterior cingulate, insula, and ventromedial prefrontal cortices, central nucleus of the amygdala, nucleus of the solitary tract, and the nucleus ambiguous. These components are reciprocally interconnected as shown in Figure 5.1. Disruption of inhibitory pathways in the CAN have been associated with disruptions in health (e.g., hypertension) and psychopathology (Malizia et al., 1998). The Anterior Executive Region is another broad network subserving executive, social, affective, attentional, and motivated behavior (AER: Devinsky, Morrell, & Vogt, 1995). Functionally, the AER and its projections regulate behavior by monitoring the motivational aspects of internal and external stimuli. The AER and its projections include the anterior, insula, and orbitofrontal cortices, the amygdala, the periaquaductal gray, ventral striatum, and autonomic brainstem motor nuclei. Damasio (1998) has identified another functional unit as the neural substrate for emotions. The structural overlap of these circuits is substantial (see Thayer & Lane, 2000), potentially suggesting they are part of an integrated network that controls response organization and selection, and serves to modulate psychophysiological resources in attention and emotion (Friedman & Thayer, 1998a, b; Thayer & Friedman, 1997). Disruption of these circuits has been associated with a variety of perseverative behaviors including a lack of habituation and inappropriate affect (cf. Crestani et al., 1999) and may thus be associated with rumination-like processes.

Detection of disruptions in these circuits involves measuring central peripheral physiological indicators. For example, the primary output of the CAN is mediated through the preganglionic sympathetic and parasympathetic neurons that innervate the heart via the stellate ganglia and the vagus nerve. The interplay of these inputs to the sinoatrial node of the heart generates complex variability that characterizes the heart rate time series (Saul, 1990). Thus, the output of the CAN is directly linked to HRV. Alternate measures of CAN activity include skin conductance and blood pressure. Skin conductance is an atypical measure of sympathetic nervous system activity that has been linked to physiological arousal in a number of research settings (Johnsen, Thayer, & Hugdahl, 1995; Lang, Greenwald, Bradley, & Hamm, 1993). The eccrine sweat glands in the hands and feet are innervated by the sympathetic nervous system. However, the neurotransmitter is acetylcholine—the parasympathetic neurotransmitter. It has been suggested that skin conductance activity may be an indicator of peripheral parasympathetic nervous system activity (Lehrer et al., 1996). The CAN also regulates blood pressure control in part via the baroreflex.

Empirical data—Physiological responses to rumination induction

Perhaps the most direct test of whether a physiological marker can be used to understand rumination is whether it changes during tasks in which rumination is induced. Though procedures for rumination induction have been available for years (e.g., Lyubomirsky & Nolen-Hoeksema, 1993), few physiological investigations of these procedures have been examined. Vickers and Vogeltanz-Holm (2003) provide an elegant test in which dysphoric and non-dysphoric individuals underwent a rumination induction procedure (viewing slides with self-relevant or neutral statements) during measurement of a number of peripheral measures of autonomic activity including heart rate, blood pressure, and galvanic skin response. The rumination condition was associated with increased systolic blood pressure (a measure of diffuse autonomic activity), suggesting that this autonomic nervous system activity may be associated with rumination. Yet, individuals who were dysphoric did not reliably display greater levels of any physiological variable in the presence of the rumination induction than never-depressed individuals, suggesting that this diffuse state may not uniquely reflect depressive rumination.

In a similar study, Sigmon, Dorhofer, Rohan, and Boulard (2000) administered a rumination induction procedure to women with high and low anxiety sensitivity (a tendency to experience frequent self-relevant anxious thoughts). Rumination induction was associated with increased levels of skin conductance in both groups. Women with high anxiety sensitivity, which was highly correlated with depressive symptomatology, displayed greater levels of skin conductance in response to both rumination and distraction tasks; their responses to the rumination condition were particularly exaggerated in comparison with other women.

Though these results suggest that something about the process of rumination is associated with autonomic nervous system activity, they also suggest that it is probably not unique to dysphoria. Rather, as both blood pressure and skin conductance have been shown to vary in response to different levels of arousal (e.g., Lang et al., 1993), these findings could better reflect general arousal in the presence of self-focus rather than dysphoric rumination *per se*.

Empirical data—trait rumination-related increases in blood pressure

Bermudez and Perez-Garcia (1996) divided students into ruminators and non-ruminators. The ruminating group showed higher levels of resting systolic blood pressure than controls. This finding could suggest either that systolic blood pressure acts as a trait-like marker for rumination or that individuals who are prone to ruminate were doing so in the authors' lab even when no nominal task was present.

More recently, Neumann, Waldstein, Sollers III, Thayer, and Sorkin (2001) reported that trait rumination was associated with a slower recovery of cardiac output (a major component of blood pressure), heart rate, and more relative sympathetic autonomic cardiac control (measured as the ratio of low-frequency to high-frequency heart rate spectral power). These findings suggest that the slower recovery associated with rumination was due to an autonomic imbalance in the direction of sympathetic overactivity. These results are consistent with the laboratory studies of worry, indicating that worry is associated with a decreased vagally mediated HRV and thus a relative sympathetic overactivity. Similarly, Gerin and colleagues (e.g., Gerin, 2000) have reported that rumination is associated with slower blood pressure recovery from emotional tasks. When participants were not allowed to ruminate (via distraction), blood pressure recovered more quickly. In addition, Neumann et al. (2001) reported that distraction was associated with quicker heart rate and pre-ejection period recovery and that this was associated with less low-frequency heart rate spectral power (a measure that indexes both sympathetic and parasympathetic HRV). Taken together these results suggest that relative sympathetic nervous system activity (or decreased parasympathetic activity) is associated with rumination and that trait rumination may dispose one to a chronic pathogenic state associated with negative psychological and physiological health outcomes.

SUSTAINED PUPIL DILATION TO EMOTIONAL STIMULI

Theoretical considerations

Muscles controlling pupil dilation are innervated by the same structures we have implicated in rumination. The frontal lobes project to the midbrain reticulum, which is in turn connected to the oculomotor nuclei. Activity in structures associated with emotional activity along the hypothalamo-thalamocortical axis and limbic structures connected to them have also been shown to result in pupil dilation (for a review, see Hess, 1972). Pupil dilation has been demonstrated in response to stimulation of the midbrain reticulum (Beatty, 1986) and amygdala (Fernandez de Molina & Hunsberger, 1962; Koikegami & Yoshida, 1953).

Pupil dilation has been demonstrated to reflect cognitive and emotional load; the pupil dilates more under conditions of higher attentional allocation, memory use, or interpretation of more difficult material (for reviews, see Beatty 1982a; Steinhauer & Hakerem 1992). As individuals are asked to remember larger numbers of digits, for example, their pupils reliably dilate (e.g., Granholm, Asarnow, Sarkin, & Dykes, 1996). Pupil dilation has also been observed to increase with the difficulty of mental arithmetic (e.g., Ahern & Beatty; 1979). Of particular interest is the finding that pupils remain dilated during conditions of sustained cognitive load (Beatty, 1982b). Sustained pupil dilation to emotional information might therefore be expected for ruminators.

Empirical data—sustained pupil dilation in depressed ruminators

Compared with never-depressed individuals, depressed individuals exhibit pupil dilation seconds after their decision time on an emotion identification task, but not on non-emotional processing tasks, such as cued reaction time tasks (Siegle, Granholm, Ingram, & Matt, 2001; Siegle, Steinhauer, Carter, & Thase, 2002). A follow-up study found that sustained pupil dilation was particularly apparent in response to negative and personally relevant information in depressed individuals and was not attenuated when a cognitive task designed to engage prefrontal cortex (e.g., a Sternberg memory task) followed negative information (Siegle, Steinhauer, Carter, & Thase, 2002). Moreover, sustained pupil dilation following negative personally relevant (vs. neutral non-personally relevant) words was significantly correlated with multiple trait measures of rumination-like constructs, including Fritz's (1999) emotion-focused and searching-for-meaning rumination measures, Luminet et al.'s (submitted) general rumination factor, and a measure of self-punishment (Wells & Davies, 1994). Other rumination scales, including Nolen-Hoeksema et al.'s (1993) measure, were also moderately correlated. In some but not all cases, these relationships were present above and beyond depressive severity. To assure specificity to depressive rumination in each of these experiments, no threat stimuli were used; stimuli were equated for word frequency and were pre-exposed to decrease novelty effects. There were no effects of subjective arousal. These data are consistent with the idea that pupil dilation indexes sustained processing of negative information and, potentially, rumination in depressed individuals.

ELECTROENCEPHALOGRAPHIC INDICES OF DECREASED FRONTAL AND SUSTAINED EMOTIONAL PROCESSING

Theoretical considerations

Scalp event encephalography (EEG) indexes brain activity through electrodes placed on the scalp. A venerable literature has demonstrated sensitivity of event-related changes in EEG signal (event-related potentials: ERPs) to the emotional content of stimuli shortly (within 500 ms) after they are presented. As rumination is hypothesized to occur on a longer timescale, seconds or minutes after an emotional event, prolonged ERPs to following presentation of negative information could index rumination.

Empirical data—event encephalography alpha asymmetry and potentiated startle

Tomarken and Davidson (1994) associate lower left prefrontal activity (specifically, EEG alpha band asymmetry) with a lower predisposition to repress negative affect. Jackson, Burghy, Hanna, Larson, and Davidson (2000) find that tonic left prefrontal activity is particularly associated with ability to suppress negative affect.

A common measure of affective processing associated with amygdala activity involves the magnitude of blink in response to a startling stimulus, such as a loud noise or air puff. Projections from the amygdala to the brainstem nucleus pontine reticularis mediate this response (e.g., Davis, Hitchcock, & Rosen, 1987); thus startle responses could also be used to index amygdala activity. Larson, Sutton, and Davidson (1998) examined the extent to which startle responses were potentiated seconds after the presentation of emotional information. Individuals with increased right prefrontal EEG asymmetry had greater startle responses to acoustical stimuli up to 8.5 seconds after negative pictures were shown than right hypofrontal individuals. This phenomenon was present even after startle during presentation of the emotional information was statistically controlled for. These data are consistent with the idea that decreased left prefrontal activity is associated with delayed recovery from emotional events. Larson and Davidson (2001) have further shown that such sustained startle potentiation up to 8.5 seconds after stimulus onset is common to dysphoric individuals with EEG alpha asymmetry, further suggesting a role for decreased prefrontal activity in depressive rumination.

Empirical data—event-related potentials to emotional information

Late positive-going shifts throughout the scalp in response to positive and negative stimuli, relative to neutral information, 500–1200 ms after their presentation have been observed (e.g., Diedrich, Naumann, Maier, Becker, & Bartussek, 1997; Schupp et al., 2000; Vanderploeg, Brown, & Marsh, 1987), suggesting that ERPs could tap sustained processing of emotionally valenced material. Much longer valence-dependent changes in ERPs have also been noted. Fretska, Bauer, Leodolter, and Leodolter (1999) presented individuals with sets of easily solvable and generally unsolvable sequence completion items, with the idea that the unsolvable items would be associated with a feeling of loss of control. Unsolvable items were associated with a significant negative potential at frontal sites and positive potential at temporal sites 11 s after stimulus presentation, relative to solvable items. Highly emotional reactive subjects displayed a general late positivity over both conditions. Few studies have examined whether greater sustained brain activity to emotional information is observed in clinical populations. Deldin, Deveney, Kim, Casas, and Best (2001) show that depressed individuals display enhanced slow wave amplitude up to 5 s post stimulus in response to negative information, and Deldin (2001) has shown that these changes last over 13 s.

Empirical data—disrupted sleep event encephalography

Hall et al. (2000) find marginal relationships between self-reported intrusive thoughts and increased EEG beta power, an index of hyperarousal, during sleep in individuals with insomnia; relationships with overall depressive severity were weaker, though both intrusive thoughts and depression were associated with decreased sleep quality. These data could suggest that aspects of rumination and worry persist into sleep.

DISRUPTIONS IN IMMUNE FUNCTION AND STRESS REACTIVITY

Theoretical considerations

Stress leads to increased cortisol production, which is frequently associated with decreased immune system responses. If depressive rumination involves sustained brain activity characteristic of responses to stress, as suggested by the idea of sustained amygdala and hippocampal activity, as well as decreased prefrontal activity, it is likely that measures associated with cortisol and immune function may be useful indices of rumination.

Empirical data—cortisol secretion following stress

Young and Nolen-Hoeksema (2001) examined whether social stress was differently associated with salivary cortisol secretion over time for ruminators and non-ruminators. While stress reliably provoked changes in cortisol secretion, and longer preparation for the stressor provoked greater changes, trait rumination as measured by Nolen-Hoeksema's Response Styles Questionnaire was not reliably associated with these effects. The authors note that the stressor did not reliably provoke increases in ruminative thoughts among trait ruminators, so the authors draw few conclusions regarding relationships between rumination and salivary cortisol secretion.

Empirical data—disrupted immune activity

Hall et al. (1998) find relationships between bereavement-related intrusive and avoidant thoughts and natural killer cell (NKC) counts in bereaved individuals. Similarly, Segerstrom, Solomon, Kemeny, and Fahey (1998) reported that participants high on trait worry had fewer natural killer cells in the wake of the Northridge earthquake. In another study, Segerstom, Glover, Craske, and Fahey (1999) reported that individuals scoring high on worry failed to show the expected increase in NKCs when exposed to a fearful situation. To the extent that these constructs reflect rumination, similar immune mechanisms may be involved.

CAUTIONS ON INTERPRETATION OF PHYSIOLOGICAL MEASURES

A number of cautions are useful to consider before wholeheartedly adopting measures of sustained physiological processing as proxies for rumination. Foremost, few studies have made these links explicit. Moreover, some of the literature we have cited has discussed these same mechanisms in contexts other than depressive rumination (e.g., anxiety sensitivity), and, thus, the specificity of the mechanisms to rumination is currently unclear. Uncertainty regarding the extent to which many similar constructs overlap with rumination—for example, worry (Papageorgiou & Wells, 1999; Segerstrom, Tsao, Alden, & Craske, 2000) and perseverative thinking (Thayer & Lane, 2002)—is cause for further caution. Further research assessing relationships between self-reported depressive rumination and physiological measures could help to flesh out this story.

Another caution involves how to interpret the functional implications of obtained physiological signals. For example, some researchers report associations of rumination-relevant constructs and excessive frontal activity, whereas others find associations with decreased frontal activity. Potentially, researchers are measuring related but functionally distinct sites. Animal studies have shown that areas with opposite functional effects (increased vs. decreased cardiovascular activity) may be adjacent to each other within a structure. Alternatively, measurements of inhibitory processes may not be adequately quantified by current assessment methodologies, such as PET and fMRI. Evidence suggests a less than linear relationship between inhibitory neurotransmitter (GABA [γ-aminobutyric acid]) activity and glucose utilization (Thayer & Balaban, in preparation), leading to the possibility that measures of frontal cortex activity derived from PET or fMRI may not accurately portray the true inhibitory functional activity. Thus, we suggest exercising caution, at least currently, toward claims regarding correspondences between observed sustained brain activity, or lack of activity, and rumination.

SOME IMPLICATIONS FOR TREATMENT

The physiological models discussed in this chapter present a number of implications for treatment. For example, feedback in Siegle's (1999) computational model affects the extent to which learning positive associations can help to overcome depressive information processing biases. Because considering new associations is an important component of cognitive therapy, depressed individuals who ruminate may be expected to be delayed in recovery in cognitive therapy relative to other depressed individuals. Preliminary data support this hypothesis (Siegle, Sagratti, & Crawford, 1999). Thus, understanding the physiology of rumination could help to estimate the length of treatment necessary for recovery.

Understanding physiology could also help to motivate treatment for depression. For example, based on the S-REF (Self-Regulatory Executive Function) model (Wells & Matthews, 1994), Wells (2000) proposes an intervention for anxious and depressed individuals that involves instructing individuals to attend to and make decisions about sounds occurring throughout a room (e.g., counting the sounds or shifting attention between them). This intervention has shown promise in treating depression (Papageorgiou & Wells, 2000). The current models suggest a physiological basis for why this treatment might work. Active manipulation of information is likely to involve prefrontal areas that we have described as important for inhibiting rumination. If this intervention effectively trains ruminators to use and thereby strengthen connections in the brain area responsible for shutting off rumination, it may act by helping depressed individuals to stop ruminating.

FUTURE DIRECTIONS

Arguably, the assessment of physiological aspects of depressive rumination is in its infancy, and there are many promising future directions. Foremost, there are few published studies in which self-report measures of rumination have been explicitly linked to physiological measures. In many cases in which such measures were employed, only one measure of depressive rumination was administered; as we have suggested, different self-report measures of rumination may index different constructs. Similarly, there have been few attempts to examine convergence between different physiological measures that could index rumination. Given that we have suggested many physiological measures could be sensitive but not specific to depressive rumination, it would be interesting to examine whether some combination of measures could yield a more specific measure of the construct. A final future direction we have not touched on at all in this chapter involves interpersonal aspects of rumination. Many theoretical accounts of rumination emphasize interpersonal processes either leading to or involved in rumination (e.g., Philippot & Rime, 1998). Physiological measures inherently allow intraperson assessment. Yet, examining physiological reactivity in dyads could be a useful extension of this literature.

SUMMARY—TYING RUMINATION AND SUSTAINED PROCESSING TOGETHER

We have suggested that understanding the physiology associated with depressive rumination could help to specify what is meant by rumination and could lead to understanding of mechanisms underlying this phenomenon. More specifically, literature suggests that depression may be characterized by increased feedback between subcortical limbic structures responsible for affective identification of information and decreased inhibition of these affective processing structures by prefrontal cortical regions. We have suggested that these processes underlie depressive rumination. Both rumination and sustained processing have been shown to share theoretical similarities: they are discussed as (1) runaway feedback processes that can be difficult to shut off and (2) a function of interactions between cognitive and affective processing systems. They also share empirical features: they (1) occur in response to rumination inductions, (2) occur in response to affective stimuli, (3) appear to be trait-like, (4) interfere with subsequent non-affective processing, (5) vary with depression and sad mood. Finally, a few studies demonstrate correlations between sustained physiological processing and rumination.

We have further suggested that these mechanisms may be reflected in changes in multiple central and peripheral physiological variables. Thus, evidence from common physiological and neuroimaging assessment technologies—including PET, fMRI—and measurement of pupil dilation, heart rate, HRV, and blood pressure have all been used to index physiological mechanisms underlying rumination. While the field is still young, we suggest this type of investigation is promising. Examination of physiological aspects of rumination in depression could thus be an important area for investigation in coming years.

REFERENCES

Abercrombie, H. C., Schaefer, S. M., Larson, C. L., Oakes, T. R., Lindgren, K. A., Holden, J. E., Perlman, S. B., Turski, P. A., Krahn, D. D., Benca, R. M., &

Davidson, R. J. (1998). Metabolic rate in the right amygdala predicts negative affect in depressed patients. *Neuroreport*, **9**, 3301–3307.

Ahern, S. K. & Beatty, J. (1979). Physiological signs of information processing vary with intelligence. *Science*, **205**, 1289–1292.

Baker, S. C., Frith, C. D., & Dolan, R. J. (1997). The interaction between mood and cognitive function studied with PET. *Psychological Medicine*, **27**, 565–578.

Baxter, L. R., Schwartz, J. M., Phelps, M. E., Mazziotta, J. C., Guze, B. H., Selin, C. E., Gerner, R. H., & Sumida, R. M. (1989). Reduction of prefrontal glucose metabolism common to three types of depression. *Archives of General Psychiatry*, **46**, 243–250.

Beatty, J. (1982a). Task-evoked pupillary responses, processing load, and the structure of processing resources. *Psychological Bulletin*, **91**, 276–292.

Beatty, J. (1982b). Phasic not tonic pupillary responses vary with auditory vigilance performance. *Psychophysiology*, **19**, 167–172.

Beatty, J. (1986). The pupil system. In: M. G. H. Coles et al. (eds), *Psychophysiology: Systems, Processes, and Applications*. New York: Guilford Press.

Benarroch, E. E. (1993). The central autonomic network: Functional organization, dysfunction, and perspective. *Mayo Clinic Proceedings*, **68**, 988–1001.

Benarroch, E. E. (1997). The central autonomic network. In: P. A. Low (ed.), *Clinical Autonomic Disorders* (2nd edn, pp. 17–23). Philadelphia: Lippincott-Raven.

Bench, C. J., Friston, K. J., Brown, R. G., Frankowiak, R. S., & Dolan, R. J. (1993). Regional cerebral blood flow in depression measured by positron emission tomography: The relationship with clinical dimensions. *Psychological Medicine*, **23**, 579–590.

Bermudez, J. & Perez-Garcia, A. M. (1996). Cardiovascular reactivity, affective responses and performance related to the risk dimensions of coronary-prone behaviour. *Personality and Individual Differences*, **21**(6), 919–927.

Botvinick, M., Nystrom, L. E., Fissell, K., Carter, C. S., & Cohen, J. D. (1999). Conflict monitoring versus selection-for-action in anterior cingulate cortex. *Nature*, **402**, 179–181.

Bower, G. (1981). Mood and memory. *American Psychologist*, **36**, 129 148.

Brosschot, J. F. & Thayer, J. F. (1998). Anger, inhibition, cardiovascular recovery, and vagal function: A model of the link between hostility and cardiovascular disease. *Annals of Behavioral Medicine*, **20**, 1–8.

Butters, M. A., Zmuda, M., Varhola, M., Reynolds, C. F., & Becker, J. (2000). Functional CNS abnormalities in late life depression. *Neuroimage*, **11**, S227.

Carter, C. S., Macdonald, A. M., Botvinick, M., Ross, L. L., Stenger, V. A., Noll, D., & Cohen, J. D. (2000). Parsing executive processes: Strategic vs. evaluative functions of the anterior cingulate cortex. *Proceedings of the National Academy of Sciences USA*, **97**, 1944–1948.

Crestani, F., Lorez, M., Baer, K., Essrich, C., Benke, D., Laurent, J. P., Belzung, C., Fritschy, J. M., Lüscher, B., & Mohler, H. (1999). Decreased $GABA_A$-receptor clustering results in enhanced anxiety and a bias for threat cues. *Nature Neuroscience*, **2**, 833–839.

Damasio, A. R. (1998). Emotion in the perspective of an integrated nervous system. *Brain Research Reviews*, **26**, 83–86.

Davidson, R. J. (1994). Assymetric brain function, affective style, and psychopathology: The role of early experience and plasticity. *Development and Psychopathology*, **6**, 741–758.

Davidson, R. J. (2000). Affective style, psychopathology, and resilience: Brain mechanisms and plasticity. *American Psychologist*, **55**, 1196–1214.

Davis, M., Hitchcock, J., & Rosen, J. (1987). Anxiety and the amygdala: Pharmacological and anatomical analysis of the fear potentiated startle paradigm. In: G. H. Bower (ed.), *Psychology of Learning and Motivation* (Vol. 2, pp. 263–305). New York: Academic Press.

Deldin, P. (2001). ERP investigations of memory biases in major depression. *Psychophysiology*, **3**, 59.

Deldin, P. J., Deveney, C. M., Kim, A. S., Casas, B. R., & Best, J. L. (1999). A slow wave investigation of working memory biases in mood disorders. *Journal of Abnormal Psychology*, **310**, 267–281.

Devinsky, O., Morrell, M. J., & Vogt, B. A. (1995). Contributions of anterior cingulate cortex to behavior. *Brain*, **118**, 279–306.

Diedrich, O., Naumann, E., Maier, S., Becker, G., & Bartussek, D. (1997). A frontal positive slow wave in the ERP associated with emotional slides. *Psychophysiology*, **11**, 71–84.

Dougherty, D. & Rauch, S. L. (1997). Neuroimaging and neurobiological models of depression. *Harvard Review of Psychiatry*, **5**, 138–159.

Drevets, W. C. (1999). Prefrontal cortical-amygdalar metabolism in major depression. In: J. F. McGinty (ed.), *Advancing from the Ventral Striatum to the Extended Amygdala: Implications for Neuropsychiatry and Drug Use* (pp. 614–637). New York: New York Academy of Sciences.

Drevets, W. C. (2000). Neuroimaging studies of mood disorders. *Biological Psychiatry*, **48**, 813–829.

Drevets, W. C., Price, J. L., Simpson, Jr, J. R., Todd, R. D., Reich, T., Vannier, M., & Raichle, M. E. (1997). Subgenual prefrontal cortex abnormalities in mood disorders. *Nature*, **386**, 824–827.

Drevets, W. C. & Raichle, M. (1998). Reciprocal suppression of regional cerebral blood flow during emotional versus higher cognitive processes: Implications for interactions between emotion and cognition. *Cognition and Emotion*, **12**, 353–385.

Drevets, W. C., Videen, T. O., Price, J. L., Preskorn, S. H., Carmichael, S. T., & Raichle, M. E. (1992). A functional anatomical study of unipolar depression. *Journal of Neuroscience*, **12**, 3628–3641.

Fernandez de Molina, A. & Hunsberger, R. W. (1962). Organization of the subcortical system governing defence and flight reactions in the cat. *Journal of Physiology*, **7**, 200–213.

Fretska, E., Bauer, H., Leodolter, M., & Leodolter, U. (1999). Loss of control and negative emotions: A cortical slow potential topography study. *International Journal of Psychophysiology*, **33**, 127–141.

Friedman, B. H. & Thayer, J. F. (1998a). Anxiety and autonomic flexibility: A cardiovascular approach. *Biological Psychology*, **49**, 303–323.

Friedman, B. H. & Thayer, J. F. (1998b). Autonomic balance revisited: Panic anxiety and heart rate variability. *Journal of Psychosomatic Research*, **44**, 133–151.

Fritz, H. L. (1999). Rumination and adjustment to a first coronary event. *Psychosomatic Medicine*, **61**, 105.

Gemar, M. C., Kapur, S., Segal, Z. V., Brown, G. M., & Houle, S. (1996). Effects of self-generated sad mood on regional cerebral activity: A PET study in normal subjects. *Depression*, **4**, 81–88.

Gerin, W. (2000). Emotional and cognitive determinants of poststress cardiovascular recovery: Role of rumination in sustained blood pressure elevation. *Psychophysiology*, **37**(Suppl.), S12.

Granholm, E., Asarnow, R. F., Sarkin, A. J., & Dykes, K. L. (1996). Pupillary responses index cognitive resource limitations. *Psychophysiology*, **33**, 457–461.

Hall, M., Baum, A., Buysse, D. J., Prigerson, H. G., Kupfer, D. J., & Reynolds, C. F. (1998). Sleep as a mediator of the stress-immune relationship. *Psychosomatic Medicine*, **60**, 48–51.

Hall, M., Buysse, D. J., Nowell, P. D., Nofzinger, E. A., Houk, P., Reynolds, C. F., & Kupfer, D. J. (2000). Symptoms of stress and depression as correlates of sleep in primary insomnia. *Psychosomatic Medicine*, **62**, 227–330.

Heinriques, J. B. & Davidson, R. J. (1991). Left frontal hypoactivation in depression. *Journal of Abnormal Psychology*, **100**, 535–545.

Hess, E. H. (1972). Pupillometrics: A method of studying mental, emotional, and sensory processes. In: N. S. Greenfield & R. A. Sternbach (eds), *Handbook of Psychophysiology* (pp. 491–531). New York: Holt, Rinehart & Winston.

Hornig, M., Mozley, P. D., & Amsterdam, J. D. (1997). HMPAO spect brain imaging in treatment-resistant depression. *Progress in Neuro-Psychopharmacology and Biological Psychiatry*, **21**, 1097–1114.

Horowitz, M. J., Wilner, N., & Alvarez, W. (1979). Impact of Event Scale: A measure of subjective stress. *Psychosomatic Medicine*, **41**(3), 209–218.

Ingram, R. E. (1984). Toward an information processing analysis of depression. *Cognitive Therapy and Research*, **8**, 443–478.

Irwin, W., Davidson, R. J., Kalin, N. H., Sorenson, J. A., & Turski, P. A. (1998). Relations between human amygdalar activation and self-reported dispositional affect. *Journal of Cognitive Neuroscience*, 109–109 Suppl. S. Described in Davidson, 2000.

Jackson, D. C., Burghy, C. A., Hanna, A. J., Larson, C. L., & Davidson, R. J. (2000). Resting frontal and anterior temporal EEG asymmetry predicts ability to regulate negative emotion. Presentation at the *Meeting of the Society for Psychophysiological Research, San Diego*.

Johnsen, B. H., Thayer, J. F., & Hugdahl, K. (1995). Affective judgment of the Ekman faces: A dimensional approach. *Journal of Psychophysiology*, **9**, 193–202.

Johnsen, B. H., Thayer, J. F., Laberg, J. C., Wormnes, B., Raadal, M., Skaret, E., Kvale, G., & Berg, E. (2002). Attentional and physiological characteristics of patients with dental anxiety. *Journal of Anxiety Disorders*, **17**, 75–87.

Koikegami, H. & Yoshida, K. (1953). Pupillary dilation induced by stimulation of amygdaloid nuclei. *Folia Pychiatrica Neurologica Japonica*, **7**, 109–125.

Kubzansky, L. D., Kawachi, I., Spiro, A., Weiss, S. T., Vokonas, P. S., & Sparrow, D. (1997). Is worrying bad for your heart? A prospective study of worry and coronary heart disease in the Normative Aging Study. *Circulation*, **95**, 818–824.

Lane, R. D., Reiman E. M., Ahern, G. L., & Thayer, J. F. (2000). Activity in medial prefrontal cortex correlates with vagal component of heart rate variability during emotion. *Psychosomatic Medicine*, **62**, 100.

Lang, P. J., Greenewald, M. K., Bradley, M. M., & Hamm, A. O. (1993). Looking at pictures: Affective, facial, visceral, and behavioral reactions. *Psychophysiology*, **30**, 261–273.

Larson, C. L. & Davidson, R. J. (2001). Prolonged startle blink potentiation to negative stimuli among individuals with relative right frontal EEG asymmetry. *Psychophysiology*, **3**, S9.

Larson, C. L., Sutton, S. K., & Davidson, R. J. (1998). Affective style, frontal EEG asymmetry, and the time course of the emotion modulated startle. *Psychophysiology*, **35**, S52.

LeDoux, J. (1996). *The Emotional Brain*. New York: Simon & Schuster.

Lehrer, P. M., Hochron, S., Carr, R., Edelberg, R., Hamer, R., Jackson, A., & Porges, S. (1996). Behavioral task-induced bronchodilation in asthma during active and passive tasks: A possible cholinergic link to psychologically induced airway changes. *Psychosomatic Medicine*, **58**, 413–422.

Levy, M. N. (1990). Autonomic interactions in cardiac control. *Annals of the New York Academy of Sciences*, **601**, 209–221.

Liotti, M., Mayberg, H. S., Brannan, S. K., McGinnis, S., Jerabek, P., & Fox, P. T. (2000). Differential limbic–cortical correlates of sadness and anxiety in healthy subjects: Implications for affective disorders. *Biological Psychiatry*, **48**, 30–42.

Luminet, O., Rime, B., & Wagner, H. (submitted). Intrusive thoughts in the laboratory and their long-lasting consequences.

Lyonfields, J., Borkovec, T. D., and Thayer, J. F. (1995). Vagal tone in generalized anxiety disorder and the effects of aversive imagery and worrisome thinking. *Behavior Therapy*, **26**, 457–466.

Lyubomirsky, S. & Nolen-Hoeksema, S. (1993). Self-perpetuating properties of dysphoric rumination. *Journal of Personality and Social Psychology*, **65**, 339–349.

Malizia, A. L., Cunningham, V. J., Bell, C. J., Liddle, P. F., Jones, T., & Nutt, D. J. (1998). Decreased brain $GABA_A$-benzodiazepine receptor binding in panic disorder. *Archives of General Psychiatry*, **55**, 715–720.

Martin, L. L. & Tesser, A. (1989). Toward a motivational and structural theory of ruminative thought. In: J. S. Uleman & J. A. Bargh (eds), *Unintended Thought* (pp. 306–326). New York: Guilford Press.

Mayberg, H. S. (1997). Limbic–cortical dysregulation: A proposed model of depression. *Journal of Neuropsychiatry and Clinical Neurosciences*, **9**, 471–481.

Mayberg, H. S., Brannan, S. K., Roderick, K. M., Jerabek, P. A., Brickman, J. S., Tekell, J. L., Silva, A., McGinnis, S., Glass, T. G., Martin, C. C., & Fox, P. T. (1997). Cingulate function in depression: A potential predictor of treatment response. *NeuroReport*, **8**, 1057–1061.

Mayberg, H. S., Liotti, M., Brannan, S. K., McGinnis, B. S., Mahurin, R. K., Jerabek, P. A., Silva, J. A., Janet, L. T., Martin, C. C., Lancaster, J. L., & Fox, P. T. (1999). Reciprocal limbic–cortical function and negative mood: Converging PET findings in depression and normal sadness. *American Journal of Psychiatry*, **156**, 675–682.

Nolen-Hoeksema, S. (1987). Sex differences in unipolar depression: Evidence and theory. *Psychological Bulletin*, **101**, 259–282.

Nolen-Hoeksema, S., Morrow, J., & Fredrickson, B. L. (1993). Response styles and the duration of episodes of depressed mood. *Journal of Abnormal Psychology*, **102**, 20–28.

Neumann, S. A., Waldstein, S. R., Sollers III, J. J., Thayer, J. F., & Sorkin, J. D. (2001). The relation of hostility, rumination, and distraction to cardiovascular reactivity and recovery responses to anger. *Annals of Behavioral Medicine*, **23**(Suppl.), 140.

Papageorgiou, C. & Wells, A. (1999). Process and meta-cognitive dimensions of depressive and anxious thoughts and relationships with emotional intensity. *Clinical Psychology and Psychotherapy*, **6**, 156–162.

Papageorgiou, C. & Wells, A. (2000). Treatment of recurrent major depression with attention training. *Cognitive and Behavioral Practice*, **7**(4), 407–413.

Philippot, P. & Rime, B. (1998). Social and cognitive processing in emotion: A heuristic for psychopathology. In: W. F. Flack and J. D. Laird (eds), *Emotions in Psychopathology* (pp. 114–130). New York: Oxford University Press.

Ray, J. P. & Price, J. L. (1993). The organization of projections from the mediodorsal nucleus of the thalamus to orbital and medial prefrontal cortex in macaque monkeys. *Journal of Comparative Neurology*, **337**, 1–37.

Rolls, E. T. (2000). Memory systems in the brain. *Annual Review of Psychology*, **51**, 599–630.

Sarason, I. G. (1960). Empirical findings and theoretical problems in the use of anxiety scales. *Psychological Bulletin*, **57**, 403–415.

Saul, J. P. (1990). Beat-to-beat variations of heart rate reflect modulation of cardiac autonomic outflow. *News in Physiological Science*, **5**, 32–37.

Schupp, H. T., Cuthbert, B. N., Bradley, M. M., Cacioppo, J. T., Ito, T., & Lang, P. J. (2000). Affective picture processing: The late positive potential is modulated by motivational relevance. *Psychophysiology*, **37**, 257–261.

Schwartzer, R. (1996). Thought control of action. In: I. G. Sarason, G. R. Pierce, & B. R. Sarason (eds), *Cognitive Interference: Theories, Methods, and Findings* (pp. 90–115). Mahwah, NJ: Lawrence Erlbaum.

Segerstrom, S. C., Glover, D. A., Craske, M. G., & Fahey, J. L. (1999). Worry affects the immune responses to phobic fear. *Brain, Behavior, and Immunity*, **13**, 80–92.

Segerstrom, S. C., Solomon, G. F., Kemeny, M. E., & Fahey, J. L. (1998). Relationship of worry to immune sequelae of the Northridge earthquake. *Journal of Behavioral Medicine*, **21**, 433–450.

Segerstrom, S. C., Tsao, J. C. I., Alden, L. E., & Craske, M. G. (2000). Worry and rumination: Repetitive thought as a concomitant and predictor of negative mood. *Cognitive Therapy and Research*, **24**, 671–688.

Sheline, Y. I., Mokhtar, H. G., & Price, J. L. (1998). Amygdala core nuclei volumes are decreased in recurrent major depression. *Neuroreport*, **9**, 2023–2028.

Sheline, Y. I., Sanghavi, M., Mintun, M. A., & Gado, M. H. (1999). Depression duration but not age predicts hippocampal volume loss in medically healthy women with recurrent major depression. *Journal of Neuroscience*, **19**, 5034–5043.

Siegle, G. J. (1999). A neural network model of attention biases in depression. In: J. A. Reggia, E. Ruppin, & D. L. Glanzman (eds), *Disorders of Brain, Behavior, and Cognition: The Neurocomputational Perspective* (pp. 415–441). New York: Elsevier.

Siegle, G. J., Granholm, E., Ingram, R. E., & Matt, G. E. (2001). Pupillary response and reaction time measures of sustained processing of negative information in depression. *Biological Psychiatry*, **49**, 624–636.

Siegle, G. J. & Hasselmo, M. (2002). Using connectionist models to guide assessment of psychological disorder. *Psychological Assessment*, **14**, 263–278.

Siegle, G. J. & Ingram, R. (1997). Modeling individual differences in negative information processing biases. In: G. Matthews (ed.), *Cognitive Science Perspectives on Personality and Emotion*. New York: Elsevier.

Siegle, G. J., Konecky, R. O., Thase, M. E., & Carter, C. S. (2002). Relationships between amygdala volume and activity during emotional information processing tasks in depressed and never-depressed individuals: An fMRI investigation. *Annals of the New York Academy of Sciences*, **985**, 481–484.

Siegle, G. J., Sagratti, S., & Crawford, C. (1999). Effects of rumination and initial severity on response to cognitive therapy for depression. *Meeting of the Association for the Advancement of Behavior Therapy, Toronto*.

Siegle, G. J., Steinhauer, S. R., Carter, C. S., & Thase, M. E. (2003, in press). Do the seconds turn into hours? Relationships between sustained processing of emotional information and self-reported rumination. *Cognitive Therapy and Research*.

Siegle, G. J., Steinhauer, S. R., Stenger, V. A., Thase, M. E., & Carter, C. S. (2002). Can't shake that feeling: fMRI assessment of sustained amygdala activity in response to emotional information in depressed individuals. *Biological Psychiatry*, **51**, 693–707.

Sigmon, S. T., Dorhofer, D. M., Rohan, K. J., & Boulard, N. E. (2000). The impact of anxiety, sensitivity, bodily expectations, and cultural beliefs on menstrual symptom reporting: A test of the menstrual reactivity hypothesis. *Journal of Anxiety Disorders*, **14**, 615–633.

Skinner, J. E. (1985). Regulation of cardiac vulnerability by the cerebral defense system. *Journal of the American College of Cardiology*, **5**, 88B–94B.

Stein, P. K. & Kleiger, R. E. (1999). Insights from the study of heart rate variability. *Annual Review of Medicine*, **50**, 249–261.

Steinhauer, S. R. & Hakerem, G. (1992). The pupillary response in cognitive psychophysiology and schizophrenia. In: D. Friedman & G. E. Bruder (eds), *Psychophysiology and Experimental Psychopathology: A Tribute to Samuel Sutton* (pp. 182–204). New York: New York Academy of Sciences.

Teasdale, J. D. (1988). Cognitive vulnerability to persistent depression. *Cognition and Emotion*, **2**, 247–274.

Ter Horst, G. J. (1999). Central autonomic control of the heart, angina, and pathogenic mechanisms of post-myocardial infarction depression. *European Journal of Morphology*, **37**, 257–266.

Ter Horst, G. J., & Postema, F. (1997). Forebrain parasympathetic control of heart activity: Retrograde transneuronal viral labeling in rats. *American Journal of Physiology*, **273**, H2926–H2930.

Thayer, J. F. & Balaban, C. (in preparation). Inhibitory neural processes and brain imaging.

Thayer, J. F. & Friedman, B. H. (1997). The heart of anxiety: A dynamical systems approach. In: A. Vingerhoets (ed.), *The (Non)Expression of Emotions in Health and Disease*. Amsterdam: Springer-Verlag.

Thayer, J. F., Friedman, B. H., & Borkovec, T. D. (1996). Autonomic characteristics of generalized anxiety disorder and worry. *Biological Psychiatry*, **39**, 255–266.

Thayer, J. F. & Lane, R. D. (2000). A model of neurovisceral integration in emotion regulation and dysregulation. *Journal of Affective Disorders*, **61**, 201–216.

Thayer, J. F. & Lane, R. D. (2002). Perseverative thinking and health: Neurovisceral concomitants. *Psychology and Health*, **17**(5), 685–695.

Thayer, J. F., & Siegle, G. J. (2002). Neurovisceral integration in cardiac and emotional regulation. *IEEE Engineering in Medicine and Biology*, **21**(4), 24–29.

Thayer, J. F., Smith, M., Rossy, L. A., Sollers, J. J., & Friedman, B. H. (1998). Heart period variability and depressive symptoms: Gender differences. *Biological Psychiatry*, **44**, 304–306.

Tomarken, A. J. & Davidson, R. J. (1994). Frontal brain activation in repressors and nonrepressors. *Journal of Abnormal Psychology*, **103**, 339–349.

Tucker, D. M. & Derryberry, D. (1992). Motivated attention: Anxiety and the frontal executive functions. *Neuropsychiatry, Neuropsychology, and Behavioral Neurology*, **5**, 233–252.

Vanderploeg, R. D., Brown, W. S., & Marsh, J. T. (1987). Judgement of emotion in words and faces: ERP correlates. *International Journal of Psychophysiology*, **5**, 193–205.

Vickers, K. S. & Vogeltanz-Holm, N. D. (2003, in press). The effects of rumination and distraction tasks on psychophysiological responses and mood in dysphoric and nondysphoric individuals. *Cognitive Therapy and Research*.

Wells, A. (2000). *Emotional Disorders and Metacognition: Innovative Cognitive Therapy*. New York: John Wiley & Sons.

Wells, A. & Davies, M. I. (1994). The thought control questionnaire: A measure of individual differences in the control of unwanted thoughts. *Behaviour Research and Therapy*, **32**, 871–878.

Wells, A. & Matthews, G. (1994). *Attention and Emotion: A Clinical Perspective*. Hove, UK: Lawrence Erlbaum.

Whalen, P. J., Bush, G., McNally, R. J., Wilhelm, S., McInerney, S. C., Jenike, M. A., & Rauch, S. L. (1998). The emotional counting Stroop paradigm: A functional magnetic resonance imaging probe of the anterior cingulate affective division. *Biological Psychiatry*, **44**, 1219–1228.

Young, E. A. & Nolen-Hoeksema, S. (2001). Effect of ruminations on the saliva cortisol response to a social stressor. *Psychoneuroendocrinology*, **26**, 319–329.

Zangen, A., Overstreet, D. H., & Yadid, G. (1999). Increased catecholamine levels in specific brain regions of a rat model of depression: Normalization by chronic antidepressant treatment. *Brain Research*, **824**, 243–250.

II   Theories of Rumination

6 The Response Styles Theory

SUSAN NOLEN-HOEKSEMA

Department of Psychology, University of Michigan, USA

When people are distressed, they can respond to their mood in several ways (Gross, 1998; Lazarus & Folkman, 1984; Nolen-Hoeksema, 1991). They may deny or avoid thinking about how they feel. They may quickly take action to alter their environment and change their mood. They may seek out social support. Or they may ruminate.

The response styles theory (Nolen-Hoeksema, 1991) defines rumination as repetitive and passive thinking about one's symptoms of depression and the possible causes and consequences of these symptoms. Thus, when ruminating, people repeatedly entertain such thoughts as "Why can't I get going? What's wrong with me? I don't feel I'll ever get over this." These thoughts do not lead to planful problem-solving focused on resolving the issues identified during rumination. Instead, people simply remain in cycles of ruminative thinking. Rumination is considered a thought process people engage in when sad or depressed. Although most people may ruminate at least somewhat when they are sad or depressed, longitudinal, community-based studies have shown that the tendency to engage in a ruminative process when distressed is a stable individual difference characteristic (Nolen-Hoeksema & Davis, 1999). Specifically, whereas many individuals may engage in some rumination when depressed or sad, some people ruminate a great deal and others engage in little or no rumination; these individual differences tend to be stable over time, even as depressed moods wax and wane.

According to the response styles theory, this form of rumination in the context of depressive symptoms exacerbates and prolongs these symptoms, increasing the likelihood that the symptoms become chronic and that moderate depressive symptoms will evolve into episodes of major depression. There are at least four mechanisms by which rumination may prolong depression. First, rumination enhances the effects of depressed mood on thinking, making it more likely that people will use the negative thoughts and memories activated by their depressed mood to understand their current circumstances. Second, rumination interferes with effective problem-solving, in part by making thinking more pessimistic and fatalistic. Third, rumination interferes with instrumental behavior. Fourth, people who chronically ruminate will lose social support, which in turn will feed their depression.

Lyubomirsky and Tkach (Chapter 2 in this book) have reviewed the large number of studies, mostly experimental in design, showing the effects of rumination on thinking, problem-solving, instrumental behavior, and social support. Below, I describe the mental health effects of rumination.

THE MENTAL HEALTH EFFECTS OF RUMINATION

We have conducted a number of longitudinal studies to address the prediction that people prone to ruminate when distressed (hereafter referred to as ruminators) will experience more severe and prolonged bouts of depressive symptoms than non-ruminators. In many of the studies we have conducted on rumination, we have used the Ruminative Responses Scale (RRS) of the Response Styles Questionnaire (RSQ) to assess people's tendencies to ruminate when distressed (Nolen-Hoeksema & Larson, 1999; Nolen-Hoeksema, Larson, & Grayson, 1999; Nolen-Hoeksema & Morrow, 1991). Respondents are asked to indicate how often they engage in each of 22 ruminative thoughts or behaviors when they feel sad, blue, or depressed. These 22 items describe responses to depressed mood that are self-focused (e.g., I think "Why do I react this way?"), symptom-focused (e.g., I think about how hard it is to concentrate), and focused on the possible consequences and causes of their mood (e.g., I think "I won't be able to do my job if I don't snap out of this"). The internal consistency of this scale is high in all studies (Cronbach's alphas about 0.90), and the scale has acceptable convergent and predictive validity (Butler & Nolen-Hoeksema, 1994; Nolen-Hoeksema & Morrow, 1991). For example, participants' responses to this scale correlated significantly ($r = 0.62$) with their uses of ruminative responses to depressed mood in a 30-day diary study (Nolen-Hoeksema, Morrow, & Fredrickson, 1993). In addition, in a controlled laboratory study participants who scored above the median on the scale were significantly more likely than participants who scored below the median to choose to engage in an emotion-focused task rather than a task unrelated to emotion while they were in a depressed mood (Butler & Nolen-Hoeksema, 1994). The tendency to ruminate appears to be a stable individual difference (Nolen-Hoeksema et al., 1993). In a longitudinal study of recently bereaved people spanning 18 months, the intraclass correlation for the RRS across 5 interviews was 0.75 ($p < 0.0001$).

In one of the first studies conducted with the RRS, rumination and depression were assessed in 137 college students just before the earthquake that hit the San Francisco Bay area in 1987 (Nolen-Hoeksema & Morrow, 1991). Depression was reassessed in these students 10 days and 2 weeks after the earthquake. We also assessed how much stress the students endured as a result of their earthquake (e.g., severe damage to their dwelling, injury). Students who were ruminators before the earthquake had more severe levels of depressive symptoms both 10 days and 7 weeks after the earthquake, even after statistically controlling for their levels of depression before the earthquake and the earthquake-related stress they endured.

Another study followed over 300 adults who lost a loved one to a terminal illness to assess the impact of a ruminative response style on bereavement-related depressions (Nolen-Hoeksema & Larson, 1999; Nolen-Hoeksema, Parker & Larson, 1994). The participants in this study were interviewed once before their loved one died and then again at 1, 6, 13, and 18 months post loss. Ruminators were consistently more likely to experience elevated depressive symptoms than non-ruminators, even after we statistically controlled for previous levels of depression and a number of other variables previously shown to predict bereavement-related depression, such as social support.

In both this bereavement study and in a subsequent study of 1,300 adults chosen randomly from the community, we have found that rumination not only predicts depressive symptoms but also episodes of major depression (Nolen-Hoeksema, 2000; Nolen-Hoeksema & Larson, 1999). That is, ruminators are significantly more likely to develop episodes of major depression over time, even after statistically controlling for previous levels of depression.

Recently, we have begun to investigate the relationship of rumination to syndromes that are highly co-morbid with depression (namely, anxiety and alcohol abuse). In the community sample of 1,300 adults, I found that ruminators were just as likely to develop severe anxiety symptoms as they were to develop severe depressive symptoms (Nolen-Hoeksema, 2000). Moreover, rumination was especially strongly related to the development of a mixed anxiety–depression syndrome. Rumination may predict anxiety simply because anxiety is co-morbid with depression. There may be more substantive reasons to expect rumination to predict anxiety and mixed anxiety–depression as well. Content analyses of ruminators' ruminations suggest that many of these thoughts reflect an uncertainty over whether important situations will be manageable or controllable (e.g., "What if I can't pull myself together?" "What did my spouse's comment mean?": Lyubomirsky, Tucker, Caldwell, & Berg, 1999). Several theorists have argued that uncertainty over whether one will be able to control one's environment is key to anxiety (Alloy, Kelly, Mineka, & Clements, 1990; Barlow, 1988; Garber, Miller, & Abramson, 1980). Yet, rumination also contributes to a hopelessness about the future and negative evaluations about the self, as we will describe below, and these cognitions are key to depression (Abramson, Metalsky, & Alloy, 1989; Beck, 1967). Ruminators may vacillate between anxiety and depression as their cognitions vacillate between uncertainty and hopelessness (see Alloy et al., 1990; Garber et al., 1980; Mineka, Watson, & Clark, 1998).

In analyses of both the community-based study and the bereavement study, we found that rumination also predicts alcohol abuse (Nolen-Hoeksema & Harrell, 2002). Ruminators were significantly more likely than non-ruminators to report drinking alcohol to cope with negative emotions and in turn ruminators had significantly more problems related to alcohol use, such as being fired from work for alcohol use, frequent hangovers, and arrests for drunken driving. Work by other investigators on the methods people use to escape from high self-consciousness (e.g., Baumeister, Heatherton, & Tice, 1994; Hull, 1981) suggests that rumination may be related to alcohol abuse because some ruminators use alcohol to escape from the negative arousal caused by their rumination.

SOURCES OF INDIVIDUAL DIFFERENCES IN RUMINATION

If rumination is so toxic, why do people do it? Matthews and Wells (2000; see also Wells & Matthews, 1994) have suggested that rumination can be the result of a strategic choice to allocate attention to analysis of past events and worry about future events. The choice to ruminate is based on a metacognitive belief in the functionality of rumination. Papageorgiou and Wells (2001a, b) developed a self-report instrument to measure positive beliefs about depressive rumination (e.g., "I need to ruminate about my problems to find answers to my depression," "ruminating about the past helps me to prevent future mistakes and failures"). They found that an excess of such beliefs were associated with a greater tendency to ruminate and in turn with higher levels of state and trait depression. The sources of these positive beliefs are not currently known.

Similarly, we found that dysphoric people induced to ruminate felt they were gaining insight to themselves and their problems, even though they were generating relatively poor solutions to their problems (Lyubomirsky & Nolen-Hoeksema, 1993). Anecdotally, ruminators often say they have a sense that they are finally being realistic about their problems and facing them when they are ruminating. This sense of insight, and the compelling nature of the problems ruminators think about, could make withdrawing from rumination very difficult once it starts.

In another set of experimental studies, we found that people who self-identify as ruminators exhibit more uncertainty and lack of confidence when devising plans to overcome difficult social problems than non-ruminators (Ward, Lyubomirsky, Sousa, & Nolen-Hoeksema, 2003). This uncertainty could reflect the negative thinking that often accompanies rumination. It also could stem from a history of difficulties in overcoming the problems in one's life, which in turn results from a tendency to ruminate.

Indeed, we have evidence from community studies that ruminators report more chronic problems in their lives and that rumination both predicts and is predicted by a history of chronic stressors. For example, in one study of adults randomly selected from the community we found that people who faced chronic stressors, such as low income, unsatisfying marriages, and ungratifying jobs, were more likely to ruminate (Nolen-Hoeksema et al., 1999). This was true even when we controlled for participants' levels of depression. Similarly, in our bereavement study, people who faced stressors in addition to the loss of their loved one, such as the loss of a job or their own chronic illness, were more likely to ruminate. People who face chronic stress may continually search for some understanding of why their lives are not going as they wish and why they are frustrated so much of the time, which is manifested as rumination. In the bereavement study, some people reported that they believed they could have coped with the loss of their loved one, but it was the cumulation of stressors that pushed them into rumination and despair.

Personality characteristics are also associated with the tendency to ruminate. Rumination is correlated significantly with neuroticism (Nolen-Hoeksema et al., 1994). Importantly, however, rumination continues to predict depression after controlling for neuroticism, suggesting it is not just a proxy for neuroticism. Instead, rumination may be a mechanism by which neuroticism may contribute to depression. Dispositional pessimism and a sense of helplessness are also associated with the tendency to ruminate (Nolen-Hoeksema et al., 1994, 1999). Again, however, rumination continues to predict depression after controlling for dispositional pessimism or helplessness. It may be that the combination of pessimism or helplessness and rumination is an especially potent contributor to depression.

GENDER DIFFERENCES IN RUMINATION AND DEPRESSION

One of the most robust findings in the literature on depression is that about twice as many women as men suffer from major depression and more minor symptoms of depression (Nolen-Hoeksema, 2002). Women are also significantly more likely than men to be ruminators, as assessed both by self-report and laboratory observation (Butler & Nolen-Hoeksema, 1994; Nolen-Hoeksema et al., 1999). We have found that the gender difference in rumination mediates the gender difference in depression (Butler & Nolen-Hoeksema, 1994; Nolen-Hoeksema et al., 1999)—that is, when we statistically control for gender differences in rumination, the gender difference in depression becomes non-significant. I do not believe that a greater tendency to ruminate is the sole source of women's greater vulnerability to depression. Indeed, there appear to be a multitude of possible contributors to the gender difference in depression (Nolen-Hoeksema, 2002). A greater tendency to ruminate, however, may keep women stuck in cycles of passivity and impair their ability to overcome other problems contributing to their depression, such as inequities in their marriages (Nolen-Hoeksema et al., 1999).

The sources of the gender difference in rumination may also be numerous. In our community study, we found that women report more chronic stressors, such as low income and unsatisfying marriages, than men, and this gender difference in chronic stressors partially mediated the gender difference in rumination (Nolen-Hoeksema et al., 1999). Women are also more likely than men to suffer certain traumatic events, particularly sexual abuse, and in turn a history of major stressors, such as childhood sexual abuse, was associated with the tendency to ruminate. Specifically, women who reported they had been abused as children were more likely to be ruminators as adults, again even after we controlled for their levels of depression (Nolen-Hoeksema, 1998). Experiences of abuse can shatter assumptions about the safety of the world and the trustworthiness of others, which in turn could feed ruminations.

In another community-based study, we found that a trio of personality characteristics tied to women's social roles may also contribute to the gender difference in rumination (Nolen-Hoeksema & Jackson, 2001). First, women were more likely than men to believe that negative emotions, such as sadness, fear, and anger, are difficult to control. In turn, difficulty in controlling negative emotions was related to a greater tendency to ruminate and helped to account for the gender difference in rumination. Women may believe that negative emotions are more difficult to control because they were not socialized to use active coping strategies during childhood as much as men were. Women may also believe that they are highly emotional compared with men and that the sources of their negative emotions (e.g., hormones) are less controllable than the sources of men's negative emotions.

Second, women were more likely than men to report feeling responsible for the emotional tone of their relationships and for maintaining positive relationships with others at all costs, and feeling too responsible would be associated with greater rumination. Feeling responsible for the emotional tone of relationships may lead women to attend to every nuance of their relationships, always vigilant for trouble, always wondering what others' comments or behaviors mean, always thinking of how they might make others happier. This, in turn, may make women vigilant to their own emotional states as barometers of how their relationships are going, contributing to rumination.

Third, women were more likely than men to report feeling little control over important events in their lives, and people who were lower on mastery reported more rumination. In turn, low perceived mastery helped to mediate the gender difference in rumination. Indeed, low perceived mastery appeared to be the strongest partial mediator of the gender difference in rumination. This suggests that women's sense that they have less control over important events in their lives compared with men is a particularly important contributor to the gender difference in rumination.

None of these three variables fully mediated the gender difference in rumination on its own. This suggests that both women high and low on beliefs about the controllability of emotions, feeling responsible for relationships and perceived mastery may be more prone to rumination than men. But the combination of these three characteristics together did mediate the gender difference in rumination. Many women may carry some, but not all three, of these risk factors for rumination. For example, even women who are high in perceived mastery may have a tendency to ruminate, perhaps because they are concerned about the emotional tone of their relationships and vigilant for problems in these relationships. In addition, even women who believe that the events in their lives are controllable may feel that negative emotions, when they inevitably arise, are not so controllable, and this contributes to their tendency to ruminate.

DEVELOPMENTAL ANTECEDENTS OF RUMINATION

There has been relatively little research on the developmental origins of rumination. Nolen-Hoeksema (1991) speculated that parents might model a ruminative style for their children. Nolen-Hoeksema, Wolfson, Mumme and Guskin (1995) found that 5–7-year-old children of depressed mothers were more likely to show passive, helpless responses to frustrating situations than children of non-depressed mothers. Moreover, children whose mothers showed more ruminative styles of responding to depressed mood were more likely to have passive, helpless styles of responding to challenge.

Children may also learn a ruminative style of responding to their negative moods if they are not explicitly taught more active problem-solving approaches. In the study of depressed and non-depressed mothers and their children, mothers' styles of responding to their children when they were frustrated predicted children's problem-solving and affect regulation strategies (Nolen-Hoeksema et al., 1995). Specifically, mothers who were intrusive and did not allow their children to solve problems, who did not explicitly teach their children to try new approaches when frustrated, or who were critical when their children failed had children who were more prone to become helpless when upset and who had poorer problem-solving skills.

Parents may be even more unlikely to teach their daughters than their sons problem-solving approaches to dealing with negative affect. Parents appear very concerned that their sons do not express stereotypically feminine emotions, such as sadness or fear, and that they "be strong" and "act like a little man" when distressed (Maccoby & Jacklin, 1974). Sanctions against males displaying sadness continue in adulthood. Siegel and Alloy (1990) found that depressed men were evaluated much more negatively than depressed women. These social reinforcements and punishments may motivate boys and men to develop active styles of responding to their depressed moods. At times, these active responses may be inappropriate (e.g., engaging in reckless behavior to avoid thinking about one's depressed mood). But much of the time, these active strategies may involve either using positive distractions or constructive problem-solving. Parents may not directly reinforce rumination in girls— they may simply fail to encourage active problem-solving when girls are sad or upset. Indeed, their learning history may be one reason women are more likely than men to say that such negative emotions as sadness and fear are uncontrollable once you have them (Nolen-Hoeksema & Jackson, 2001).

Biological factors may also play a role in the development of a ruminative style. Children who are more physiologically reactive to stress may find their negative emotional states more compelling and more difficult to overcome, leading them to focus on these states and feel helpless to cope with them. Recent evidence suggests that children with a history of sexual or physical abuse, or severe neglect, may develop dysregulated stress responses, as measured by cortisol levels, adrenocorticotropic hormone levels, and cardiac measures compared with people who did not suffer child abuse or neglect (Heim et al., 2000; Zahn-Waxler, 2000). In turn, this greater biological reactivity is associated with a greater adult prevalence of major depression. It may also be that the greater biological reactivity that results from childhood abuse or neglect could lead to a ruminative style. Children who have more poorly regulated biological responses to stress will find it more difficult to engage in efficacious behavioral responses to new stressors and thus may fall into a ruminative pattern.

DISTINGUISHING RUMINATION FROM OTHER COGNITIVE CONSTRUCTS

Rumination shares similarities with worry, but can be distinguished from it (Nolen-Hoeksema, 2000; Papageorgiou & Wells, 1999a). Rumination tends to involve more thinking about the past, particularly about loss and failure, compared with worry (Wells & Matthews, 1994). Worry is more likely to focus on anticipated threats in the future (Beck, Brown, Steer, Eidelson, & Riskind, 1987; Borkovec, Robinson, Pruzinsky, & DePree, 1983). Papageorgiou and Wells (1999a, b) found that rumination is associated with less verbal content, less compulsion to act, and lower effort and confidence in problem-solving than worry. But both rumination and worry focus on both the past and the future (Borkovec et al., 1983; Lyubomirsky et al., 1999). Further, both rumination and worry may serve to inhibit effective emotional processing (Segerstrom, Tsao, Alden, & Craske, 2000; Teasdale & Barnard, 1993). As noted above, Nolen-Hoeksema (2000) found that her rumination measure predicted both major depression and anxiety symptoms and that a mixed anxiety–depression syndrome may be best predicted by rumination.

Rumination can also be distinguished from negative automatic thoughts as described by Beck, Rush, Shaw, and Emery (1979) and Burns (1980). Principally, rumination is a process of turning attention to one's symptoms and analysis of the causes and consequences of those symptoms. If the individual is in a depressed mood when engaging in rumination, the thoughts he or she focuses on are likely to be negative. Indeed, Lyubomirsky and Nolen-Hoeksema (1995) showed that inducing dysphoric people to ruminate increased their endorsement of the kind of negative cognitive distortions described by Beck and Burns (see also Needles & Abramson, 1990). These thoughts may then increase depressed mood. Rumination predicts depression over and above its shared variance with different forms of negative cognitions, including measures of dispositional optimism and dysfunctional attitudes (Nolen-Hoeksema et al., 1994; Spasojevic & Alloy, 2001).

Finally, rumination can be distinguished from private self-consciousness, a disposition to self-focus and self-analyze regardless of mood (Fenigstein, Scheier, & Buss, 1975). Rumination remained a significant predictor of depression after statistically controlling for private self-consciousness, whereas private self-consciousness was not a significant predictor of depression after controlling for rumination (Nolen-Hoeksema & Morrow, 1993). These results suggest that, although ruminative coping is related to private self-consciousness, it is a better predictor of changes in depression over time than this more global self-focusing construct and may mediate the relationship between private self-consciousness and depression.

ALTERNATIVE CONCEPTUALIZATIONS OF RUMINATION

A number of theorists have provided alternative, and in most cases complementary, conceptualizations of rumination and self-focus (for a series of essays on different conceptualizations of rumination, see Wyer, 1996). Most rumination theorists argue that rumination is instigated when there is a perceived discrepancy between a current state and a desired state (e.g., Carver & Scheier, 1981; Klinger, 1977; Martin & Tesser, 1996; Matthews & Wells, 2000; Pyszczynski & Greenberg, 1987). Many researchers confine their analysis to rumination instigated by a negative event (e.g., Pyszczynski & Greenberg, 1987), whereas Nolen-Hoeksema (1991) focused on rumination instigated by perceived negative affect, whether that affect is the result of an obvious negative event or arises in the absence of a negative event (e.g., as in people with biologically based depressions).

But the greatest debate is over whether rumination is adaptive or maladaptive. Martin and Tesser (1996) argue that rumination is instrumental and is generally adaptive in assisting a person toward solving a problem. Carver and Scheier (1981), Matthews and Wells (2000) and Pyszczynski and Greenberg

(1987) noted that rumination can become maladaptive when an individual cannot resolve the discrepancy between current and desired states and cannot relinquish goals. Nolen-Hoeksema (1996) has focused almost exclusively on the maladaptive consequences of rumination, suggesting that even self-reflection intended to be problem-solving can draw one into negative cycles of thinking and thus impair mood.

Recent analyses by Treynor, Gonzalez, and Nolen-Hoeksema (in press) suggest that finding support for any of these viewpoints depends on how you operationalize rumination. They factor-analyzed the RRS and found two factors. The items on the first factor suggest a purposeful turning inward to engage in cognitive problem-solving to alleviate one's depressive symptoms, and we labeled that factor "reflection." In contrast, the items on the second factor reflect a passive comparison of one's current situation with some unachieved standard, and we labeled that factor "brooding." These two factors resemble those that other researchers have found. For example, the reflection factor is related to the "RRS Self-focus" factor Cox et al. (2001) and the "Introspection/Self-isolation" factor Roberts, Gilboa, & Gotlib (1998) found when they factor-analyzed the RRS. Bagby and Parker (2001) found a "Self-focused Rumination" factor when they analyzed the RSQ. In addition, the brooding factor is similar to the "Self-blame" subfactor Roberts et al. (1998) found in analyzing the RRS.

The reflection factor of rumination was associated with less depression over time in longitudinal analyses, although it was correlated with more depression concurrently. This suggests that reflection is either instigated by negative affect or leads to negative affect in the short term, but is eventually adaptive in reducing negative affect, perhaps because it leads to effective problem-solving. In contrast, the brooding factor of rumination was associated with more depression both concurrently and in longitudinal analyses, suggesting it is not adaptive.

Teasdale and Barnard (1993; see also Barnard & Teasdale, 1991) captured this distinction in their Interacting Cognitive Subsystems Theory. They suggest there are multiple forms of emotional processing in depression, with very different outcomes. The form they label "conceptualizing/doing" most closely resembles the brooding factor found by Treynor et al. (in press)— thoughts *about* the self or emotion and *about* evaluations of present-ideal discrepancies in relation to goals, that do not move the individual into active problem-solving. Watkins and Teasdale (2001) have argued that the overgeneral memory characteristic of depression may be the result of a chronic ruminative analysis of current or past difficulties. In contrast, the form they label "mindful experiencing/being" resembles the reflection factor found by Treynor et al. (in press)—a use of present feelings as a guide to problem solution and resolution, and a non-evaluative awareness of present experiences. This form of emotional processing is associated with good psychotherapeutic outcomes. Indeed, "mindfulness therapy," developed by Teasdale and colleagues to teach depressed people how to engage in mindful emotional processing, has proven effective in reducing depression and preventing relapse (Segal, Williams, & Teasdale, 2002; Teasdale et al., 2000).

A key question then is why some people, when they contemplate their problems and feelings of distress, are able to engage in adaptive reflection whereas others fall into brooding. Teasdale and Barnard (1993) have suggested that people whose negative self-schemas have become easily accessible because of previous episodes of depression should fall into the brooding form of rumination more easily, and I would agree.

Treynor et al. (in press) also found that a personal sense of mastery and a history of chronic stressors were differentially related to brooding and reflection. Brooding was more strongly associated with both mastery and chronic strain than was reflection. The relationship between reflection and mastery did not even reach statistical significance. Chronic stressors probably give people much to brood about, but for some people instigate problem-solving. A low sense of mastery, however, contributes primarily to brooding—that is, to a passive contemplation of what's wrong in your life and how you wish it were better.

Further exploration of the factors that differentiate people who engage in adaptive reflection and those who engage in maladaptive brooding could provide clues as to how to assist depressed people to engage in problem-solving without falling into brooding. If our *post hoc* results, showing that low mastery contributes to brooding but not reflection, can be replicated, this suggests that graded task assignments designed to provide people with evidence of their control over their problems are a critical aspect of cognitive therapy. It may also be useful to assess and explicitly respond to an individual's tendency to engage in negative social comparisons (e.g., "Why do I have problems other people don't have?"), because this was a key aspect of the brooding factor in this study.

IMPLICATIONS FOR THERAPY

The type of therapy that would appear to most directly address the tendency to ruminate is cognitive–behavioral therapy (Beck et al., 1979). In CBT, patients are encouraged to identify the negative thoughts that occur to them in the process of rumination and to challenge these thoughts rather than accepting them. Barber and DeRubeis (1989) and Teasdale, Segal, and Williams (1995) suggest that CBT works not by changing the content of depressed people's cognitions, but by teaching them methods for standing apart from those cognitions and questioning them when they occur. In other words, the key to therapy is for people to stop automatically accepting the truth value of their negative thoughts and to choose to substitute these thoughts with more rational or adaptive thoughts. In a similar vein, Papageorgiou and Wells (2001a, b) argue that interventions with depressed people should include explicit focus on the metacognitive beliefs about rumination that maintain this choice of coping strategies. Ruminators need to be convinced that rumination is not adaptive and encouraged to choose more adaptive modes of coping.

Mindfulness therapy (Segal et al., 2002; Teasdale et al., 2000; see also Kabat-Zinn, 1990) takes a somewhat different approach, suggesting that depressed people stand back and observe their ruminative thoughts in a non-judgmental and non-evaluative manner. The intent is to help people become detached from ways of thinking that have become automatic and that they believe they cannot control. This detached status then gives them a better opportunity to reject irrational or maladaptive thoughts and embrace more adaptive thoughts. Mindfulness interventions have been shown to reduce depression (Teasdale et al., 2000).

The behavioral component of CBT includes training in the use of techniques for interrupting negative ruminations (e.g., thought-stopping exercises, the use of positive distractions) and training in problem-solving skills. The evidence from several of our laboratory studies suggests these are important components of therapy for ruminators. Positive distractions are highly effective at breaking ruminative streams of thought, leading to less negative thinking and more instrumental behavior (Lyubomirsky & Nolen-Hoeksema, 1993, 1995). Positive distractions that interrupt rumination also improve problem-solving skills (Lyubomirsky & Nolen-Hoeksema, 1995). Ruminators may benefit from explicit training in problem-solving, however, focusing particularly on their tendency to feel uncertain about the implementation of any solution they generate and thus to remain immobilized (Ward et al., 2002).

I have argued (Nolen-Hoeksema, 1996) that any type of therapy that provides a ruminator with an explanation of why he or she is depressed and a set of steps to overcome problems may interrupt rumination and thus improve depression (see also Frank, 1973). As long as the ruminator believes the explanation the therapist is providing, she or he has answers to ruminative questions about what is wrong with life and has a set of strategies for facing the future. Of course, if the explanation provided by the therapist is wrong, the problems that led to the depression may remain and cause it to relapse. However, the fact that several different therapies for depression seem equally effective (Robinson, Berman, & Neimeyer, 1990) suggests that some common element of these therapies effectively fights depression. Providing depressed people with a plausible rationale for their depression and the hope they can overcome it by following the therapist's prescriptions may go a long way in interrupting the depression–rumination–inaction cycle. This may be a common characteristic of many effective forms of psychotherapy.

CONCLUSIONS

Rumination in the context of depressed mood would appear to have a number of negative effects. Perhaps most perniciously, rumination can make people keenly aware of the problems in their lives, but simultaneously lead them to be unable to generate good solutions to those problems and to be hopeless about being able to change their lives. Thus, ruminators remain caught in cycles of passivity and despair, occasionally engaging in impulsive or unwise attempts to "do something." Rumination may be the engine that keeps depression running chronically and the link between depression and some of its co-morbid syndromes, such as anxiety and alcohol abuse.

REFERENCES

Abramson, L. Y., Metalsky, G. L., & Alloy, L. B. (1989). Hopelessness depression: A theory based subtype of depression. *Psychological Review*, **96**, 358–372.

Alloy, L., Kelly, K., Mineka, S., & Clements, C. (1990). Comorbidity in anxiety and depressive disorders: A helplessness/hopelessness perspective. In: J. D. Maser & C. R. Cloninger (eds.), *Comorbidity of Mood and Anxiety Disorders* (pp. 3–12). Washington, DC: American Psychiatric Association.

Bagby, R. M. & Parker, J. D. A. (2001). Relation of rumination and distraction with neuroticism and extraversion in a sample of patients with major depression. *Cognitive Therapy and Research*, **25**(1), 91–102.

Barber, J. P. & DeRubeis, R. J. (1989). On second thought: Where the action is in cognitive therapy for depression. *Cognitive Therapy and Research*, **13**, 441–457.

Barlow, D. H. (1988). *Anxiety and Its Disorders: The Nature and Treatment of Anxiety and Panic*. New York: Guilford Press.

Barnard, P. J. & Teasdale, J. D. (1991). Interacting cognitive subsystems: A systemic approach to cognitive-affective interaction and change. *Cognition and Emotion*, **5**, 1–39.

Baumeister, R. F., Heatherton, T. F., & Tice, D. M. (1994). *Losing Control: How and Why People Fail at Self-regulation*. San Diego: Academic Press.

Beck, A. T. (1967). *Depression: Clinical, Experimental and Theoretical Aspects*. New York: Harper & Row.

Beck, A. T., Brown, G., Steer, R. A., Eidelson, J. I., & Riskind, J. H. (1987). Differentiating anxiety and depression: A test of the cognitive-content specificity hypothesis. *Journal of Abnormal Psychology*, **96**, 179–183.

Beck, A. T., Rush, A. J., Shaw, B. F., & Emery, G. (1979). *Cognitive Therapy of Depression*. New York: Guilford Press.

Borkovec, T., Robinson, E., Pruzinsky, T., & DePree, J. (1983). Preliminary exploration of worry: Some characteristics and processes. *Behaviour Research and Therapy*, **21**, 9–16.

Burns, D. (1980). *Feeling Good: The New Mood Therapy*. New York: Morrow.

Butler, L. D. & Nolen-Hoeksema, S. (1994). Gender differences in responses to depressed mood in a college sample. *Sex Roles*, **30**, 331–346.

Carver, C. S. & Scheier, M. F. (1981). *Attention and Self-regulation: A Control-theory Approach to Human Behavior*. New York: Springer-Verlag.

Cox, B. J., Enns, M. W., & Taylor, S. (2001). The effect of rumination as a mediator of elevated anxiety sensitivity in major depression. *Cognitive Therapy and Research*, **25**(5), 525–534.

Fenigstein, A., Scheier, M. F., & Buss, A. H. (1975). Public and private self-consciousness: Assessment and theory. *Journal of Consulting and Clinical Psychology*, **43**, 522–527.

Frank, J. (1973). *Persuasion and Healing: A Comparative Study of Psychotherapy* (2nd edn). Baltimore: Johns Hopkins University Press.

Garber, J., Miller, S. M., & Abramson, L. Y. (1980). On the distinction between anxiety states and depression: Perceived control, certainty, and probability of goal attainment. In: J. Garber & M. E. P. Seligman (eds), *Human Helplessness: Theory and Applications*. New York: Academic Press.

Gross, J. J. (1998). Antecedent- and response-focused emotion regulation: Divergent consequences for experience, expression, and physiology. *Journal of Personality and Social Psychology*, **74**, 224–237.

Heim, C., Newport, J., Heit, S., Graham, Y., Wilcox, M., Bonsall, R., Miller, A., & Nemeroff, C. (2000). Pituitary-adrenal and autonomic responses to stress in women after sexual and physical abuse in childhood. *Journal of the American Medical Association*, **284**, 592–596.

Hull, J. G. (1981). A self-awareness model of the causes and effects of alcohol consumption. *Journal of Abnormal Psychology*, **90**, 586–600.

Kabat-Zinn, J. (1990). *Full Catastrophe Living: The Program of the Stress Reduction Clinic at the University of Massachusetts Medical Center*. New York: Dell.

Klinger, E. (1977). *Meaning and Void: Inner Experience and the Incentives in People's Lives*. Minneapolis, MN: University of Minnesota Press.

Lazarus, R. S. & Folkman, S. (1984). *Stress, Appraisal and Coping*. New York: Springer-Verlag.

Lyubomirsky, S., Caldwell, N. D., & Nolen-Hoeksema, S. (1998). Effects of ruminative and distracting responses to depressed mood on retrieval of autobiographical memories. *Journal of Personality and Social Psychology*, **75**, 166–177.

Lyubomirsky, S. & Nolen-Hoeksema, S. (1993). Self-perpetuating properties of dysphoric rumination. *Journal of Personality and Social Psychology*, **65**, 339–349.

Lyubomirsky, S. & Nolen-Hoeksema, S. (1995). Effects of self-focused rumination on negative thinking and interpersonal problem solving. *Journal of Personality and Social Psychology*, **69**, 176–190.

Lyubomirsky, S., Tucker, K., Caldwell, N. D., & Berg, K. (1999). Why ruminators are poor problem solvers: Clues from the phenomenology of dysphoric rumination. *Journal of Personality and Social Psychology*, **77**, 1041–1060.

Maccoby, E. E. & Jacklin, C. N. (1974). *The Psychology of Sex Differences*. Stanford, CA: Stanford University Press.

Martin, L. L. & Tesser, A. (1996). Some ruminative thoughts. In: R. S. Wyer, Jr (ed.), *Advances in Social Cognition* (pp. 1–47). Hillsdale, NJ: Lawrence Erlbaum.

Matthews, G. & Wells, A. (2000). Attention, automaticity, and affective disorder. *Behavior Modification*, **24**, 69–93.

Mineka, S., Watson, D., & Clark, L. A. (1998). Comorbidity of anxiety and unipolar mood disorders. *Annual Review of Psychology*, **49**, 377–412.

Needles, D. J. & Abramson, L. Y. (1990). Response to depressed mood: Cognitive and affective affects of rumination and distraction. Unpublished manuscript, University of Wisconsin.

Nolen-Hoeksema, S. (1991). Responses to depression and their effects on the duration of depressive episodes. *Journal of Abnormal Psychology*, **100**, 569–582.

Nolen-Hoeksema, S. (1993). Sex differences in control of depression. In: D. M. Wegner & J. W. Pennebaker (eds), *Handbook of Mental Control* (pp. 306–324). Englewood Cliffs, NJ: Prentice Hall.

Nolen-Hoeksema, S. (1996). Chewing the cud and other ruminations. In: R. S. Wyer, Jr (ed.), *Ruminative Thoughts* (pp. 135–144). Mahwah, NJ: Lawrence Erlbaum.

Nolen-Hoeksema, S. (1998). Contributors to the gender difference in rumination. Paper presented to the *Annual Meeting of the American Psychological Association, San Francisco, CA*.

Nolen-Hoeksema, S. (2000). The role of rumination in depressive disorders and mixed anxiety/depressive symptoms. *Journal of Abnormal Psychology*, **109**, 504–511.

Nolen-Hoeksema, S. (2002). Gender differences in depression. In: I. Gotlib & C. Hammen (eds), *Handbook of Depression* (pp. 492–509). New York: Guilford Press.

Nolen-Hoeksema, S. & Davis, C. G. (1999). "Thanks for sharing that": Ruminators and their social support networks. *Journal of Personality and Social Psychology*, **77**, 801–814.

Nolen-Hoeksema, S. & Harrell, Z. A. T. (2002). Rumination, depression and alcohol use: Tests of gender differences. *Journal of Cognitive Psychotherapy: An International Journal*, **16**, 391–404.

Nolen-Hoeksema, S. & Jackson, B. (2001). Mediators of the gender difference in rumination. *Psychology of Women Quarterly*, **25**, 37–47.

Nolen-Hoeksema, S. & Larson, J. (1999). *Coping with Loss*. Mahwah, NJ: Lawrence Erlbaum.

Nolen-Hoeksema, S., Larson, J., & Grayson, C. (1999). Explaining the gender difference in depressive symptoms. *Journal of Personality and Social Psychology*, **77**, 1061–1072.

Nolen-Hoeksema, S. & Morrow, J. (1991). A prospective study of depression and posttraumatic stress symptoms after a natural disaster: The 1989 Loma Prieta earthquake. *Journal of Personality and Social Psychology*, **61**, 115–121.

Nolen-Hoeksema, S. & Morrow, J. (1993). Effects of rumination and distraction on naturally occurring depressed mood. *Cognition and Emotion*, 7(6), 561–570.

Nolen-Hoeksema, S., Morrow, J., & Fredrickson, B. L. (1993). Response styles and the duration of episodes of depressed mood. *Journal of Abnormal Psychology*, **102**, 20–28.

Nolen-Hoeksema, S., Parker, L. E., & Larson, J. (1994). Ruminative coping with depressed mood following loss. *Journal of Personality and Social Psychology*, **67**, 92–104.

Nolen-Hoeksema, S., Wolfson, A., Mumme, G., & Guskin, K. (1995). Helplessness in children of depressed and nondepressed mothers. *Developmental Psychology*, **31**, 377–387.

Papageorgiou, C. & Wells, A. (1999a). Process and metacognitive dimensions of depressive and anxious thoughts and relationships with emotional intensity. *Clinical Psychology and Psychotherapy*, **6**, 156–162.

Papageorgiou, C. & Wells, A. (1999b). Dimensions of depressive rumination and anxious worry: A comparative study. Paper presented at the *33rd Annual Convention of the Association for Advancement of Behavior Therapy*, Toronto.

Papageorgiou, C. & Wells, A. (2001a). Metacognitive beliefs about rumination in recurrent major depression. *Cognitive and Behavioral Practice*, **8**, 160–164.

Papageorgiou, C. & Wells, A. (2001b). Positive beliefs about depressive rumination: Development and preliminary validation of a self-report scale. *Behavior Therapy*, **32**, 13–26.

Pyszczynski, T. & Greenberg, J. (1987). Self-regulatory perseveration and the depressive self-focusing style: A self-awareness theory of reactive depression. *Psychological Bulletin*, **201**, 122–138.

Roberts, J. E., Gilboa, E., & Gotlib, I. H. (1998). Ruminative response style and vulnerability to episodes of dysphoria: Gender, neuroticism, and episode duration. *Cognitive Therapy and Research*, **22**(4), 401–423.

Robinson, L. A., Berman, J. S., & Neimeyer, R. A. (1990). Psychotherapy for the treatment of depression: A comprehensive review of controlled outcome research. *Psychological Bulletin*, **108**, 30–49.

Segal, A., Williams, J. M. G., & Teasdale, J. D. (2002). *Mindfulness-based Cognitive Therapy for Depression: A New Approach to Preventing Relapse*. New York: Guilford Press.

Segerstrom, S. C., Tsao, J. C. I., Alden, L. E., & Craske, M. G. (2000). Worry and rumination: Repetitive thought as a concomitant and predictor of negative mood. *Cognitive Therapy and Research*, **24**, 671–688.

Siegel, S. J. & Alloy, L. B. (1990). Interpersonal perceptions and consequences of depressive-significant other relationships: A naturalistic study of college roommates. *Journal of Abnormal Psychology*, **99**, 361–373.

Spasojevic, J. & Alloy, L. B. (2001). Rumination as a common mechanism relating depressive risk factors to depression. *Emotion*, **1**, 25–37.

Teasdale, J. D. & Barnard, P. J. (1993). *Affect, Cognition, and Change: Re-modelling Depressive Thought*. Hillsdale, NJ: Lawrence Erlbaum.

Teasdale, J. D., Segal, Z., & Williams, J. M. G. (1995). How does cognitive therapy prevent depressive relapse and why should attentional control (mindfulness) training help? *Behavior Research and Therapy*, **33**, 25–39.

Teasdale, J. D., Segal, Z., Williams, J. M. G., Ridgeway, J. A., Sousby, J. M., & Lau, M. A. (2000). Prevention of relapse/recurrence in major depression by mindfulness-based cognitive therapy. *Journal of Consulting and Clinical Psychology*, **68**, 615–623.

Treynor, W., Gonzalez, R., & Nolen-Hoeksema, S. (in press). Rumination reconsidered: A psychometric analysis. *Cognitive Therapy and Research*.

Ward, A., Lyubomirsky, S., Sousa, L., & Nolen-Hoeksema, S. (2003). Can't quite commit: Rumination and uncertainty. *Personality and Social Psychology Bulletin*, **29**, 96–107.

Watkins, E. & Teasdale, J. D. (2001). Rumination and overgeneral memory in depression: Effects of self-focus and analytic thinking. *Journal of Abnormal Psychology*, **110**, 333–357.

Wells, A. & Matthews, G. (1994). *Attention and Emotion: A Clinical Perspective*. Hove, UK: Lawrence Erlbaum.

Wyer, Jr, R. S. (ed.) (1996). *Advances in Social Cognition*. Hillsdale, NJ: Lawrence Erlbaum.

Zahn-Waxler, C. (2000). The development of empathy, guilt, and internalization of distress: Implications for gender differences in internalizing and externalizing problems. In: R. Davidson (ed.), *Anxiety, Depression, and Emotion: Wisconsin Symposium on Emotion* (Vol. 1, pp. 222–265). Oxford, UK: Oxford University Press.

7 Rumination, Depression, and Metacognition: the S-REF Model

GERALD MATTHEWS
Department of Psychology, University of Cincinnati, USA

ADRIAN WELLS
Academic Division of Clinical Psychology, University of Manchester, UK

Typically, rumination refers to repetitive thoughts about personal problems that may be experienced as involuntary and unintended. Ruminative thought occurs in both normal individuals and clinical patients, but especially in the latter group tends to possess a morbid, brooding quality. An early focus for interest in rumination was its role in the symptomatology of obsessive–compulsive disorder (OCD: Rachman, 1971). However, rumination is also a feature of various anxiety and mood disorders (e.g., Paykel & Weissman, 1973 observed that anxious rumination was closely related to symptomatic depression). Current work on the topic centres on a general consensus that rumination is a predominantly maladaptive process that may serve to maintain or even initiate depression. Nolen-Hoeksema has conducted an influential series of studies of rumination that show, for example, that, even with initial symptom levels controlled, rumination predicts future distress and depression (e.g. Nolen-Hoeksema, Parker, & Larson, 1994). Rumination predicts both anxiety and depression symptoms (Nolen-Hoeksema, 2000). The broad consensus that rumination is maladaptive conceals various theoretical uncertainties over the role of rumination in normal and abnormal affective functioning:

- *Differences in conceptualization.* Different authors have proposed somewhat different conceptualizations of rumination. Martin and Tesser (1989, 1996), for example, offer a rather broad definition of rumination as, in effect, any recurring set of thoughts that revolve around a common instrumental theme. Ruminations may be positive or negative and may focus on either goal attainment or discrepancies between goals and current progress. These authors also see rumination as potentially focusing on past, present, or future goals. By contrast, other authors adopt more

Depressive Rumination: Nature, Theory and Treatment
Edited by Costas Papageorgiou and Adrian Wells. © 2004 John Wiley & Sons Ltd

narrow definitions. Nolen-Hoeksema (e.g., 2000) defines rumination in terms of thoughts specifically about depressive symptoms (i.e., referring more to discrepancies than to goal attainment). Roger and Jamieson (1988) claim that rumination over *past* failures to manage interpersonal conflict is a key determinant of stress vulnerability, but other work sees rumination primarily as an attempt to reduce *future* uncertainty, through the establishment of a "future event" schema (Anderson & Limpert, 2001).

- *Assessment issues.* The importance of rumination is attested by the convergence of findings between studies using experimental manipulations to induce rumination and studies that measure individual differences in rumination using questionnaires. However, interpretation of data from questionnaire studies is hindered by difficulties in assessment. It is not clear that different questionnaires (e.g. Nolen-Hoeksema et al., 1994; Roger & Jamieson, 1988; Scott & McIntosh, 1999) are actually measuring the same construct. Indeed, Scott and McIntosh (1999) obtained three orthogonal factors relating to motivation, distraction, and emotionality. A recent confirmatory factor analysis (Bagby & Parker, 2001) shows that Nolen-Hoeksema's scale for ruminative response style is not unidimensional: it actually comprises two modestly intercorrelated factors of symptom-focused rumination (e.g., thinking about negative emotions) and self-focused rumination (e.g., thinking about why you are experiencing negative emotions). In this study, self-focused rumination predicted anxious and depressive personality traits, but symptom-focused rumination did not.

- *Overlap with other constructs.* Scales for rumination tend to correlate with other constructs, such as worry (Papageorgiou & Wells, 1999a, b). Indeed, rumination and worry are substantially correlated empirically (Segerstrom, Tsao, Alden, & Craske, 2000). Rumination also overlaps with the general personality dimension of neuroticism (Bagby & Parker, 2001; Roberts, Gilboa, & Gotlib, 1998). Other possible confounds of rumination include: *emotion-focused coping*, in the sense of self-criticism and blaming oneself for problems; *self-focus of attention*, in the sense of excessive selective attention to self-referent cognitions; and *metacognition*, in the sense of believing it important to focus attention on one's thoughts.

- *Mechanisms for rumination effects.* An account of rumination should specify the information-processing mechanisms that initiate and maintain ruminative activity. Two somewhat conflicting notions appear to dominate the theoretical literature. The first idea is that rumination represents a prolonged episode of "recycling" thoughts that serve no conscious purpose or goal. From this perspective, rumination is somewhat automatic[1] in that it is non-intentional, although it may require some

---

[1] In common with most current thought, we recognize that there are dissociations between criteria for automaticity, of which the most important are lack of volition, few demands for general purpose processing resources, and unconsciousness, implying that there is no simple dichotomy between automatic and controlled processing.

attentional capacity and impinge on consciousness (Uleman, 1989). Siegle (1999) has developed a connectionist model of this type, in which rumination is supported by stronger feedback connections between affective and non-affective feature modules. That is, rumination may be entirely stimulus-driven (although perhaps also moderated by top-down control). The second idea (Martin & Tesser, 1989) is that rumination is a response to goal frustration, functioning initially as a controlled search for an alternative route to the goal, but becoming increasingly non-instrumental. In addition, the character of rumination may change and develop over time: Segerstrom et al. (2000) suggest that rumination may begin as strategic (i.e., controlled), but become increasingly automatic with practice.

- *Rumination as a pathological process.* There appear to be multiple routes through which rumination might contribute to emotional dysfunction. Young and Nolen-Hoeksema (2001), for example, list four mechanisms for prolongation of distress. Rumination may (1) enhance depressogenic thinking, (2) interfere with interpersonal problem-solving, (3) sap motivation to engage in instrumental behaviour, and (4) impair social relationships because other people tire of listening to ruminations. These are all plausible mechanisms, but it is not clear that they are exclusive to rumination (i.e., to repetitive, self-referent thinking). For example, depressogenic thinking may reflect content as well as process factors, formulating coping strategies may interfere with problem-solving and externally directed attention (Matthews & Wells, 1988), and loss of motivation may reflect beliefs about helplessness and lack of self-agency. Existing theory also neglects the role of dynamic person–environment interaction. The person's attempts to manage exposure to events that trigger rumination, for example, by avoiding problematic situations, may in themselves be a source of pathology (Wells, 1997). In short, it is likely that rumination correlates with a variety of other content and process factors, and it is difficult to discriminate causal and incidental factors in studies of emotional distress.

- *Treatment implications.* Uncertainties about the conceptualization, causes and consequences of rumination limit the application of theory to clinical practice. Any attempt to address rumination clinically requires a coherent conceptualization of the construct that defines its relations with other correlated factors. Perhaps the most fundamental issue is whether rumination is a causal factor in emotional disorder and hence a potential target for intervention, as opposed to being merely a symptom of some more fundamental underlying process. Another important issue for the clinical psychologist is the degree of similarity of the ruminative process in different mood and anxiety disorders. Anxious, depressed, and obsessional patients all ruminate, but do their ruminations reflect the same form of maladaptive processing or do they have differing theoretical and clinical implications? Identification of a configuration of cognitive processes common to a range of emotional disorders may facilitate therapy.

AIMS OF THIS CHAPTER

There is general agreement that rumination is important (1) as an element of the cognitive theory of negative affect, (2) as a predictor of depression and emotional distress in empirical studies, and (3) as a clinical symptom that may require treatment. However, the preceding analysis has identified various sources of uncertainty. There is no precise consensual definition of rumination, and so different scales for measuring rumination may not converge well. Similarly, rumination appears to overlap considerably with other constructs related to personality and cognition. Theoretical uncertainties revolve around the extent to which rumination is "automatic" or "controlled", and how it should be distinguished from other cognitive processes, such as worry, self-focus of attention, negative self-appraisal and dysfunctional emotion-focused processing (other than in terms of duration). In consequence, its relevance to clinical practice is unclear.

In the remainder of this chapter, we will argue that the source of many of the uncertainties listed is that rumination has not been conceptualized within an explicit and comprehensive architecture for negative affect and cognition. We will describe our Self-Regulatory Executive Function (S-REF: Wells & Matthews, 1994, 1996) model of affective dysfunction, which links rumination to self-regulation within a multilevel architecture. The model emphasizes the role of metacognitive beliefs and coping processes in initiating and perpetuating ruminative thought. It also supports a dynamic perspective on the negative consequences of rumination for maintaining adaptive self-knowledge. After describing how the model clarifies the conceptualization of rumination, we will briefly review some illustrative research that supports its predictions concerning the interrelationships of rumination, metacognition, coping, and emotional disturbance. The S-REF model emphasizes that rumination is common to a variety of emotional disorders, and it should be understood as a generic dysfunctional process, not as a quality of depression alone. The final part of the chapter applies the S-REF account to clinical issues and treatment implications.

THE S-REF MODEL

ACTIVATION OF THE SUPERVISORY EXECUTIVE

The architecture of the S-REF model comprises three levels: a set of lower level processing networks, a supervisory executive system (cf. Norman & Shallice, 1986), and a self-knowledge level that represents self-beliefs and generic plans for coping (Matthews & Wells, 1999; Wells and Matthews, 1994). Lower level networks support processing that is automatic, in that it is reflexively triggered by incoming stimuli. It represents various types of information, including codings of stimuli, descriptions of internal cognitive state, and representations of somatic states. Much routine processing operates at this level, which has an associative, schematic quality. Processing at this level may be experienced as the "negative automatic thoughts" characteristic of depression that intrude into conscious awareness for no apparent reason (Beck, Emery, & Greenberg, 1985).

Motivationally significant external stimuli and intruding thoughts activate the supervisory executive. Once activated, the operations of the S-REF are guided by closed loop control that aims to reduce any discrepancy between current status and some target status. First, the intruding stimulus must be appraised (i.e., evaluated with respect to personal goals and social constraints) and any discrepancy computed. In the event of discrepancy, a search is conducted for coping options, and a particular coping strategy is selected, adapted to immediate situational needs, implemented, and monitored. Coping responses are implemented by biasing lower level processing networks, so that level of control of processing shifts dynamically between executive and lower level systems, until discrepancy is resolved and the episode can "finish". Emotion-focused coping feeds back into the processing and modification of internal representations, whereas problem-focused coping initiates responses intended to change external reality (Lazarus & Folkman, 1984; Matthews & Wells, 1996). Emotions are generated as an integration of appraisal and coping processes that signals the relational or "transactional" meaning of the encounter to the person (Lazarus, 1999; Matthews et al., 2003).

These processing operations depend on interaction between the executive and the third level of the model: the self-knowledge level. Both appraisal and coping require the accessing of self-relevant knowledge (Lazarus, 1999). Appraisal requires self-knowledge as a frame of reference for computing current and desired status. Coping requires the accessing of generic procedures for coping, which are modified online to deal with the immediate problem at hand, as specified by skill theory (Anderson, 1996).

In recent work, Wells (2000) has emphasized the importance of *metacognition* in executive control. Especially when the S-REF is activated by internally generated intrusions, appraisal and coping are influenced by metacognitive beliefs that specify (1) the personal significance and (2) the coping implications of thoughts, corresponding to a theoretical distinction made between metacognitive knowledge and metacognitive regulation (Brown, Bransford, Campione, & Ferrara, 1983). Wells (2000) gives the example of an obsessional patient disturbed by intrusive images of the Devil. He appraised these images as dangerous and evil, and coped with them by concentrating on every word, while praying and forming a mental image of Christ. Metacognitive beliefs and control strategies are themselves shaped by self-knowledge. For example, beliefs about the harmfulness of anxiety symptoms ("anxiety sensitivity") may derive from childhood learning experiences (Schmidt & Woolaway-Bickel, in press).

Rumination in the S-REF model derives in part from the person's metacognitive beliefs that specify the use of rumination as a strategy for coping and self-regulation. These beliefs exist as implicit plans that guide self-regulative processing and as explicit, declarative beliefs that are accessible to verbal report (e.g., "ruminating about the past helps me to prevent future mistakes and failures": see Papageorgiou & Wells, 2001a). Rumination is not always volitionally triggered, as the initial impetus for rumination in the S-REF model may be supplied by lower level processes that detect discrepancies between the self and a goal and thereby refresh the need for continual processing. The choice of ruminative emotion-focused coping as a self-regulative strategy, in preference to alternative strategies focused on immediate action, is a consequence of the availability and accessibility of self-knowledge in the form of information for interpreting the significance of one's internal cognitive events. As discussed below, the harmful effects of rumination may be closely related to metacognitive beliefs that exaggerate the importance of thoughts and to control strategies that serve to perpetuate maladaptive cognitions (Wells & Matthews, 1994).

CONSEQUENCES OF S-REF ACTIVATION

The cognitive and behavioural responses generated by S-REF function produce a variety of consequences in parallel (Matthews & Wells, 1999, 2000). The most immediate consequence is that the person's choice of coping strategy directly impacts low-level processing operations and hence behaviour (although strategies do not always function as intended). In addition, the resource demands of self-regulative activity may divert resources away from other processing, leading to disruption of attention. Sometimes, coping will successfully eliminate self-discrepancy, terminating S-REF processing successfully. However, under other circumstances, self-discrepancy will remain, most obviously if coping fails to solve the problem, which as Martin and Tesser (1989) discuss may lead over time to increasingly unproductive ruminative thoughts.

There are also dynamic factors that may serve to perpetuate S-REF processing and worry (Matthews & Wells, 1999, 2000). Various internally directed coping strategies intended to reduce self-discrepancy may backfire and actually maintain negative self-beliefs. Self-referent processing necessarily involves heightened self-focus of attention and awareness of discrepancy, a slippery slope leading to pathological sensitivity to threat in vulnerable individuals. The interaction between the executive system and self-knowledge may perpetuate pathology, if it operates to increase the availability and/or accessibility of negative items of knowledge. S-REF activity may increase availability of negative self-knowledge through establishing a more elaborated and extensive set of negative associations to concepts and events.

In addition, individuals who are distressed and worried may use *thought control* strategies (i.e., metacognitive coping strategies that seek to control the content of thought directly). Such strategies may increase the accessibility of negative self-beliefs. The best known strategy of this kind is suppression of disturbing thoughts, which may sometimes lead to a paradoxical rebound of the unwanted thought (Wenzlaff & Wegner, 2000), although data are rather inconsistent across studies (Purdon, 1999). As further discussed below, other thought control strategies, such as seeking to punish oneself for the thought, may also serve to maintain distress through maintaining the activation of maladaptive beliefs (Wells & Davies, 1994). Hence, the continued use of rumination is likely to lead to a range of problems, such as incubation of intrusions following stress (e.g., Wells & Papageorgiou, 1995) and a perpetuation of mood disturbance (Nolen-Hoeksema, 2000), which contribute to the development of negative beliefs about emotional and thinking processes. In the S-REF model these responses have been referred to as "secondary emotion" (Wells & Matthews, 1994) and are a component of metacognition contributing to emotional disturbance.

S-REF activity also tends to promote maladaptive patterns of interaction with the outside world, a process mediated by choice of coping strategy (Matthews & Wells, 1996, 1999). For example, one form of coping associated with depression is avoidance of troubling situations (Fichman, Koestner, Zuroff, & Gordon, 1999). However, this strategy prevents the acquisition of task-focused skills for management of such situations, maintaining a sense of powerlessness. Another coping strategy typical of depressed individuals is self-criticism. A recent experience-sampling study (Fichman et al., 1999) suggests that self-criticism may promote both behavioural avoidance and venting negative emotions, a behaviour pattern that may encourage other persons to avoid the depressed individual. Similarly, anxiety patients engage in "safety behaviours" (e.g., mentally rehearsing sentences) that are designed to prevent feared catastrophes (saying something "stupid"). These behaviours are likely to enhance self-consciousness and maintain awareness of self-discrepancies (Wells, 1997). In addition, the non-occurrence of catastrophes can be attributed to the safety behaviour, so there is no challenging to the fundamental cognitive error (i.e., assuming the catastrophe is likely). Thus, the coping strategies of both depressed and anxious individuals tend (1) to elicit negative feedback from the outside world, (2) to maintain negative self-referent cognitions including rumination, and (3) to block the acquisition of more effective skills, such as being able to profit from interaction with other people.

CONCEPTUALIZATION OF RUMINATION IN THE S-REF MODEL

This general account of dysfunctional emotion allows a more precise definition of rumination: as repetitive thoughts generated by attempts to cope with self-discrepancy that are directed primarily toward processing the content of self-referent information and not toward immediate goal-directed action. In other words, given some threatening or damaging event, rumination seeks the answers to questions, such as "how do I feel about this event?", "how can I change my thoughts and feelings about the event?", and "how can I prevent disturbing thoughts and feelings in the future?". Although there is considerable overlap between rumination and worry, the definition establishes rumination as a subset of worry. Worry not only includes rumination but also intrusive thoughts that are directed toward immediate action in the troubling situation.

The S-REF model also clarifies both process and content in rumination, as shown in Figure 7.1, which illustrates some of the self-regulative processes that operate during depression. Similar to Martin and Tesser (1996), the S-REF model sees ruminative thought as a response to self-discrepancy (i.e., it is fundamentally goal-directed). However, the model extends this conceptualization by linking rumination to an explicit cognitive architecture. Rumination appears to possess both automatic and controlled qualities (Uleman, 1989) because both types of processing are involved. On the one hand, rumination is maintained by executive (S-REF) processing routines driven by dysfunctional metacognitive knowledge that support self-reflective, emotion-focused processing as a coping strategy. On the other hand, executive processing operates through initiating attempts at thought control that bias lower level, "automatic" processing, which generates intrusive thoughts autonomously. Figure 7.1 shows that rumination is supported by several distinct cyclical processes. First, rumination supported by interlocked cycles of appraisal and emotion-focused coping is entirely controlled. The person may believe these processing efforts are directed toward problem-solving, but typically rumination interferes with systematic, task-directed action. In this sense, rumination is emotion-focused coping masquerading as problem-focus. Second, executive processing may provoke sequences of automatic processing (experienced as intrusive thoughts or bodily sensations) that, if appraised as threatening, damaging or uncontrollable, continue to elicit attempts at coping through thought control. Third, an ecological perspective might see person and environment as an integrated system, with rumination tending to promote continued exposure to depressogenic events and trigger stimuli that in turn maintain ruminative cognitions.

As previously discussed, theories of rumination differ considerably in the scope of thought content considered "ruminative". In the S-REF model, ruminative thought content must be related (1) (even if only indirectly) to the initiating self-discrepancy (e.g., through, referring to lack of self-worth or self-efficacy) and (2) to coping responses that are primarily internally rather than externally directed. For example, in test anxiety (cf. Sarason, Sarason, Keefe, Hayes, & Shearin, 1986) persistent intrusive thoughts may include both those directed toward answering the test ("this question is too hard for me") and those directed toward the broader status of the self ("I must be really stupid to fail this test"). The first thought is not necessarily ruminative

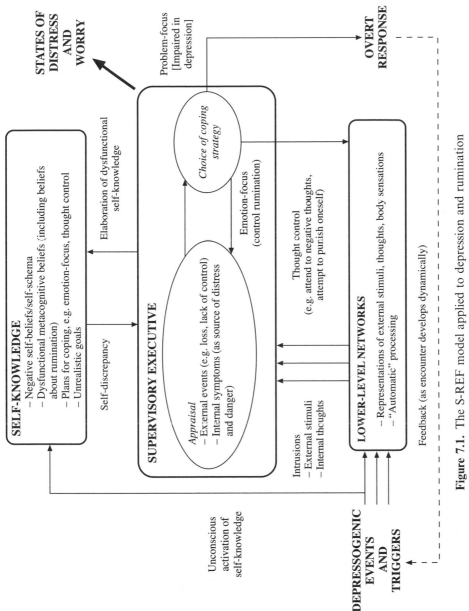

Figure 7.1. The S-REF model applied to depression and rumination

because, even if the person blames themselves rather than the test, they may cope by moving onto the next question. Conversely, the second of the two thoughts is likely to be ruminative, in that it implies self-discrepancy and coping efforts that entail processing the self as "stupid".

Thus, the S-REF conceptualization of rumination is narrower than that of Martin and Tesser (1989, 1996), in excluding positively toned reflection and immediate instrumental problem-solving efforts from the definition. It is broader than Nolen-Hoeksema's (e.g., 2000) definition in that the content of rumination is not restricted to depressive symptomatology, and, indeed, important evidence on rumination comes from studies of anxiety and OCDs. It is also more action-oriented, in that rumination implies some goal-directed coping strategy (although conscious awareness of the goal may be incomplete). A final distinctive feature of our conceptualization is that rumination should not be seen as a typically free-running process that proceeds independently of environmental contingencies. Rather, because of the key role of environmental triggers in activating self-discrepancy, the onset and offset of rumination depend on both personal and situational factors. Indeed, the person may try to control rumination through avoiding situations that trigger it.

IMPLICATIONS FOR ASSESSMENT

So far as assessment is concerned, rumination from the S-REF perspective represents a higher order processing syndrome, rather than any single process. Hence, scales for negative self-appraisal, emotion-focused coping (especially self-criticism), thought control, metacognition, and worry may all capture some elements of rumination, but no single scale seems ideal as an index of the complete syndrome. Similarly, existing scales are probably biased toward one or more of the various components of the syndrome. The scale closest to our conceptualization is the metaworry scale from the Anxious Thoughts Inventory (AnTI: Wells, 1994), which refers to "worries about worry". Metaworry appears to be a stronger predictor of pathological worry than worries about more specific concerns (Wells & Carter, 1999, 2001). Furthermore, metaworry is elevated in both depressed and anxious patient groups (Wells & Carter, 2001). More generally, the S-REF model suggests that care is needed in operationalizing different aspects of rumination: it is essential to distinguish *self-knowledge*, *situational processes*, and *outcome* constructs. Self-knowledge is indexed by dispositional scales that assess, for example, typical metacognitions or coping strategies, showing high test–retest reliability. Such scales include the Metacognitions Questionnaire (MCQ: Cartwright-Hatton & Wells, 1997) and the Thought Control Questionnaire (TCQ: Wells & Davies, 1994), which measure metacognitive beliefs and individual differences in use of a range of strategies for controlling distressing thoughts.

Such standard personality traits as neuroticism may also represent individual differences in self-knowledge (Matthews, Schwean, Campbell, Saklofske, & Mohamed, 2000). Scales for situational appraisal and coping provide an index of the executive processing elicited during a specific encounter (to the extent that processing can be validly measured through self-report). Normally, such processing reflects both dispositional and situational factors: correlations between dispositional and situational coping, for example, are positive but moderate in magnitude (Matthews, Hillyard, & Campbell, 1999).

Stress outcome variables represent the overall emotional, motivational, and cognitive state of the person, as indexed by such variables as mood, state anxiety, and cognitive interference (Matthews, 2001; Matthews et al., 2003). Outcomes may reflect an integration of more specific processes, perhaps representing some relational or transactional theme (Lazarus & Folkman, 1984). Hence, a scale for rumination could index: (1) the general disposition of rumination proneness; (2) the underlying processes that cause rumination, such as choosing to reflect on a problem; or (3) the immediate rumination state of experiencing many intrusive thoughts in a given situation. Rumination measures, such as those previously reviewed, are dispositional in nature, although measures of intrusive thought frequency or state worry may serve as a partial index of the ruminative state (e.g., Wells & Papageorgiou, 1995). Recent work grounded in the S-REF model has developed scales to assess the metacognitions underlying rumination: the Positive Beliefs about Rumination Scale (PBRS: Papageorgiou & Wells, 2001b) and the Negative Beliefs about Rumination Scale (NBRS: Papageorgiou, Wells, & Meina, in preparation).

TESTING PREDICTIONS FROM THE S-REF MODEL

Next, we survey some illustrative examples of empirical studies that have tested predictions from the S-REF model in normal and clinical samples (for more extended accounts, see Wells, 2000 and Matthews, Schwean et al., 2000). As indicated above, the model suggests that the rumination process will be functionally similar in different emotional disorders, and so these studies investigate several forms of emotional pathology. Figure 7.2 illustrates some of the principal constructs assessed, classified as referring to dispositional self-knowledge, in-situation processing and outcomes, respectively. The figure also lists the various questionnaires used in our research, which are described in context below. Constructs shown in square brackets were not assessed directly in these studies. The figure is not intended to portray a detailed model, such as the model shown in Figure 7.1, but it includes some broad causal relations. It is assumed that self-knowledge biases situational processing, which in turn generates acute and chronic outcomes signalling dysfunction. Rumination is seen as a configuration of self-referent situational processing as described above; our studies have focused on various components of this configuration.

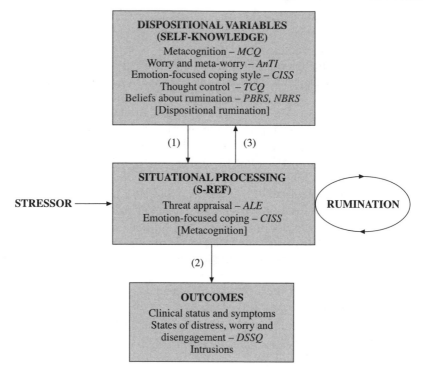

Figure 7.2. Constructs related to self-knowledge, situational processing, and outcomes. Abbreviations: MCQ = Metacognitions Questionnaire (Cartwright-Hatton & Wells, 1997); AnTI = Anxious Thoughts Investory (Wells, 1994); CISS = Coping Inventory for Stressful Situations (Endler & Parker, 1990); TCQ = Thought Control Questionnaire (Wells & Davies, 1994); PBRS = Positive Beliefs about Rumination Scale (Papageorgiou & Wells, 2001b; NBRS = Negative Beliefs about Rumination Scale (Papageorgiou, Wells, & Meina, in press; ALE = Assessment of Life Events scale (Ferguson, Matthews, & Cox, 1999); Coping Inventory for Task Stress (CITS: Matthews & Campbell, 1998); DSSQ = Dundee Stress State Questionnaire (Matthews et al., in press)

We discuss evidence relating to three classes of prediction, tested by the paths between constructs (1)–(3) in the figure:

(1) *Metacognitions as a source of maladaptive coping.* According to the S-REF model, maladaptive metacognitions are a source of inner-directed coping strategies, such as emotion focus, thought control, and rumination. (Likelihood of strategy use also depends on appraisals of the situation and availability of generic coping procedures.) Thus, metacognitive beliefs should be positively associated with maladaptive coping styles (the link from "self-knowledge" to the "supervisory executive" in Figure 7.1).

(2) *Maladaptive coping as a cause of emotional dysfunction and pathology.* A further prediction from the model is that use of maladaptive coping strategies should generate various symptoms of dysfunction (including clinical pathology) and subclinical disturbances of subjective state. This prediction has been tested in studies of (1) the relationship between thought control strategies and emotional pathology, and (2) the relationship between coping and stress outcomes in experimental studies of performance (links between the "supervisory executive" and (1) overt response and (2) states of distress and worry in Figure 7.1).

(3) *Rumination as a source of further cognitive dysfunction.* In addition to exacerbating immediate emotional distress, the ruminative cycle may also produce more far-reaching deleterious effects, associated with elaboration of self-knowledge and blocking of adaptive restructuring. Studies of experimental induction of worry and social phobia test this prediction (feedback loop between "supervisory executive" and "self-knowledge" in Figure 7.1).

METACOGNITIONS AS A SOURCE OF MALADAPTIVE COPING

Several studies testing predictions from the S-REF model have made use of the MCQ developed by Cartwright-Hatton and Wells (1997). It comprises five internally consistent scales that assess: positive beliefs about worry, negative beliefs about worry concerning themes of danger and uncontrollability, lack of cognitive confidence; negative beliefs concerning themes of responsibility, punishment and superstition; and cognitive self-consciousness. The MCQ scales correlate with worry proneness in non-clinical samples (Cartwright-Hatton & Wells, 1997), and both anxious and depressed patient groups show elevated negative metacognitive belief scores (Wells & Carter, 2001).

Wells and Matthews (1994) suggest that disturbed metacognition is central to OCD, in that the patient's plans for dealing with disturbing thoughts specify use of control strategies, such as (depending on the patient) thought suppression, monitoring for thoughts, and performing behavioural rituals like checking (see Wells, 2000). Wells and Papageorgiou (1998) investigated the MCQ as a predictor of OCD symptoms. They found a general tendency for MCQ scales to correlate positively with both cognitive and behavioural symptom clusters. In addition, multiple regression showed that the MCQ was predictive of maladaptive cognition even with general worry proneness statistically controlled. For example, positive beliefs and danger/uncontrollability beliefs predicted obsessional thinking independently of worry, and of one another. Positive beliefs also made an independent contribution to prediction of checking.

Another line of research has been concerned with predictors of maladaptive coping and chronic emotional distress in college students. In a study of test anxiety, Matthews et al. (1999) assessed how students coped with an impending examination, using the MCQ, the Wells (1994) questionnaire for dispositional worry and metaworry, and a standard coping measure that assessed task focus (i.e., problem focus), emotion focus, and avoidance (Endler & Parker's, 1990, Coping Inventory for Stressful Situations: CISS). Factor analysis of these scales distinguished two factors that were independently predictive of test anxiety: one defined primarily by metacognitive and worry scales and one defined primarily by coping scales. However, emotion-focused coping had substantial loadings on both metacognitive and coping factors, showing that metacognition is especially linked to such emotion-focused strategies as self-criticism (which tend to be maladaptive). In two studies of homesickness, Mohamed (1996) showed that the Wells (1994) metaworry scale was correlated with negative appraisals of being away from home, use of emotion-focused coping, and chronic emotional disturbance, including both depression and anxiety. Furthermore, these relationships remained significant when neuroticism was statistically controlled. Thus, pathological "worry about worry", a concept close to rumination, is closely related to coping style.

COPING AS A SOURCE OF EMOTIONAL DYSFUNCTION AND PATHOLOGY

The S-REF model accommodates the consensus view that, although effects of coping on outcome are somewhat context-dependent, self-critical emotion-focused coping tends to be associated with more adverse outcomes to stressful encounters (Matthews & Wells, 1996). The S-REF model also provides a more fine-grained account of different forms of emotion-focused coping that may contribute to pathology. Emotion-focused coping is typically conceptualized as strategies, such as self-criticism and wishful thinking (Lazarus & Folkman, 1984). However, especially in the clinical context, it may also be important to discriminate thought control strategies. In a study of flood victims, Morgan, Matthews and Winton (1995) showed that emotion-focused coping predicted trauma symptoms, even with severity of appraisal controlled. Rated use of suppression, as a thought control strategy, was independently predictive.

The TCQ (Wells & Davies, 1994) measures strategies of distraction, social control (i.e., consulting with a friend), punishment, reappraisal, and worry (in the sense of choosing to direct attention toward negative thoughts). Use of worry and punishment strategies are associated with pathological worry and proneness to emotional problems in both non-patient and patient groups (Reynolds & Wells, 1999; Wells & Davies, 1994). Punishment and worry strategy use also discriminates OCD patients from non-patients (Amir, Cashman, & Foa, 1997), and motor vehicle accident victims with and without acute stress disorder (Warda & Bryant, 1998). Holeva, Tarrier, and Wells (2001) tested the prediction derived from the S-REF model that coping strategies characterized by worry would be positively associated with the development of PTSD following trauma (road traffic accidents). In cross-sectional analyses, worry and punishment strategies emerged as positive predictors while distraction and social control were negative predictors. Worry at time 1 predicted PTSD at time 2 (four to six months later), when acute stress disorder at time 1 was controlled.

The studies of Matthews et al. (1999) and Mohamed (1996) showed robust correlations between dispositional worry, emotion-focused coping, and such outcomes as depression and anxiety, consistent with the S-REF model. However, these studies, in looking at general styles of coping with such challenges as being away from home, provide limited insight into the situational processes controlling stress outcomes. Experimental studies of acute distress and worry have investigated appraisal and coping with a specific, situational stressor. Matthews et al. (in press) developed the Dundee Stress State Questionnaire (DSSQ) to measure three fundamental dimensions of subjective state disturbance: distress (negative emotions, lack of confidence); worry (intrusive thoughts, self-focused attention); and task disengagement (mental fatigue, demotivation). Here, "worry" refers to the *state* of experiencing frequent intrusive, self-referent thoughts, rather than the underlying *process* that generates the thoughts. In two studies (Matthews & Falconer, 2000; Matthews, Derryberry, & Siegle, 2000), subjective states were assessed before and after performance of stressful, high-workload cognitive tasks. Two validated measures of situational appraisal and coping were also administered post task: the Appraisal of Life Events Scale (ALE: Ferguson, Matthews, & Cox, 1999) and the Coping Inventory for Task Stress (CITS: Matthews & Campbell, 1998). Multiple regressions showed that increases in distress over initial baseline level were reliably associated with threat appraisal and emotion-focused coping (self-criticism), whereas increased worry was independently predicted by both emotion-focused and avoidant coping. Thus, how the person chooses to cope with the immediate stressor has a strong impact on levels of worry. Further work might investigate how metacognitive coping strategies contribute to the maintenance of the worry state following its initiation. Coping may both initiate and perpetuate rumination.

RUMINATION AS A SOURCE OF FURTHER COGNITIVE DYSFUNCTION

The S-REF model proposes that the deleterious effects of rumination operate in part through its dynamic interaction with stable long-term memories (Wells & Matthews, in press). Rumination is likely to lead to more elaborated representations of negative beliefs and stressful events, making negative self-referent information more easily accessed. Rumination appears to block this adaptive restructuring of self-knowledge (e.g., following trauma). Wells (2000) reviews various experimental studies showing that experimental manipulations of worry tend to increase subsequent negative thinking and disrupt cognitive self-regulation. For example, Wells and Papageorgiou (1995) had subjects watch a gruesome film depicting a workshop accident. Following exposure, subjects were assigned to one of five groups instructed to use different strategies for processing the stressful event. The frequency of intruding thoughts during the subsequent three-day period was then assessed. Groups explicitly instructed to worry about the film reported higher frequencies of intrusive images than groups in other conditions. Wells and Papageorgiou suggest that worries "incubate" intrusive thoughts under these conditions, because (1) the worry instruction blocks adaptive emotion processing and (2) through elaborative processing the stressor representation in memory becomes "tagged" and more easily accessed.

Similarly, Mellings and Alden (2000) found that socially anxious individuals reported higher self-focus, greater rumination, and larger negative cognitive biases in judgement and recall, during a social interaction. Rumination predicted negative bias in judgement and recall of negative self-related information, implying that, consistent with the Wells and Papageorgiou (1995) finding, rumination increases accessibility of negative, self-referent memory. These findings support the Clark and Wells (1995) model of social phobia that states social phobics engage in post-event rumination following stressful social encounters, centring on anxious feelings and negative self-perceptions, which tends to induce a negative bias in recall.

RUMINATION IN CLINICAL PATIENTS

Our definition of rumination suggests that it occurs as a subset of worry and is a general feature of emotional disturbance. However, important differences are likely to exist between normal and clinical forms of rumination, and between the properties of rumination across different disorders.

NORMAL VS. ABNORMAL RUMINATION

The S-REF model implies that distinctions can be made between normal and clinical forms of rumination. Normal individuals may sometimes engage in prolonged processing of self-referent information, especially if the person is dispositionally neurotic (Matthews, Derryberry et al., 2000). "Normal" rumination may serve to perpetuate negative affect, but, typically, the person will also use additional coping strategies that are likely to be more successful in dealing with the problem eliciting rumination. For example, the person might brood on the problem for some time and then take some direct problem-focused action, or turn their attention to other matters entirely. Indeed, rumination may occasionally lead to useful insights into the problem. In clinical patients, however, rumination may be indefinitely self-perpetuating, so that it sustains perseverative negative thinking as the primary focus of coping attempts, which in turn thwarts self-regulation and the compilation of more adaptive knowledge. What is it about clinical forms of rumination that contributes to such problems?

First, rumination may be used inflexibly as the predominant means of dealing with particular stressors, when alternative responses may provide more favourable outcomes, such as exposure to information that can restructure maladaptive beliefs. Second, patients may have negative metacognitive beliefs about the meaning and consequences of rumination itself that lead to negative interpretation of rumination. In generalized anxiety disorder (GAD), which is characterized by repeated worrying about a number of topics, negative beliefs about the dangers and controllability of worrying are thought to play a central role in problem maintenance (Wells, 1995, 1997). Similarly, rumination in depression may become problematic for well-being when negative metacognitive beliefs about rumination are activated, thereby perpetuating self-discrepancies and refreshing the need for sustained rumination (cf. Wells, 2000).

Third, the internal rules that individuals use to signal the cessation or continuation of rumination may contribute to prolonged rumination that is difficult to stop. A distinctive contribution of the metacognitive approach to understanding emotional disorder (Wells, 2000) is its emphasis on maladaptive internal criteria that people use to regulate behaviour and processing. In emotional disorder, patients' metacognitions direct them to monitor for internal feeling states as a sign of safety or competency in coping with future threats. For example, in the absence of distractions, some GAD patients worry until they "feel" that it is safe to stop. In OCD, patients engage in overt and mental rituals such as repeating behaviours until some desired internal state is satisfied (e.g., a perfect and complete memory of performing an action). Such criteria are unhelpful since they maintain self-focus, are demanding to accomplish, and do not provide accurate information about events, increasing the likelihood of experiencing self-discrepancies.

METACOGNITION AND RUMINATION IN EMOTIONAL DISORDER

In the S-REF model, emotional disorder is linked to the activation of a cognitive–attentional processing configuration in which perseverative self-focused processing is a key constituent (Wells & Matthews, 1994). This perseverative processing occurs as repetitive negative thinking (i.e., worry/rumination). We have discussed various mechanisms through which rumination may produce disturbances in affect and cognition. However, in clinical patients, metacognition seems to play a dominant role in mediating detrimental effects of rumination, through the development of "secondary" negative beliefs about emotional and thinking processes. In GAD, patients have both positive and negative beliefs about worry, and it is the negative appraisal of worrying based on negative beliefs that leads to an escalation of distress. In depression, the S-REF model similarly predicts that, irrespective of positive beliefs about rumination, negative beliefs and associated negative interpretation of internal events will contribute to a downward spiralling of mood and concomitant anxiety about loss of emotional control.

Prompted by the S-REF model, a series of recent studies have set out to explore the nature of metacognitive beliefs about rumination in depression, and relationships among such beliefs and depression (see also Chapter 1). Papageorgiou and Wells (2001a) examined the presence and content of positive and negative beliefs about rumination in patients suffering from recurrent major depression. All patients reported positive and negative beliefs about rumination. Positive beliefs reflected themes concerning rumination as a coping strategy (e.g., "I need to ruminate about my problems to find answers to my depression," "ruminating about the past helps me to prevent future mistakes and failures"). Negative beliefs contained themes concerning uncontrollability and harm, and the interpersonal consequences of rumination (e.g., "ruminating about my problems is uncontrollable," "ruminating about my depression could make me kill myself"). Papageorgiou and Wells (2001b) developed the PBRS to further explore relationships between metacognition, rumination, and depression. The PBRS is a nine-item unifactorial instrument possessing good psychometric properties. PBRS scores were positively correlated with Beck depression scores ($r = 0.45$) and the state–trait anxiety inventory depression subcomponent score ($r = 0.43$) in students ($n = 119$). The correlation between PBRS and scores on the Nolen-Hoeksema and Morrow (1993) short-form rumination scale were $r = 0.53$. Path models relating positive metacognitive beliefs, rumination, and depression showed that the relationships between positive beliefs and state depression, and between positive beliefs and trait depression, were both mediated by rumination. The PBRS discriminates between patients diagnosed with major depression, panic disorder, social phobia, and non-patient controls. Patients suffering from major depression endorsed significantly higher positive belief scores than patients in the other groups (Papageorgiou & Wells, 2001b). In a recent structural equation modelling study, Papageorgiou and Wells (2001c, 2003) obtained a good fit to data for an S-REF-grounded model in which the relationship between rumination and depression in depressed patients was mediated by negative beliefs about rumination.

RUMINATION IN DIFFERENT DISORDERS

One of the key issues in the cognitive psychology of emotional disorders is the extent to which different disorders depend on common and specific abnormalities of processing (Wells & Matthews, in press). Increasingly, excessive rumination is seen as an abnormality common to various disorders that, as just discussed, may relate to the harmful effects of negative metacognitions. However, differences in the content and objectives of rumination in different disorders may also be clinically significant. Data on the characteristics of rumination across different disorders are limited. However, studies have begun to investigate the nature of different types of perseverative thoughts in non-clinical samples. Wells and Morrison (1994) explored the comparative dimensions of normal worry and normal obsessions. They found that worry and obsessions possessed both similarities and differences on the dimensions measured. Compared with obsessional thoughts, worry was rated as longer in duration, associated with a greater compulsion to act, more verbal, and more voluntary. In a later study, Clark and Claybourn (1997) showed that, compared with obsessive thoughts, worry was focused more on the consequences of negative events, was more distressing, more likely to lead to effective solutions to everyday problems, caused more worry about feeling distressed, and caused more interference in daily living.

Comparisons have also been made between anxious thoughts and depressive thoughts (i.e., between worry and depressive rumination). In two studies by Papagcorgiou and Wells (1999a, b) anxious and depressive thinking showed many similarities in the process and metacognitive dimensions assessed, but some differences did emerge. In particular, compared with anxious thoughts, depressed thoughts were associated with ratings of lower effort to problem-solve, lower confidence in problem-solving ability, and a greater past orientation.

While these studies have focused on the process and metacognitive component of thoughts, there is a larger literature on the content of thinking in disorders. Disorders appear to show a reasonable degree of content specificity, such that anxiety is associated with thoughts concerned with themes of danger, while depression is associated with thoughts concerning loss and hopelessness. Within these domains further distinctions are possible. So, for instance, social phobia is characterized by thoughts concerning the negative consequences of performance failure, and panic disorder is associated with thoughts concerning catastrophic interpretations of bodily symptoms.

The concept of intrusive thoughts as *ego-dystonic* (unwanted or unacceptable to the self) has diagnostic utility in discriminating between obsessional thoughts and other ruminations, such as worry. It also suggests theoretical implications for understanding the interface between obsessional thoughts and broader aspects of the self-concept (Purdon & Clark, 1999). Obsessional thoughts are experienced as ego-dystonic in that they are seen as uncharacteristic of the self, abhorrent, and repugnant. Worry and depressive rumination in contrast do not appear to evoke this type of response. Indeed, worry and depressive rumination may well be seen as characteristic of the self rather than as uncharacteristic. Many patients with GAD report that they have been worriers for most of their lives and see this as part of their personality, and so worrying does not pose a threat to personal identity.

TREATMENT IMPLICATIONS OF THE S-REF MODEL
OF RUMINATION

The S-REF model provides several implications for developing more effective cognitive–behavioural treatments for depression. General and specific implications for cognitive–behavioural theory (CBT) of emotional disorder have been described in detail elsewhere (Wells, 2000), and space does not permit a detailed examination here. This section will be confined to a consideration of factors relating to depression.

First, the model provides an account of vulnerability factors related to the onset and maintenance of depression that specifies the mechanisms that lead patients to repeatedly engage in dysfunctional thinking styles. Schema theory does not adequately address such mechanisms because it emphasizes the role of belief domains outside of the metacognitive domain concerning self, world, and future. It therefore does not explain the mechanisms underlying rumination.

Second, a metacognitive model helps to explain why traditional CBT is only moderately effective and why relapse following treatment continues to be a problem. Treatment typically fails to modify the metacognitions that repeatedly give rise to rumination as a means of dealing with stress and self-discrepancies. Thus, an item of dysfunctional self-knowledge, such as the belief "I'm inadequate," may be modified in treatment, but if the patient maintains the propensity to deal with problems by ruminating on them (i.e., metacognitive beliefs are unchanged), negative mood and negative beliefs will be reinstated.

Third, the dynamic and interactive multilevel nature of disturbances in the S-REF suggests that cognitive modification is likely to be more efficient if the maladaptive ruminative processing style can be disrupted early in treatment. This will have several beneficial effects, including freeing up attentional resources needed for the processing of disconfirmatory information (i.e., increase the flow of new information into consciousness) and for the internal computations that are required for changing stable self-knowledge. Interruption of ruminative self-focused thinking also enables patients to exercise metacognitive control over the stream of consciousness, thereby strengthening metacognitive control plans that facilitate adaptive regulation of cognition under stress. The model suggests specific therapeutic strategies that reduce self-focused attention, lead to a suspension of rumination, and promote flexible control over attention. This analysis has led to the development of attention training as a strategy for modifying locked-in perseverative processing in anxiety (Wells, 1990, 2000) and in depression (Papageorgiou & Wells, 2000; see Chapter 13 for more details).

Fourth, self-regulatory processing is goal-directed, and the S-REF suggests that in clinical disorder inappropriate internal guides are used to regulate behaviour. Hence, treatment should focus on at least two parameters: (1) elucidating and modifying unrealistic goals or rules that patients hold for making judgements about themselves or regulating behaviour (e.g., "I must always do a perfect job otherwise ..."); (2) exploring and modifying inappropriate internal criteria used to signal the cessation or continuation of rumination.

Fifth, negative beliefs about emotional responses and cognition are likely to feed the cycle of depression. Secondary emotion of this kind will contribute to fear of depression and a tendency to catastrophize normal mood deviation or mild symptom occurrences, such as motivational changes or fatigue. As a result, an increasing range of factors fuel the need to engage in rumination in order to cope with all of the attendant problems that this brings. Thus, therapists should assess the role of negative beliefs about symptoms and fear of depression, and facilitate the development of normalizing attributions for symptoms (e.g., by identifying cognitive distortions like "catastrophizing"). Worry about symptoms can be seen as another manifestation of rumination, or "metarumination," and belief in these metaruminations should be challenged by verbal and behavioural strategies.

Finally, the negative effects of rumination on other cognitive–emotional mechanisms, such as those involved in emotional processing of trauma, imply that individuals who ruminate may be more prone to other disorders, such as acute stress reactions and PTSD. Chronic or recurrent depression may be complicated by failures of emotional processing caused by rumination as individuals encounter stresses in daily life. Thus, depression becomes compounded over time because rumination prevents the resolution of particular anxiety reactions that subsequently combine with depression. Depression may become more resistant to treatment because the cessation of depressive thinking will be associated with an upsurge of anxious thoughts, which may be experienced as more distressing than depression itself. In such circumstances depressive responses may be negatively reinforced by the anxious distress they suppress. The implication here is that anxiety may have to be treated first before depression, and the patient should be directed in the gradual reduction of rumination combined with exposure to anxious thoughts and feelings in a way that facilitates modification of anxious beliefs and facilitates habituation.

A METACOGNITIVE FOCUS FOR COGNITIVE THERAPY

The S-REF model suggests that positive and negative beliefs about rumination are involved in the development and maintenance of clinical depression. Positive beliefs about the utility of rumination as a coping strategy promote sustained rumination. When such rumination is appraised as failing to meet its goals or as potentially causing further hazards, the individual will experience depression or anxiety depending on the content of the negative appraisal. When rumination is appraised as dangerous this will lead to anxiety; when it is appraised as a sign of loss, failure, or hopelessness it will contribute to depression.

Because of the similarities in metacognitive factors thought to underlie pathological worry in GAD and rumination in depression, it is possible that metacognitive treatment techniques developed for GAD (Wells, 1995, 1997) will also be useful in depression. Thus, in the treatment of depressive rumination, the emphasis should be on challenging negative beliefs about rumination, which includes the use of rumination postponement experiments to challenge beliefs about the uncontrollability of rumination. Specific strategies that have been developed for challenging positive beliefs about worry (e.g., Wells, 1997) may also be used to challenge positive beliefs about rumination. An appropriate treatment goal is to enable patients to encounter depressogenic situations without activating the need for sustained rumination, but to divert resources to external-focused, problem-oriented, and present moment processing. This goal is likely to be most effective when combined with modification of maladaptive positive and negative metacognitive beliefs about rumination and depressive experiences.

CONCLUSIONS

Rumination is attracting increasing research interest as a source of both subclinical dysphoria and of emotional disorder. However, progress has been limited by differing conceptualizations of the construct and failure to discriminate rumination from other, related aspects of disordered cognition. We have suggested that the S-REF model of affective dysfunction may contribute to resolving such difficulties. Within the model, rumination has been defined as repetitive thoughts generated by attempts to cope with self-discrepancy that are directed primarily toward processing the content of self-referent information. This definition points toward rumination as a *configuration of multiple processes* that, within the multilevel architecture described by the S-REF model, may be supported by both "controlled" and "automatic" processing, as well as dynamic interaction with the external environment. The choice of a ruminative coping strategy is a consequence of stable metacognitive self-knowledge, referring to the importance of controlling thoughts and feelings, and attending to their content.

Although rumination represents an attempt at problem-solving, it frequently fails to reach its goal and perpetuates negative affect and cognition. Rumination may in the short term serve to maintain awareness of threats, losses, and negative self-beliefs and may interfere with potentially more effective task-directed coping. In the longer term, rumination may block adaptive restructuring of self-knowledge, initiate potentially damaging thought control strategies, and facilitate the development of harmful metacognitive beliefs about rumination itself (e.g., "metaworry"). Furthermore, rumination may contribute to dysfunctional person–environment cycles of interactions that block adaptive learning of effective strategies for coping with external sources of threat. Empirical studies confirm that (1) metacognitions contribute to maladaptive coping associated with processing self-referent information (e.g., worry/rumination), (2) such coping styles contribute to emotional dysfunction and pathology, and (3) rumination leads to additional cognitive dysfunctions, such as negative cognitive bias and incubation of intrusive thoughts.

The S-REF model focuses on the metacognitive concomitants of rumination as a source of general emotional pathology. Patients' beliefs about their own cognitions and emotions serve to perpetuate ruminative cycles to the extent that they block alternative coping strategies and adaptive restructuring of self-knowledge, and the patient becomes locked into a never-ending cycle of worry about their own symptoms. Pathology is a consequence of a continuing dynamic pattern of maladaptive interaction with the external physical and social environment. Rumination may operate somewhat differently in different disorders, although more evidence is required. For example, anxious rumination appears to relate especially to appraising one's worries as threatening and uncontrollable, whereas the ego-dystonic nature of worries in OCD appears to be unique to that condition. Depressive rumination overlaps with anxious rumination (e.g., in referring to the uncontrollability of thoughts), but it appears to be more past-oriented and accompanied by lowered confidence in problem-solving.

The S-REF model highlights some shortcomings of existing CBTs for rumination, as an aspect of emotional disorders. Metacognitive vulnerability factors are often neglected in case conceptualization. Effective cognitive modification requires targeting these maladaptive metacognitions and the maladaptive cognitive–attentional configuration that they generate at an early stage of treatment. For example, modification of self-beliefs may focus on identifying unrealistic self-regulative goals that may trigger rumination or harmful metacognitive beliefs about rumination itself. Hence, treatment for depressive rumination requires a focus on techniques that challenge both the positive and negative metacognitive beliefs that perpetuate dysfunctional cognition. Inflexibility of self-focused preoccupations may be treated directly by such techniques as attention training (Wells, 1990, 2000) that reduce self-focus and enhance metacognitive control of cognition.

REFERENCES

Amir, N., Cashman, L., & Foa, E. B. (1997). Strategies of thought control in obsessive–compulsive disorder. *Behaviour Research and Therapy*, **35**, 775–777.

Andersen, S. M. & Limpert, C. (2001). Future-event schemas: Automaticity and rumination in major depression. *Cognitive Therapy and Research*, **25**, 311–333.

Anderson, J. R. (1996). ACT: A simple theory of complex cognition. *American Psychologist*, **51**, 355–365.

Bagby, R. M. & Parker, J. D. A. (2001). Relation of rumination and distraction with neuroticism and extraversion in a sample of patients with major depression. *Cognitive Therapy and Research*, **25**, 91–102.

Beck, A. T., Emery, G., & Greenberg, R. L. (1985). *Anxiety Disorders and Phobias: A Cognitive Perspective*. New York: Basic Books.

Brown, A. L., Bransford, J. D., Campione, J. C., & Ferrara, R. A. (1983). Learning, remembering and understanding. In: J. Flavell & E. Markman (eds), *Handbook of Child Psychology. Vol. 3: Cognitive Development*. New York: John Wiley & Sons.

Cartwright-Hatton, S. & Wells, A. (1997). Beliefs about worry and intrusions: The Metacognitions Questionnaire and its correlates. *Journal of Anxiety Disorders*, **11**, 279–296.

Clark, D. A. & Claybourn, M. (1997). Process characteristics of worry and obsessive intrusive thoughts. *Behaviour Research and Therapy*, **35**, 1139–1141.

Clark, D. M. & Wells, A. (1995). A cognitive model of social phobia. In: R. Heimberg, M. Liebowitz, D. A. Hope & F. R. Schneier (eds), *Social Phobia: Diagnosis, Assessment and Treatment*. New York: Guilford Press.

Endler, N. & Parker, J. (1990). Multi dimensional assessment of coping: A critical review. *Journal of Personality and Social Psychology*, **58**, 844–854.

Ferguson, E., Matthews, G., & Cox, T. (1999) The Appraisal of Life Events (ALE) Scale: Reliability and validity. *British Journal of Health Psychology*, **4**, 97–116.

Fichman, L., Koestner, R., Zuroff, D. C., & Gordon, L. (1999) Depressive styles and the regulation of negative affect: A daily experience study. *Cognitive Therapy and Research*, **23**, 483–495.

Holeva, V., Tarrier, N., & Wells, A. (2001). Prevalence and predictors of acute PTSD following road traffic accidents: Thought control strategies and social support. *Behavior Therapy*, **32**, 65–84.

Lazarus, R. S. (1999). *Stress and Emotion: A New Synthesis*. New York: Springer-Verlag.

Lazarus, R. S. & Folkman, S. (1984) *Stress, Appraisal and Coping*. New York: Springer-Verlag.

Martin, L. L. & Tesser, A. (1989). Toward a motivational and structural theory of ruminative thought. In: J. S. Uleman & J. A. Bargh (eds), *Unintended Thought* (pp. 306–326). New York: Guilford Press.

Martin, L. L. & Tesser, A. (1996). Some ruminative thoughts. In: R. S. Wyer, Jr (ed), *Ruminative Thoughts* (pp. 1–47). Hillsdale, NJ: Lawrence Erlbaum.

Matthews, G. (2001). Levels of transaction: A cognitive science framework for operator stress. In: P. A. Hancock & P. A. Desmond (eds), *Stress, Workload and Fatigue* (pp. 5–33). Mahwah, NJ: Lawrence Erlbaum.

Matthews, G. & Campbell, S. E. (1998). Task-induced stress and individual differences in coping. In: *Proceedings of the Human Factors and Ergonomics Society 42nd Annual Meeting* (pp. 821–825). Santa Monica, CA: Human Factors and Ergonomics Society.

Matthews, G., Campbell, S. E., Falconer, S., Joyner, L., Huggins, J., Gilliland, K., Grier, R., & Warm, J. S. (2003). Fundamental dimensions of subjective state in performance settings: Task engagement, distress and worry. *Emotion*, **2**, 315–340.

Matthews, G., Derryberry, D., & Siegle, G. J. (2000). Personality and emotion: Cognitive science perspectives. In: S. E. Hampson (ed.), *Advances in Personality Psychology* (Vol. 1, pp. 199–237). London: Routledge.

Matthews, G. & Falconer, S. (2000). Individual differences in task-induced stress in customer service personnel. In: *Proceedings of the Human Factors and Ergonomics Society 44th Annual Meeting*. Santa Monica, CA: Human Factors and Ergonomics Society.

Matthews, G., Hillyard, E. J., & Campbell, S. E. (1999). Metacognition and maladaptive coping as components of test anxiety. *Clinical Psychology and Psychotherapy*, **6**, 111–125.

Matthews, G., Schwean, V. L., Campbell, S. E., Saklofske, D. H., & Mohamed A. A. R. (2000). Personality, self-regulation and adaptation: A cognitive–social framework. In: M. Boekarts, P. R. Pintrich, & M. Zeidner (eds), *Handbook of Self-regulation* (pp. 171–207). New York: Academic Press.

Matthews, G. & Wells, A. (1988). Relationships between anxiety, self-consciousness and cognitive failures. *Cognition and Emotion*, **2**, 123–132.

Matthews, G. & Wells, A. (1996). Attentional processes, coping strategies and clinical intervention. In: M. Zeidner & N. S. Endler (eds), *Handbook of Coping: Theory, Research, Applications* (pp. 573–601). New York: John Wiley & Sons.

Matthews, G. & Wells, A. (1999). The cognitive science of attention and emotion. In: T. Dalgleish & M. Power (eds), *Handbook of Cognition and Emotion* (pp. 171–192). New York: John Wiley & Sons.

Matthews, G. & Wells, A. (2000). Attention, automaticity and affective disorder. *Behavior Modification*, **24**, 69–93.

Mellings, T. M. B. & Alden, L. E. (2000). Cognitive processes in social anxiety: The effects of self-focus, rumination and anticipatory processing. *Behaviour Research and Therapy*, **38**, 243–257.

Mohamed, A. A. R. (1996). Stress processes in British and overseas students. Unpublished doctoral dissertation, University of Dundee, UK.

Morgan, I. A., Matthews, G., & Winton, M. (1995). Coping and personality as predictors of post-traumatic intrusions, numbing, avoidance and general distress: A study of victims of the Perth flood. *Behavioural and Cognitive Psychotherapy*, **23**, 251–264.

Nolen-Hoeksema, S. (2000). The role of rumination in depressive disorders and mixed anxiety/depressive symptoms. *Journal of Abnormal Psychology*, **109**, 504–511.

Nolen-Hoeksema, S. & Morrow, J. (1993). Effects of rumination and distraction on naturally occurring depressed mood. *Cognition and Emotion*, **7**, 561–570.

Nolen-Hoeksema, S., Parker, L. E., & Larson, J. (1994). Ruminative coping with depressed mood following loss. *Journal of Personality and Social Psychology*, **67**, 92–104.

Norman, D. A. & Shallice, T. (1986) Attention to action: Willed and automatic control of behaviour. In: R. J. Davidson, G. E. Schwartz, & D. Shapiro (eds), *Consciousness and Self-Regulation: Advances in Research* (Vol. 4, pp. 1–18). New York: Plenum Press.

Papageorgiou, C. & Wells, A. (1999a). Process and metacognitive dimensions of depressive and anxious thoughts and relationships with emotional intensity. *Clinical Psychology and Psychotherapy*, **6**, 156–162.

Papageorgiou, C. & Wells, A. (1999b). Dimensions of depressive rumination and anxious worry: A comparative study. Paper presented at the *33rd Annual Convention of the Association for the Advancement of Behavior Therapy*, Toronto.

Papageorgiou, C. & Wells, A. (2000). Treatment of recurrent major depression with attention training. *Cognitive and Behavioral Practice*, **7**, 407–413.

Papageorgiou, C. & Wells, A. (2001a). Metacognitive beliefs about rumination in recurrent major depression. *Cognitive and Behavioral Practice*, **8**, 160–164.

Papageorgiou, C. & Wells, A. (2001b). Positive beliefs about depressive rumination: Development and preliminary validation of a self-report scale. *Behavior Therapy*, **32**, 13–26.

Papageorgiou, C. & Wells, A. (2001c). Does metacognition play a role in rumination and depression? Paper presented at the *World Congress of Behavioral and Cognitive Therapies, Vancouver*.

Papageorgiou, C. & Wells, A. (2003). An empirical test of a clinical metacognitive model of rumination and depression. *Cognitive Therapy and Research*, **27**, 261–273.

Papageorgiou, C., Wells, A. & Meina, L. J. (in preparation). Development and preliminary validation of the Negative Beliefs about Rumination Scale. Manuscript in preparation.

Paykel, E. S. & Weissman, M. M. (1973). Social adjustment and depression: A longitudinal study. *Archives of General Psychiatry*, **28**, 659–663.

Purdon, C. (1999). Thought suppression and psychopathology. *Behaviour Research and Therapy*, **37**, 1029–1054.

Purdon, C. & Clark, D. A. (1999). Metacognition and obsessions. *Clinical Psychology and Psychotherapy*, **6**, 102–110.

Rachman, S. (1971). Obsessional ruminations. *Behaviour Research and Therapy*, **9**, 229–235.

Reynolds, M. & Wells, A. (1999). The Thought Control Questionnaire—psychometric properties in a clinical sample, and relationships with PTSD and depression. *Psychological Medicine*, **29**, 1089–1099.

Roberts, J. E., Gilboa, E., & Gotlib, I. H. (1998). Ruminative response style and vulnerability to episodes of dysphoria: Gender, neuroticism, and episode duration. *Cognitive Therapy and Research*, **22**, 401–423.

Roger, D. & Jamieson, J. (1988). Individual differences in delayed heart-rate recovery following stress: The role of extraversion, neuroticism and emotional control. *Personality and Individual Differences*, **9**, 721–726.

Sarason, I. G., Sarason, B. R., Keefe, D. E., Hayes, B. E., & Shearin, E. N. (1986) Cognitive interference: Situational determinants and traitlike characteristics. *Journal of Personality and Social Psychology*, **31**, 215–226.

Schmidt, N. B. & Woolaway-Bickel, K. (in press). Cognitive vulnerability to panic disorder. In: L. B. Alloy & J. H. Riskind (eds), *Cognitive Vulnerability to Emotional Disorders*. Hillsdale, NJ: Lawrence Erlbaum.

Scott, Jr, V. B. & McIntosh, W. D. (1999). The development of a trait measure of ruminative thought. *Personality and Individual Differences*, **26**, 1045–1056.

Segerstrom, S. C., Tsao, J. C. I., Alden, L. E., & Craske, M. G. (2000). Worry and rumination: Repetitive thought as a concomitant and predictor of negative mood. *Cognitive Therapy and Research*, **24**, 671–688.

Siegle, G. J. (1999). A neural network model of attention biases in depression. In: E. Ruppin, J. Reggia, & D. Glanzman (eds), *Progress in Brain Research* (Vol. 121, pp. 415–441). Mahwah, NJ: Elsevier.

Uleman, J. S. (1989). A framework for thinking intentionally about unintended thoughts. In: J. S. Uleman & J. A. Bargh (eds), *Unintended Thought* (pp. 425–449). New York: Guilford Press.

Warda, G. & Bryant, R. (1998). Cognitive bias in acute stress disorder. *Behaviour Research and Therapy*, **36**, 1177–1183.

Wells, A. (1990). Panic disorder in association with relaxation induced anxiety: An attentional training approach to treatment. *Behaviour Therapy*, **21**, 272–280.

Wells, A. (1994). A multi-dimensional measure of worry: Development and preliminary validation of the Anxious Thoughts Inventory. *Anxiety, Stress and Coping*, **6**, 280–299.

Wells, A. (1995). Meta-cognition and worry: A cognitive model of Generalised Anxiety Disorder. *Behavioural and Cognitive Psychotherapy*, **23**, 301–320.

Wells, A. (1997). *Cognitive Therapy of Anxiety Disorders: A Practice Manual and Conceptual Guide*. Chichester, UK: John Wiley & Sons.

Wells, A. (2000). *Emotional Disorders and Metacognition: Innovative Cognitive Therapy*. Chichester, UK: John Wiley & Sons.

Wells, A. & Carter, K. (1999). Preliminary tests of a cognitive model of GAD. *Behaviour Research and Therapy*, **37**, 585–594.

Wells, A. & Carter, K. (2001). Further tests of a cognitive model of generalized anxiety disorder: Metacognitions and worry in GAD, panic disorder, social phobia, depression, and non-patients. *Behavior Therapy*, **32**, 85–102.

Wells, A. & Davies, M. (1994). The Thought Control Questionnaire: A measure of individual differences in the control of unwanted thoughts. *Behaviour Research and Therapy*, **32**, 871–878.

Wells, A. & Matthews, G. (1994). *Attention and Emotion: A Clinical Perspective*. Hove, UK: Lawrence Erlbaum.

Wells, A. & Matthews, G. (1996). Modelling cognition in emotional disorders: The S-REF model. *Behaviour Research and Therapy*, **34**, 881–888.

Wells, A. & Matthews, G. (in press). Cognitive vulnerability to anxiety disorders: An integrative approach. In: L. B. Alloy & J. H. Riskind (eds), *Cognitive Vulnerability to Emotional Disorders*. Hillsdale, NJ: Lawrence Erlbaum.

Wells, A. & Morrison, A. P. (1994). Qualitative dimensions of normal worry and normal obsessions: A comparative study. *Behaviour Research and Therapy*, **32**, 867–870.

Wells, A. & Papageorgiou, C. (1995). Worry and the incubation of intrusive images following stress. *Behaviour Research and Therapy*, **33**, 579–583.

Wells, A. & Papageorgiou, C. (1998). Relationships between worry, obsessive–compulsive symptoms, and meta-cognitive beliefs. *Behaviour Research and Therapy*, **36**, 899–913.

Wenzlaff, R. M. & Wegner, D. M. (2000). Thought suppression. *Annual Review of Psychology*, **51**, 59–91.

Young, E. A. & Nolen-Hoeksema, S. (2001). Effects of ruminations on the saliva cortisol response to a social stressor. *Psychoneuroendocrinology*, **26**, 319–329.

8 Rumination as a Function of Goal Progress, Stop Rules, and Cerebral Lateralization

LEONARD L. MARTIN* AND ILAN SHRIRA
Department of Psychology, University of Georgia, Athens, USA

HELEN M. STARTUP
Department of Psychology, Institute of Psychiatry, London, UK

In previous publications, we suggested that rumination is a function of goal progress (Martin, 1999; Martin & Tesser, 1989, 1996; Martin, Tesser, & McIntosh, 1993). Specifically, we suggested that when individuals do not receive clear, consistent feedback that they are progressing toward their goals, they engage in mental activities designed to get them such feedback. These activities include formulating alternate paths to the goal, re-evaluating the desirability of the goal, and reconstruing one's behavior in relation to various goals (e.g., "I am not simply walking to work; I am exercising"). When these activities recur for extended periods of time, we call them rumination. Although rumination does not always lead individuals back to goal progress, that is its function.

In this chapter, we build upon these earlier suggestions by exploring some connections between rumination and cerebral hemisphere specialization. We do this not to explain away rumination by assigning it to a specific brain location, but to see if research on hemisphere specialization can help us refine our theories of rumination. For example, if rumination does indeed reflect attempts to find alternative paths to a goal and if the generation of alternative strategies is largely a right hemisphere operation (Goldberg & Costa, 1981; Rotenberg & Weinberg, 1999), then individuals should display relatively greater right hemisphere activation when ruminating. If this turns out to be the case, then it would not prove the goal progress view correct, but it

* Author for correspondence.

Depressive Rumination: Nature, Theory and Treatment
Edited by Costas Papageorgiou and Adrian Wells. © 2004 John Wiley & Sons Ltd

may be seen as converging evidence for the goal progress view and could increase our confidence in that view.

We begin by reviewing the goal progress theory of rumination. Then, we discuss some findings on hemisphere specialization that appear relevant to rumination. After that, we discuss some studies that explored more directly the links between goal progress, rumination, and hemisphere activation. Finally, we synthesize these various strands of thought into what we hope is a more coherent view of rumination.

THE GOAL PROGRESS THEORY OF RUMINATION

According to Martin and Tesser (1989, 1996; Martin et al., 1993; see also Martin, 1999), rumination is essentially an instance of the Zeigarnik effect. Zeigarnik (1938) demonstrated that information related to incomplete tasks tends to remain in memory longer than information related to completed tasks. From the goal progress view, rumination is essentially the tendency to think recurrently about important, higher order goals that have not yet been attained. Rumination is instigated not just by failure to attain a goal, however, but also by failure to progress toward a goal at a rate that matches the individual's standard for progress (Carver & Scheier, 1990). For example, a new faculty member may want but not have tenure. He or she is not likely to ruminate about getting tenure, however, if he or she is publishing consistently, receiving high teaching evaluations, and getting along well with other members of the department. In short, rumination occurs when individuals are not making progress toward their higher order goals.

The theory further assumes that the proximate underlying cause of rumination is the accessibility of goal-related information. Specifically, failure to attain a goal keeps information related to that goal highly accessible (Zeigarnik, 1938). When in this state, the information can be easily cued and is more likely to be used than equally relevant, but less accessible information (Bruner, 1957; Higgins, Rholes, & Jones, 1977; Martin, Strack, & Stapel, 2001). As a result, otherwise innocuous stimuli might easily instigate rumination. For example, a woman who wants to conceive a child but who cannot do so may have highly accessible thoughts related to infertility. So, if the woman walks past displays of baby food in a grocery store, she may be induced to ruminate about her infertility, even though exposure to the same display would have little or no effect on individuals in whom thoughts related to infertility were not so accessible (Clark, Henry, & Taylor, 1991).

As can be seen, in the context of the goal progress view, rumination is a form of self-regulation (Wells & Matthews, 1994). It keeps goal-related information highly accessible making it more likely that individuals will detect and process information related to the non-attained goal. This, in turn, could facilitate problem-solving and help individuals get back on track toward their goals

(Bowden & Beeman, 1998; Kuiken & Mathews, 1986–87; Schooler, Fallshore, & Fiore, 1995). Once individuals are back on track, the rumination has in essence done its job. Therefore, it ceases. More generally, rumination terminates when individuals either attain the higher order goal, make sufficient progress toward it, or give it up.

EVIDENCE FOR THE GOAL PROGRESS THEORY

Evidence for the role of goal progress in rumination was reported by Martin, Tesser, and McIntosh (1993). In one study, they allowed one group of participants to think about a white bear, but instructed two other groups to keep thoughts of a white bear from coming to mind. As Wegner, Schneider, Carter, and White (1987) showed, attempting to suppress a thought can heighten its accessibility. According to the goal progress view, however, this heightened accessibility is not a direct result of attempted thought suppression. It is the result of individuals experiencing difficulty attempting to suppress their thoughts, or, more accurately, failing at the higher order goal of maintaining self-control. If individuals perceive themselves to be successful at their thought control, then their attempted suppression would not increase the accessibility of the to-be-suppressed thought.

To test this hypothesis, Martin et al. gave success feedback to half of the suppression participants. Specifically, they told some participants that they had performed better than most at suppressing white bear thoughts and that they seemed to be good at controlling their thoughts. Finally, all participants were asked to recognize words presented one letter at a time on the computer screen. Some of the words were related to a white bear (e.g., snow, polar). It was assumed that the more accessible white bear-related information was to a participant the faster he or she would be at recognizing the white bear-related words. Specifically, it was predicted that participants who felt they had not succeeded at the thought suppression task would recognize white bear-related words faster than participants who succeeded or who did not attempt to suppress the white bear thoughts.

The results were consistent with these predictions. Participants who attempted to suppress thoughts of a white bear and who did not receive success feedback showed the highest accessibility of white bear thoughts. The recognition times of the suppress/success group were no different from those of the control group. In other words, telling participants they had attained the goal of being in control of their thoughts reduced the heightened accessibility of goal-related thoughts that otherwise would have followed attempts at thought suppression. The reduction in accessibility would presumably result in a lower likelihood of rumination.

Another implication of the goal progress view is that rumination results from the failure to progress toward higher order as opposed to lower order goals.

Lower order goals are, by definition, ways of attaining higher order goals. In addition, there are more ways to attain a higher order goal than a lower order goal. The only way not to think about a white bear, for example, is not to think about a white bear. If someone wants to attain a higher order goal, such as self-control, however, then he or she can do this by successfully suppressing thoughts of a white bear, being polite when he or she does not wish to be, or refusing to spend too much money while shopping. What is important in turning off rumination is attainment of the higher order goal regardless of the lower order means by which this is done (Steele, 1988; Tesser, Martin, & Cornell, 1996).

The role that attainment of higher order goals plays in terminating rumination was demonstrated by Koole, Smeets, van Knippenberg, and Dijksterhuis (1999). They had participants take what ostensibly was an intelligence test. All participants were informed that they had done poorly on this test. Presumably, participants would want to do well as a sign that they were maintaining progress toward their higher order goal of being intelligent. So, receiving negative feedback would frustrate their progress toward this higher order goal and induce rumination.

Following the failure feedback, all participants had a chance to express some values on a series of rating scales. For some participants, these values were ones they had earlier indicated were central to their self-concept. For others, the values were ones they had earlier indicated were peripheral to their self-concept. Expressing the central values could serve as a self-affirmation (Steele, 1988). That is, it could remind participants that they were competent, adaptive individuals. In goal progress terms, expressing central values could remind participants that overall they had attained their higher order goal of being competent despite their poor performance on this one intelligence test. If so, then participants who expressed their central values should ruminate less about their intelligence than participants who did not express such values.

Koole et al. measured the accessibility of goal-related information by asking participants to decide as quickly as possible whether a series of letter strings were real words. In cases in which the letter strings were real words, some of the words were related to intelligence. It was assumed that participants who were ruminating about their failure on the intelligence test would recognize these words faster than those who were not ruminating. Consistent with the goal progress view, participants who had not expressed their central values were faster to recognize intelligence-related words than participants who had expressed such values. In other words, all participants failed the intelligence test, but only those who had not attained the higher order goal (e.g., intelligence, competence) still had this information highly accessible in mind. This heightened accessibility would presumably leave them vulnerable to rumination.

To summarize, the goal progress view suggests that failure to make sufficient progress toward a higher order goal causes individuals to formulate alternative paths to the goal, reevaluate the desirability of the goal, or reconstrue their behavior in relation to various goals. When this thinking recurs for an extended period of time, we call it rumination. Rumination may not always place individuals back on track toward their goals, but that is its function.

In the next section, we examine whether research on hemisphere specialization can tell us anything about the relations among goal progress, rumination, and the generation of alternate strategies. Before we discuss this research, however, we should mention a few caveats. First, we do not assume that biopsychologists have a lock on the truth such that if there is an inconsistency between their findings and ours that they are necessarily correct. In their area, as in any other, we can have more confidence in some findings than in others. Second, we do not assume that all of the conclusions drawn about hemisphere differences are non-controversial. As in any area, there are conflicting findings and competing theories. On the other hand, there is consensus on a number of points, and it is on this consensus that we focus. Third, in normal individuals the hemispheres do not comprise two independent, distinctly different brains. There is overlap in the functions of the two, and most complex processing involves activation in both hemispheres (de Zubicaray, Andrew, Zelaya, Williams, & Dumanoir, 2000; Knecht, Henningsen, Deppe, & Huber, 1996). Having said this, though, it is also important to keep in mind that there are some well-established differences between the left and right hemispheres and a consideration of these differences may help us in our theorizing about rumination.

HEMISPHERE FUNCTIONS RELATED TO GOAL PROGRESS AND RUMINATION

Several provocative reviews of hemisphere functions have been published (e.g., Davidson, Ekman, Saron, Senulis, & Friesen, 1990; Gazzaniga, 2000; Goldberg, Podell, & Lovell, 1994; Moller, 2000; Ramachandran & Hirstein, 1997; Rotenberg & Weinberg, 1999; Tomarken & Keener, 1998; Tucker & Williamson, 1984). A reiteration of these reviews, of course, is beyond the scope of this chapter. What we do instead is focus on those aspects of hemisphere functions that appear particularly relevant to an understanding of rumination.

FIXATION VS. FLEXIBILITY: THE ROLES OF THE HEMISPHERES IN GOAL PURSUIT

To progress toward a goal, individuals need at least two general skills. First, they need to stay focused on the goal even in the face of frustrations and distractions. If individuals have the goal of writing a chapter, for example, then they would not make much progress if they were repeatedly watching TV, taking a walk, or surfing the web. The second skill individuals need, oddly enough, is the ability to disengage from pursuit of a goal. This skill is important when the initial strategies for attaining a goal are not working. In this case, individuals may want to stop what they are doing and try something new. In sum, to pursue a goal successfully, individuals need to persist despite distractions, and they need to switch to alternate strategies when necessary. Interestingly, these two skills map very cleanly onto the functions of the left and right hemisphere, respectively.

The left hemisphere uses tight internal representations (e.g., schemata, scripts) to guide behavior. This allows for an ongoing internal determination of behavior even in the face of environmental distractions. In fact, the left hemisphere does more than persist in the face of distraction. It represses potential distractions. More specifically, the left hemisphere represses information not central to its current aims. This glossing over of discrepancies increases certainty and fosters rapid and effective action, but it also restricts an individual's responses to high probability ones that will be performed repetitively.

The right hemisphere, by comparison, does not guide behavior in accordance with internal representations. Instead, it is attuned to external contingencies and activates information that deviates from existing representations (e.g., non-dominant meanings of words). This makes the right hemisphere more useful than the left in building an experiential base and in navigating novel situations for which individuals have no pre-existing representations. On the other hand, the right hemisphere's attraction to alternative paths and meanings leaves it vulnerable to distraction by seemingly irrelevant cues (e.g., word meanings not pertinent to the current context).

Perhaps most pertinent to our discussion of rumination and goal progress is the characterization of the right hemisphere as an anomaly detector (Ramachandran & Hirstein, 1997). With its shift away from prior representations and its focus on external contingencies, the right hemisphere can generate (in fact seems necessary for generating) a shift in the left hemisphere's representation of the situation. As long as the situation is predictable, the left hemisphere can guide behavior using its internal representations. When these representations are not mapping well onto the current situation, it is up to the right hemisphere to note this and to make available a new perspective. It is this last function we think is most closely related to rumination. Specifically, when individuals receive feedback that they are progressing toward their goals, they can take this as a sign that their goal attainment strategies are working. The strategies are allowing the individuals to move toward their goals. When individuals receive negative feedback regarding their goal progress, however, they can infer that their strategies are not working, and that they need to find an alternative path toward their goal.

We think the right hemisphere is involved in the ruminative search for alternative paths to a goal.

THE RIGHT HEMISPHERE PROVIDES ALTERNATIVES

Evidence that the left hemisphere follows well-practiced routines, whereas the right deviates from these routines was obtained by Burgess and Simpson (1988). They presented to participants' right or left visual fields (i.e., to their left and right hemispheres, respectively) cue words that had more than one meaning. For each of these words, though, one meaning was dominant. Exposure to the word "bank," for example, is more likely to make individuals think of "money" than "river." Following presentation of the cue words, participants saw a string of letters and had to decide as quickly as possible whether each string represented a real word.

On some trials, the letter string followed the initial prime word by 35 ms, whereas on other trials it followed the prime word by 750 ms. These different time intervals were included to foster automatic and controlled processing, respectively. In addition, the letter strings sometimes represented the dominant meaning of the cue word and sometimes represented the subordinate meaning. It was assumed that participants would be faster at identifying words representing the dominant meaning if that meaning had been primed by the cue word, but would be faster at identifying words representing the subordinate meaning if that meaning had been primed by the cue word. The question, though, was whether priming of these different meanings would depend on the hemisphere to which the cue word had been presented and on the time between the cue and the letter string. It did.

Specifically, the left hemisphere was quick to identify associates of both the dominant and subordinate meanings when the delay was short, but was quick to identify associates of only the dominant meaning when the delay was longer. In contrast, the right hemisphere was quick to identify associates of only the dominant meaning when the delay was short, but was quick to identify associates of both meanings when the delay was longer. In other words, the left hemisphere had initial access to both meanings, but inhibited the non-central one, whereas the right hemisphere had initial access to the dominant meaning and used this as a starting point to find alternate meanings (see also Atchley, Burgess, & Keeney, 1999; Meyer & Peterson, 2000).

The differing tendencies of the hemispheres to maintain or shift from an established, dominant response could be especially consequential when individuals are attempting to discern relations in the environment. Rauch (1977) found that the left hemisphere tends to maintain a pre-existing hypothesis even in the face of non-supportive feedback, whereas the right hemisphere tends to switch even when its prior hypothesis was shown to be correct. Specifically, she presented participants with a concept formation task in which two letters varied from trial to trial in size, color, and location. Participants had to guess on each trial which of the two letters was the correct one. The correct response on any given trial was determined by a rule selected a priori by the experimenter (e.g., the larger of the two letters regardless of letter, size, or location). To respond correctly, participants had to discern the nature of this rule. On every fourth trial, the experimenter told participants whether their responses had been correct or incorrect, and participants could use this feedback to generate their hypotheses. Participants included normal individuals as well as individuals with damage to either the left or right hemisphere.

Not surprisingly, participants with brain damage performed worse than participants without such damage. What was interesting, though, was the nature of the mistakes made by participants with left or right brain damage. Those with an intact left hemisphere (i.e., right damage) tended to stay with the same hypothesis from trial to trial even when given feedback that their responses were wrong. Those with an intact right hemisphere (i.e., left damage) tended to shift to a new hypothesis from trial to trial even after receiving feedback that their responses were correct. These results, like those of Burgess and Simpson, suggest that the left hemisphere tries to apply pre-existing structures, whereas the right hemisphere attempts to find alternatives to these structures. The tendency of the right hemisphere to provide alternative hypotheses fits with our characterization of rumination as a search for alternate hypotheses (i.e., alternative paths to the goal).

THE RIGHT DOMINATES WHEN THE OLD RULES DON'T APPLY

If the left hemisphere tends to operate from existing representations, then it may not be as useful as the right when individuals face a novel task. Here, the right hemisphere's ability to explore alternative strategies might facilitate the learning of new skills. Once the task is learned, however, the left hemisphere can take over again and guide behavior in accordance with its newly established representations. This analysis suggests a shift from right to left dominance as individuals move from learning a new task to performing a well-learned task. This is precisely the pattern found by Gordon and Carmon (1976; see also Goldberg & Costa, 1981).

They flashed items to either participants' left or right visual fields. These items ranged from familiar (e.g., Arabic numbers) to unfamiliar (e.g., binary numbers, novel geometric symbols), and participants had to name the items as quickly as possible. Overall, participants identified the familiar items faster when the problems were presented to the left hemisphere, but identified the unfamiliar items faster when the problems were presented to the right hemisphere. This relation, however, was qualified by the number of times participants had been exposed to the items. Specifically, the right hemisphere's superiority for unfamiliar items was observed only during the first half of the trials. During the second half, the superiority shifted to the left. According to Gordon and Carmon, with continued exposure the unusual patterns became familiar and the left hemisphere took over processing (see also Bever & Chiarello, 1974; Fink et al., 1999). These results fit with the more general pattern of the left hemisphere guiding behavior when all is going according to plan and the right hemisphere becoming dominant when individuals need to explore alternatives to the established routines. In rumination terms, the right hemisphere is likely to become active in situations in which the established patterns are no longer applicable and individuals must think of alternatives.

THE RIGHT MAINTAINS UNSOLVED PROBLEMS

The tendency of the right hemisphere to shift away from previous representations and consider the situation from different perspectives is consistent with the nature of rumination as suggested in the goal progress view. When individuals are having difficulty progressing toward their goal, they begin to rethink the situation from different perspectives (e.g., "How else can I attain the goal?" "Do I really want it?"). The goal progress view, however, also makes a more specific claim about rumination. It assumes that rumination keeps goal-related information in mind until individuals either attain the goal, progress toward it, or disengage themselves from it. Is the right hemisphere involved in operations of this kind? Evidence by Bowden and Beeman (1998) suggests that it is.

Bowden and Beeman presented participants with three cue words and asked the participants to generate a fourth word. This word had to be one that would produce meaningful word pairs when combined with each of the cue words. If the cue words were "high," "district," and "house," for example, the correct solution word would be "school." The question was whether the solution words would be processed more readily by the left or the right hemisphere.

To answer this question, Bowden and Beeman presented the three cue words either to participants' left or right visual fields. Then, they presented (to both hemispheres) words that either were or were not the solution to the problem, and participants had to name this word as quickly as possible. When participants had solved the word problem, they named the solution words faster when the problem had been presented to the right as compared with the left hemisphere. When participants failed to solve the problem, they named the solution words quickly only when the problems had been presented to the right hemisphere. In other words, information related to solved problems was active in both hemispheres, whereas information related to unsolved problems was active only in the right hemisphere. In rumination terms, these results suggest that the right hemisphere is the locus of the Zeigarnik effect. It maintains activation of information related to non-attained goals.

In a follow-up study, Bowden and Beeman examined whether the right hemisphere could actually help individuals in solving the problem. This study was similar to the first, but this time, instead of simply naming the solution-relevant or irrelevant words, participants had to say whether these words were in fact the solution. Again, there was a right hemisphere advantage. Participants correctly identified words as solutions more quickly when the problems had been presented to the right as compared with the left hemisphere.

Taken together, these two studies suggest that when individuals fail to solve a problem, they have solution-related information in the right but not the left hemisphere, and this information can help them identify the solution (see also Fiore & Schooler, 1998). This is essentially rumination as described in the goal progress view (Martin & Tesser, 1989, 1996). From that perspective, rumination maintains the accessibility of problem-related information and uses that information in the recognition of solutions.

SUMMARY OF THE RUMINATION/ HEMISPHERE PARALLELS

In sum, when individuals perceive the environment as stable and predictable, their left hemisphere uses established representations as internal guides for behavior. When it is clear that these representations do not fit, the right hemisphere provides alternative ways of construing the situation. The right hemisphere also keeps problem-related information in mind for use in identifying a solution when it becomes available. Once a solution is found, the left hemisphere can take over again and guide behavior in accordance with the newly established representations.

The parallel of these findings to the goal progress view of rumination should be obvious. According to the goal progress view, when individuals are progressing successfully on the basis of their internal models (left hemisphere), there is no rumination. When this progress breaks down, individuals begin to reconstrue events in an attempt to restore goal progress (right hemisphere). Once they have re-established progress (left hemisphere), they stop ruminating. If this parallel is meaningful, then we should find that active rumination is associated with relatively more right than left hemisphere activation. Some evidence for this association was obtained by Martin and Shrira (2002) using a variant of the thought suppression paradigm (Wegner et al., 1987).

RUMINATION AND RIGHT HEMISPHERE ACTIVATION

Wegner et al. (1987) showed that attempting to keep a thought from one's mind can have the paradoxical effect of increasing the accessibility of that thought (i.e., a rebound effect). They explained this rebound effect by suggesting that individuals need to bring the thought to mind in order to determine whether they are thinking about it (e.g., "Am I thinking about a white bear? No. Actually, I just did." "How about now? No. Except that I just did again"). This repeated checking heightens the thought's accessibility. As long as individuals are actively suppressing, however, the increased accessibility may not reveal itself in a rebound. When individuals stop their active suppression, the heightened accessibility can lead the thought to return to mind at a level greater than if the individuals had not attempted to suppress the thought in the first place.

According to the goal progress view, however, the rebound reflects failure to attain the higher order goal of suppressing one's thoughts. This is why the receipt of success feedback eliminates the rebound effect (Koole et al., 1999; Martin & Tesser, 1996). Thinking in terms of the cerebral hemispheres may help us tease apart these two explanations.

Recall that the left hemisphere is better than the right in suppressing thoughts not central to its current processing objective (Burgess & Simpson, 1988). So, as individuals attempt to keep a thought from their mind, they are likely to experience relatively greater activation of their left hemisphere—at least initially. As we know, attempting to keep a thought from mind can be difficult if not impossible. When individuals detect deviations from their intentions, they experience greater right hemisphere activation (Blakemore et al., 1997; Fink et al., 1999; Paavilainen et al., 1991). So, if individuals experience failure in their attempted thought suppression, then they may move from relative left hemisphere activation to relative right hemisphere activation. Not only is the right hemisphere not adept at suppressing task-irrelevant information but it may actually maintain activation of information suppressed by the left (Burgess & Simpson, 1988; Fiore & Schooler, 1998). So, if individuals switch from greater left hemisphere activation to greater right hemisphere activation in the course of thought suppression, then they may be moving away from control (left hemisphere) into greater contact with the to-be-suppressed thought (right hemisphere). This would produce a rebound effect.

We tested this hypothesis by assessing relative hemisphere activation on four separate occasions in a within-subject design. Specifically, we obtained a baseline level of activation by having participants complete the line bisection task at the beginning of the experimental session (Bowers & Heilman, 1980; Milner, Brechmann, & Pagliarini, 1992). We first gave participants five sheets of paper with a small mark in the middle of each. Participants were asked to draw a line of a specified size on each sheet using the mark as the center. A tendency to draw the left side of the line longer than the right indicates relative left hemisphere activation. A tendency to draw the right side longer indicates relative right hemisphere activation.

After this baseline assessment, we told participants they would have five minutes to think about anything they wanted except a white bear. Shortly after these instructions, we had participants complete the line bisection task again. Next, we left participants alone for five minutes to suppress thoughts of a white bear. When we returned, we told participants they were free to think about whatever they wanted, and we had them perform the line bisection task again. After that, we presented participants with a list of 16 possible life goals (e.g., happiness, money) and asked participants to choose the three goals that best represented them. Finally, we had participants complete the line bisection task one last time.

If our hypothesis is correct, then participants should show greater left hemisphere activation (relative to their baseline) as they begin to suppress thoughts of a white bear. After attempting to do so, however, they should show greater right hemisphere activation. Interestingly, after participants rank their goals, they should return to relative left hemisphere activation. This last prediction was based on the finding that having participants process positive information about themselves eliminates the rebound effect (Koole et al., 1999).

This non-linear pattern was supported. A significant cubic contrast showed that, relative to the control condition, participants displayed greater left hemisphere activation when beginning to suppress thoughts of a white bear. After five minutes of attempting to suppress these thoughts, however, participants displayed greater right hemisphere activation. Finally, after ranking their self-defining goals, participants displayed an increase in left hemisphere activation. This pattern is consistent with prior research showing that individuals experience few thought intrusions while attempting actively to suppress a thought (left hemisphere), but show a rebound after attempting to suppress a thought (right hemisphere) and again show no rebound after affirming the self (left hemisphere).

Further evidence that rumination (i.e., heightened accessibility of thoughts following attempted suppression) is related to goal progress and right hemisphere activation was obtained in a second study by Martin and Shrira. According to the goal progress theory, the accessibility of goal-related information is maintained as long as individuals fail to make progress toward their higher order goals. One implication of this assumption is that individuals who feel they are making little progress in their life in general may be more susceptible to the rebound effect. The reason is that these participants may generally be experiencing greater right hemisphere activation as they attempt to find alternative ways toward their various life goals. As a result, they may display heightened accessibility of white bear thoughts whether they succeeded or failed on a white bear suppression task and maybe even if they expressed rather than suppressed white bear thoughts (Liberman & Förster, 2000).

To test this idea, Martin and Shrira first assessed participants self-reported goal progress. Specifically, participants answered such questions as: "During the last two weeks, how successful have you been?" "How competent did you feel?" and "How much were you living up to your own expectations?" After completing this inventory, some participants were given five minutes to think of anything they wanted (including a white bear), whereas others were given five minutes to keep thoughts of a white bear from coming to mind. Next, participants were given a list of incomplete words and instructed to add a letter to complete each word. Some of the words could be completed in more than one way, and in some cases one of these ways was related to a white bear (e.g., "_olar"). Presumably, the more accessible white bear thoughts were the more likely it was that participants would complete the words in a white bear-related way. Following this accessibility measure, participants completed a line bisection task to measure their relative hemisphere activation.

If the goal progress view is correct, then participants who are generally not making progress should show more right hemisphere activation (as they attempt to find alternative ways to their goal) and should display greater accessibility of white bear thoughts. Moreover, the greater accessibility should be seen whether these participants were asked to suppress thoughts of a white bear or were allowed to express those thoughts. This is because it is failure to attain higher order goals (and its attendant right hemisphere activation), not attempts to suppress a specific thought, that heightens thought accessibility.

The results were as predicted (see Figure 8.1). Only participants making progress toward their goals showed the typical rebound effect. Namely, those who attempted to suppress thoughts of a white bear produced more white bear stem completions than those allowed to think of a white bear. Those who attempted to suppress their thoughts also revealed more right hemisphere activation on the line bisection task.

A different pattern emerged, however, among participants who had not been making progress toward their goals. These participants showed a high number of white bear completions whether they expressed or suppressed thoughts of a white bear. They also showed relative right hemisphere activation whether they expressed or suppressed thoughts of a white bear.

In sum, when individuals are making progress toward their life goals as well as on their current tasks (i.e., express condition), they can continue to function according to routine. This involves left hemisphere activation and little rumination. When individuals have difficulty, however, either in life or on a specific task (i.e., suppress condition), their usual routines are not serving them well. Consequently, individuals have to switch to alternate strategies and may do so until goal progress is restored. This involves right hemisphere activation and an increased vulnerability to rumination.

RUMINATION, RIGHT HEMISPHERE ACTIVATION AND INSIGHT

In the context of the goal progress view, rumination can be beneficial. It can help individuals find alternate solutions to their problems. Evidence consistent

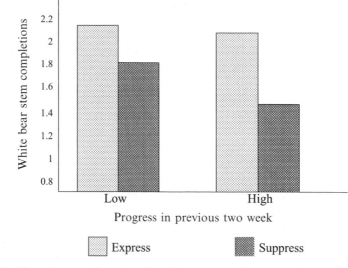

Figure 8.1. Thoughts as a function of goal progress and suppress/express instructions

with this hypothesis was obtained by Kuiken and Mathews (1986–87). They asked participants to think about a problem in their life. Some participants were asked to do so while paying attention to their feelings; others were asked to do so while searching for an explanation that helped them make sense of their problem. EEG (event encephalography) recordings revealed that the feeling-based rumination was associated with greater right hemisphere activation, whereas the explanation-based rumination was associated with greater left hemisphere activation. More interesting, though, was the observation of theta bursts, which have been shown to correlate with shifts in the meaning or significance of a problem (Don, 1977). Consistent with the hypothesis that right hemisphere rumination can facilitate insight, theta bursts were observed in 83% of the participants who engaged in feeling-based (right hemisphere) rumination, but in only 33% of the participants who engaged in explanation-based (left hemisphere) rumination.

ASSESSING ATTAINMENT AND PROGRESS WITHOUT OBJECTIVE STANDARDS

According to the goal progress view, individuals stop ruminating when they have attained their goal or are making progress toward it. As long as the situation is clear, then assessments of attainment and progress are easy. If individuals want to lose five pounds, for example, then they have attained their goal when they are five pounds lighter than they were. What happens, though, when individuals have a more diffuse goal, such as "be healthy." How do individuals know when they have accomplished this goal? Exactly what are the signs of closure, how many of these signs does an individual need, and over what period of time? In the absence of clear standards of attainment and progress, individuals have no choice but to rely upon subjective stop rules. In other words, individuals may ruminate until they feel they have attained or made progress toward their goals. The obvious next question is: "What determines one's feelings of progress?"

This question was explored by Startup and Davey (2001) in the context of catastrophic worrying. They proposed that the occurrence of catastrophic worrying might be understood in terms of the mood-as-input hypothesis (Davey, Startup, Zara, MacDonald, & Field, in press; Martin, Achee, Ward, & Wyer, 1993; Martin & Davies, 1998; Turley & Mark, 1996). Specifically, they suggested that, as individuals are working through a problem (i.e., worrying), they may ask themselves either explicitly or implicitly, "Have I thought about my problem enough?" (the enough stop rule). If they answer "yes," then they stop worrying. If they answer "no," then they continue.

Without clear, objective indicators of completion, however, the likelihood of a "yes" or a "no" answer may vary with the individual's subjective state. Specifically, if we assume mood-congruent evaluations, then individuals in a positive mood would feel better about their progress than individuals in a negative mood (Hirt, Levine, McDonald, Melton, & Martin, 1997; Martin, Achee et al., 1993). So, if individuals ask themselves, "Have I thought about my problem enough?", then those in positive moods would answer "yes," whereas those in negative moods would answer "no." Then, as a consequence of these different answers, those in positive moods would stop worrying (they've done enough), whereas those in negative moods would continue (they have not done enough).

Suppose, however, individuals asked themselves: "Am I enjoying thinking about this problem?" (enjoy stop rule). If we again assume mood-congruent evaluations, then we would again expect that individuals in positive moods would answer "yes" (they are enjoying the task), whereas individuals in negative moods would answer "no" (they are not enjoying the task). This time, though, the motivational implications of a "yes" and a "no" answer are different. When individuals are enjoying themselves, they are likely to continue thinking about their problem. When they are not enjoying themselves, they are likely to stop. Thus, with an enjoy stop rule, positive and negative moods would produce effects on worrying opposite to those produced with an enough stop rule.

This mood-as-input interpretation suggests that catastrophic worrying is not inherent to a given problem, person, mood, or stop rule. It is the product of an individual's mood combined with an individual's stop rule. Given that worrying is a form of persistent thinking, then the mood/stop rule combinations most likely to foster rumination are those that motivate individuals to continue

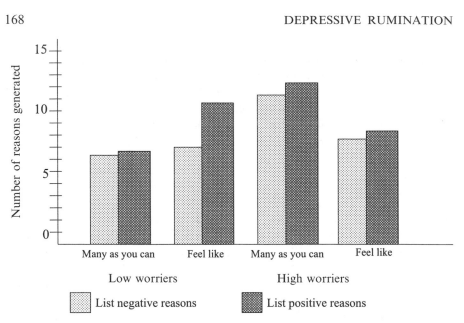

Figure 8.2. Number of reasons generated by high and low worriers as a Function of stop rule and task

processing. These would be a negative mood with an enough stop rule and a positive mood with an enjoy stop rule. Given that most worry is associated with negative moods (Borkovec, Robinson, Pruzinsky, & DePree, 1983), then the stop rule most likely to foster catastrophic worry is the enough rule.

This hypothesis was tested by Startup and Davey (2001) in the context of catastrophic worrying. Specifically, they had high and low worriers generate reasons why being the manager of a small hotel would be a good (or bad) thing. Half of the participants were instructed to generate reasons until they had "generated as many as they could" (enough rule), whereas half were instructed to generate reasons as long as they "felt like continuing" (enjoy rule). Measures of trait and state mood indicated that high worriers were in a more negative mood than low worriers. So, high worriers should generate more reasons than low worriers when provided with the enough rule. Their negative mood would tell them they had not thought about the issue enough. When provided with the enjoy rule, however, high worriers should actually generate fewer reasons than low worriers. In this case, their negative mood would tell them they were not enjoying thinking about the issue.

This predicted crossover was obtained by Startup and Davey (see Figure 8.2). Moreover, the crossover was obtained whether participants elucidated positive or negative features (i.e., why being manager of a small hotel would be good/bad). These results suggest that catastrophic worrying is not a function of a particular person, topic, mood, or stop rule. It is an interactive function of individuals' moods and stop rules.

By explicitly providing participants with a stop rule, Startup and Davey allowed us to see the effects of stop rules on catastrophic worrying. Explicit provision of the stop rules, however, did not allow us to see what individuals might do on their own. For example, do high worriers adopt an enough rule even when not prompted to do so? This question was addressed by Davey and Levy (1998) using the catastrophizing interview. This interview is essentially a method of externalizing individuals' worrisome cognitions (see Davey & Levy 1998; Vasey & Borkovec, 1992). It begins with participants identifying the topic of their main worry. If a participant reports being worried about exams, for example, then the experimenter would ask, "What is it that worries you about exams?" A typical response would be, "I might fail them." The experimenter would then ask, "What is it that worries you about failing exams?" If the participant answered, "I won't get a good job," then the experimenter would ask, "What is it that worries you about not getting a good job?" This proce- dure would continue until the participant could no longer come up with responses.

Davey and Levy used this procedure not only with regard to participants' main worry but also with regard to a novel, hypothetical worry (being the Statue of Liberty) and to a positive feature of the participants' life. Participants were also asked to reverse-catastrophize (i.e., say what is good about) their main worry and the novel worry. Davey and Levy found that high worriers, even without being instructed to do so, operated in accordance with an enough rule. That is, they generated significantly more catastrophizing steps than low worriers and did so not only with their main worry but also with the novel, hypothetical worry. High worriers also generated more steps than low worriers when iterating good as well as bad aspects of these worries.

Together, these studies suggest that rumination (i.e., catastrophic worrying) is a function of perceived goal progress. Individuals who worry tend to approach ruminative tasks with an enough stop rule. Use of this rule in the context of their negative mood makes high worriers continue worrying because they feel they have not made sufficient progress on their problem. When high worriers are provided with an enjoy rule, however, they actually generate fewer iterative steps than low worriers. Clearly, catastrophic worrying is the result of a subjective assessment of goal progress, which in turn is an interactive function of individuals' moods and stop rules.

DEPRESSION, RUMINATION, AND THE RIGHT HEMISPHERE

Our research has suggested that there are close connections among rumination, goal progress, right hemisphere activation, and use of an enough rule to determine sufficiency of processing. There are other, relevant connections to rumination, however, that we have not yet addressed. For example, rumination has been found to be associated with depression (Morrow & Nolen-Hoeksema, 1990) and with augmented pessimism (Lyubomirsky & Nolen-Hoeksema, 1995). Does the goal progress view account for these connections as well? Yes, it does. We simply have to consider rumination in the context of right hemisphere activation.

Right hemisphere activation has been shown to be associated with greater negative affect (Merckelbach & Van Oppen, 1989), greater depression (Tomarken & Keener, 1998), more negative self-evaluation (Ahern, Herring, Tackenburg, & Schwartz, 1994), and greater pessimism (Drake & Ulrich, 1992). In addition, activation of the left hemisphere is associated with action, whereas activation of the right hemisphere is associated with a slowdown in action (Tucker & Williamson, 1984). So, when individuals are unable to rely upon established routines (left hemisphere) to proceed toward their goals, they search for alternatives. This search is associated with greater right hemisphere activation, which in turn is associated with greater rumination, pessimism, sadness, depression, and negative self-evaluation, as well as a reduced tendency to act.

SUMMARY AND IMPLICATIONS

We began by asking if research on differential hemisphere activation could provide converging evidence for aspects of the goal progress view of rumination (Martin & Tesser, 1989, 1996; Martin, Tesser et al., 1993). We believe it has. Research in both areas suggests that when individuals are able to guide their behavior using established internal representations, they do so and do not ruminate. When it is clear to individuals that their current representations are not allowing them to progress toward their goals, they begin to entertain alternate perspectives. Moreover, they entertain these perspectives until they can use them to identity alternate solutions to their problems and regain progress toward their goals. In determining whether they have or have not progressed sufficiently toward their goals, individuals may rely upon subjective experiences (i.e., mood and stop rules).

From a goal perspective, all of this is as it should be. After all, when individuals are failing to progress toward their goals, it probably means that their established routines are not working for them (Schwartzberg & Janoff-Bulman, 1991). A new approach may be needed. If so, then the right hemisphere activation that accompanies rumination might help individuals find non-obvious, alternative paths to their goal (Kuiken & Matthews, 1986–87). In finding these paths, individuals can resume progress toward their goals and can terminate their rumination.

More generally, the juxtaposition of the goal progress view and the hemisphere research suggests that rumination is a natural, normal phenomenon, although it may not always be interpreted as such by those experiencing the rumination (Papageorgiou & Wells, 1999, 2001a, b; Wells & Matthews, 1994). It is simply an individual's way of getting back on track to his or her goals. Of course, there are times when rumination can be undesired and counter productive. For example, individuals may apply left hemisphere logic to insight problems or right hemisphere insight to logic problems. Neither application would be likely to produce an appropriate solution (Schooler, Ohlsson, & Brooks, 1993). As a result, individuals would not be likely to regain progress toward their goals and their rumination would continue.

A related contributor to prolonged, counterproductive rumination is the restriction of acceptable solutions. For example, if individuals believe they can be happy only if they get a promotion, then they will ruminate until they get the promotion (McIntosh, 1996). They may not even consider an alternative approach, such as changing jobs. The consequence, of course, is that they would remain in their current job and would ruminate until they obtained the promotion or abandoned their desire for it.

Rumination may also be maintained if individuals interpret their rumination as a sign of inadequacy (Ehlers & Steil, 1995; Papageorgiou & Wells, 1999, 2001a, b; Wells & Matthews, 1994). For example, some individuals see their rumination as a sign they are losing control. For these individuals, rumination moves from being a potentially fruitful response to a problem in itself. Once this happens, individuals may attempt to suppress the rumination and any potential insights it could provide (Horowitz, Znoj, & Stinson, 1996). To the extent they are successful with this, then individuals may fail to regain progress toward their goals and their rumination would continue.

Finally, rumination may be maintained if individuals make an inappropriate interpretation of their subjective state. When individuals are not making progress toward their goals, they experience negative affect (Carver & Scheier, 1990). If they interpret this affect in the context of an enough rule, then they may continue ruminating even if objectively they have found an appropriate solution. Their negative feelings in the context of their enough rule would tell them their progress had not been sufficient, even though it had.

If individuals wish to terminate their rumination, then the goal progress view suggests several solutions. Most of these involve rectifying the conditions just discussed. Specifically, rumination is likely to terminate when individuals (a) attain the goal or return to progress toward it, (b) use a form of rumination that can provide a solution for the type of problem they are facing, (c) expand their preconceptions of what constitutes an acceptable solution, (d) accept rumination as simply a way of finding an alternative path to the goal (as opposed to signifying loss of control), or (e) adopt moods and stop rules that give them a sense that they have attained or made progress toward their goal.

REFERENCES

Ahern, G. L., Herring, A. M., Tackenburg, J. N., & Schwartz, G. E. (1994). Affective self-report during the intracarotid sodium amobarbital test. *Journal of Clinical and Experimental Neuropsychology*, **16**, 372–376.

Atchley, R. A., Burgess, C., & Keeney, M. (1999). The effect of time course and context on the facilitation of semantic features in the cerebral hemispheres. *Neuropsychology*, **13**, 389–403.

Bever, T. G. & Chiarello, R. J. (1974). Cerebral dominance in musicians and non-musicians. *Science*, **185**, 537–539.

Blakemore, S., Rees, G., & Firth, C. D. (1997). How do we predict the consequences of our actions? A functional imaging study. *Neuropsychologia*, **36**, 521–529.

Bowden, E. M. & Beeman, M. J. (1998). Getting the right idea: Semantic activation in the right hemisphere may help solve insight problems. *Psychological Science*, **9**, 435–440.

Bowers, D. & Heilman, K. M. (1980). Pseudoneglect: Effects of hemispace on a tactile line bisection task. *Neuropsychologia*, **18**, 491–498.

Borkovec, T. D., Robinson, E., Pruzinsky, T., & DePree, J. A. (1983). Preliminary exploration of worry: Some characteristics and processes. *Behaviour Research and Therapy*, **21**, 9–16.

Bruner, J. S. (1957). On perceptual readiness. *Psychological Review*, **64**, 123–152.

Burgess, C. & Simpson, G. B. (1988). Cerebral hemispheric mechanisms in the retrieval of ambiguous word meanings. *Brain and Language*, **33**, 86–103.

Carver, C. S. & Scheier, M. F. (1990). Origins and functions of positive and negative affect: A control-process view. *Psychological Review*, **97**, 19–35.

Clark, L. F., Henry, S. M., & Taylor, D. M. (1991). Cognitive examination of motivation for childbearing as a factor in adjustment to infertility. In: A. L. Stanton & C. Dunkel-Schetter (eds), *Infertility: Perspectives from Stress and Coping Research* (the Plenum Series on Stress and Coping, pp. 157–180). New York: Plenum Press.

Davey, G. C. L. & Levy, S. (1998). Catastrophic worrying: Personal inadequacy and a perseverative iterative style as features of the catastrophizing process. *Journal of Abnormal Psychology*, **107**, 576–586.

Davey, G. C. L., Startup, H. M., Zara, A., MacDonald, C., & Field, A. (in press). The perseveration of checking thoughts and mood-as-input-hypothesis. *Journal of Behavior Therapy and Experimental Psychiatry*.

Davidson, R. J., Ekman, P., Saron, C. D., Senulis, J. A., & Friesen, W. V. (1990). Approach-withdrawal and cerebral asymmetry: Emotional expression and brain physiology, I. *Journal of Personality and Social Psychology*, **58**, 330–341.

De Zubicaray, G. I., Andrew, C., Zelaya, F. O., Williams, S. C. R., & Dumanoir, C. (2000). Motor response suppression and the prepotent tendency to respond: A parametric fMRI study. *Neuropsychologia*, **38**, 1280–1291.

Don, N. S. (1977). The transformation of conscious experience and its EEG correlates. *Journal of Altered States of Consciousness*, **3**, 147–168.

Drake, R. A. & Ulrich, G. (1992). Line bisecting as a predictor of personal optimism and desirability of risky behaviors. *Acta Psychologica*, **79**, 219–226.

Ehlers, A. & Steil, R. (1995). Maintenance of intrusive memories in posttraumatic stress disorder: A cognitive approach. *Behavioral and Cognitive Psychotherapy*, **23**, 217–249.

Fink, G. R., Marshall, J. C., Halligan, P. W., Frith, C. D., Drover, J., Frackowiak, R. S. J., & Dolan, R. J. (1999). The neural consequences of conflict between intention and the senses. *Brain*, **122**, 497–512.

Fiore, S. M. & Schooler, J. W. (1998). Right hemisphere contributions to creative problem solving: Converging evidence for divergent thinking. In: R. J. Sternberg & J. E. Davidson (eds), *The Nature of Insight* (pp. 559–587). Cambridge, MA: MIT Press.

Gazzaniga, M. S. (2000). Cerebral specialization and interhemispheric communication: Does the corpus callosum enable the human condition? *Brain*, **123**, 1293–1326.

Goldberg, E. & Costa, L. D. (1981). Hemisphere differences in the acquisition and use of descriptive systems. *Brain and Language*, **14**, 144–173.

Goldberg, E., Podell, K., & Lovell, M. (1994). Lateralization of frontal lobe functions and cognitive novelty. *Journal of Neuropsychiatry*, **6**, 371–378.

Gordon, H. W. & Carmon, A. (1976). Transfer of dominance in speed of verbal response to visually presented stimuli from right to left hemisphere. *Perceptual and Motor Skills*, **42**, 1091–1100.

Higgins, E. T., Rhodes, W. S., & Jones, C. R. (1957). Category accessibility and impression formation. *Journal of Experimental Social Psychology*, **13**, 141–154.

Hirt, E. R., Levine, G. M., McDonald, H. E., Melton, R. J., & Martin, L. L. (1997). The role of mood in quantitative and qualitative aspects of performance: Single or multiple mechanisms? *Journal of Experimental Social Psychology*, **33**, 602–629.

Horowitz, M. J., Znoj, H. J., & Stinson, C. H. (1996). Defensive control processes: Use of theory in research, formulation, and therapy of stress response syndromes. In: M. Zeidner & N. S. Endler (eds), *Handbook of Coping: Theory, Research, Applications* (pp. 532–553). New York: John Wiley & Sons.

Knecht, S., Henningsen, H., Deppe, M., & Huber, T. (1996). Successive activation of both hemispheres during cued word generation. *Neuroreport: An International Journal for the Rapid Communication of Research in Neuroscience*, **7**, 820–824.

Koole, S. L., Smeets, K., van Knippenberg, A., & Dijksterhuis, A. (1999). The cessation of rumination through self-affirmation. *Journal of Personality and Social Psychology*, **77**, 111–125.

Kuiken, D. & Mathews, J. (1986–87). EEG and facial EMG changes during self-reflection with affective imagery. *Imagination, Cognition, and Personality*, **6**, 55–66.

Libermann, N. & Förster, J. (2000). Expression after suppression: A motivational explanation of postsuppressional rebound. *Journal of Personality and Social Psychology*, **79**, 190–203.

Lyubomirsky, S. & Nolen-Hoeksema, S. (1995). Self-perpetuating properties of dysphoric rumination. *Journal of Personality and Social Psychology*, **65**, 339–349.

Martin, L. L. (1999). I-D [Immediate-Delayed] compensation theory: Some implications of trying to satisfy immediate-return needs in a delayed-return culture. *Psychological Inquiry*, **10**, 195–208.

Martin, L. L., Achee, J., Ward, D., & Wyer, R. S. (1993). Mood as input: People have to interpret the motivational implications of their moods. *Journal of Personality and Social Psychology*, **64**, 317–326.

Martin, L. L. & Davies, B. (1998). Beyond hedonism and associationism: A configural view of the role of affect in evaluation, processing, and self-regulation. *Motivation and Emotion*, **22**, 33–51.

Martin, L. L. & Shrira, I. (2002). Unpublished data, University of Georgia, Athens, GA.

Martin, L. L., Strack, F., & Stapel, D. A. (2001). How the mind moves: Knowledge accessibility and the fine-tuning of the cognitive system. In: A. Tesser & N. Schwarz (eds), *Blackwell International Handbook of Social Psychology: Intra-individual Processes* (Vol. 1, pp. 236–256). London: Blackwell.

Martin, L. L. & Tesser, A. (1989). Toward a motivational and structural theory of ruminative thought. In: J. S. Uleman & J. A. Bargh (eds), *Unintended Thought* (pp. 306–326). New York: Guilford Press.

Martin, L. L. & Tesser, A. (1996). Some ruminative thoughts. In: R. S. Wyer (ed.), *Advances in Social Cognition* (Vol. 9, pp. 1–47). Mahwah: Lawrence Erlbaum Associates.

Martin, L. L. Tesser, A., & McIntosh, W. D. (1993). Wanting but not having: The effects of unattained goals on thoughts and feelings. In: D. M. Wegner, & J. W. Pennebaker (eds), *Handbook of Mental Control* (pp. 552–572). Englewood Cliffs: Prentice Hall, Inc.

McIntosh, W. D. (1996). When does goal nonattainment lead to negative emotional reactions, and when doesn't it?: The role of linking and rumination. In: L. L. Martin, & A. Tesser (eds), *Striving and Feeling: Interactions among Goals, Affect, and Self-regulation* (pp. 53–77). Mahwah: Lawrence Erlbaum Associates.

Merkelbach, H. & Van Oppen, P. (1989). Effects of gaze manipulation on subjective evaluation of neutral and phobia-relevant stimuli: A comment on Drake's (1987) "Effects of gaze manipulation on aesthetic judgments: Hemisphere priming of affect." *Acta Psychologica*, **70**, 147–151.

Meyer, A. M. & Peterson, R. R. (2000). Structural influences on the resolution of lexical ambiguity: An analysis of hemispheric asymmetries. *Brain and Cognition*, **43**, 341–345.

Milner, A. D., Brechmann, M., & Pagliarini, L. (1992). To halve and to halve not: An analysis of line bisection judgments in normal subjects. *Neuropsychologia*, **30**, 515–526.

Moller, E. (2000). Have dual survival systems created the human mind? *Psychiatry*, **63**, 178–201.

Morrow, J. & Nolen-Hoeksema, S. (1990). Effects of responses to depression on the remediation of depressive affect. *Journal of Personality and Social Psychology*, **58**, 519–527.

Paavilainen, P., Alho, K., Reinikainen, K., Sams, M., & Näätänen, R. (1991). Right hemisphere dominance of different mismatch negatives. *Electroencephalography and Clinical Neurophysiology*, **78**, 466–479.

Papageorgiou, C. & Wells, A. (1999). Process and meta-cognitive dimensions of depressive and anxious thoughts and relationships with emotional intensity. *Clinical Psychology and Psychotherapy*, **6**, 156–162.

Papageorgiou, C. & Wells, A. (2001a). Metacognitive beliefs about rumination in recurrent major depression. *Cognitive and Behavioral Practice*, **8**, 160–164.

Papageorgiou, C. & Wells, A. (2001b). Positive beliefs about depressive rumination: Development and preliminary validation of a self-report scale. *Behavior Therapy*, **32**, 13–26.

Ramachandran, V. S. & Hirstein, W. (1997). Three laws of qualia: What neurology tells us about the biological functions of consciousness. *Journal of Consciousness Studies*, **4**, 429–457.

Rauch, R. (1977). Cognitive strategies in patients with unilateral temporal lobe excisions. *Neuropsychologia*, **15**, 385–395.

Rotenberg, V. S. & Weinberg, I. (1999). Human memory, cerebral hemispheres, and the limbic system: A new approach. *Genetic, Social, and General Psychology Monographs*, **125**, 45–70.

Sanna, L. J., Turley, K. J., & Mark, M. M. (1996). Expected evaluation, goals, and performance: Mood as input. *Personality and Social Psychology Bulletin*, **22**, 323–335.

Schooler, J. W., Fallshore, M., & Fiore, S. M. (1995). Epilogue: Putting insight into perspective. In: R. J. Sternberg & J. E. Davidson (eds), *The Nature of Insight* (pp. 559–587). Cambridge, MA: MIT Press.

Schooler, J. W., Ohlsson, S., & Brooks, K. (1993). Thoughts beyond words: When language overshadows insight. *Journal of Experimental Psychology: General*, **122**, 166–183.

Schwartzberg, S. S. & Janoff-Bulman, R. (1991). Grief and the search for meaning: Exploring the assumptive worlds of bereaved college students. *Journal of Social and Clinical Psychology*, **10**, 270–288.

Startup, H. M. & Davey, G. C. L. (2001). Mood as input and catastrophic worrying. *Journal of Abnormal Psychology*, **110**, 83–96.

Steele, C. (1988). The psychology of self-affirmation: Sustaining the integrity of the self. *Advances in Experimental Social Psychology*, **21**, 261–302.

Tesser, A., Martin, L. L., & Cornell, D. P. (1996). On the substitutability of self-protective mechanisms. In: P. M. Gollwitzer & J. A. Bargh (eds), *The Psychology of Action: Linking Cognition and Motivation to Behavior* (pp. 48–68). New York: Guilford Press.

Tomarken, A. J. & Keener, A. D. (1998). Frontal brain asymmetry and depression: A self-regulation perspective. *Cognition and Emotion*, **12**, 387–420.

Tucker, D. M. & Williamson, P. A. (1984). Asymmetric neural control systems in human self-regulation. *Psychological Review*, **91**, 185–215.

Vasey, M. W. & Borkovec, T. D. (1992). A catastrophizing assessment of worrisome thoughts. *Cognitive Therapy and Research*, **16**, 505–520.

Wegner, D. M., Schneider, D. J., Carter, S. R., & White, T. L. (1987). Paradoxical effects of thought suppression. *Journal of Personality and Social Psychology*, **53**, 5–13.

Wells, A. & Matthews, G. (1994). *Attention and Emotion: A Clinical Perspective*. Hove, UK: Lawrence Erlbaum.

Zeigarnik, B. (1938). On finished and unfinished tasks. In: W. D. Ellis (ed.), *A Source Book of Gestalt Psychology* (pp. 300–314). New York: Harcourt, Brace, & World. (Reprinted and condensed from *Psychologishe Forschung*, 1927, **9**, 1–85.)

9 A Comparison and Appraisal of Theories of Rumination

MELISSA A. BROTMAN AND ROBERT J. DERUBEIS

Department of Psychology, University of Pennsylvania, USA

Theories of rumination have elucidated our understanding of this often vague concept. Although theorists have different views of the mechanisms involved, rumination is consistently referred to as some form of repetitive and/or recursive set of thoughts. In the preceding three chapters, Nolen-Hoeksema presents findings from research generated by her response styles theory, Matthews and Wells discuss their Self-Regulatory Executive Function (S-REF) model, and Martin, Shrira, and Startup articulate their conceptualization of rumination as integral to the assessment of goal progress. Each perspective has unique strengths and the theories may be viewed as complementary, so that a consideration of the similarities and differences among these perspectives may yield a more comprehensive conceptualization.

Nolen-Hoeksema's (Chapter 6) approach to rumination is the most focused because it is meant to refer only to responses to negative (primarily sad) moods. In her response styles theory (Nolen-Hoeksema, 1991), rumination is a process whereby one turns one's attention to the causes and consequences of symptoms of depression. Rumination in response to a negative mood is seen as less adaptive than the two alternatives: engaging in distraction techniques, or using active problem-solving strategies.

Nolen-Hoeksema's studies have revealed that ruminating in response to a stressor has negative mental health effects. Specifically, she and her colleagues find that rumination, in the context of depressive moods, prolongs and exacerbates depressive symptoms and may lead to later depressive episodes. Compared with the other theorists, Nolen-Hoeksema maintains a singular focus on rumination as a pathological process. Rumination activates negative thoughts and memories, makes problem-solving less effective, interferes with instrumental behavior, and leads to social isolation and more depressive symptoms.

A strength of Nolen-Hoeksema's research program is its use of longitudinal methods. She identifies those with a propensity to ruminate and finds that,

Depressive Rumination: Nature, Theory and Treatment
Edited by Costas Papageorgiou and Adrian Wells © 2004 John Wiley & Sons Ltd

relative to those who are action-oriented, those who ruminate when distressed experience more severe and prolonged depressive symptoms following stressful life events. However, what remains unclear is what leads to individual differences in the tendency to ruminate. Clearly, ruminating produces additional and future problems, but is rumination a cause or a consequence of a larger problem? If it is established that rumination exacerbates depressive symptoms, the nature of the relationship between the tendency to ruminate and the experience of depression needs to be more thoroughly documented.

Nolen-Hoeksema has begun to examine the developmental antecedents of rumination. She hypothesizes that children are more likely to ruminate when their parents model a ruminative style. For some children, rumination may be the default (inborn) mode in the face of a negative mood. These children may develop a ruminative style if they are not explicitly taught more active problem-solving approaches. Given the gender differences in rumination, learning active strategies may be particularly important for girls compared with boys.

Nolen-Hoeksema's findings suggest that gender differences in rumination account for the large gender difference in incidence of depression. Women both ruminate more than men and are more likely to experience episodes of depression. Her group has reported that gender differences in rumination mediate the gender differences in depression. In other words, when the gender differences in rumination are statistically controlled, there are no longer gender differences in depression.

There are many potential explanations for the gender differences in rumination. Women report more stressors and traumatic events, and such experiences partially mediate the gender differences in rumination. In addition, women, more frequently than men, believe that negative emotions are difficult to control. Although differences in socialization may partially account for such findings, Nolen-Hoeksema and other researchers have found vast individual differences in rumination even among women.

Matthews and Wells (Chapter 7) seek a more differentiated view of rumination. Their focus on the importance of metacognition shifts the source of the problem with rumination to a different level. Their S-REF model (Wells & Matthews, 1994, 1996) aims to clarify the processes and effects of rumination. It portrays ruminative thought as a response to self-discrepancy. From this perspective, similar to Martin and Tesser (1989, 1996), ruminations are recurring thoughts that revolve around a common instrumental theme, but they can be either positive or negative. Whereas for Nolen-Hoeksema, rumination is a close cousin of (negative) mood, Matthews and Wells view rumination as a coping mechanism driven by metacognitive beliefs that inhibits emotional processing and interferes with adaptive coping. Although in both theories rumination is an ineffective strategy for dealing with emotional upset, Papageorgiou and Wells (2001) find that those who ruminate often have positive beliefs about ruminating. Thus, perhaps an important individual difference in rumination is the belief of the individual who is engaged in this recursive process. In support of this view, a confirmatory factor analysis by Bagby and Parker (2001) found that Nolen-Hoeksema's scale for ruminative response style is comprised of two intercorrelated factors: symptom-focused rumination and self-focused rumination. While the former is defined as thoughts about negative emotions, the latter is characterized by metacognitive thoughts about why one is experiencing negative emotions. In this analysis, self-focused rumination was correlated with anxiety and depression, whereas symptom-focused rumination did not show this relationship. Thus, above and beyond merely experiencing negative moods, the interpretation of these moods can further influence thinking about one's negative thoughts and emotions.

Nolen-Hoeksema's response style theory and Matthews and Wells' metacognitive view of rumination are complementary. Both theories suggest that rumination is maladaptive, although ruminators may not be aware of the negative consequences. Nolen-Hoeksema focuses on ruminations about one's symptoms of depression and examines the mental health effects of engaging in this response style. In contrast, Matthews and Wells argue that rumination is a dysfunctional process that is common to a variety of emotional disorders, in addition to depression.

In their S-REF model of affective dysfunction, Matthews and Wells link rumination to self-regulation within a dynamic, three-level network system. First, lower level networks process incoming stimuli in an automatic fashion. If these stimuli are coded as motivationally significant, the second level—the supervisory executive system—is activated. At this level, information is appraised and evaluated for potential personal discrepancies. Coping responses are implemented by biasing the lower level system until the discrepancy is resolved.

There are two forms of coping: emotion-focused coping and problem-focused coping. Whereas the former modifies internal representations, the latter attempts to change external realities. Emotions, in turn, are generated as appraisals, and coping processes are integrated and assessed. Appraisal and coping requires access to the third level in the system, which is comprised of self-relevant knowledge in the form of schema and dysfunctional metacognitive beliefs. The plans for coping are determined at this level. An integrative view of Nolen-Hoeksema's and Matthews and Wells' work may focus on individual differences in the third level of processing.

In the S-REF model, the effects of metacognition on the emotions are presumed to vary greatly across people. In so far as the S-REF model is conceived as a top-down processing model, one's metacognitive beliefs influence the automatic processing of information, the coping strategies one chooses, and the personal significance applied to a given discrepancy. From a response styles perspective, there are individual differences, gender differences, and developmental antecedents that lead to varying response styles. Given the consistent findings of gender differences in rumination, future investigations should attempt to map the gender differences in information processing in the

S-REF model. Do men and women differ in their automatic processing of incoming stimuli in the lower level networks? Are there gender differences in the number and degree of automatic thoughts? Are there gender differences in the appraisal of external events? One might hypothesize gender differences in all three levels of the S-REF model, beginning at the metacognitive level, given Nolen-Hoeksema's findings that women and men differ in their perception of control over negative emotions.

Another way both the response styles theory and the S-REF model might explain the gender differences in rumination would be to focus on differences in coping responses once a discrepancy is perceived and goal frustration is experienced. Rumination is initiated as a coping response if a discrepancy is perceived between one's current status and goal. In response to such goal frustration, men may engage in more problem-focused coping, whereas women may be more likely to engage in emotion-focused coping, or rumination. Thus, rumination is closely linked to goal frustration.

Martin et al. (Chapter 8) discuss rumination in the context of the assessment of goal progress. The authors support Martin and Tesser's (1989) conceptualization of rumination as an instance of the Zeigarnik effect. Information regarding incomplete tasks remains in memory longer than information regarding completed tasks and is more accessible and more readily and easily cued as well. When individuals do not perceive themselves as progressing toward their goals, they are easily reminded of their lack of progress. Rumination, then, is the tendency to think about unattained goals. Martin et al.'s goal process theory can be understood in the framework of the S-REF model. Specifically, rumination promotes self-regulation, in that goal-related information remains activated for as long as the discrepancy is detected. Lower level networks are biased toward processing information consistent with the ruminative content. This information remains highly accessible until the discrepancy is resolved.

How is such a discrepancy resolved? According to the S-REF theory, coping mechanisms either bias lower level networks to make the discrepancy less apparent, or they change external circumstances so as to minimize the discrepancy. In the context of the goal process view, rumination can facilitate either of these coping processes. Once the discrepant information is highly accessible, one is motivated to modify the discrepancy. In other words, rumination may facilitate more ruminative strategies (i.e., emotion-focused coping) or it may facilitate problem-solving strategies (i.e., problem-focused coping). Thus, both the goal progress theory and S-REF model state that insufficient progress toward a goal leads to one of two responses. An individual may engage in a problem-focused approach whereby he or she formulates an alternative path to the goal and changes his behavior, or an individual may recursively think about the discrepancy for an extended period of time. While the former strategy may be effective, the latter is pathological. From this perspective Martin et al.'s conception of rumination is broader than Nolen-Hoeksema's on two fronts: ruminative processes can lead to effective action, and the pathological effects of rumination can pertain to a variety of emotional states, not just depression.

Following their presentation of the goal progress theory, Martin et al. investigate the relationship between rumination, self-regulation, cerebral hemisphere specialization, and the biological correlates of goal attainment. The goal progress theory garners support in so far as right hemisphere activity correlates with attempts toward goal attainment and rumination.

How does one make progress toward a goal? In order to attain a goal, one must pursue the goal in the face of challenges, changing strategies as necessary. Whereas left hemisphere activity promotes convergent, routinized thinking, right hemisphere activation may be associated with divergent thinking that can either result in the generation of an alternative path to a goal, or in the unsuccessful (ruminative) search for an alternative path. Studies in both normal and brain-damaged populations suggest that the right hemisphere is more responsible for changing strategies and generating novel solutions to complex problems. In other words, the right hemisphere becomes activated when established patterns (i.e., situations easily interpreted by the left hemisphere) are no longer achievable and alternative paths must be accessed. Thus, Martin et al. argue that rumination and the Zeigarnik effect more generally may be the result of activity in the right hemisphere. From a goal process perspective, when feedback regarding one's progress toward a goal is positive, the left hemisphere is successfully responding to the environmental contingencies. When feedback suggests that the progress is unacceptable, the right hemisphere becomes activated in an attempt to generate an alternative strategy. If the strategy is effective, the left hemisphere is reactivated; however, if the new plan is not producing substantial gains, the right hemisphere remains activated, in principle indefinitely.

Applying the S-REF model to the brain-based model of rumination, both hemispheres are activated by lower level networks. If incongruency is determined, the right hemisphere then becomes activated to generate a new alternative. If this alternative is an effective problem-solving technique, the left hemisphere becomes activated. However, if the right hemisphere does not generate an effective solution, it remains active and rumination persists. It is unclear what areas of the brain are most involved in the metacognitive assessment. If metacognition is similar to Martin et al.'s conception of an "enough rule," the right hemisphere determines if progress toward a goal is satisfactory. However, one might also hypothesize that metacognition is a left hemisphere phenomenon, in so far as one's self-schema is invariant over time and thus an enduring feature in the assessment of progress toward a goal.

Perhaps the strongest work on hemisphere specialization is in the depression literature. As discussed by Nolen-Hoeksema, rumination and depression may be causally related. Davidson's findings with depressed patients (1992, 1993) integrate Martin and colleagues', Nolen-Hoeksema and colleagues', and

Matthews and Wells' work. Davidson and Irwin (1999) proposed two basic systems involved in emotion: the approach system and the withdrawal system. The approach system facilitates appetitive behaviors and generates certain types of positive affect, whereas the withdrawal system facilitates escape from aversive stimulation. Depressed individuals, in fact, show less left-sided activation (Henriques & Davidson, 1991) and brain metabolism (Mathew et al., 1980), relative to controls. Martin et al. might hypothesize that such individuals with less left brain activity, relative to right brain activity, are likely to become depressed because they are not able to pursue a goal effectively. When a depression-prone person correctly identifies a goal, he or she is apt to engage the right hemisphere in an unsuccessful pursuit of a goal. The fact that males and females differ in both depression and rumination suggests that there may be gender differences in hemisphere activation. However, such differences have yet to be consistently reported.

Even if gender differences in hemispheric activation can account for observed gender differences in rumination, this would not point to the origins of such differences. It is possible that differential socialization would lead both to differences in the interpretation of stimuli that would lead one to ruminate and to differential activation of the two hemispheres. Since cultures vary substantially in the degree of sex role differentiation (Costa, Terracciano, & McCrae, 2001), this is a testable hypothesis. On the other hand, the hypothesis that these gender differences are (at least in part) genetic begs for an evolutionary account of these differences.

From an evolutionary perspective, it might be argued that engaging in ruminative strategies may have been more lethal for males compared with females in the evolutionary environment in which gender differences in behavior developed. If, for example, a hunter (typically male), following a near-death experience, began to ruminate about the interaction, he may have been more likely to die during his next encounter, compared with the hunter who was able to engage in a more active, problem-solving technique. If lower order networks were biased to interpret information in a way that is consistent with rumination or if the hunter paused too long before taking action, the likelihood of grave consequences would have been high. Females, in contrast, may have benefited from a more ruminative style, as it may be more advantageous to offspring to have a caretaker who engages, at least in the short-term, in emotion-focused coping. Moreover, the negative consequences of rumination are unlikely to be as extreme as those that can befall the hunter. In addition, the hunter's ability to measure his progress toward his goal (e.g., killing an animal for food) is perhaps more concrete relative to that of the caretaker, for whom the assessment of goal progress may be more elusive. In turn, goal frustration for the caretaker may be less salient. Thus, ruminative strategies may have been both less common and less lethal for the caretaker, relative to the hunter in the evolutionary environment, which may have influenced later gender differences in rumination.

CONCLUSION

Nolen-Hoeksema's response styles theory, Matthews and Wells' S-REF model, and Martin et al.'s view of rumination as a function of goal frustration and right hemisphere activation have provided distinct perspectives on this process. A critical and practical test of these theories would be whether they lead to more successful treatment interventions. As discussed by Nolen-Hoeksema, early interventions with children that teach active, problem-solving coping may be most effective in preventing rumination and depression. But it may be difficult to treat individuals who are continuously engaging in ruminative strategies. Given Matthews and Wells' S-REF model, one might hypothesize that a most effective strategy would be to induce the ruminator to examine his or her metacognitive beliefs about his or her ruminative strategy, much as might be done in cognitive therapy (Beck, Rush, Shaw, & Emery, 1979). If, as suggested by the S-REF model and shown by Papageorgiou and Wells (2001), ruminators tend to have positive beliefs about these strategies, such conceptions should be challenged. Interventions can be applied to every level of the S-REF: lower level networks and automatic thoughts can be analyzed; supervisory executive coping strategies can be examined pragmatically; and, perhaps most importantly, metacognitive beliefs about the process can be challenged. In so far as rumination is most likely to evolve from goal frustration, as discussed by Martin et al., effective problem-solving techniques can be examined and the meaning of goal frustrations can be explored.

REFERENCES

Bagby, R. M. & Parker, J. D. A. (2001). Relation of rumination and distraction with neuroticism and extraversion in a sample of patients with major depression. *Cognitive Therapy and Research*, **25**, 91–102.

Beck, A. T., Rush, A. J., Shaw, B. F., & Emery, G. (1979). *Cognitive Therapy of Depression*. New York: Guilford Press.

Costa, P. T., Terracciano, A., & McCrae, R. R. (2001). Gender differences in personality traits across cultures: Robust and surprising findings. *Journal of Personality and Social Psychology*, **81**, 322–331.

Davidson, R. J. (1992). Anterior cerebral asymmetry and the nature of emotion. *Brain and Cognition*, **20**, 125–151.

Davidson, R. J. (1993). Cerebral asymmetry and emotion: Conceptual and methodological conundrums. *Cognition and Emotion*, **7**, 115–138.

Davidson, R. J. & Irwin, W. (1999). The functional neuroanatomy of emotion and affective style. *Trends in Cognitive Science*, **3**, 11–21.

Henriques, J. B. & Davidson, R. J. (1991). Left frontal hypoactivation in depression. *Journal of Abnormal Psychology*, **4**, 535–545.

Martin, L. L. & Tesser, A. (1989). Toward a motivational and structural theory of ruminative thought. In: J. S. Uleman & J. A. Bargh (eds), *Unintended Thought.* New York: Guilford Press.

Martin, L. L. & Tesser, A. (1996). Some ruminative thoughts. In: R. S. Wyer (ed.), *Advances in Social Cognition.* Mahwah, NJ: Lawrence Erlbaum.

Mathew, R. J., Meyer, J. S., Francis, D. J., Semchuk, K. M., Morte, K., & Claghorn, J. L. (1980). Cerebral blood flow in depression. *American Journal of Psychiatry,* **137**, 1449–1450.

Nolen-Hoeksema, S. (1991). Responses to depression and their effects on the duration of depressive episodes. *Journal of Abnormal Psychology,* **100**, 569–582.

Papageorgiou, C. & Wells, A. (2001). Metacognitive beliefs about rumination in recurrent major depression. *Cognitive and Behavioral Practice,* **8**, 160–164.

Wells, A. & Matthews, G. (1994). *Attention and Emotion: A Clinical Perspective.* Hove, UK: Lawrence Erlbaum.

Wells, A. & Matthews, G. (1996). Modelling cognition in emotional disorder: The S-REF model. *Behaviour Research and Therapy,* **34**, 881–888.

III   Measurement and Treatment of Rumination

10 Measurement of Depressive Rumination and Associated Constructs

OLIVIER LUMINET

Belgian National Fund for Scientific Research, University of Louvain at Louvain-la-Neuve, Belgium

The present chapter first reviews two instruments specifically related to depressive rumination. The first instrument reviewed is the Response Styles Questionnaire (RSQ), which derived from the response styles theory of Nolen-Hoeksema (1987). A strong emphasis is given to this measure as it is well supported by a theoretical model and a number of empirical studies. Then, a new instrument assessing depressive rumination (the Rumination on Sadness Scale) is presented. The second section of the chapter is dedicated to measures of metacognition about rumination. These are beliefs that individuals have about rumination and the preference for certain thought control strategies. The instruments reviewed are the Positive Beliefs about Rumination Scale (PBRS), the Negative Beliefs about Rumination Scale (NBRS), the Thought Control Questionnaire (TCQ), the Metacognitions Questionnaire (MCQ), the White Bear Suppression Inventory (WBSI) and diary methods. For each instrument, examples of items are presented along with data on their reliability, such as internal consistency and test–retest correlations, the factorial structure, validity (concurrent, convergent, discriminant, and predictive), and when avail-able data on the sensitivity to change following treatment.

Most measures of rumination are based on self-report scales. Although self-reports are easy to administer, they raise some important questions about how accurately they measure the frequency and content of mental processes. The third section describes an indirect method for assessing rumination as an alternative to self-reports.

The final section examines convergence and divergence in measures of rumination. There has been a tendency up to now to develop new instruments rather than look at the overlaps between the existing measures. A recent study

Depressive Rumination: Nature, Theory and Treatment
Edited by Costas Papageorgiou and Adrian Wells. © 2004 John Wiley & Sons Ltd

addressed this issue and made interesting suggestions on the possibilities of aggregating scales.

SELF-REPORT INSTRUMENTS FOR MEASURING DEPRESSIVE RUMINATION

THE RESPONSE STYLES QUESTIONNAIRE (RSQ)

Background

The RSQ was derived from Nolen-Hoeksema's (1987) observation that women are twice more likely to become depressed than men. For Nolen-Hoeksema, the difference is explained by two antagonistic ways to respond to depressive mood. The first is *distraction*, in which people focus their attention on external aspects, unrelated to their current mood state. The second is *rumination*, in which people focus their attention on symptoms, meaning, causes, and consequences of the dysphoric state. A large set of studies showed that women have a greater tendency to engage in rumination than men when in a depressive mood. A ruminative thinking style will then maintain the depressed mood previously instated. Following Nolen-Hoeksema's view, rumination is a passive response to depressive mood that needs to be distinguished from adaptive emotion-focused coping responses, such as reappraisal or seeking social support. Rumination maintains all the available attention toward the symptoms of depression, which does not allow any space for emotion regulation (e.g., in the form of emotion repair: for more details, see Chapter 6 by Nolen-Hoeksema in this book).

Assessment

Items, Reliability, Stability, and Factor Structure
Nolen-Hoeksema and Morrow (1991) developed a self-report questionnaire intended to assess four different types of reactions to negative mood. This initial version of the RSQ included 71 items measuring ruminative, distracting, problem-solving, and dangerous activities. Respondents were instructed to focus on their thoughts when they feel "sad, blue, or depressed." For each item, they indicate overall how often they experience each response on a four-point scale ranging from 1 ("almost never") to 4 ("almost always"). The problem-solving and the dangerous activities scales were dropped in further studies due to very low reliability coefficients.

The RSQ comprises a Ruminative Responses Scale (RRS) and a Distracting Responses Scale (DRS). The RRS is a 22-item scale evidencing high internal reliability, with Cronbach alphas ranging from 0.88 to 0.92 (Bagby et al., 1999; Just & Alloy, 1997; Nolan, Roberts, & Gotlib, 1998; Nolen-Hoeksema &

Davis, 1999; Nolen-Hoeksema, Larson, & Grayson, 1999; Nolen-Hoeksema & Morrow, 1991; Nolen-Hoeksema, Parker, & Larson, 1994). Items focus either on the *meaning* of rumination ("I write down what I am thinking about and analyze it"), on the *feelings* related to the depressed mood ("I think about how sad I feel"), on *symptoms* ("I think about how hard it is to concentrate"), and on *consequences* and *causes* of the mood ("I think I won't be able to do my job if I don't snap out of this"). Recently, a short version of the scale has been developed (Nolen-Hoeksema & Jackson, 2001) that contains 10 items from the original list of 22. The scale was obtained by selecting the items that had the highest item–total correlations with the total score. Authors also made sure that they covered the range of self-focused and symptom-focused constructs (Nolen-Hoeksema, 2001, pers. commun.). The short version is highly related to the full version of the scale ($r = 0.90$) and has a high internal reliability (Cronbach $\alpha = 0.85$). The construct validity and test–retest reliability of this short version of the RRS still needs to be demonstrated.

Several studies support the view that the RRS measures a *stable* tendency to ruminate. In a longitudinal study looking at people who lost a loved one (Nolen-Hoeksema & Davis, 1999), the RRS was administered before the loss and 1, 6, 13, and 18 months after the loss. The intraclass correlation across five times of measurement was high ($r = 0.75$). In another study with recently bereaved people, Nolen-Hoeksema et al. (1994) obtained a strong test–retest correlation of the RRS ($r = 0.80$) after a six-month interval. In a study looking at the effects of chronic strain, low mastery, and ruminative style on depressive symptoms in men and women (Nolen-Hoeksema et al., 1999), 1,100 community-based adults were interviewed twice at 12 months intervals. The test–retest correlation for the RRS was 0.67. However, Just and Alloy (1997) found a lower correlation in a group of clinically depressed people after a 12-month interval.

The RRS is supposed to be independent of the scale that measures preferences for distracting activities (i.e., the DRS). The DRS is a 13-item scale describing active, distracting responses to depression that are not dangerous or reckless. Examples of items on the DRS include: "When I feel depressed I go to a favorite place to get my mind off my feelings" and "I talk with friends about something other than how I am feeling." The assumption of independence between the RRS and the DRS is confirmed by a non-significant correlation ($r = 0.08$) between the scales in a clinical sample of severely depressed patients (Bagby et al., 1999) and in a sample of initially non-depressed freshmen followed up longitudinally ($r = 0.14$) (Just & Alloy, 1997).

The *factor structure* of the RRS was examined in two college samples (Roberts, Gilboa, & Gotlib, 1998). In the first sample ($N = 299$), an exploratory factor analysis yielded a three-factor solution that accounted for 55.7% of the variance. The first factor labeled "symptom-based rumination" accounted for 17.4% of the variance. It included seven items ($\alpha = 0.81$), such as "think about how passive and unmotivated you feel" or "think about how you don't feel up to doing anything." The second factor, which was composed of five items ($\alpha = 0.84$), was labeled "introspection/self-isolation" and accounted for 21.2% of the variance. Example items were "go someplace alone to think about your feelings" or "isolate yourself and think about the reasons why you feel sad." The third factor ("self-blame") was composed of three items ($\alpha = 71$) and accounted for 17.1% of the variance. Example items include: "think about a recent situation wishing it had gone better" or "think about how angry you are with yourself." Although the three-factor solution accounted for a large part of the variance, six items were not retained in the final solution. The second sample ($N = 317$) was used to run a confirmatory factor analysis in order to test the replicability of the three-factor solution obtained in the first sample. The solution was confirmed with the small modification that one item loaded on two factors. Indices of fit reached the criterion thresholds. Moreover, all factor loadings were statistically significant. Despite these encouraging findings, six items from the RRS were not retained in the factor analysis. Further studies need to test the replicability of the factor structure obtained by Roberts et al. (1998).

Validity

The *predictive* validity of the RRS has been examined in a large number of studies. The first part of this subsection examines studies conducted with non-clinical populations, while the second part extends it to clinically depressed patients.

In a study with non-clinical populations, a group of students completed by chance the RRS and the DRS together with the Inventory to Diagnose Depression (IDD: Zimmerman, Coryell, Corenthal, & Wilson, 1986), a scale assessing depression severity, two weeks before a major earthquake (Nolen-Hoeksema & Morrow, 1991). The group was then followed up ten days and seven weeks after the stressful event. A regression analysis revealed that the more people adopted a ruminative response style following the earthquake the more severely depressed they were after seven weeks, irrespective of their initial level of depression or their initial level of stress.

In another longitudinal study with recently bereaved people, Nolen-Hoeksema et al. (1994) examined *additional predictors* of depression severity six months after the death of a family member. The additional predictors were optimism measured by the Life Orientation Test (LOT: Scheier & Carver, 1985) and social support assessed by the Social Support and Activities Scale (O'Brien, Wortman, Kessler, & Joseph, 1989). Results showed that the propensity to ruminate measured by the RRS made a significant contribution in predicting depression severity over and above the contribution of depression at one month. The other variables (optimism, social support, and additional stressors) made only a small contribution in predicting depression severity. Nolen-Hoeksema et al. (1994, p. 102) concluded that: "The results of this study suggest that the ways people respond to their initial symptoms of distress following their loss may influence the long-term impact of the loss on their emotional well-being. Specifically, people who cope with those initial negative emotions with rumination have trouble adjusting to their loss and are at risk for long-term emotional difficulties."

A recent study examined the predictive validity of the RRS for depression by including dimensions of the *social context* (Nolen-Hoeksema & Davis, 1999). A group of people recently traumatized by the loss of a loved one were interviewed before the loss and then again 1, 6, 13, and 18 months following the loss. Results indicated that people scoring high on the RRS (high ruminators) were actively seeking more social support. Although social support *per se* is generally beneficial, it also depends on the type of feedback offered by the social environment and the accuracy of the perception from the traumatized individual. The study revealed that people with high RRS scores were more sensitive to the type of feedback they received than low RRS scorers. However, a high level of rumination was not systematically associated with a high level of distress. When the social context was favorable (high level of emotional support, low level of social friction, and high level of comfort when discussing loss), high RRS scorers were less distressed throughout the 18 months following the loss as compared with high RRS scorers for whom the social network was critical about their reactions. Third, a strong negative relationship was observed only among high ruminators between scores on the RRS and the subjective perception of the quality of social support received, after controlling for level of distress. This result suggests that, despite a greater desire for social support, high ruminators perceive their social support as poor and not fulfilling their expectancies. As noted by Nolen-Hoeksema and Davis (1999, p. 812): "People may be less supportive of ruminators because ruminators go over and over their loss and persistently discuss their feelings and grief-related symptoms without making much progress toward 'resolving' their loss." On the other hand, the impact of social support on distress was only of small magnitude in the low ruminators group.

The respective contribution of a ruminative response style and *social conditions* in the prediction of depression has been recently investigated (Nolen-Hoeksema et al., 1999). Social conditions were related to chronic strain (e.g., lack of affirmation in close relationships, housework or childcare inequities) and to lack of control (or low mastery). The study was conducted with a large community sample. Results from structural equation modeling showed that, while the level of preference for a ruminative response style measured by the RRS was directly related to the level of depression severity, the level of strain and the level of mastery had only an indirect effect on depression, both being mediated by scores on the RRS (Nolen-Hoeksema et al., 1999). This suggests that low mastery and high level of strain would only contribute to depression severity when associated with a high preference for rumination. Results showed that low mastery and high level of strain are more prevalent in women than in men. Women generally experience more chronic strain by feeling less valued in their family and working role, and they are also more likely to feel a chronic lack of control over their environment.

The data reviewed up to now support the predictive validity of the RRS for non-clinical, untreated individuals with mild to moderate depression. A study conducted in a group of patients diagnosed with a primary, unipolar, non-psychotic major depression did not provide the expected relationship between scores on the RRS and either the *number* of previous depressive episodes ($r = 0.01$) or the *duration* of current depressive episodes ($r = -0.05$) (Bagby et al., 1999). Just and Alloy (1997) also failed to find that the degree of ruminative responses would predict the duration of depressive episodes in a longitudinal prospective study with initially non-depressed freshmen. These studies suggest that the effects of ruminative style on depression severity appear to be restricted to non-clinical populations.

In contrast with these results, two studies with clinically depressed partici-pants have shown that a preference for ruminative responses represents a vulnerability factor to depression (Nolan et al., 1998; Roberts et al., 1998). Elevated levels of rumination were found in currently and previously dysphoric individuals, but not in never dysphoric participants. Results from Roberts et al. (1998) also indicated that rumination tendency measured by the RRS is asso-ciated with *prolonged* episodes of depression. Nolan et al. (1998) then showed that elevated scores of *both* neuroticism and rumination without a previous history of depression are good predictors of subsequent elevated depressive symptoms. A path model indicated that neuroticism does not directly affect mood state. Rather, high levels of neuroticism determine a specific *cognitive* style that involves a particular attentional focus on depressed mood. In turn, this cognitive style increases the probability of developing a ruminative style that then directly contributes to predict subsequent depression.

A recent *prospective* study suggests that rumination can predict depression severity among clinically depressed people (Nolen-Hoeksema, 2000). The first goal of the study was to test the relationship between ruminative responses measured by the RRS and depression severity one year later in a large community sample. Depression was assessed with the Beck Depression Inventory (BDI: Beck, Ward, Mendelson, Mock, & Eerbaugh, 1961), the Hamilton Rating Scale for Depression (HRSD: Hamilton, 1960) and the Structured Clinical Interview for *DSM-IV* Axis I Disorders (First et al., 1995). Separate analyses with clinically depressed and non-depressed people at time 1 showed that ruminative response score on the RRS predicted depression severity at time 2 over and above depression severity at time 1 in both groups.

The second purpose of the study was to examine if a propensity to ruminate could predict anxiety and mixed anxiety/depression symptomatology. Content analysis of ruminators' thoughts indicated that uncertainty over whether important situations are controllable and manageable is a central component of their cognitive activity (Lyubomirsky, Tucker, Caldwell, & Berg, 1999). At the same time, several theorists argued that uncertainty about being able to control one's environment is a key feature of anxiety (e.g., Alloy, Kelly, Mineka, & Clements, 1990). Taken together with the propensity of ruminators for negative evaluations of the self and hopelessness about the future (Abramson, Metalsky, & Alloy, 1989), these data suggest that people scoring high on the RRS would also be particularly prone to a mixed anxiety/depression syndrome. Four groups (no-symptom, depression only, anxiety only, mixed anxiety/depression) were created based on their depression and anxiety scores (measured by the Beck Anxiety Inventory: Beck & Steer, 1990). Results revealed an identical pattern at both times of measurement with the mixed depression/anxiety group having a significantly higher RRS score than the three other groups. The depression only and the anxiety only groups did not differ from each other, but were significantly higher than the no-symptom group. These results show a similar relationship between ruminative response style on the one hand and depressive and anxious symptomatology on the other hand. Moreover, when depression and anxiety are combined they seem to make ruminative cognitions even more pervasive. As a consequence, the instructions for completing the RRS have been recently revised (Nolen-Hoeksema & Jackson, 2001). Instead of asking people to think about situations when they feel "sad, blue, or depressed" the new instructions refer to situations when people feel "upset—sad, blue, nervous." In that way, the RRS now includes situations in which people feel depressed and/or anxious.

Although these results need further replications, they raise the question of the specificity of the RRS to predict depressive symptoms. If a ruminative style predicts both anxiety and depression this would suggest that a propensity for rumination represents a vulnerability factor for emotional disorders in general as suggested in a recent metacognitive theory of emotional disorders (Wells, 2000; Wells & Matthews, 1994).

More recently, Treynor, Gonzalez, and Nolen-Hoeksema (2003) revised the original 22-item RRS and produced a new measure of rumination that is unconfounded with depression content. Twelve depression-related items of the RRS were first removed. A principal components analysis with the remaining ten items yieded a two-factor solution with one factor labeled "reflection" and the other "brooding." Reflection involves efforts to deal with and attempt to overcome problems and difficulties. Brooding is related to thinking anxiously or gloomily about things. Interestingly, both factors evidenced different relationships with depression. Reflection was associated with less depression over time, while brooding was associated with more depression, suggesting that the first factor is related to adaptive rumination and the second to maladaptive rumination. These results indicate refinements in the Response Styles Theory of Nolen-Hoeksema and the need for examining these two factors separately in future studies.

The *convergent* and the *discriminant* validity of the RRS have been examined in various studies. First, the assumption of a moderate relationship with depressive symptoms has been consistently supported. Roberts et al. (1998) showed that the three factors of the RRS (symptom-based rumination, introspection/self-isolation, and self-blame) were correlated with current depressive symptoms measured by the IDD ($r = 0.23$ to 0.43), worst lifetime depressive symptoms measured by the IDD-Lifetime Version (Zimmerman & Coryell, 1987) ($r = 0.34$ to 0.45), and neuroticism measured by the Eysenck Personality Inventory (EPI: Eysenck & Eysenck, 1964) ($r = 0.16$ to 0.19 for "introspection/isolation," $r = 0.33$ to 0.41 for "symptom-base rumination," and $r = 0.43$ to 0.44 for "self-blame"). High correlations were also found between the *total* RRS score and current depressive symptoms measured by the IDD ($r = 0.53$ to 0.57), worst lifetime depressive symptoms measured by the IDD-Lifetime Version ($r = 0.61$) and neuroticism measured by the EPI ($r = 0.57$) (Nolan et al., 1998).

With respect to discriminant validity, the RRS was found to be negatively related to dispositional optimism measured by the LOT (Scheier & Carver, 1985), correlations ranging from -0.30 to -0.36, and to social support measured by the Social Support and Activities Scale (O'Brien et al., 1989) from -0.38 to -0.40 (Nolen-Hoeksema et al., 1994). These results suggest that people with low dispositional optimism and poor social support are more likely to report ruminative coping.

A ruminative response style is related to different *beliefs* about emotional coping. People who ruminate more as measured by the short version of the RRS (Jackson & Nolen-Hoeksema, 1998) think that rumination is a response they should have following symptoms of negative emotion ($r = 0.38$). Higher scores on the short version of the RRS are also associated with a lower belief of control over experiencing negative emotions ($r = -0.21$) and a lower sense of mastery about people's own lives ($r = -0.44$) (Nolen-Hoeksema & Jackson, 2001).

Finally, sensitivity of the RRS to therapeutic change is evident in one study looking at the effectiveness of attention training treatment (ATT: Wells, 1990) in the management of recurrent major depression (Papageorgiou & Wells, 2000). Patients were first assigned to no-treatment baseline for three to five weeks. They were then administered five to eight weekly sessions of ATT and followed up at three, six, and twelve months post treatment. Scores on the RRS showed substantial decrements at post treatment, which were maintained in the three follow-up assessments.

Critical evaluation

From the observation of a higher prevalence of depression in women, Nolen-Hoeksema developed a theoretical model that can account for these differences. She showed that women consistently orient their responses toward a ruminative style when feeling depressed. This orientation toward depression leads to the maintenance or even to the growth of depressive symptoms. On the other hand, men would favor distractive responses. Two scales were developed to measure these orientations: the RRS and the DRS. A large set of studies support the reliability of the RRS, with high scores of internal consistency and test–retest stability. However, the factor structure of the scale has not been investigated systematically. Further studies using confirmatory factor analyses need to be conducted to test the replicability of the three-factor solution suggested by Roberts et al. (1998). Conway, Csank, Holm, & Blake (2000) also emphasized that one factor of the RRS ("symptom-based rumination") is more related to previous symptoms of dysphoria than to rumination, suggesting some problems of content validity.

The predictive validity of the scale is evident in a large set of studies showing its ability to predict depression at follow-up, over and above other variables, such as initial depression or additional stressors. Further studies showed that particular beliefs related to social status and emotion regulation in women also have an effect on depression. However, this effect is indirect, being mediated by score on the RRS. Some authors have questioned the predictive validity of the RRS for clinical populations with major depression. However, a recent prospective study suggests that the scale predicts depression severity at 12 months over and above initial depression severity. Finally, recent findings question the specificity of the relationship between a preference for a ruminative style and depression by showing that scores on the RRS are higher for mixed depression/ anxiety than for depression. One important step for the validation of the RRS will be to conduct experimental studies that will allow direct tests of causal effect of rumination on depression and anxiety.

Although the predictive validity of the RRS is well supported, there are few studies that have assessed its discriminant validity. Conclusions about the DRS are more difficult to draw as only a few studies have included the scale. This can be explained by the lack of empirical support for the assumption of a higher level of distractive responses in men when in a depressed mood and the assumption that a higher preference for the distractive style would reduce depression severity (e.g., Nolen-Hoeksema & Morrow, 1991; Nolen-Hoeksema, Morrow & Frederickson, 1993). In fact, Nolen-Hoeksema and colleagues have not included the DRS in their most recent studies.

THE RUMINATION ON SADNESS SCALE (RSS)

Background

A new scale has recently been developed and validated that aims to specifically assess rumination on current feelings of distress (Conway et al., 2000). The authors define rumination on distress as "repetitive thoughts concerning one's present distress and the circumstances surrounding the sadness" (Conway et al., 2000, p. 404). They make an important distinction with Nolen-Hoeksema's view of rumination by excluding social sharing about sadness as part of rumination, while for Nolen-Hoeksema rumination includes disclosing feelings of sadness to others.

Assessment

Items, reliability, stability, and factor structure
Items of the RSS were conceptually derived with the goal of assessing various aspects of rumination specifically related to sadness and distress. For each item, people are asked to refer to situations in which they feel sad, down, or blue. Responses are recorded on a five-point scale ranging from "not at all" to "very much." The RSS includes items measuring the intensity and repetitive quality of ruminative thoughts ("I repeatedly analyze and keep thinking about the reasons for my sadness"), the difficulty with stopping ruminative thoughts ("I have difficulty getting myself to stop thinking about how sad I am"), attempts at understanding the nature of one's distress ("I search my mind repeatedly for events or experiences in my childhood that may help me understand my sad feelings"), and lack of instrumental goal orientation ("I lie in bed and keep thinking about my lack of motivation and wonder about whether it will ever return").

Internal consistency was found to be high ($\alpha = 0.91$) in a sample of 220 students. Test–retest reliability was satisfactory ($r = 0.70$), although it was assessed over a short time interval (two to three weeks). A principal component analysis revealed a one-factor solution (Conway et al., 2000, study 1), which was replicated in a second sample of 201 students (Conway et al., 2000, study 2).

Validity
Evidence for the *concurrent* validity of the scale was provided by high correlation with the RRS ($r = 0.81$) (Conway et al., 2000). The *convergent* and *discriminant* validity of the RSS was assessed by examining its relationship with other sets of constructs. Expected correlations were found ($r = 0.56$) with depression severity as assessed by the BDI (Beck et al., 1961). Partial correlations were computed to assess the overlap between the RSS and the RRS and the severity of depressive symptoms. Results showed that the correlation between the RSS and the BDI, after controlling for the RRS, remained significant ($r = 0.30$), while the correlation between the RRS and the BDI, after controlling for the RSS, did not ($r = 0.88$). This is an indication that the RSS may be a better predictor of depression than the RRS when the overlap between the RRS and RSS is controlled. The relationship between the RSS and the Five-Factor Model was assessed by using the NEO-FFI (Neuroticism Extraversion Openness-Five Factor Inventory) (Costa & McCrae, 1989). A significant and positive correlation was found with neuroticism ($r = 0.66$) and a moderate negative correlation was found with

extraversion $(r = -0.39)$. Low negative correlations were also found with agreeableness $(r = -0.26)$ and with conscientiousness $(r = -0.24)$. As suggested by Conway et al. (2000, p. 422) these results imply that "individuals are more likely to ruminate to the extent that they are more introverted, more antagonistic toward others, and less oriented in a disciplined manner toward goal achievement." Low but significant positive relationships were also found with the tendency for habitual use of imagery $(r = 0.21)$ and for vividness of dreams, daydreams, and imagination $(r = 0.23)$, both assessed by the Individual Differences Questionnaire (Paivio & Harshman, 1983). A moderate relation was observed with absorption $(r = 0.37)$ as assessed by the absorption scale of the Multidimensional Personality Questionnaire (Tellegen, 1982), which suggests that people who ruminate can become highly involved in their own thoughts. Self-reflectiveness, which includes attempts at better identifying one's own needs or feelings, and analyse, the causes of one's own thoughts, feelings, and actions, was strongly related to the RSS $(r = 0.50)$. The RSS was also negatively related to self-deception $(r = -0.28)$ and to impression management $(r = -0.15)$. These results suggest that people with a high tendency for depressive rumination are less likely to be overconfident in their judgments and to present themselves in a socially desirable manner. Finally, the RSS was not related to emotional expression or self-disclosure.

The *predictive* validity of the RSS was investigated in one study (Conway et al., 2000, study 3). People scoring high and low on the scale were exposed to a sad mood induction. Immediately afterwards, half of the participants were asked to wait before completing a self-report measure of how distressed they felt about their two most pressing current concerns (delay condition), while for the other half no waiting period was provided (no-delay condition). Results showed that high RSS scorers were more distressed in the delay condition than in the non-delay condition and that within the delay condition high RSS scorers reported being more distressed than low RSS scorers. On the other hand, low RSS scorers did not differ significantly in the delay and the non-delay condition. These results would suggest that providing high ruminators with an opportunity to ruminate (delay condition) increases their level of distress. Although there was no control on the mental activity of participants during the delay condition, it is assumed that the higher level of reported distress for high RSS scorers was the result of spending a higher proportion of their time ruminating about their sadness.

Critical evaluation

The RSS seems to be a promising scale for assessing depressive rumination. The scale is internally consistent and reliable and assesses a single dimension. The scale also shares a higher proportion of variance with depression severity than the RRS. The convergent and discriminant validity has been demonstrated by expected relationships with broad dimensions of personality, cognitive functions related to imagery, self-deception, and impression management or emotional expressiveness. These results are only preliminary and require further replications. Additional data are also needed to assess the predictive validity of the scale.

MEASUREMENT OF METACOGNITION IN DEPRESSIVE RUMINATION

Metacognition refers to beliefs and appraisals about one's thinking and the ability and strategies used to monitor and regulate cognition (Flavell, 1979; Wells, 2000). Recent theory has closely linked metacognition with repetitive styles of thinking (Wells, 2000; Wells & Matthews, 1994), and instruments have been developed to assess metacognition. A number of measures indexing metacognition are described including: the PBRS (Papageorgiou & Wells, 2001a, b), the NBRS (Papageorgiou, Wells, & Meina, in preparation), the MCQ (Cartwright-Hatton & Wells, 1997), the TCQ (Wells & Davies, 1994), and the White Bear Suppression Inventory (WBSI: Wegner & Zanakos, 1994). Moreover, the results from two naturalistic diary studies aiming at differentiating depressive rumination and anxious worry in terms of metacognitive dimensions (Papageorgiou & Wells, 1999a, b) are presented.

THE POSITIVE AND NEGATIVE BELIEFS ABOUT RUMINATION SCALES (PBRS AND NBRS)

Background

In their S-REF model of emotional disorders, Wells and Matthews (1994) proposed that the knowledge base of emotionally vulnerable individuals could predispose them to select and engage in active and perseverative thinking (i.e., rumination or worry) as a coping strategy. Negative appraisals of this style of thinking are hypothesized to be made once this process is activated. Beliefs that individuals hold about rumination can represent a predisposition for rumination and vulnerability for depression. Positive metacognitive beliefs relate to advantages of rumination while negative metacognitive beliefs reflect disadvantages of rumination. Based on this, two separate measures of positive and negative metacognitive beliefs about rumination have been developed (Papageorgiou & Wells, 2001a, b; Papageorgiou et al., in preparation).

Assessment

Development of the instruments, items, reliability, and validity
Papageorgiou and Wells (2001a) conducted a semistructured interview with 14 patients who met *DSM-IV* criteria for major depressive disorder and did not meet criteria for concurrent Axis I disorders. Patients were asked to think

about the most recent time in which they felt depressed and were ruminating. Various probe questions were then asked concerning the presence and content of metacognitive beliefs about rumination. All of the patients reported advantages and disadvantages of rumination, supporting the assumption that individuals with depression hold both positive and negative metacognitive beliefs about rumination. Positive beliefs were related to rumination as a coping strategy, such as "if I did not ruminate about my feelings, they would never end" or "ruminating about my feelings helps me to understand what went wrong in the past." Negative beliefs were related to the uncontrollability and harm of rumination as well as the interpersonal and social consequences of ruminating (e.g., "ruminating about my problems is uncontrollable," "ruminating could make me harm myself," "everyone would desert me if they knew how much I ruminate about myself," "I could become a complete loser, if I continue to ruminate").

The Positive Beliefs about Rumination Scale (PBRS)

A pool of 16 items was derived from the positive beliefs reported by patients in the study conducted by Papageorgiou and Wells (2001a). Seven items were dropped due to skewness in their distribution. An exploratory factor analysis based on the nine remaining items was performed with a large non-clinical sample. This nine-item PBRS yielded a one-factor solution accounting for 53.5% of the variance. The internal consistency was high ($\alpha = 0.89$). The test–retest reliability of the scale was evidenced by a high Pearson product–moment correlation ($r = 0.85$) and non-significant difference in score over a six-week interval. Support for the concurrent validity of the PBRS was obtained from a significant correlation ($r = 0.43$) with subscale 1 (positive beliefs about worrying) of the MCQ. Evidence supporting the convergent validity of the scale was provided by significant correlations with the RRS ($r = 0.53$), BDI ($r = 0.45$), and trait depression ($r = 0.43$). There was also support for the discriminant validity of the scale as evidenced by a significantly higher correlation with the RRS than the Penn State Worry Questionnaire (PSWQ: Meyer et al., 1990), which specifically measures proneness to anxious worry. Papageorgiou and Wells (2001b) also found that the relationship between PBRS and both state and trait depression was mediated by actual rumination. Finally, the discriminant clinical validity of the scale was investigated with three clinical groups (recurrent major depression, panic disorder with agoraphobia, and social phobia) and a non-clinical control group. As predicted, patients with recurrent major depression scored significantly higher than the other patient groups and the control group. No other significant differences in PBRS scores were found.

The Negative Beliefs about Rumination Scale (NBRS)

An initial pool of 17 items was derived from the negative metacognitive beliefs about rumination reported by patients with depression in the study by

Papageorgiou and Wells (2001a). A factor analysis performed on the data of a large sample of clinically depressed individuals revealed a two-factor solution accounting for 66.4% of the variance and consisting of 13 items. The two factors that emerged were concerned with the uncontrollability and harm of rumination (NBRS1) and the interpersonal and social consequences of ruminating (NBRS2). The Cronbach alphas for the NBRS1 and NBRS2 were 0.80 and 0.83, respectively. Both scales also evidenced acceptable levels of test–retest reliability over a 12-week interval. These instruments have also been found to have good psychometric properties of validity (Papageorgiou et al., in preparation). In terms of concurrent validity, both the NBRS1 and NBRS2 are significantly and positively correlated ($r = 0.66$ and 0.38, respectively) with subscale 2 (negative beliefs about worry) of the MCQ. Moreover, the convergent validity of NBRS1 and NBRS2 is provided by significant correlations with the RRS ($r = 0.51$ and 0.39, respectively), IDD ($r = 0.46$ and 0.35, respectively), and trait depression ($r = 0.45$ and 0.37, respectively). The scales also appear to be correlated more highly with RRS than the PSWQ. Finally, preliminary data indicate that scores on the NBRS1 and NBRS2 can discriminate significantly patients with depression from those with panic disorder and agoraphobia, patients with social phobia, and non-patients.

Critical evaluation

Overall, the PBRS and NBRS seem to be promising scales for assessing a range of positive and negative metacognitive beliefs about rumination in depression. Although initial studies provide good support for the reliability and validity of the PBRS and NBRS, future studies are required to further establish the psychometric properties of these scales. However, both instruments may be useful for eliciting metacognitive beliefs about rumination in clinical assessment and case formulation. With the development of the PBRS and NBRS, Papageorgiou and Wells (2003) have examined the relationships between rumination, depression, and specific metacognitions. Grounded on Wells and Matthews' (1994) generic information processing model of emotional disorders, Papageorgiou and Wells (2003) have proposed a specific clinical metacognitive model of rumination and depression. Recent tests of this model provide evidence of its fit.

THE METACOGNITIONS QUESTIONNAIRE (MCQ)

Background

Following Wells' (1995) model, people with generalized anxiety disorder (GAD) hold both negative and positive beliefs about worry. Negative beliefs are related to potential dangers of worrying, while positive ones are linked to supposedly beneficial effects of using worry as a coping strategy. These beliefs can lead to the development of dysfunctional worry, especially when people start to worry about worry. Given the importance of metacognitions in the development and maintenance of problematic worry, Cartwright-Hatton and Wells (1997) developed the MCQ, a self-report measure to assess beliefs about worry, and other metacognitive judgments and processes.

Assessment

Items, reliability, stability, and factor structure
The MCQ is a 65-item scale that assesses 5 factors. The first one (*positive beliefs about worrying*) includes items concerning the beneficial outcomes of worrying for planning, problem-solving, and coping, such as "worrying helps me to avoid disastrous situations" or "worrying helps me to plan the future more effectively." The second one (*negative beliefs about worry*) reflects the belief that worry is uncontrollable together with beliefs about the dangers of worry. Example items are: "when I start worrying I cannot stop" and "worrying is dangerous for me." Factor 3 deals with *lack of cognitive confidence for one's own memory and attentional abilities*, with such items as "my memory can mislead me at times" or "I have difficulty keeping my mind focused on one thing for a long time." Factor 4 involves items related to *negative beliefs about thoughts* like "if I did not control a worrying thought, and then it happened, it would be my fault" or "I could be punished for not having certain thoughts." Factor 5 is related to preoccupation with one's own thought processes or *cognitive self-consciousness*. Example items are: "I think a lot about my thoughts" or "I pay close attention to the way my mind works." The internal reliability of the scale is satisfactory with Cronbach alphas ranging from 0.72 (factor 5) to 0.89 (factor 2). The intercorrelations between the factors were relatively low, ranging from 0.08 to 0.43, suggesting that relatively distinct aspects of metacognitions are assessed by the MCQ. Test–retest at five weeks for the total scale was high ($r = 0.94$).

Validity
Data on the convergent validity of the scale support its close relationship with anxious symptomatology as evidenced by strong correlations with the Spielberger Trait Anxiety Inventory ($r = 0.68$) (STAI: Spielberger, Gorsuch, Lushene, Vagg, & Jacobs, 1983) and with the Anxious Thoughts Inventory ($r = 0.74$) (AnTI: Wells, 1994). The discriminant validity of the scale was supported by comparing scores on the MCQ in a group of people with GAD, obsessive–compulsive disorder (OCD), a clinical group with other emotional disorders and a control group. The GAD and OCD groups scored higher than the two other groups on factor 2 (negative beliefs). GAD and OCD groups also scored higher than the other clinical group on factor 3 (cognitive confidence) and higher than the non-clinical group on factor 4 (negative beliefs about worry). Regression analyses also showed that proneness

to worry was predicted by most of the factors of the MCQ. Importantly, both negative and positive beliefs were related to higher prevalence of worry. Sensitivity to change was demonstrated by Papageorgiou and Wells (2000). Scores on the MCQ decreased post treatment and remained low during the follow-up assessments at three, six, and twelve months in patients with recurrent major depression.

Critical evaluation

The MCQ was devised along the lines of the model developed by Wells (1995) of the importance of metacognitions related to worry in GAD. The scale consists of five factors, among which three are related to positive and negative beliefs people hold about their worries. Empirical data suggest that negative beliefs about uncontrollability and danger are particularly characteristic of GAD and OCD.

THE THOUGHT CONTROL QUESTIONNAIRE (TCQ)

Background

Wells and Davies (1994) reported that intrusive thoughts are a frequent phenomenon in normal and clinical populations with both anxiety disorders (such as OCD or PTSD) and depression. These intrusive thoughts usually elicit feelings of distress and discomfort. In reaction to these negative feelings, people develop various strategies for controlling further occurrences of intrusive thoughts. "The Thought Control Questionnaire (TCQ) was developed to provide a measure of the various techniques which individuals use to control unpleasant and unwanted thoughts" (Wells & Davies, 1994, p. 875).

Assessment

Items, reliability, stability, and factor structure
The TCQ is a five-factor instrument (distraction, social control, worry, punishment, and reappraisal), with six items for each factor. People are instructed to indicate the techniques they generally use to control unpleasant and/or unwanted thoughts on a four-point rating scale, ranging from "never" to "almost always." Examples of items include: "I occupy myself with work instead" (*distraction*), "I ask my friends if they have similar thoughts" (*social control*), "I focus on different negative thoughts" (*worry*), "I punish myself for thinking the thought" (*punishment*), and "I question the reasons for having the thought" (*reappraisal*). Item content suggests that three factors can be used as potential measures of rumination (worry, punishment, and reappraisal). The distraction measure is similar to the DRS scale from the RSQ (Nolen-Hoeksema & Morrow, 1991), and the social control factor investigates

aspects related to inhibition vs. free expression through interpersonal ways ("I keep the thought to myself") or interpersonal ones ("I talk to a friend about the thought").

Internal consistency was found to be acceptable ($\alpha = 0.64$ for punishment, $\alpha = 0.67$ for reappraisal) to good ($\alpha = 0.72$ for distraction, $\alpha = 0.79$ for social control, and $\alpha = 0.71$ for worry). Test–retest reliability was examined at six-week intervals. Coefficients ranged from 0.67 for punishment to 0.83 for social control, demonstrating acceptable to very good stability (Wells & Davies, 1994).

Validity
Discriminant and *convergent* validity was assessed by administrating the TCQ together with measures of stress vulnerability (such as neuroticism and extra-version), trait anxiety, self-consciousness, and measures of perceived lack of control over thinking (such as worry). Among the three factors assessing rumination, worry and punishment presented a very similar pattern of significant relationships with neuroticism, trait anxiety, social and metaworry. Reappraisal, on the other hand, was only related to private self-consciousness. These results suggest that worry and punishment subscales are specifically related to emotional vulnerability, while reappraisal may not. The relatively modest intercorrelations between the subscales (maximum $r = 0.27$ between worry and punishment) suggests that the subscales are measuring empirically distinct dimensions of thought control. Three of the strategies investigated seem to be related to rumination. Among them, two (worry and punishment) are primarily related to anxious symptomatology as evidenced by moderate correlations with trait anxiety, while the relationship with depression as measured by the BDI is low for worry ($r = 0.22$) and for punishment ($r = 0.19$) (Siegle, 2000). The reappraisal subscale, however, is neither related to anxious symptomatology, nor to depression (both $r = 0.14$) (Siegle, 2000). The TCQ subscales appear sensitive to recovery in a group of mixed patients with PTSD and depression (Reynolds & Wells, 1999). Endorsement of TCQ worry following road traffic accidents is positively associated with the development of PTSD three months later (Holeva, Tarrier, & Wells, 2001).

Critical evaluation

The TCQ appears to be a reliable instrument that is able to discriminate among different thought control strategies following the experience of intrusive thoughts. Further data are necessary, however, in order to replicate results obtained by Wells and Davies (1994) and to collect data on the predictive validity of the subscales and the total TCQ score. As noted by these authors: "The development of the TCQ is an initial step in research currently in progress which is aimed at developing measures of metacognition that may contribute to our understanding of the problem of unwanted intrusive thoughts" (Wells & Davies, 1994, p. 877).

THE WHITE BEAR SUPPRESSION INVENTORY (WBSI)

Background

Wegner and his colleagues have conducted extensive research on the paradoxical effects of thought suppression as a strategy of mental control (see Wegner & Pennebaker, 1993). Thought suppression has two main consequences. First, it is only successful for a short time. The suppressed thought usually bounces back quickly. Second, the occurrence of the suppressed thought in mind is higher than before the strategy of thought suppression has been initiated. This delayed increase in the frequency of the suppressed thought has been called the rebound effect (see Wegner, 1992, 1994). Automatic and voluntary processes are thought to explain this effect (e.g., Wegner & Erber, 1992).

An important finding from Wegner's studies was that "suppressing distressing emotional thoughts increases the likelihood that the individual will fail to habituate to emotional stimuli relevant to those thoughts" (Wegner & Zanakos, 1994, p. 619). A direct outcome is that chronic thought suppression would be related to hypersensitivity to depressive and anxious thoughts and would lead to symptoms of depression and anxiety. The WBSI (Wegner & Zanakos, 1994) was developed to assess people's tendency for chronic thought suppression.

Assessment

Items, reliability, stability, and factor structure
A list of 72 items that tapped suppression and control of thoughts and emotions was first developed. A three-factor solution (thought suppression, negative affectivity, and concentration) was found. Only items that specifically loaded on the thought suppression factor were retained. The resulting 33 items were administered to a large group of psychology students. A factor analysis was then conducted with the same purpose of isolating items that loaded specifically on the thought suppression factor. This led to a retention of 15 items that loaded on a single factor. The scale includes such items as "there are things that I try not to think about," "I have thoughts I cannot stop," or "there are thoughts that keep jumping into my head." Higher scores on the scale represent a higher tendency to suppress thoughts. Reliability was high with Cronbach alphas ranging from 0.87 to 0.89. The measure was found to be reliable over time as evidenced by test–retest after one week ($r = 0.92$) and one month ($r = 0.69$) (Wegner & Zanakos, 1994).

Validity

The WBSI was consistently related to depression as measured by the BDI, with correlations ranging from 0.44 to 0.52 (Wegner & Zanakos, 1994). This result is consistent with observations that depressed individuals report frequent attempts to suppress negative thoughts (Wenzlaff, Wegner, & Klein, 1991: Wenzlaff, Wegner, & Roper, 1988). Wegner and Zanakos tested the possibility that among depressed people those who chronically suppress their thoughts related to their depressed mood and particularly dislike having these thoughts are more at risk for later depression (Wegner & Zanakos, 1994, study 5). They developed a brief measure called "depression sensitivity" to assess the extent to which people find it disturbing, scary, or socially unacceptable having these negative thoughts. To test their hypothesis, they conducted a hierarchical regression analysis to predict BDI scores from WBSI scores, depression sensitivity scores, and the interaction between these two scales. Results showed that using thought suppression as a mental control strategy (as evidenced by high scores on the WBSI) that is sensitive to depressing thoughts and the interaction of both variables predicted BDI scores. As Wegner and Zanakos (1994, p. 631) noted: "The link between thought suppression and depression suggests that any tendency to suppress thoughts, even without a strong desire to avoid depression, may be tied to depression. The association of depression sensitivity with depression, in turn, suggests that a desire to escape the negative affective state may be associated with depression even when thought suppression is not present."

Critical evaluation

The WBSI is a reliable and valid scale. However, the items do not appear to solely assess suppression, as some of them appear to focus on the uncontrollability of thoughts. The instrument does not provide a means of assessing different types of suppression strategies. The interaction of chronic thought suppression with depression sensitivity (i.e., people who are particularly averse to negative thoughts) seems to make people even more at risk for depression.

DIARY ASSESSMENT OF METACOGNITIVE DIMENSIONS OF DEPRESSIVE AND ANXIOUS THOUGHTS

Papageorgiou and Wells (1999a) examined the similarities and differences in naturally occurring depressive thoughts (rumination) and anxious thoughts (worry) and whether people have different metacognitions in relation to them. Fifty-four non-clinical participants were asked to report two depressive and two anxious thoughts that occurred naturally during a two-week period in a diary that assessed the content, duration, process, and metacognitive dimensions for each type of thought. Overall, the two categories of thought were found to be similar, although some differences emerged. Anxious (worrisome) thoughts were reported as consisting of more verbal content, greater compulsion to act, more effort in problem-solving, and more confidence in the ability to problem-solve, while depressive (ruminative) thoughts were assessed as more past-oriented. Relationships between dimensions of depressive and anxious thoughts and affective responses for each type of thoughts were also found. When the overlap between depression and anxiety was controlled, specific dimensions of thinking were found to be associated with emotional intensity. These data show that ruminative thinking is associated with metacognitive processes and that the metacognitions people hold about their depressive and anxious thoughts evidence some specificity that can be distinguished empirically. The generalizability of these findings has been demonstrated in samples of patients with major depressive disorder and patients with panic disorder and agoraphobia (Papageorgiou & Wells, 1999b).

INDIRECT MEASURES OF RUMINATION

BACKGROUND

All the measures of rumination reviewed up to now are based on self-report measures. Self-report measures are based on the assumptions that people have direct access to their internal responses and that they are willing to give an accurate report of them. However, self-reports increase the risk of reconstruction biases (e.g., Brewer, 1986; Conway, 1990). Also, people have only a very low level of awareness of the cognitive processes that mediate inferences and the production of complex behaviors (Nisbett & Wilson, 1977a, b). To overcome these problems, some recent attempts have been made to rely more on performance measures or on psychophysiological or neuroanatomical correlates of rumination. We will present one recent empirical study supporting these alternatives to self-report measures (for physiological and neuroanatomical correlates of rumination, see Chapter 5 by Siegle and Thayer in this book).

We recently conducted two studies investigating the relationship between the number of intrusive ruminations measured immediately after participants were exposed to a negatively valenced situation (immediate intrusive ruminations or IIRs) and an index of the severity of intrusive ruminations that occurred in the following 24 hours (retrospective intrusive ruminations, or RIRs) (Luminet, Rimé, & Wagner, 2003). The existing literature does not provide a consensus as regards the most appropriate way of assessing intrusive ruminations related to a specific stressful situation. Two different approaches are typically found. The first one (later referred to as the "intrusion-signaling approach") investigates intrusive ruminations in the laboratory immediately after participants have been exposed to an emotion-inducing stimulus (e.g., Horowitz, 1969, 1975; Horowitz & Becker, 1971a, b, c, 1973). The second approach (later referred to as the "retrospective approach") investigates the degree of severity of intrusive ruminations related to personal emotional events using self-report scales. Measures are generally taken some weeks or some months after the event occurred. This approach commonly involves clinical populations with a high prevalence of intrusive rumination (e.g., de Silva & Marks, 1999; Janoff-Bulman, 1989; Rachman & de Silva, 1978; Tait & Silver, 1989; Timko & Janoff-Bulman, 1985; Wortman & Silver, 1987, 1989), but was also conducted with non-clinical populations (e.g., Rimé, Mesquita, Philippot, & Boca, 1991). If these two types of measure are highly correlated, it would indicate that the two categories of research presented above support each other rather well in assessing intrusive ruminations. The goal of the studies conducted by Luminet et al. (2003) was, first, to test whether an ecologically valid measure of intrusive rumination can reliably predict a set of self-report measures and, second, to establish the degree of relationship between the intrusion-signaling approach and the retrospective approach.

Participants ($N = 61$ in study 1, $N = 41$ in study 2) first listened to a negatively valenced situation (testimony of a woman who had been severely injured and burned in a car accident). Pilot investigations showed that the story was able to elicit a moderate level of disruptiveness, that the main emotion involved was sadness, and that the story was perceived as highly self-relevant. Next, participants performed an attentional task during which they were asked to press a key on a computer keyboard each time they had a thought or an image related to the story they had heard. This measure was designed to parallel the occurrence of intrusive ruminations in a natural context (i.e., thoughts that interrupt ongoing activities). During the second session, participants completed a set of questionnaires, including the RIRs. The RIRs are composed of six seven-point scales that were selected as assessing important aspects of intrusive ruminations. They were all related to the occurrence of intrusive ruminations from the time participants left the laboratory to the time they came back to the laboratory 24 hours later. Scales were about the extent to which the thoughts were (1) vivid, (2) captivated attention, (3) disrupted people's ongoing activities, (4) entered people's minds suddenly, (5) were difficult to dismiss, and (6) if people actively tried to dismiss the thoughts when they appeared. The internal reliability of the scale was satisfactory ($\alpha = 0.75$ for study 1, $\alpha = 0.84$ for study 2). Results showed a positive correlation between IIRs and RIRs ($r = 0.41$) in study 1 and ($r = 0.34$) in study 2. The significant relationships obtained suggest that the intrusion-signaling approach and the retrospective approach do to some extent assess the same features of intrusive ruminations. Thus, these studies represent a step in filling the gap between the "retrospective approach," in which people report still having intrusive ruminations several months or years after experiencing highly emotional situations (e.g., Lehman, Wortman, & Williams, 1987; Tait & Silver, 1989), and the "intrusion-signaling approach," in which reports of intrusive ruminations were restricted to the few minutes following an emotional stimulus (e.g., Horowitz, 1969, 1975; Horowitz

& Becker, 1971a, b, 1973). However, the relatively small amount of shared variance between the IIRs and RIRs indicates that they may not assess the same aspects of depressive rumination. The two approaches for assessing intrusive ruminations are probably worth using together.

Siegle (2000) recently brought additional information on the discriminant and the convergent validity of the RIRs. First, RIRs were related to the RRS (Nolen-Hoeksema & Morrow, 1991), $r = 0.29$ and they correlate with the BDI (Beck et al., 1961), $r = 0.28$. A non-significant relationship was found with the Emotion Control Questionnaire (ECQ: Roger & Najarian, 1989), a measure assessing the degree to which individuals inhibit unwanted thoughts and that is related to trait anxiety. Together, these results suggest that RIRs are more related to depressive than to anxious rumination.

Critical evaluation

The two reported studies suggest a positive relation between an ecologically valid measure of intrusive ruminations following a stressful situation and a self-report retrospective measure assessing the main aspects of intrusive rumination. However, the modest correlation between the IIRs and RIRs suggests they may not be measuring the same construct.

CONVERGENCE AND DIVERGENCE IN MEASURES OF RUMINATION

A large number of instruments have been reported, with only very few studies examining whether these instruments represent similar aspects of rumination. Recently, Siegle (2000) examined convergence and divergence in a large set of self-report measures of rumination. A sample of 189 undergraduate students completed seven measures of rumination including: the RRS (Nolen-Hoeksema & Morrow, 1991), the TCQ (Wells & Davies, 1994), the diary of process and metacognitive dimensions of depressive and anxious thoughts (Papageorgiou & Wells, 1999a, b), the Impact of Event Scale (IES: Horowitz, Wilner, & Alvarez, 1979), the Retrospective Intrusive Ruminations Scale (RIRS: Luminet et al., 2002), the Multidimensional Rumination Questionnaire (MRQ: Fritz, 1999), and the rehearsal subscale of the ECQ (Roger & Najarian, 1989). Siegle (2000) first examined the extent to which these measures index a single construct. Results indicated that both at the scale level and at the item level the instruments used measure different types of rumination rather than a single construct. The intercorrelations between the scales further support these results with correlations ranging from 0.10 to 0.81. The highest correlations were found among the subscales of the MRQ. High correlations were also found between the RRS and the MRQ subscales on emotion ($r = 0.50$) and on search for meaning ($r = 0.46$), between the RRS and the TCQ subscales on reappraisal ($r = 0.49$) and worry ($r = 0.44$), and between the IES and the RIRS ($r = 0.47$), and the MRQ subscale on emotion ($r = 0.45$).

The factor structure was then examined by an exploratory principal component analysis in which participants' scores on the rumination scales were entered. Three factors were retained, explaining 62.5% of the total variance. Factor 1 represented all scales from the MRQ. Factor 2 included *trait-related* measures of rumination (such as the RRS), the TCQ subscales on worry, punishment, and reappraisal. Factor 3 typically assessed *state-related* dimensions of ruminations, including the IES, the diary of metacognitive dimensions of depressive and anxious thoughts and the RIRs.

The relationship of these scales with depressive symptomatology was assessed by administering the BDI to the whole sample. A multiple regression analysis was performed in which all of the rumination scales served as potential predictors of depression. Highest semipartial correlations with BDI were found for the RRS, the TCQ subscale on reappraisal, and the ECQ subscale on rehearsal. Together, the rumination scales explained 36.4% of the variance in dysphoria, 25% being accounted for by the RRS on its own.

Critical evaluation

Overall, the results reported by Siegle (2000) suggest that studies investigating rumination by using single scales need to specify the type of rumination being examined. When investigating broad aspects of rumination, a battery of several scales is highly recommended. Techniques that aggregate scales also offer a more internally consistent solution than examining the scales separately. Finally, although the different scales examined share some variance with depression, they investigate distinct content and processes.

SUMMARY AND CONCLUSIONS

This chapter started with an extensive review of two instruments that are specifically intended to measure depressive rumination. Both the RRS and RSS show good internal consistency and test–retest reliability. The scales differ in the content of depressive rumination considered. In the RSS, the items are only related to the ideation part of rumination, while in the RRS other aspects are considered, such as disclosing sadness to others. The RSS has a single factor structure while the RRS has three factors. The data on the RSS suggest a higher relationship with depression than for the RRS. Recent investigations on the RRS suggest that people scoring high on the scale are equally likely to be anxious or depressed and that the highest scores are found in people presenting with a mixed anxiety/depressive symptomatology

(Nolen-Hoeksema, 2000). These results indicate that the border between anxious and depressive rumination may not be delineated with the RRS. Predictive validity has only been investigated extensively for the RRS.

Measures of metacognitions in depressive rumination represent a promising area that may contribute to understanding the maintenance of rumination and the shift from functional to dysfunctional rumination. The PBRS and the NBRS represent two new tools for the assessment of metacognitions in depressive rumination. Other measures of metacognition also focus on particular strategies people develop in reaction to the negative feelings triggered by their ruminations (TCQ) and a range of specific beliefs about worry (MCQ).

Most measures of depressive rumination are self-report scales. Future investigations need to focus on indirect measures that rely less on introspective abilities. More ecologically valid techniques, using indirect techniques, are required. Self-report measures are still important as they are easy to administer to large groups.

The goal of future investigations should be to assess the overlap of existing scales, rather than the development of new scales. The study conducted by Siegle (2000) clearly emphasized the lack of convergence in some self-report measures of depressive rumination. However, rumination may well be a multi-component process and high levels of convergence in different measures of separate components would not be expected.

ACKNOWLEDGMENTS

Olivier Luminet is research associate at the Belgian National Fund for Scientific Research and associate professor at the University of Louvain in Louvain-la-Neuve (UCL) and at the University of Brussels (ULB). Preparation of this chapter was supported by grants 1.5.124.00 and 1.5.146.02 from the Belgian National Fund for Scientific Research. The author would like to thank Costas Papageorgiou and Adrian Wells for their helpful comments in previous versions of this manuscript.

REFERENCES

Abramson, L. Y., Metalsky, G. L., & Alloy, L. B. (1989). Hopelessness depression: A theory based subtype of depression. *Psychological Review*, **96**, 358–372.

Alloy, L. B., Kelly, K., Mineka, S., & Clements, C. (1990). Comorbidity in anxiety and depressive disorders: A helplessness/hopelessness perspective. In: J. D. Maser & C. R. Cloninger (eds), *Comorbidity of Mood and Anxiety Disorders* (pp. 3–12). Washington, DC: American Psychiatric Association.

Bagby, R. M., Rector, N. A., Segal, Z. V., Joffe, R. T., Levitt, A. J., Kennedy, S. H., & Levitan, R. D. (1999). Rumination and distraction in major depression: Assessing response to pharmacological treatment. *Journal of Affective Disorders*, **55**, 225–229.

Beck, A. T. & Steer, R. A. (1990). *Manual for the Revised Beck Anxiety Inventory*. San Antonio, TX: Psychological Corporation.

Beck, A. T., Ward, C. H., Mendelson, M., Mock, J., & Eerbaugh, J. (1961). An inventory for measuring depression. *Archives of General Psychiatry*, **4**, 561–571.

Brewer, W. F. (1986). What is autobiographical memory? In: D. Rubin (ed.), *Autobiographical Memory* (pp. 25–49). Cambridge, UK: Cambridge University Press.

Cartwright-Hatton, S. & Wells, A. (1997). Beliefs about worry and intrusions: The metacognitions questionnaire and its correlates. *Journal of Anxiety Disorders*, **11**, 279–296.

Conway, M., Csank, P. A. R., Holm, S. L., & Blake, C. K. (2000). On assessing individual differences in rumination on sadness. *Journal of Personality Assessment*, **75**, 404–425.

Conway, M. A. (1990). *Autobiographical Memory: An Introduction*. Milton Keynes, UK: Open University Press.

Costa, P. T. J. & McCrae, R. R. (1989). *The NEO-PI/FFI Manual Supplement*. Odessa, FL: Psychological Assessment Resources.

de Silva, P. & Marks, M. (1999). Intrusive thinking in post-traumatic stress disorder. In: W. Yule (eds), *Post-traumatic Stress Disorders: Concepts and Therapy* (pp. 161–175). Chichester, UK: John Wiley and Sons.

Eysenck, H. J. & Eysenck, S. B. G. (1964). *Eysenck Personality Inventory*. San Diego, CA: Educational and Industrial Testing Service.

First, M. B., Spitzer, R. L., Gibbon, M., & Williams, J. B. W. (1995). *Structured Clinical Interview for DSM-IV Axis I Disorders* (Patient Edition, SCID-I/P). New York: New York State Psychiatric Institute.

Flavell, J. H. (1979). Metacognition and metacognitive monitoring: A new area of cognitive-developmental inquiry. *American Psychologist*, **34**, 906–911.

Fritz, H. L. (1999). Rumination and adjustment to a first coronary event. *Psychosomatic Medicine*, **61**, 105.

Hamilton, M. (1960). A rating scale for depression. *Journal of Neurology, Neurosurgery, and Psychiatry*, **23**, 56–62.

Holeva, V., Tarrier, N., & Wells, A. (2001). Prevalence and predictors of acute stress disorder and PTSD following road traffic accidents: Thought control strategies and social support. *Behavior Therapy*, **32**, 65–83.

Horowitz, M. J. (1969). Psychic trauma: Return of images after a stressful film. *Archives of General Psychiatry*, **20**, 552–559.

Horowitz, M. J. (1975). Intrusive and repetitive thoughts after experimental stress. *Archives of General Psychiatry*, **32**, 1457–1463.

Horowitz, M. J. & Becker, S. S. (1971a). Cognitive response to stress and experimental demand. *Journal of Abnormal Psychology*, **78**(1), 86–92.

Horowitz, M. J. & Becker, S. S. (1971b). Cognitive response to stressful stimuli. *Archives of General Psychiatry*, **25**, 419–428.

Horowitz, M. J. & Becker, S. S. (1971c). The compulsion to repeat trauma: Experimental study of intrusive thinking after stress. *Journal of Nervous and Mental Disease*, **153**, 32–34.

Horowitz, M. J. & Becker, S. S. (1973). Cognitive response to erotic and stressful films. *Archives of General Psychiatry*, **29**, 81–84.

Horowitz, M. J., Wilner, N., & Alvarez, W. (1979). Impact of Event Scale: A study of subjective stress. *Psychosomatic Medicine*, **41**, 209–218.

Jackson, B. & Nolen-Hoeksema, S. (1998). The Emotion-Focused Coping Questionnaire. Unpublished manuscript, University of Michigan at Ann Arbor.

Janoff-Bulman, R. (1989). Assumptive worlds and the stress of traumatic events: Applications of the schema construct. *Social Cognition*, **7**, 113–136.

Just, N. & Alloy, L. B. (1997). The response styles theory of depression: Tests and an extension of the theory. *Journal of Abnormal Psychology*, **106**, 221–229.

Lehman, D. R., Wortman, C. B., & Williams, A. F. (1987). Long-term effects of losing a spouse or child in a motor vehicle crash. *Journal of Personality and Social Psychology*, **52**, 218–231.

Luminet, O., Rimé, B., & Wagner, H. L. (2003). Intrusive ruminations, meta-cognitions about intrusive ruminations, and social sharing of emotion following exposure to a negatively valenced situation. Manuscript submitted for publication.

Lyubomirsky, S., Tucker, K., Caldwell, N. D., & Berg, K. (1999). Why ruminators are poor problem solvers: Clues from the phenomenology of dysphoric rumination. *Journal of Personality and Social Psychology*, **77**, 1041–1060.

Meyer, T. J., Miller, M. L., Metzger, R. L., & Borkovec, T. D. (1990). Development and validation of the Penn State Worry Questionnaire. *Behaviour Research and Therapy*, **28**, 487–495.

Nisbett, J. & Wilson, T. D. (1977a). Telling more than we can know: Verbal reports of mental processes. *Psychological Review*, **84**, 231–259.

Nisbett, J. & Wilson, T. D. (1977b). The halo effect: Evidence for unconscious alteration of judgment. *Journal of Personality and Social Psychology*, **35**, 250–256.

Nolan, S. A., Roberts, J. E., & Gotlib, I. H. (1998). Neuroticism and ruminative response style as predictors of change in depressive symptomatology. *Cognitive Therapy and Research*, **22**, 445–455.

Nolen-Hoeksema, S. (1987). Sex differences in unipolar depression: Evidence and theory. *Psychological Bulletin*, **101**(2), 259–282.

Nolen-Hoeksema, S. (2000). The role of rumination in depressive disorders and mixed anxiety/depressive symptoms. *Journal of Abnormal Psychology*, **109**, 504–511.

Nolen-Hoeksema, S. & Davis, C. G. (1999). "Thanks for sharing that": Ruminators and their social support network. *Journal of Personality and Social Psychology*, **77**, 801–814.

Nolen-Hoeksema, S. & Jackson, B. (2001). Mediators of the gender difference in rumination. *Woman Psychology Quarterly*, **25**, 37–47.

Nolen-Hoeksema, S., Larson, J., & Grayson, C. (1999). Explaining the gender difference in depressive symptoms. *Journal of Personality and Social Psychology*, **77**, 1061–1072.

Nolen-Hoeksema, S. & Morrow, J. (1991). A prospective study of depression and posttraumatic stress symptoms after a natural disaster: The 1989 Loma Prieta earthquake. *Journal of Personality and Social Psychology*, **61**, 115–121.

Nolen-Hoeksema, S., Morrow, J., & Frederickson, B. L. (1993). Response styles and the duration of episodes of depressed mood. *Journal of Abnormal Psychology*, **102**, 20–28.

Nolen-Hoeksema, S., Parker, L. E., & Larson, J. (1994). Ruminative coping with depressed mood following loss. *Journal of Personality and Social Psychology*, **67**, 92–104.

O'Brien, K., Wortman, C. B., Kessler, R. C., & Joseph, J. G. (1989). Social conflict and social support in a cohort at risk for AIDS. Unpublished manuscript, Institute for Social Research, University of Michigan, Ann Arbor.

Paivio, A. & Harshman, R. (1983). Factor analysis of a questionnaire on imagery and verbal habits and skills. *Canadian Journal of Psychology*, **37**, 461–483.

Papageorgiou, C. & Wells, A. (1999a). Process and metacognitive dimensions of depressive and anxious thoughts and relationships with emotional intensity. *Clinical Psychology and Psychotherapy*, **6**, 156–162.

Papageorgiou, C. & Wells, A. (1999b). Dimensions of depressive rumination and anxious worry: A comparative study. Paper presented at the *33rd Annual Convention of the Association for Advancement of Behavior Therapy*, Toronto.

Papageorgiou, C. & Wells, A. (2000). Treatment of recurrent major depression with attention training. *Cognitive and Behavioral Practice*, **7**, 407–413.

Papageorgiou, C. & Wells, A. (2001a). Metacognitive beliefs about rumination in recurrent major depression. *Cognitive and Behavioral Practice*, **8**, 160–164.

Papageorgiou, C. & Wells, A. (2001b). Positive beliefs about depressive rumination: Development and preliminary validation of a self-report scale. *Behavior Therapy*, **32**, 13–26.

Papageorgiou, C. & Wells, A. (2003). An empirical test of a clinical metacognitive model of rumination and depression. *Cognitive Therapy and Research*, **27**, 261–273.

Papageorgiou, C., Wells, A., & Meina, L. J. (2003). Development and preliminary validation of the Negative Beliefs about Rumination Scale. Manuscript in preparation.

Rachman, S. J. & de Silva, P. (1978). Abnormal and normal obsessions. *Behavior Research and Therapy*, **16**, 233–248.

Reynolds, M. & Wells, A. (1999). The Thought Control Questionnaire: Psychometric properties in a clinical sample, and relationships with PTSD and depression. *Psychological Medicine*, **29**, 1089–1099.

Rimé, B., Mesquita, B., Philippot, P., & Boca, S. (1991). Beyond the emotional event: Six studies on the social sharing of emotion. *Cognition and Emotion*, **5**, 435–465.

Roberts, J. E., Gilboa, E., & Gotlib, I. H. (1998). Ruminative response style and vulnerability to episodes of dysphoria: Gender, neuroticism, and episode duration. *Cognitive Therapy and Research*, **22**, 401–423.

Roger, D. & Najarian, B. (1989). The construction and validation of a new scale for measuring emotion control. *Personality and Individual Differences*, **10**, 845–853.

Scheier, M. F. & Carver, C. S. (1985). Optimism, coping, and health: Assessment and implications of generalized outcome expectancies. *Health Psychology*, **4**, 219–247.

Siegle, G. (2000). Convergence and divergence in measures of rumination. Paper presented at the *Annual Convention of the Association for Advancement of Behavior Therapy, New Orleans*.

Spielberger, C. D., Gorsuch, R. L., Lushene, R., Vagg, P. R., & Jacobs, G. A. (1983). *Manual for the State–trait Anxiety Inventory (STAI: form Y)*. Palo Alto, CA: Consulting Psychologists Press.

Tait, R. & Silver, R. C. (1989). Coming to terms with major negative life events. In: J. S. Uleman & J. A. Bargh (eds), *Unintended Thoughts* (pp. 351–382). New York: Guilford Press.

Tellegen, A. (1982). *Brief Manual for the Differential Personality Questionnaire.* Minneapolis, MN: Author.

Timko, C. & Janoff-Bulman, R. (1985). Attributions, vulnerability, and psychological adjustment: The case of breast cancer. *Health Psychology*, **4**, 521–544.

Treynor, W., Gonzalez, R., & Nolen-Hoeksema, S. (2003). Rumination reconsidered: A psychometric analysis. *Cognitive Therapy and Research.*

Wegner, D. M. (1992). You can't always think what you want: Problems in the suppression of unwanted thoughts. *Advances in Experimental Social Psychology*, **25**, 193–225.

Wegner, D. M. (1994). Ironic processes of mental control. *Psychological Review*, **101**, 34–52.

Wegner, D. M. & Erber, R. (1992). The hyperaccessibility of suppressed thoughts. *Journal of Personality and Social Psychology*, **63**, 903–912.

Wegner, D. M. & Pennebaker, J. W. (1993). *Handbook of Mental Control.* Englewood Cliffs, NJ: Prentice Hall.

Wegner, D. M. & Zanakos, S. (1994). Chronic thought suppression. *Journal of Personality*, **62**, 615–640.

Wells, A. (1990). Panic disorder in association with relaxation-induced anxiety: An attentional training approach to treatment. *Behavior Therapy*, **21**, 273–280.

Wells, A. (1994). A multidimensional measure of worry: Development and preliminary validation of the Anxious Thoughts Inventory. *Anxiety, Stress, and Coping*, **6**, 288–299.

Wells, A. (1995). Meta-cognition and worry: A cognitive model of generalised anxiety disorder. *Behavioural and Cognitive Psychotherapy*, **23**, 301–320.

Wells, A. (2000). *Emotional Disorders and Metacognition: Innovative Cognitive Therapy.* Chichester, UK: John Wiley & Sons.

Wells, A. & Davies, M. I. (1994). The thought control questionnaire: A measure of individual differences in the control of unwanted thoughts. *Behaviour Research and Therapy*, **32**, 871–878.

Wells, A. & Matthews, G. (1994). *Attention and Emotion: A Clinical Perspective.* Hillsdale, NJ: Lawrence Erlbaum.

Wenzlaff, R. M., Wegner, D. M., & Klein, S. B. (1991). The role of thought suppression in the bonding of thoughts and mood. *Journal of Personality and Social Psychology*, **60**, 500–508.

Wenzlaff, R. M., Wegner, D. M., & Roper, D. W. (1988). Depression and mental control: The resurgence of unwanted negative thoughts. *Journal of Personality and Social Psychology*, **55**, 882–892.

Wortman, C. B. & Silver, R. C. (1987). Coping with irrevocable loss. In: G. R. V. Bos & B. K. Bryant (eds), *Cataclysms, Crises, and Catastrophes: Psychology in Action* (pp. 189–235). Washington, DC: American Psychological Association.

Wortman, C. B. & Silver, R. C. (1989). The myths of coping with loss. *Journal of Consulting and Clinical Psychology*, **57**, 349–357.

Zimmerman, M. & Coryell, W. (1987). The Inventory to Diagnose Depression, Lifetime Version. *Acta Psychiatrica Scandinavica*, **75**, 495–499.

Zimmerman, M., Coryell, W., Corenthal, C., & Wilson, S. (1986). A self-report scale to diagnose major depressive disorder. *Archives of General Psychiatry*, **43**, 1076–1081.

11 Psychological Treatment of Rumination

CHRISTINE PURDON

Department of Psychology, University of Waterloo, Ontario, Canada

Negative, unwelcome thoughts are the primary complaint of sufferers of many psychological disorders. In depression, individuals are plagued by frequent rumination about perceived past mistakes, wrongs, and character shortcomings. In obsessive–compulsive disorder (OCD), sufferers experience repeated occurrences of upsetting or discomfiting thoughts that typically require complex, repetitive, time-consuming and/or embarrassing ameliorative strategies. Individuals with OCD may ruminate at length about why they feel compelled to perform the ritual and why they experience the obsessional thought. Post-traumatic stress disorder (PTSD) is characterized by the relentless return of images or thoughts about the traumatic event and often is accompanied by rumination over why the event happened and/or getting revenge. People with generalized anxiety disorder (GAD) catastrophize at length about events that may occur in the future. The "anxious apprehension" of the worrier can also be a secondary characteristic of other anxiety disorders (e.g., individuals with panic disorder often worry at length about their next panic attack, individuals with social anxiety may worry about their next social event, individuals with hypochondriasis worry about their health).

In all cases, the unwanted thoughts are unwelcome at some point, even if people hold beliefs about the utility of focusing on them. For example, people don't report that they wished they worried more, or had more obsessional thoughts, or examined "mistakes of the past" more. The unwanted thoughts are also actively resisted at some point, even if initially the thoughts are actively generated as a coping strategy. Various approaches have been developed to treat rumination in its different forms, including thought stopping, *in vivo* and imaginal exposure, systematic desensitization and relaxation training, cognitive–behavioural therapy and metacognitive therapy, mindfulness meditation, and attention training. This chapter describes these interventions and their theoretical rationale, and offers general comments on their success.

Depressive Rumination: Nature, Theory and Treatment
Edited by Costas Papageorgiou and Adrian Wells. © 2004 John Wiley & Sons Ltd

THOUGHT STOPPING

Thought stopping is a form of aversion training that is based on the assumption that the introduction of an aversive stimulus will produce a response that is different from the undesirable, habitual emotional response (e.g., anxiety) (Wolpe, 1973). In the thought stopping procedure, the therapist yells "stop!" or delivers a painful shock when the individual signals that an unwanted thought has appeared. In some adaptations of the procedure, the patient is instructed to replace the obsession with a more positive thought. Gradually, patients are trained to conduct the thought stopping procedure on their own by saying "stop" to themselves, pinching themselves, or snapping an elastic band on their wrist. This procedure has been used as one component of treatment of PTSD (see Kilpatrick, Veronen, & Resick, 1982), in which patients are instructed to think about the thought for 30–45 seconds and then yell "stop!" It has been most commonly applied to treatment of OCD. While a few single case studies reveal some empirical support for the success of the procedure with certain patients with OCD (Hackman & McLean, 1975; Stern, Lipsedge, & Marks, 1973; Yamagami, 1971), others have found no evidence for the efficacy of this procedure in treating obsessions (Blue, 1978; Emmelkamp & Kwee, 1977; Likierman & Rachman, 1982).

Major criticisms of thought stopping have been raised. For example, Reed (1985) noted that the "aversive" consequences used in the procedure are likely to enhance anxiety. At the same time, the association between the aversive strategy and the thought may cause that strategy to become a cue for further ruminations, as was found by Blue (1978). Rachman and Hodgson (1980) suggested that decreases in the frequency of intrusions that are associated with use of thought stopping are likely due to the patient's perceived ability to control thinking and decreased concern about the thought's occurrence rather than by the dissociation of the thought from anxiety.

Thought suppression is actually contraindicated by leading models of anxiety disorders. For example, in their models of OCD, Rachman (1997, 1998), Salkovskis (1985, 1998), and Wells (1997, 2000) argue that suppression of the obsession sustains its frequency and sustains erroneous beliefs about the meaning of the obsession. These models are emphatic that a key ingredient to treatment of OCD is exposure to the obsession so as to "detoxify" its personal meaning, thereby decreasing its aversiveness and making ameliorative strategies (i.e., compulsions) obsolete. At the same time, Foa and Kozak (1986) argue that in order for a threatening stimulus to be processed emotionally, the threat must be experienced while all of the fear structures are activated. That is, the person must be aware of and attending to all aspects of the threatening situation. In their treatment of PTSD, Foa and colleagues thus emphasize exposure to thoughts about the traumatic event (e.g., Foa, Rothbaum, Riggs, & Murdock, 1991). Ehlers and Clark (2000) argue that suppression of thoughts about the trauma directly increases the frequency of those thoughts, prevents negative appraisals about the meaning of the trauma symptoms from being challenged, and prevents elaboration of the memory that would allow it to be placed in context, all of which are necessary for over-coming trauma symptoms. Finally, in his model of GAD, Borkovec argues that worry is a form of cognitive avoidance used to suppress thoughts about threatening events as well as physiological responses to threat. Both features of worry interfere with the emotional processing of threat and therefore with habituation. Treatment is directed at exposure to the primary source of threat and developing strategies for coping with threat without avoiding or suppressing it (Borkovec, Ray, & Stöber, 1998; Borkovec, Shadick, & Hopkins, 1991). Thus, all of these approaches proscribe the use of thought stopping or suppression as a means of coping with unwanted thoughts.

Work by Wegner and colleagues (e.g., Wegner, Schneider, Carter, & White, 1987) suggests that suppression leads to a rebound of thought occurrences once control efforts have ceased. Does suppression indeed have an ironic effect on thought frequency? Purdon (1999) and Rassin, Merckelbach, and Muris (2000) both note that studies investigating the effects of suppression have yielded highly inconsistent findings. Abramowitz, Tolin, and Street (2001) conducted a meta-analysis of thought suppression studies and found a "small to moder-ate" rebound effect of thought suppression that varied according to the nature of the target thought (discrete vs. non-discrete) and the method by which target thought occurrences were recorded. Few studies have examined the effects of suppression of ruminative or repetitive thoughts symptomatic of mood and anxiety disorders in clinical samples, but there is an emerging body of work on the effects of suppression in PTSD, OCD, and depression. Research on the effects of suppressing the upsetting thoughts characteristic of PTSD has consistently found an ironic effect, such that suppression is associated with more frequent thought occurrences and more distress over thoughts of the trauma (e.g., Harvey & Bryant, 1998; Shipherd & Beck, 1999). Furthermore, Davies and Clark (1998) found that tendency to suppress unwanted thoughts was associated with greater frequency of trauma-related thoughts later on. Similarly, Holeva, Tarrier, and Wells (2001) found that individuals who attempted to suppress their thoughts about a traumatic event by worrying were more likely to develop PTSD.

Given the emphasis on suppression in leading models of OCD, there have been surprisingly few studies of the effects of thought suppression in this group. Tolin, Abramowitz, Przeworski, & Foa (2002) found that individuals with OCD reported significantly more occurrences of a neutral thought during suppression than did non-clinical and anxious control groups, suggesting that this group may have a general deficit in their ability to control thoughts. However, studies examining the effects of suppression of obsessions in indi-viduals with OCD have found no paradoxical increase in the frequency of obsessions, either while suppression efforts were in operation or afterwards (Janeck & Calamari, 1999; Purdon, Rowa, & Antony, 2001). Indeed, Purdon et al. (2001) observed that greater self-reported suppression effort was associated with fewer recurrences of the obsession in the short term.

Despite these negative findings, it is important to note that in neither study was any participant able to achieve perfect suppression (i.e., zero thought occurrences). Furthermore, Purdon et al. did find that thought recurrences while suppression efforts were in operation were associated with more negative appraisal of the thought and more negative mood state. This is consistent with Tolin, Abramowitz, Hamlin, Foa, & Synodi (2002) who found that individuals with OCD were more likely to attribute failures in thought control to internal factors (e.g., "there is something wrong with my brain") than were control groups. Thus, the inevitable recurrence of thoughts while suppression efforts are in operation may have insidious effects on people's response to their obsessional thoughts. Suppression may play a key role in the persistence of the disorder, even if it doesn't result in increased frequency.

Thought stopping or suppression has not been widely used to treat depressive rumination. However, the Response Styles Theory of depression (Nolen-Hoeksema, 1991) argues that rumination about a depressed mood (i.e., thinking about the mood itself, its causes, and its consequences) sustains that depressed mood whereas distraction from the negative mood (i.e., focusing one's attention on matters other than the mood, which is a form of thought suppression) ameliorates it. Distraction can be viewed as one method of suppression, and it is possible that some types of suppression are more effective than others or more effective in certain disorders. Empirical work using non-clinical samples suggests that rumination about an experimentally induced mood is associated with sustained negative mood, negatively biased interpretations of situations, and poorer problem-solving abilities, whereas distraction is associated with better mood, less negative bias, and better problem-solving (e.g., Lyubomirsky, Caldwell & Nolen-Hoeksema, 1998; Lyubomirsky & Nolen-Hoeksema, 1995; Trask & Sigmon, 1999). Consistent with this, Blagden and Craske (1996) found that distraction was associated with a greater reduction in anxiety and negative mood than was rumination.

Research on the role of rumination and distraction on mood in clinical samples (as opposed to non-clincial samples who have undergone a mood induction) has yielded inconsistent findings. Nolen-Hoeksema and Morrow (1993) found that rumination worsened depressed mood in a sample of mild-to-moderately depressed individuals, whereas distraction was associated with mood improvement. However, Kuehner and Weber (1999) found that rumination over negative mood was associated with depressive symptoms later on, but that use of distraction as a means of coping with negative mood was only marginally associated with depressive symptoms. On the other hand, Burns and Nolen-Hoeksema (1991) found that use of distraction was associated with a better response to cognitive–behavioural therapy (CBT). Bagby et al. (1999) examined the relationship between response style and response to antidepressants and found that greater use of distraction predicted positive change in depression severity over the course of treatment, as well as overall treatment outcome. This is consistent with Reynolds and Wells (1999), who found that use of distraction as a thought control strategy was associated with lower depression. However, in the Bagby et al. study, rumination was not associated with change in severity and neither rumination nor distraction was associated with number of past depressive episodes or length of current episode prior to treatment. At the same time, studies examining the effects of deliberate suppression on worry and depressive rumination have failed to detect an ironic effect of suppression on frequency (e.g., Mathews & Milroy, 1994; Roemer & Borkovec, 1994). Overall, this might suggest that distraction from depressive rumination is a useful strategy for coping with depressed mood.

However, Roemer and Borkovec (1994) did find that suppression of thoughts about neutral, depressing, or anxiety-evoking situations was associated with greater anxiety over that situation, suggesting that suppression serves to incubate negative affect. Meanwhile, Wegner, Erber, and Zanakos (1993) found that when attempts to suppress stimuli related to a negative mood were thwarted by a cognitive load, mood state became more negative. In a closer examination of the relationship between mood state and suppression, Wenzlaff and Eisenberg (2001) found that remitted dysphoric individuals did engage in active suppression of negative stimuli and that this effort ameliorated the negative cognitive bias symptomatic of depression. However, when suppression efforts were disrupted by the introduction of a cognitive load, the negative cognitive bias in thinking re-emerged. Wenzlaff, Rude, and West (2002) found that formerly depressed individuals reported having the most uncertainty in their adaptive beliefs as opposed to their maladaptive beliefs.

Similarly, Wenzlaff, Meier, and Salas (2002) found that formerly depressed individuals had greater negative memory biases than did a sample of never-depressed individuals and this bias was associated with higher levels of self-reported thought suppression. Thus, suppression may have a short-term, adaptive function in "staving off" a negative mood, but suppression may also be quite vulnerable to disruption. Research to date on the role of distraction in the maintenance of depressive symptoms has not taken into account potential disruptions in distraction, which may help account for the inconsistent findings. It may be the case that distraction is a more adaptive response to depressive rumination than ruminating about the rumination, but distraction may be vulnerable to disruption and therefore may not be an ideal ameliorative strategy.

In sum, thought suppression appears to have a negative impact on the frequency of thoughts related to a traumatic event in PTSD and insidious effects on thought appraisal and mood state in thoughts characteristic of OCD and GAD. Suppression of depression-related thoughts appears to be somewhat successful in the short term, but these efforts may be highly vulnerable to disruption and therefore rather inefficient as a long-term strategy for managing depressive rumination.

IN VIVO AND IMAGINAL EXPOSURE

In vivo exposure involves graduated exposure to the upsetting stimulus itself (i.e., in OCD, exposure to the obsession, in PTSD, exposure to images of the trauma). The goal is to repeatedly activate all the fear structures (e.g., memories, emotion, cognition) without allowing avoidance or escape behaviours (e.g., neutralizing, suppressing, fleeing), until the anxiety decreases on its own. In treatment of obsessions, the patient identifies a target obsession and its associated rituals. A graded hierarchy is developed that reflects gradual exposure to the most feared stimulus (e.g., a hierarchy for a contamination obsession might start with touching the door to a public bathroom and end with touching the toilet itself and then touching one's face). The patient is then put in the situation and is directed to focus on the obsession, but is not allowed to complete any rituals, overt or covert. The person remains in the situation until anxiety reduces substantially. The exposure is repeated until the situation and its concomitant obsession result in minimal anxious arousal. At that point, exposure begins to the next situation on the hierarchy. Salkovskis and Westbrook (1989) developed an exposure procedure for obsessions that are accompanied by a covert (i.e., mental), rather than overt compulsive act in which the obsession is repeated on audiotape. The tape is fixed in a loop so that it repeats itself. In this manner the individual is exposed to the obsession without having the opportunity to use the mental ritual. Imaginal exposure might also be used in OCD when it is difficult to recreate the feared situation or as a preliminary step to *in vivo* exposure (see Antony & Swinson, 2000; Foa, Steketee, Grayson, Turner, & Latimer, 1984; Foa & Wilson, 1991; Steketee, 1999). The crucial aspect of the exposure in treatment of obsessions is that the individual be fully aware of all the details of the scene and the exposure session not be terminated until there has been a significant reduction in anxiety.

Treatment outcome studies consistently support the efficacy of *in vivo* exposure with response prevention (ERP) in the treatment of OCD, in comparison with other forms of treatment, with around 63% showing at least some improvement (e.g., Abramowitz, 1996; Foa, Franklin, & Kozak, 1998; Stanley & Turner, 1995). Franklin, Abramowitz, Kozak, Levitt, and Foa (2000) found comparable rates of improvement even when participants were not excluded from clinical trials on the basis of such factors as treatment history, concurrent psychotherapy, co-morbidity, age, or OCD severity. ERP appears to be more effective when the exposure sessions are therapist-controlled rather than self-controlled and when they are longer in duration (Abramowitz, 1996). However, as Salkovskis and colleagues note (Salkovskis & Westbrook, 1989;

Salkovskis, Richards, & Forrester, 2000), these efficacy rates do not take into account treatment dropouts and treatment refusers; when such rates are taken into account, the success rate of ERP falls to about 50%.

In vivo exposure is used in the treatment of PTSD as a means of overcoming avoidance of stimuli associated with the trauma. The primary component of most current treatment protocols for PTSD derives from the seminal work of Foa and her colleagues (e.g., Foa et al., 1991) and is based on imaginal exposure, which follows the same theoretical principles as *in vivo* exposure. In imaginal exposure, individuals are instructed to imagine the trauma scene, with an increasing focus on the upsetting details of the scene (e.g., Ehlers & Clark, 2000). They may "speak" the details of the scene aloud and have it audiotaped so that they can then listen to the tape in-between sessions (e.g., Foa et al., 1991), or they may write the scene out in detail (e.g., Calhoun & Resick, 1993; Ellis, Black, & Resick, 1992). Treatment outcome studies suggest that exposure-based treatments are effective for PTSD relative to other psychological treatments (e.g., Foa et al., 1991; Keane, Fairbank, Caddell, & Zimering, 1989), with high end state functioning observed in 40–60% of individuals (for a discussion, see Craske, 2000).

EYE MOVEMENT DESENSITIZATION RETRAINING (EMDR)

EMDR was developed by Shapiro (1995) to treat PTSD. Shapiro reported that rapid back-and-forth eye movements reduced her own anxiety and, based on this observation, went on to develop a treatment protocol for PTSD integrating eye movement with imaginal exposure to trauma. There is little empirical or theoretical basis for the eye movement component of the treatment, and the procedure has been strongly criticized on that basis (e.g., Lohr et al., 1992). EMDR is listed as an empirically supported treatment by the American Psychological Association (Chambless et al., 1998). However, a recent comprehensive meta-analysis has concluded that treatment gains are largely accounted for by exposure to traumatic events and that the eye movement component of EMDR does not have any additional therapeutic value (Davidson & Parker, 2001).

RELAXATION TRAINING AND SYSTEMATIC DESENSITIZATION

Early approaches to treatment of anxiety problems drew upon the behavioural theory of Wolpe (1958) and were based on the principle of reciprocal inhibition. The term "reciprocal inhibition" refers to the inhibition of an undesirable response through the evocation of another, mutually incompatible response. In the case of anxiety, the undesirable response is anxiety arousal and the incompatible response is relaxation. In systematic desensitization (SD), scenes related to the source of anxiety are presented to the patient in a graded sequence while she or he is in a relaxed state. The goal is to achieve presentation of the stimulus without an anxiety response.

Relaxation and desensitization have most commonly been applied to the treatment of GAD. Borkovec's leading model of GAD understands worry as a verbal–linguistic activity that (a) distracts the individual from more upsetting mental images related to a threat, and (b) establishes an emotional distance from the threat, thereby facilitating avoidance of the unpleasant physiological symptoms of autonomic arousal. Consistent with this, individuals with GAD show decreased sympathetic nervous system response, or "autonomic inflexibility" (Borkovec et al., 1991, 1998). Borkovec also notes that individuals with GAD have a preattentive bias to signs of threat. Yet, the threat to which individuals with GAD react is existent only in the future, so the typical fight/flight responses to threat are not helpful. Instead, the individual inhibits motor behaviour (i.e., "freezes") while attempting to remove the source of threat (i.e., by worrying) (Lyonsfield, Borkovec, & Thayer, 1995).

Worrying consumes attentional resources and does not allow full activation of the fear structures (Borkovec et al., 1998), so the person is unable to habituate to the source of threat. Thus, individuals with GAD are in a constant state of tension while they engage in the strenuous mental activity of worrying in order to protect themselves against greater anxiety and its physical and emotional concomitants. Borkovec argues that successful treatment of GAD should involve exposure to cues that trigger anxiety in addition to development of coping strategies and relaxation skills in response to such cues. Relaxation should serve to improve flexibility of responding at various levels by ameliorating the bodily tension associated with motoric inhibition and facilitating habituation to the true source of threat (Borkovec & Costello, 1993). In a key study on treatment of GAD, Borkovec and Costello (1993) compared the relative efficacy of a non-directive treatment control, applied relaxation, and CBT. The applied relaxation treatment involved training in progressive muscle relaxation, early detection of cues for anxiety, and use of relaxation in response to the cues. The CBT treatment involved identification and modification of erroneous thoughts associated with an anxious response, and desensitization during which the client relaxed in response to cues for anxiety and then imagined her or himself using relaxation skills in the anxious situation. This latter intervention is quite similar to systematic desensitization. The results indicated that the applied relaxation and cognitive therapy groups were similar to each other in effectiveness and more effective than the non-directive treatment. At 12-month follow-up, significantly more clients who had undergone CBT showed high end state functioning compared with those in the applied relaxation treatment (58% vs. 27%), and 84% of those in the CBT group were rated as exhibiting "high" clinically significant change, compared with 67% of those in the applied relaxation group.

Öst and Breitholtz (2000) found applied relaxation to be as effective as cognitive therapy (with no relaxation training) in treatment of GAD, although their rates for clinically significant improvement were lower than those observed by Borkovec and Costello. In this study, 67% of those in the applied relaxation group and 56% of those in the cognitive therapy group showed clinically significant improvement at 12-month follow-up (the difference in rate was not significant). Thus, relaxation training and systematic desensitization (as developed in Borkovec and Costello's CBT intervention) do appear to be effective in treatment of GAD. Borkovec and Costello (1993) do note, however, that the success rate of these interventions is relatively low and that we need more information about the factors involved in worry persistence and how to treat them.

COGNITIVE THERAPY

Cognitive therapy teaches the client to identify negative, erroneous interpretations of thoughts, events, and situations. Specific types of appraisals and beliefs are implicated depending on the disorder.

OBSESSIVE–COMPULSIVE DISORDER (OCD)

Leading cognitive–behavioural models of OCD suggest that obsessions are thoughts whose importance has been exaggerated (e.g., Rachman, 1997, 1998; Salkovskis, 1985, 1989, 1998; Salkovskis et al., 2000). Indeed, Rachman (1997, 1998) refers to this as a "catastrophic misinterpretation" of the meaning of the occurrence of the obsession. In his model, Rachman first notes that obsessions tend to reflect moral themes. He then emphasizes the role of "thought–action fusion" appraisals, which are appraisals that (a) having the thought will increase the likelihood that the thought will come true in real life ("likelihood fusion"), and (b) that having the obsession is as bad morally as actually completing the action represented by the obsession ("moral fusion").

Salkovskis (1985, 1989, 1998; Salkovskis et al., 2000) argues that obsessions are thoughts that give rise to an overvalued sense of responsibility, such as the belief that any influence over outcome = full responsibility for the outcome, and therefore full responsibility to prevent the negative outcome, no matter how remote its probability. Other kinds of thoughts also relevant to OCD have been implicated, including the need to control thoughts (see Clark & Purdon, 1993; Purdon & Clark, 1999; Salkovskis, 1985, 1989), the need for certainty and overestimation of danger (see Freeston, Ladouceur, Gagnon, & Thibodeau, 1993; Freeston et al., 1997), and perfectionism (see Frost & Steketee, 1997; McFall & Wollersheim, 1979). The Obsessive–Compulsive

Cognitions Working Group (OCCWG) is an international group of researchers in OCD who assembled several years ago to identify the range of beliefs and appraisals relevant to the development and maintenance of OCD, according to leading models of OCD, as well as to develop standardized scales for assessing those beliefs. This group identified six domains of belief/appraisal relevant to OCD, which included thought–action fusion, importance of controlling thoughts, overestimation of the severity and probability of threat, intolerance of uncertainty and perfectionism (OCCWG, 1997).

Wells (1997, 2000) proposed a metacognitive model of OCD based on a range of beliefs about thoughts including thought–event fusion ("if I think an event happened, it did") and thought–object fusion (that an object that has been touched becomes imbued with their thoughts and feelings and can imbue other objects or people with those thoughts and feelings). In all cases, the essential problem in OCD is conceptualized as some form of misinterpretation of the significance of the obsession, which leads to neutralizing or control strategies, such as suppression, "undoing" or preventative rituals, and reassurance seeking. Wells (1997, 2000) notes that beliefs about the utility of the compulsive act or ameliorative strategy will ensure that the individual will continue to select that strategy as a means of coping and that the tendency to focus on internal feeling states will ensure that the compulsive rituals are performed in response to a "felt sense" that things are "right," rather than in response to valuable external information (e.g., seeing that the bolt on the door is engaged). Wells (1997, 2000) emphasizes the importance of modifying erroneous metacognitive beliefs about the obsession and its aftermath, as well as beliefs about failure to perform the ritual adequately in treatment success.

Rachman (1997) predicts that the obsessional problem will remain refractory to treatment until erroneous beliefs about obsessional thoughts are corrected. Salkovskis (e.g., Salkovskis, 1998) further argued that correction of erroneous beliefs about thoughts may be helpful for people who initially refuse ERP or who would otherwise drop out of ERP, as cognitive restructuring may serve to detoxify the obsession enough that the individual feels "up to" engaging in exposure. Cognitive therapy treatment protocols for OCD have been designed to address these specific domains using cognitive techniques (cognitive restructuring, behavioural experiments, Socratic dialogue) either in combination with ERP or without ERP. Freeston et al. (1997) found that 67% of individuals undergoing treatment involving cognitive restructuring targeting responsibility, threat overestimation, thought–action fusion and control beliefs, in combination with ERP, showed clinically significant improvement as compared with virtually no improvement in waiting list controls. O'Connor, Todorov, Robillard, Borgeat, & Brault (1999) used a similar treatment protocol and found it to be more effective than no intervention (i.e., as compared with controls on a waiting list for treatment) and just as effective as medication. Van Oppen et al. (1995) found that cognitive therapy using behavioural experiments (which have elements of exposure) was more effective than *in vivo* exposure in treating OCD, with 68% vs. 48% showing significant improvement (although both were superior to no treatment).

The experience of exposure itself can of course alter erroneous beliefs about thoughts (Steketee, 1993), and indeed Foa and Kozak (1986) argue that one of the goals of exposure is to disconfirm erroneous associations and beliefs (e.g., urine = contamination, bathroom floor = urine, therefore bathroom floor = contamination). As such, she advocates doing evaluation of risk assessment, probability overestimations, etc. during exposure, all of which would be targets for cognitive restructuring recommended by the OCCWG and leading theorists (see Foa et al., 1998).

Stanley and Averill (1998) observe that there have been few treatment outcome studies examining the efficacy of cognitive therapy over and above ERP, so the superiority of cognitive therapy alone or adding cognitive techniques to ERP has not been established. One concern about using cognitive therapy with OCD is the possibility that the cognitive restructuring could serve to provide temporary reassurance and could be used as a compulsive ritual. Certainly, exposure-based exercises can develop into compulsive rituals. Research on the extent to which this is problematic and on whether this is more likely to happen with certain kinds of OCD subtypes is necessary. It is also important to target the key negative automatic thoughts. For example, working on probability overestimations may not be at all helpful for individuals who have an overvalued sense of responsibility, because in their mind *any* possibility that the feared event will come true means that they are still "on the hook" to prevent harm. Indeed, for such individuals, establishing the low probability of the event happening is likely to provide temporary reassurance, which may reinforce use of probability generation as an ameliorative strategy. In such cases, it would be much more useful to target appraisals involving responsibility that drive the concern about the event happening in the first place.

GENERALIZED ANXIETY DISORDER (GAD)

Earlier studies examining the efficacy of cognitive therapy for GAD were guided by Beck and Emery's (1985) general model of anxiety, which argues that anxiety responses are maintained by negative automatic thoughts about degree of threat and vulnerability. Butler, Fennell, Robson, and Gelder (1991) found that CBT that addressed thoughts about threat and vulnerability (with no relaxation training component) was superior to applied relaxation in treatment of GAD. Cognitive therapy has also been found to be superior to psychoanalytic treatment for GAD (e.g., Durham et al., 1993). Since these earlier studies, leading theorists have offered a more detailed analysis of the types of cognitive appraisal that characterize GAD. Wells' cognitive model of GAD is grounded in the Self-Regulatory Executive Functioning (S-REF) model (see Wells & Matthews, 1994). An authoritative description and analysis of this model appears elsewhere in this book, so only a brief review of Wells's cognitive model of GAD will be provided here. Wells (1995, 1997, 2000) identifies specific beliefs about thoughts and thought processes (or "metacognitive beliefs") that are important in the persistence of worry. Metacognitive beliefs include beliefs about the utility of worry (e.g., "worrying helps me to solve problems"), about the dangerous consequences of worry (e.g., "I must control bad thoughts or I could go crazy"), and about the nature of worry (e.g., "my worries are uncontrollable").

Wells distinguishes between worry itself (Type I worry) and worry about that worry (Type II worry). Positive beliefs about worry and negative beliefs about the controllability of worry may sustain Type I worry because the individual is unlikely to attempt to look for or try strategies for coping with threats other than worry and is unlikely to attempt to actively interrupt the worry process. When worry persists, Type II worries will develop, with several insidious effects: (a) the worry episode becomes extended; (b) the individual will not be able to process the concerns that are the object of the Type I worry; (c) Type II worry primes the system for detection of worry-related thoughts and increases sensitivity to worry cues; (d) the individual may attempt to suppress worry thoughts and avoid worry cues, which can backfire, contributing to the individual's perception that worry is uncontrollable; and (e) Type II worry prolongs activation of dysfunctional metacognitive beliefs, which can influence processing of other types of thought (Wells, 1995, p. 305; Wells, 2000). As such, Wells emphasizes the importance of restructuring negative beliefs about worry that will reduce Type II worry and positive beliefs that lead to repeated use of Type I worry as a coping strategy. His treatment de-emphasizes problem-solving, as this will sustain the individual's view that he or she needs to worry about problems. Preliminary treatment outcome data indicate significant decreases in GAD symptoms and trait anxiety (Wells & King, 2002).

Dugas, Gagnon, Ladouceur, and Freeston (1998) argue that a primary problem for individuals with GAD is that they have a low tolerance for uncertainty. As such, they worry excessively, as a means of working through all the details of a problem in order to decrease the sense of uncertainty and therefore their anxiety level. This focus on the details of the problem makes it difficult to actually use problem-solving skills to solve the problem, and the intolerance of uncertainty makes it very difficult for them to abandon worrying about a problem over which they have no control. Thus, worry serves several adaptive functions for the individual. Ladouceur et al. (2000) report on a treatment protocol based on this model. As in Wells' treatment, their protocol targets positive beliefs about worry (e.g., "if I worry, I will be prepared"), while developing the individual's problem identification skills (problem orientation) so that they are able to view the problem itself without getting mired in all the details. The problem orientation training also helps individuals learn to face problems rather than avoid them, develops confidence in problem-solving abilities, and helps the worrier learn to tolerate problems that are not within one's control. Following from Borkovec's finding that worry serves to prevent exposure to upsetting events, Ladouceur et al. (2000) also incorporate exposure to scenes the individual is worried about. Ladouceur et al. (2000) report significant success in treating a small sample of individuals with GAD, with 77% no longer meeting diagnostic criteria for GAD, compared with no change in a no-treatment control condition.

POST-TRAUMATIC STRESS DISORDER (PTSD)

Ehlers and Clark (2000) posited a cognitive model of PTSD that emphasizes the role of negative appraisal of trauma and trauma sequelae in the development and persistence of the disorder. They observe that, although the symptoms of PTSD arise from a threat that was endured in the past, PTSD develops and persists because the traumatic event and/or its sequelae are interpreted as signifying current threat. Overgeneralization of the event can lead to the perception that normal activities are in fact highly dangerous, that traumatic events are highly probable, and that the individual her or himself "attracts" disaster or possesses some flaw that makes her or him more vulnerable to experiencing disaster. Negative appraisals of the individual's behaviour during the event can also lead to a sense that one's safety is currently threatened. For example, thinking that one could or should have been able to anticipate the danger, and avoid it, can lead to the perception that one can no longer trust one's instincts. Symptoms of trauma (such as flashbacks, anger, numbing) and difficulty concentrating may also be interpreted as evidence that one's personality, mind, or cognitive abilities have been permanently damaged. This, of course, would also result in a sense of current threat. Finally, if the reactions of others are interpreted in a negative way (i.e., that others perceive the individual as weak and unable to cope or that others are not sympathetic) the individual is likely to feel a sense of insecurity and doubt around inter-personal relationships. Successful treatment relies on modification of erroneous beliefs about the meaning of the traumatic event and the symptoms of PTSD.

Ehlers and Clark recommend treatment that involves imaginal exposure, or "reliving," within the session followed by immediate identification and restruc-turing of problematic thoughts and beliefs of the type described above. This is similar to cognitive processing therapy developed by Ellis, Black, and Resick (1992) in which activation of the fear structures through immersion in the details of the trauma is paired with challenging faulty beliefs and inferences about the traumatic event, in order that the fear structures will change in accordance with the new learning. Treatment outcome data on the specific protocol offered by Ehlers and Clark (2000) are not yet available, so it is unknown whether this emphasis on correcting these particular types of faulty appraisal following imaginal exposure improves treatment outcome over and above rates of success in exposure-based interventions discussed earlier. It is important to note that Ehlers and Clark also observe that individuals with PTSD often ruminate about the event and why it happened, and/or about getting revenge. Specific recommendations for treating rumination are not made.

Wells (2000) argues that exposure to the traumatic event is unnecessary, as long as factors that interfere with natural emotional processing of the event are targeted. Such factors include unhelpful coping strategies (e.g., hypervigilance, monitoring, rumination), maladaptive self-knowledge (e.g., incorrect and negative appraisal of symptoms), and situational factors (e.g., negative appraisal of one's coping strategies during the traumatic event, or appraisal of symptoms as a sign of one's failure to cope). Indeed, empirical research suggests that rumination is a significant predictor of intrusive images after a stressful event (e.g., Holeva et al., 2001; Wells & Papageorgiou, 1995). Wells recommends that treatment should include normalization of trauma symptoms, prohibition of unhelpful coping strategies, development and practice (imaginal and actual) of coping strategies, and cognitive restructuring around faulty appraisals related to all of these factors. In particular, patients should be encouraged to evaluate their efforts at coping in a positive way.

DEPRESSION

CBT for depression targets negative automatic thoughts about self, world, and future. This treatment is well established and considered one of the most, if not the most, effective treatments for overcoming depression. However, existing CBT protocols typically do not address depressive rumination, or the negative, self-generated, elaborated chains of thoughts about one's failures, one's shortcomings, or about the state of being depressed itself. Papageorgiou and Wells (2001a) distinguish depressive rumination from negative automatic thoughts and identify rumination as a coping strategy that exacerbates depression in the same way that anxious rumination (or worry) serves to maintain anxiety. Worry and depressive rumination are seen as similar but not identical because, whereas the former is highly verbal, future-oriented, effortful, and results in greater impulse to act and more confidence in problem-solving, the latter is less verbal, less effortful, and doesn't result in the same impulse to act (Papageorgiou & Wells, 1999a, b). Depressive rumination exacerbates depression because it occupies attentional resources, thereby disallowing new, positive, or corrective information from being processed. Rumination will also prime negative thoughts, emotions, memories, etc., which can trigger negative automatic thoughts.

Papageorgiou and Wells (2001b) hypothesized that rumination is selected as a coping strategy on the basis of the individual's metacognitive knowledge. They interviewed depressed individuals about their rumination and found that people hold positive beliefs about rumination, such that when dealing with the problems and feelings of depression rumination is helpful for solving problems, for gaining insight, identifying potential triggers and causes, preventing future mistakes, and prioritizing important tasks (see Papageorgiou and Wells, 2001b). They suggest that such beliefs may play a role in the development and persistence of depression, or in depressive relapse. Cognitive restructuring around these beliefs may be useful in decreasing the use of rumination as a coping strategy and therefore may reduce depressive symptoms overall. More research is needed to determine the role of positive beliefs about rumination in depression, but this could be quite promising in understanding both depression and depressive relapse.

MEDITATION

Segal, Williams, and Teasdale (2002) have developed a protocol for preventing depressive relapse in individuals with recurrent depression called mindfulness-based cognitive therapy (MBCT). This treatment strategy is grounded in Teasdale's (1983) differential activation hypothesis and his Interacting Cognitive Subsystems (ICS) model (Teasdale & Barnard, 1993). In general, this model argues that individuals who have experienced a depressive episode acquire a massive association between depressed mood and patterns of negative thinking at various levels. This association leaves them vulnerable to becoming depressed again because, after the experience of the depressive episode and the formation of the associations between mood and cognition, even a small decrease in mood state can activate negative thinking patterns, which in turn exacerbate mood. Negative mood makes negative thoughts ever-more accessible, which of course decreases mood further. This cycle can turn an episode of mild dysphoria, which would be transient in never-depressed individuals, into a major depressive episode. The purpose of MBCT is to thwart this cycle by helping vulnerable individuals learn to identify their negative mood and thoughts and respond to them in such a way that they may disengage from "ruminative depressive processing" (Teasdale et al., 2000).

MBCT trains people to develop "non-judgemental awareness" of bodily sensations, thoughts, and feelings, including difficult or discomforting ones, with a goal to developing a "decentred" perspective such that the thoughts are viewed as passing events in the mind. This allows the individual to identify negative thoughts and feelings early on and disengage from ruminative processes that might otherwise prime negative thoughts and mood, as well as thwart automatic processing. In the absence of this "non-judgemental awareness," negative thoughts and feelings would be processed in an automatic, negative way (e.g., the negative automatic thoughts would be automatically accepted as "truths," which in turn would drive negative affect, which in turn would be associated with biases in information processing such that positive cues are ignored and ambiguous ones misinterpreted as negative, which serves to escalate negative mood, etc.). Unlike in standard cognitive therapy, the individual is not expected to challenge the content of negative thoughts, but rather simply be aware of and disengaged from them. Cognitive restructuring would, however, target ideas about the nature of thoughts (e.g., "thoughts are truths"), which Wells might refer to as "metacognitive" appraisal, in order to facilitate the "decentred" view (Teasdale et al., 2000). Preliminary data found that MBCT offered in addition to treatment as usual was associated with almost half the rate of relapse for patients who had had three or more previous episodes of depression, but not for those with two or less (Teasdale et al., 2000).

ATTENTION TRAINING (ATT)

Wells (2000) critiques the model on which mindfulness meditation is predicated and argues that heightened self-awareness, which is the goal of MBCT, is a non-specific feature of emotional disorders that serves to maintain the disorder by preventing processing of information that could modify maladaptive beliefs. Wells agrees that development of a state of "detached awareness" is desirable, but emphasizes the importance of also developing skills for reducing excessive and uncontrollable self-focused attention (Wells, 2000, p. 88). Wells has developed a technique to accomplish this, called attention training treatment (ATT: Wells, 1990), which trains individuals in selective attention, attention switching, and divided attention.

Wells argues that a cognitive attentional "syndrome" is characteristic of all emotional disorder and is responsible for maintaining dysfunction. This "syndrome" is characterized by inflexible, excessive, and uncontrollable self-focused attention as well as worry/rumination, threat monitoring, and activation of negative beliefs, especially those in the metacognitive domain. Thus, ATT is applied in the same manner regardless of the disorder. Individuals are given in-session training in focusing attention on different auditory stimuli, switching their attention and attending to more than one stimuli at once. They are then given instructions to practise at least twice a day. If negative thoughts or emotions arise during practice they are to be ignored and treated as "noise" (see Papageorgiou & Wells, 2000). In an A–B [before and after] design, Papageorgiou and Wells (2000) report significant reduction in depressive symptoms, negative thoughts, negative metacognitive appraisal, and rumination in four depressed individuals. Wells and colleagues report similar success in using ATT in treatment of panic (Wells, 1990; Wells, White, & Carter, 1997), and hypochondriasis (Cavanagh & Franklin, 2001; Papageorgiou & Wells, 1998). It is noteworthy that such significant change on a variety of outcome indicators has been observed given the relative simplicity of the intervention.

SUMMARY AND CONCLUSIONS

Rumination is difficult to treat, and even the most successful interventions are still not helpful for a significant number of sufferers. One difficulty is that we lack a comprehensive understanding of rumination, the processes that sustain it, and potential factors that might thwart it. It does seem like suppression, in the form of simply attempting not to have the unwanted thought, is relatively unsuccessful, being associated with either a resurgence of thoughts (as in PTSD), insidious effects on thought appraisal and mood state (as in OCD), or is vulnerable to disruption (as in depressive rumination). Cognitive and behavioural strategies have been developed to detoxify the meaning of repetitive thoughts so that rumination or further processing becomes unnecessary. Other strategies target rumination itself, helping the individual learn to accept thoughts without reacting to them, or developing their ability to simply choose not to pay the thoughts attention. In either case, we appear to be making some progress in our ability to treat rumination, and the newer models for understanding rumination (e.g., MBCT, ATT, and new cognitive models) seem promising.

REFERENCES

Abramowitz, J. S. (1996). Variants of exposure and response prevention in the treatment of obsessive–compulsive disorder: A meta-analysis. *Behavior Therapy*, **27**, 583–600.

Abramowitz, J. S., Tolin, D. F., & Street, G. P. (2001). Paradoxical effects of thought suppression: A meta-analysis of controlled studies. *Clinical Psychology Review*, **21**, 683–703.

Antony, M. M. & Swinson, R. P. (2000). *Phobic Disorders and Panic in Adults: A Guide to Assessment and Treatment*. Washington, DC: American Psychological Association.

Bagby, R. M., Rector, N. A., Segal, Z. V., Joffe, R. T., Levitt, A. J., Kennedy, S. H., & Levitan, R. D. (1999). Rumination and distraction in major depression: Assessing response to pharmacological treatment. *Journal of Affective Disorders*, **55**, 225–229.

Beck, A. T. & Emery, G. (1985). *Anxiety Disorders and Phobias: A Cognitive Perspective*. New York: Basic Books.

Blagden, J. C. & Craske, M. G. (1996). Effects of active and passive rumination and distraction: A pilot replication with anxious mood. *Journal of Anxiety Disorders*, **10**, 243–252.

Blue, R. (1978). Ineffectiveness of an aversion therapy technique in treatment of obsessional thinking. *Psychological Reports*, **43**, 181–182.

Borkovec, T. D. & Costello, E. (1993). Efficacy of applied relaxation and cognitive–behavioral therapy in the treatment of generalized anxiety disorder. *Journal of Consulting and Clinical Psychology*, **61**, 611–619.

Borkovec, T. D., Ray, W. J., & Stöber, J. (1998). Worry: A cognitive phenomenon intimately linked to affective, physiological, and interpersonal behavioral processes. *Cognitive Therapy and Research*, **22**, 561–576.

Borkovec, T. D., Shadick, R. N., & Hopkins, M. (1991). The nature of normal and pathological worry. In: R. M. Rapee & D. H. Barlow (eds), *Chronic Anxiety: Generalized Anxiety Disorder and Mixed Anxiety-Depression* (pp. 29–51). New York: Guilford Press.

Burns, D. D. & Nolen-Hoeksema, S. (1991). Coping styles, homework compliance and the effectiveness of cognitive–behavioural therapy. *Journal of Consulting and Clinical Psychology*, **59**, 564–578.

Butler, G. B., Fennell, M., Robson, P., & Gelder, M. (1991). Comparison of behavior therapy and cognitive behavior therapy in the treatment of generalized anxiety disorder. *Journal of Consulting and Clinical Psychology*, **59**, 167–175.

Calhoun, K. S. & Resick, P. A. (1993). Post-traumatic stress disorder. In: D. H. Barlow (ed.), *Clinical Handbook of Psychological Disorders* (2nd edn, pp. 48–98). New York: Guilford Press.

Cavanagh, M. J. & Franklin, J. (2001, July). Attention training and hypochondriasis: Preliminary results of a controlled treatment trial. Paper presented at the *World Congress of Behavioral and Cognitive Therapies, Vancouver*.

Chambless, D. L., Baker, M. J., Boucom, D. H., Beutler, L. E., Calhoun, K. S., Crits-Christoph, P., Daiuto, A., DeRubeis, R., Detweiler, J., Haada, D. A. F., Bennett-Johnson, S., McCurry, S., Mueser, K. T., Pope, K. S., Sanderson, W. C., Shoham, V., Stickle, T., Williams, D. A., & Woody, S. R. (1998). Update on empirically validated therapies, II. *Clinical Psychologist*, **51**, 3–16.

Clark, D. A. & Purdon, C. (1993). New perspectives for a cognitive theory of obsessions. *Australian Psychologist*, **28**, 161–167.

Craske, M. G. (2000). *Anxiety Disorders: Psychological Approaches to Theory and Treatment*. Boulder, CO: Westview Press.

Davidson, P. R. & Parker, K. C. H. (2001). Eye movement desensitization and reprocessing (EMDR): A meta-analysis. *Journal of Consulting and Clinical Psychology*, **69**, 305–316.

Davies, M. I. & Clark, D. M. (1998). Thought suppression produces a rebound effect with analogue post-traumatic intrusions. *Behaviour Research and Therapy*, **36**, 571–582.

Dugas, M. J., Gagnon, F., Ladouceur, R., & Freeston, M. H. (1998). Generalized anxiety disorder: A preliminary test of a conceptual model. *Behaviour Research and Therapy*, **36**, 215–226.

Durham, R. C., Murphy, T., Allan, T., Richard, K., Treliving, L. R., & Fenton, G. W. (1993). Cognitive therapy, analytic psychotherapy and anxiety management training for generalized anxiety disorder. *British Journal of Psychiatry*, **165**, 315–323.

Ehlers, A. & Clark, D. M. (2000). A cognitive model of posttraumatic stress disorder. *Behaviour Research and Therapy*, **38**, 319–345.

Ellis, L. F., Black, L. D., & Resick, P. A. (1992). Cognitive–behavioural treatment approaches for victims of crime. In: P. A. Keller & S. R. Heyman (eds), *Innovations in Clinical Practice: A Sourcebook* (pp. 23–38). Sarasota, FL: Professional Resource Exchange.

Emmelkamp, P. M. G. & Kwee, K. G. (1977). Obsessional ruminations: A comparison between thought-stopping and prolonged exposure in imagination. *Behaviour Research and Therapy*, **15**, 441–444.

Foa, E. B., Franklin, M. E., & Kozak, M. J. (1998). Psychosocial treatments for obsessive compulsive disorder: Literature review. In: R. P. Swinson, M. M. Antony, S. Rachman, and M. A. Richter (eds), *Obsessive–Compulsive Disorder: Theory, Research and Treatment* (pp. 258–276). New York: Guilford Press.

Foa, E. B. & Kozak, M. J. (1986). Emotional processing of fear: Exposure to corrective information. *Psychological Bulletin*, **99**, 20–35.

Foa, E. B., Rothbaum, B. O., Riggs, D. S., & Murdock, T. B. (1991). Treatment of posttraumatic stress disorder in rape victims: A comparison between cognitive–behavioral procedures and counseling. *Journal of Consulting and Clinical Psychology*, **59**, 715–723.

Foa, E. B., Steketee, G. S., Grayson, J. B., Turner, R. M., & Latimer, P. (1984). Deliberate exposure and blocking of obsessive–compulsive rituals: Immediate and long-term effects. *Behavior Therapy*, **15**, 450–472.

Foa, E. B. & Wilson, R. (1991). *Stop Obsessing! How to Overcome Your Obsessions and Compulsions*. New York: Bantam Books.

Franklin, M. E., Abramowitz, J. S., Kozak, M. J., Levitt, J. T., & Foa, E. B. (2000). Effectiveness of exposure and ritual prevention for obsessive–compulsive disorder: Randomized compared with nonrandomized samples. *Journal of Consulting and Clinical Psychology*, **68**, 594–602.

Freeston, M. H., Ladouceur, R., Gagnon, F., & Thibodeau, N. (1993). Beliefs about obsessional thoughts. *Journal of Psychopathology and Behavioural Assessment*, **15**, 1–21.

Freeston, M. H., Ladouceur, R., Gagnon, F., Thibodeau, N., Rheaume, J., Letarte, H., & Bujold, A. (1997). Cognitive–behavioural treatment of obsessive thoughts: A controlled study. *Journal of Consulting and Clinical Psychology*, **65**, 405–413.

Frost, R. O. & Steketee, G. (1997). Perfectionism in obsessive–compulsive disorder patients. *Behaviour Research and Therapy*, **35**, 291–296.

Hackman, A. & McLean, C. (1975). A comparison of flooding and thought stopping in the treatment of obsessional neurosis. *Behaviour Research and Therapy*, **13**, 263–269.

Harvey, A. G. & Bryant, R. A. (1998). The effect of attempted thought suppression in acute stress disorder. *Behaviour Research and Therapy*, **36**, 583–590.

Holeva, V., Tarrier, N., & Wells, A. (2001). Prevalence and predictors of acute stress disorder and PTSD following road traffic accidents: Thought control strategies and social support. *Behavior Therapy*, **32**, 65–84.

Janeck, A. S. & Calamari, J. E. (1999). Thought suppression in obsessive–compulsive disorder. *Cognitive Therapy and Research*, **23**, 497–509.

Keane, T. M., Fairbank, J. A., Caddell, J. M., & Zimering, R. T. (1989). Implosive (flooding) therapy reduces symptoms of PTSD in Vietnam combat veterans. *Behavior Therapy*, **20**, 245–260.

Kilpatrick, D. G., Veronen, L. J., & Resick, P. A. (1982). Psychological sequelae to rape: Assessment and treatment strategies. In: D. M. Dolays & R. L. Meredith (eds), *Behavioral Medicine: Assessment and Treatment Strategies* (pp. 473–497). New York: Plenum Press.

Kuehner, C. & Weber, I. (1999). Responses to depression in unipolar depressed patients: An investigation of Nolen-Hoeksema's response styles theory. *Psychological Medicine*, **29**, 1323–1333.

Ladouceur, R., Dugas, M. J., Freeston, M. H., Léger, E., Gagnon, F., & Thibodeau, N. (2000). Efficacy of a cognitive–behavioral treatment of generalized anxiety disorder: Evaluation in a controlled clinical trial. *Journal of Consulting and Clinical Psychology*, **68**, 957–964.

Likierman, H. & Rachman, S. (1982). Obsessions: An experimental investigation of thought-stopping and habituation training. *Behavioural Psychotherapy*, **10**, 324–338.

Lohr, J. M., Kleinknecht, R. A., Conley, A. T., Dal Cerro, S., Schmidt, J., & Sonntag, M. E. (1992). A methodological critique of the current status of eye movement desensitization (EMD). *Journal of Behavior Therapy and Experimental Psychiatry*, **23**, 159–167.

Lyonsfield, J. D., Borkovec, T. D., & Thayer, J. F. (1995). Vagal tone in generalized anxiety disorder and the effects of aversive imagery and worrisome thinking. *Behavior Therapy*, **26**, 457–466.

Lyubomirsky, S., Caldwell, N. D., & Nolen-Hoeksema, S. (1998). Effects of ruminative and distracting responses to depressed mood on retrieval of autobiographical memories. *Journal of Personality and Social Psychology*, **75**, 166–177.

Lyubomirsky, S. & Nolen-Hoeksema, S. (1995). Effects of self-focused rumination on negative thinking and interpersonal problem solving. *Journal of Personality and Social Psychology*, **69**, 176–190.

Mathews, A. & Milroy, R. (1994). Effects of priming and suppression on worry. *Behaviour Research and Therapy*, **32**, 843–850.

McFall, M. E. & Wollersheim, J. P. (1979). Obsessive–compulsive neurosis: A cognitive behavioural formulation and approach to treatment. *Cognitive Therapy and Research*, **3**, 333–348.

Nolen-Hoeksema, S. (1991). Responses to depression and their effects on the duration of depressive episodes. *Journal of Abnormal Psychology*, **100**, 569–582.

Nolen-Hoeksema, S. & Morrow, J. (1993). Effects of rumination and distraction on naturally occurring depressed mood. *Cognition and Emotion*, **7**, 561–570.

Obsessive Compulsive Cognitions Working Group [OCCWG] (1997). Cognitive assessment of obsessive compulsive disorder. *Behaviour Research and Therapy*, **35**, 667–681.

O'Connor, K., Todorov, C., Robillard, S., Borgeat, F., & Brault, M. (1999). Cognitive–behaviour therapy in the treatment of obsessive–compulsive disorder: A controlled study. *Canadian Journal of Psychiatry*, **44**, 64–71.

Öst, L-G. & Breitholtz, E. (2000). Applied relaxation vs. cognitive therapy in the treatment of generalized anxiety disorder. *Behaviour Research and Therapy*, **38**, 777–790.

Papageorgiou, C. & Wells, A. (1998). Effects of attention training on hypochondriasis: A brief case series. *Psychological Medicine*, **28**, 193–200.

Papageorgiou, C. & Wells, A. (1999a). Process and metacognitive dimensions of depressive and anxious thoughts and relationships with emotional intensity. *Clinical Psychology and Psychotherapy*, **6**, 156–162.

Papageorgiou, C. & Wells, A. (1999b). Dimensions of depressive rumination and anxious worry: A comparative study. Paper presented at the *33rd Annual Convention of the Association for the Advancement of Behavior Therapy, Toronto.*

Papageorgiou, C. & Wells, A. (2000). Treatment of recurrent major depression with Attention Training. *Cognitive and Behavioral Practice*, **7**, 407–413.

Papageorgiou, C. & Wells, A. (2001a). Positive beliefs about depressive rumination: Development and preliminary validation of a self-report scale. *Behavior Therapy*, **32**, 13–26.

Papageorgiou, C., & Wells, A. (2001b). Metacognitive beliefs about rumination in recurrent major depression. *Cognitive and Behavioral Practice*, **8**, 160–164.

Purdon, C. (1999). Thought suppression and psychopathology. *Behaviour Research and Therapy*, **37**, 1029–1054.

Purdon, C. & Clark, D. A. (1999). Meta-cognition and obsessions. *Clinical Psychology and Psychotherapy*, **6**, 96–101.

Purdon, C., Rowa, K., & Antony, M. M. (2001). Thought suppression in OCD. Paper presented in C. Purdon & D. Tolin (chairs), Cognitive factors in the persistence of OCD. *Symposium presented at the Association for the Advancement of Behavior Therapy annual meeting, Philadelphia.*

Rachman, S. (1997). A cognitive theory of obsessions. *Behaviour Research and Therapy*, **35**, 793–802.

Rachman, S. (1998). A cognitive theory of obsessions: Elaborations. *Behaviour Research and Therapy*, **36**, 385–401.

Rachman, S. J. & Hodgson, R. J. (1980). *Obsessions and Compulsions.* Englewood Cliffs, NJ: Prentice Hall.

Rassin, E., Merckelbach, H., & Muris, P. (2000). Paradoxical and less paradoxical effects of thought suppression. *Clinical Psychology Review*, **20**, 973–995.

Reed, G. F. (1985). *Obsessional Experience and Compulsive Behaviour: A Cognitive–Structural Approach.* New York: Academic Press.

Reynolds, M. & Wells, A. (1999). The Thought Control Questionnaire—Psychometric properties in a clinical sample, and relationships with PTSD and depression. *Psychological Medicine*, **29**, 1089–1099.

Roemer, L. & Borkovec, T. D. (1994). Effects of suppressing thoughts about emotional material. *Journal of Abnormal Psychology*, **103**, 467–474.

Salkovskis, P. M. (1985). Obsessional–compulsive problems: A cognitive–behavioural analysis. *Behaviour Research and Therapy*, **23**, 571–584.

Salkovskis, P. M. (1989). Cognitive–behavioural factors and the persistence of intrusive thoughts in obsessional problems. *Behaviour Research and Therapy*, **27**, 677–682.

Salkovskis, P. M. (1998). Psychological approaches to the understanding of obsessional problems. In: R. P. Swinson, M. M. Antony, S. Rachman, & M. A. Richter (eds), *Obsessive–Compulsive Disorder: Theory, Research and Treatment* (pp. 33–50). New York: Guilford Press.

Salkovskis, P. M., Richards, C., & Forrester, E. (2000). Psychological treatment of refractory obsessive–compulsive disorder and related problems. In: W. K. Goodman, M. V. Rudorfer, and J. D. Master (eds), *Obsessive–Compulsive Disorder: Contemporary Issues in Treatment* (pp. 201–222). Mahwah, NJ: Lawrence Erlbaum.

Salkovskis, P. M. & Westbrook, D. (1989). Behavior therapy and obsessional ruminations: Can failure be turned into success? *Behaviour Research and Therapy*, **27**, 149–160.

Segal, Z. V., Williams, J. M. G., & Teasdale, J. D. (2002). *Mindfulness Based Cognitive Therapy for Depression: A New Approach for Preventing Relapse.* New York: Guilford Press.

Shapiro, F. (1995). *Eye Movement Desensitization and Reprocessing.* New York: Guilford Press.

Shipherd, J. C. & Beck, J. G. (1999). The effects of suppressing trauma-related thoughts on women with rape-related posttraumatic stress disorder. *Behaviour Research and Therapy*, **37**, 99–112.

Stanley, M. A. & Averill, P. M. (1998). Psychosocial treatment for obsessive–compulsive disorder: Clinical applications. In: R. P. Swinson, M. M. Antony, S. Rachman, and M. Richter (eds), *Obsessive–Compulsive Disorder: Theory, Research and Treatment* (pp. 277–297). New York: Guilford Press.

Stanley, M. A. & Turner, S. M. (1995). Current status of pharmacological and behavioral treatment of obsessive–compulsive disorder. *Behavior Therapy*, **26**, 163–186.

Steketee, G. (1993). *Treatment of Obsessive–Compulsive Disorder.* New York: Guilford Press.

Steketee, G. (1999). *Overcoming Obsessive–Compulsive Disorder: A Behavioral and Cognitive Protocol for the Treatment of OCD.* Oakland, CA: New Harbinger.

Stern, R. S., Lipsedge, M., & Marks, I. (1973). Obsessive ruminations: A controlled trial of a thought stopping technique. *Behaviour Research and Therapy*, **11**, 659–662.

Teasdale, J. D. (1983). Negative thinking in depression: Cause, effect or reciprocal relationship? *Advances in Behaviour Research and Therapy*, **5**, 3–25.

Teasdale, J. D. & Barnard, P. J. (1993). *Affect, Cognition and Change: Remodelling Depressive Thought.* Hove, UK: Lawrence Erlbaum.

Teasdale, J. D., Segal, Z. V., Williams, J. M. G., Ridgeway, V. A., Soulsby, J. M., & Lau, M. A. (2000). Prevention of relapse/recurrence in major depression by mindfulness-based cognitive therapy. *Journal of Consulting and Clinical Psychology*, **68**, 615–623.

Tolin, D. F., Abramowitz, J. S., Hamlin, C., Foa, E. B., & Synodi, D. S. (2002). Attributions for thought suppression failure in obsessive–compulsive disorder. *Cognitive Therapy & Research*, **26**, 505–517.

Tolin, D. F., Abramowitz, J. S., Przeworski, A., & Foa, E. B. (2002). Thought suppression in obsessive–compulsive disorder. *Behaviour Research and Therapy*, **40**, 1255–1274.

Trask, P. C. & Sigmon, S. T. (1999). Ruminating and distracting: The effects of sequential tasks on depressed mood. *Cognitive Therapy and Research*, **23**, 231–246.

Van Oppen, P., De Haan, E., Van Balkom, A. J. L. M., Spinhoven, P., Hoogduin, K., & Van Dyck, R. (1995). Cognitive therapy and exposure in vivo in the treatment of obsessive compulsive disorder. *Behaviour Research and Therapy*, **33**, 379–390.

Wegner, D. M., Erber, R., & Zanakos, S. (1993). Ironic processes in the mental control of mood and mood-related thought. *Journal of Personality and Social Psychology*, **65**, 1093–1104.

Wegner, D. M., Schneider, D. J., Carter, S. R., & White, T. L. (1987). Paradoxical effects of thought suppression. *Journal of Personality and Social Psychology*, **53**, 5–13.

Wells, A. (1990). Panic disorder in association with relaxation induced anxiety: An attentional training approach to treatment. *Behavior Therapy*, **21**, 273–280.

Wells, A. (1995). Meta-cognition and worry: A cognitive model of generalized anxiety disorder. *Behavioural and Cognitive Psychotherapy*, **23**, 301–320.

Wells, A. (1997). *Cognitive Therapy of Anxiety Disorders: A Practice Manual and Conceptual Guide*. Chichester, UK: John Wiley & Sons.

Wells, A. (2000). *Emotional Disorders and Metacognition: Innovative Cognitive Therapy*. Chichester, UK: John Wiley & Sons.

Wells, A. & King, P. (2002). Metacognitive therapy for GAD: Results from a preliminary open trial. Manuscript in preparation.

Wells, A. & Matthews, G. (1994). *Attention and Emotion: A Clinical Perspective*. Hillsdale, NJ: Lawrence Erlbaum.

Wells, A. & Papageorgiou, C. (1995). Worry and the incubation of intrusive images following stress. *Behaviour Research and Therapy*, **33**, 579–583.

Wells, A., White, J., & Carter, K. (1997). Attention training effects on anxiety and beliefs in panic and social phobia. *Clinical Psychology and Psychotherapy*, **4**, 226–232.

Wenzlaff, R. M. & Eisenberg, A. R. (2001). Mental control after dysphoria: Evidence of a suppressed, depressive bias. *Behavior Therapy*, **32**, 27–46.

Wenzlaff, R. M., Meier, J., & Salas, D. M. (2002). Thought suppression and memory biases during and after depressive moods. *Cognition and Emotion*, **16**, 403–422.

Wenzlaff, R. M., Rude, S. S., & West, L. M. (2002). Cognitive vulnerability to depression: The role of thought suppression and attitude certainty. *Cognition and Emotion*, **16**, 533–548.

Wolpe, J. (1958). *Psychotherapy by Reciprocal Inhibition*. Stanford, CA: Stanford University Press.

Wolpe, J. (1973). *The Practice of Behavior Therapy*. New York: Pergamon Press.

Yamagami, T. (1971). The treatment of an obsession by thought-stopping. *Journal of Behavior Therapy and Experimental Psychology*, **2**, 133–135.

12 Cognitive Therapy for Depressive Thinking

DEAN McMILLAN AND PETER FISHER

Academic Division of Clinical Psychology, University of Manchester, UK

Cognitive therapy (CT) for depression (Beck, Rush, Shaw, & Emery, 1979) is probably the most widely researched and evaluated of the psychological interventions for emotional disorders. Reviews of CT for depression indicate that it is an efficacious treatment for mild to moderate depression (e.g., Clark, Beck, & Alford, 1999; DeRubeis & Crits-Christoph, 1998). CT for depression also has demonstrable relapse prevention effects. Numerous studies have found CT to be more effective than antidepressant medication when both are withdrawn shortly after recovery (e.g., Blackburn, Eunson, & Bishop, 1986; Shea et al., 1992). However, a significant proportion of clients continue to relapse, estimates vary between 25% (DeRubeis & Crits-Christoph, 1998) and 50% (Nezu, Nezu, Trunzo, & McClure, 1998). Furthermore, a recent "mega-analysis" indicated that CT is as equally effective as antidepressant medication in treating severe depression (DeRubeis, Gelfand, Tang, & Simons, 1999).

CT for depression was developed from Beck's cognitive model of emotional disorders (Beck 1967, 1976). This is a clinical theory that places negative patterns of thinking at the heart of depression. The model assumes that through experience individuals develop depressogenic schemas or negative core beliefs about themselves and the world, which confers a vulnerability to developing depression. Schemas represent a useful heuristic in conceptualizing the way in which an individual makes sense of the world. In Beck's theory, the content of the schema is paramount: specifically, how an individual's core beliefs and conditional assumptions guide interpretation of events and subsequently behaviour. Schemas are thought to lie dormant until activated through a life event that runs counter to the individual's rules and assumptions (e.g., experiencing a failure, when the conditional assumption is "I must succeed at everything otherwise I am useless"). Schema activation triggers negative automatic thoughts (NATs). These thoughts or images, which appear to occur spontaneously, are perceived as reflecting reality at the time of occurrence and produce negative affect. NATs in depression fall into three distinct content domains termed the negative cognitive triad (Beck et al., 1979). This comprises negative views about the self (e.g., "I am useless"), the world/external events (e.g., "life is unenjoyable"), and the future (e.g., "my life will always be full of failures"). The final component of Beck's cognitive model of depression is the presence of systematic bias in thinking styles or thinking errors. Such errors include *selective abstraction*, focusing solely on the negative aspect of an event; *overgeneralization*, drawing all encompassing conclusions based on a single incident; and *dichotomous reasoning*, thinking in all or nothing terms.

CT for depression is a structured, time-limited problem-focused approach that aims to modify the three main domains of negative thinking outlined above; namely, negative automatic thoughts, thinking errors, and depressogenic schema. This chapter brings together the principal cognitive and behavioural techniques that are used to modify NATs and thinking errors in depression. Although NATs are conceptually distinct from depressive rumination (e.g., Papageorgiou & Wells, 2001; see also Chapter 1), it is possible that the techniques used to challenge the content of NATs could be effective in modifying the content of depressive rumination. The present chapter is a summary of techniques a clinician could use to challenge the content of depressive rumination and is not intended to be a comprehensive guide to CT for depression.

This chapter is divided into three sections. First, we present some of the behavioural strategies that are used at the beginning of CT for depression. Then we discuss the verbal reattribution and behavioural reattribution techniques that make up the main body of CT. Finally, there is a brief description of schema-focused strategies that are used in the later stages of therapy.

BEHAVIOURAL STRATEGIES

Behavioural formulations of depression essentially suggest that depression is precipitated by changes in an individual's life circumstances that result in a loss of positive reinforcement. Depression is subsequently maintained because once a person is depressed his or her behaviour (e.g., lowered activity levels and social withdrawal) presents fewer opportunities for positive reinforcement (cf. Williams, 1992). The main goal of behavioural approaches to depression is to increase the opportunity for positive reinforcement. However, in CT for depression, behavioural techniques are primarily used as a "series of small experiments designed to test the validity of the patient's hypotheses or ideas about himself" (Beck et al., 1979, p. 118). However, this does not diminish the usefulness of other behavioural strategies in improving mood and activity levels. Below are three examples of how behavioural strategies are used to produce cognitive change.

MONITORING ACTIVITY LEVELS

In the initial stages of treatment, clients are typically asked to monitor their activities on an hourly basis. In addition, the client can be asked to rate the degree of mastery and pleasure for each of the activities on a 0 (no mastery/ pleasure) to 10 (complete mastery/pleasure) scale. This enables the therapist to assess the client's current activity levels and which activities the client finds most pleasurable and feel they have the most mastery over. This facilitates discussion of thoughts, such as "I never do anything," "nothing gives me pleasure," and "everything is a chore," that are common in depression. Monitoring activities can provide good evidence to refute NATs especially when coupled with the reattribution techniques discussed on p. 244. Monitoring activity levels can be especially useful in socializing the client to the cognitive model of depression. For example, the client may have the belief "nothing I do makes any difference to my mood." Mastery and pleasure ratings can be used effectively to refute this belief and used as further evidence that challenging the veracity of depressive thoughts will help to overcome depression.

ACTIVITY SCHEDULING

Once an accurate baseline of the client's level of activity and degree of mastery and pleasure is obtained, the therapist can start to assist the client in scheduling activities. The main purpose of activity scheduling is to help the client overcome the symptoms of depression, specifically to counter depressive inertia, social withdrawal, and hopelessness. The client is provided with a rationale outlining that inactivity leads to lowered mood and reduced problem-solving. Scheduling activities provides a direct means of challenging NATs concerning hopelessness. Consider the client with the following NATs: "I am useless" and "my life will always be full of failures." Through judicious activity scheduling, these NATs can be challenged effectively. It requires careful planning, but it is comparatively easy to devise activities that give the client a sense of accomplishment and enjoyment. In summary, activity scheduling provides the client with substantial counterevidence to their NATs. The therapist can use this evidence profitably during verbal reattribution.

GRADED TASK ASSIGNMENT

Beck et al. (1979) observed that when depressed clients successfully complete tasks a temporary improvement in mood occurs. Persons (1989) notes that depressed clients often have NATs, such as "I won't be able to do it, I'll fail." Therefore, the main purpose of graded task assignment is to maximize the likelihood of successful task completion thereby disconfirming the client's negative assumptions. Task completion is achieved by breaking a task into concrete and manageable steps, combined with verbal reattribution of

NATs that interfere with task completion. Graded task assignment is also a useful technique for overcoming procrastination and hopelessness (Fennell, 1989).

In the remainder of this chapter we will review common techniques for modifying belief in NATs and schemas. Broadly, these techniques can be classified as verbal reattribution strategies and behavioural reattribution strategies.

VERBAL REATTRIBUTION

One of the challenges facing the cognitive therapist is the identification of key target NATs that are conceptualized as a source of dysfunction. Individuals may report multiple NATs and the key to effective therapy is identification of cognitions driving persistent depression. There are a number of techniques for doing this:

- ask about thoughts that occurred during a recent difficult situation in which the client felt low (Beck et al., 1979; Persons, 1989);
- when the client's mood changes noticeably during a session, ask the client what they are currently thinking about (Beck, 1995; Wells, 1997);
- ask the client to complete a Dysfunctional Thought Record (DTR) (see subsequent section for details) (Beck et al., 1979; Fennell, 1989).

If a client has difficulty identifying automatic thoughts, the therapist can use a number of strategies. For example, the client could be asked to imagine him or herself in a recent difficult situation and then describe it in the present tense, which can help activate the thoughts (Wells, 1997). Another method for doing this involves the therapist and client role-playing a difficult situation (Wells, 1997). Automatic thoughts may occur in the form of an image, and so the therapist should also ask about these (Leahy, 1996; Persons, 1989).

Once the automatic thought has been identified, the therapist should then elicit the following information:

- the client's belief in the automatic thought (e.g., 0–100% scale);
- the emotion accompanying the thought;
- the intensity of this emotional response (e.g., 0–100 scale).

DEFINITION OF KEY TERMS

A NAT can be upsetting even when its contents are vague or undefined; in fact, the client may continue to believe the thought because of its vagueness. The process of defining key terms can help the client realize that, once clearly defined, the thought is not true (Leahy, 1996).

This technique can be introduced by saying something like "the same word might mean different things to different people; we'll first need to work out exactly what you mean by ____ (e.g., 'a failure')." The therapist then asks the client to come up with a definition of the key term using such questions as:

- How would you define ____?
- What characteristics make someone ____?
- How does a person who is ____ behave?

Once the term is defined, the therapist asks the client to identify the opposite pole of the construct (Leahy, 1996). Here the client is asked what word or phrase would be used to describe the opposite of the key term (e.g., "a success"), and the client is asked to define this opposite pole.

With the terms clearly defined, the validity of the thought can be discussed. The therapist asks the client about the extent to which he or she shares the characteristics of the key term and then asks the same question about the opposite construct. This can be combined with other verbal reattribution techniques, such as asking for evidence and counterevidence.

For example, a client described how he shouted at his adolescent daughter because she wanted to stay out later than midnight. After she had gone out, he spent the rest of the evening brooding about being a bad father. In the therapy session the therapist and client worked to define the term "bad father" and "good father." Although the client mentioned "shouting at your child" as a feature of being a bad parent, he realized that there was more to it than just this characteristic. He also realized that he shared many of the characteristics of a good father, such as spending time with his daughter and taking interest in her hobbies.

Even if defining key terms does not produce a shift in the client's belief, it has several benefits for the therapist. It is difficult to challenge a thought if the meaning is unclear (Wells, 1997). The act of defining a term can reveal distortions to the therapist, and this may then lead to the use of other verbal reattribution techniques (Persons, 1989). For example, the client believes he is a bad father on the basis of shouting at his daughter, which indicates an "overgeneralization" thinking error (see section on thinking errors).

EVALUATING AND QUESTIONING THE EVIDENCE

The initial goal of the therapist is to question the evidence supporting negative automatic thoughts. Demonstration of the lack of evidence can weaken the client's belief level. Preliminary questions may be, "what evidence do you have that supports that thought?" or "what makes you think that this is the reality?" Follow-up questions should be used to explore in detail the evidence provided by the client. Occasionally, the client recognizes that he or she has somewhat limited evidence, which in itself can weaken the belief. Of course, it is more probable that the client will supply evidence in support of the NAT. In this situation, the quality and nature of the evidence should be carefully ascertained.

ESTABLISHING AND EVALUATING COUNTEREVIDENCE

Once the evidence supporting the NAT has been established, counterevidence to the NAT is then explored. For example, a client may have the NAT, "no one likes me"; the therapist's task is to elicit any existing counterevidence. Useful questions in eliciting counterevidence to the NAT "no one likes me" may include:

- "Is there any evidence that people do like you?"
- "Do you have any evidence to suggest that the thought 'no one likes me' is not true?"
- "How do you know the thought 'no one likes me' is accurate?"

The main goal is to obtain concrete counterevidence to the NAT. In this example, the therapist can widen the search for counterevidence to the NAT "no one likes me" by asking the client exactly how different subgroups of people (family, friends, work colleagues, and so on) demonstrate they like her (e.g., asking her for lunch, offers of help, inquiring about her life). Helping clients provide their own rich vein of counterevidence to the NAT can be extremely effective in belief modification.

ALTERNATIVE EXPLANATIONS

When NATs represent inaccurate or biased interpretations of events, reattribution can focus on identifying alternative explanations. This technique simply requires the client and therapist to brainstorm alternative explanations or solutions to the identified problem (Beck et al., 1979). Generation of alternative explanations is typically straightforward. For example, a client may interpret his partner's quietness over the course of an evening or week as proof she is no longer in love with him. By developing a list of alternative explanations, the client can discover that there are many other explanations. This technique can be used to illustrate how attention is focused solely on the negative appraisal and other explanations are ignored or discounted. As with all CT techniques the effectiveness of this approach varies considerably across clients, but can be very effective when one of the alternative explanations matches perfectly with the client's experience (Persons, 1989).

PIE CHARTS

Simply generating a list of alternative explanations can produce belief change. However, the effectiveness of verbal reattribution can be maximized through appropriately combining and layering techniques. The use of a pie chart following generation of alternative explanations can be useful in modifying the client's negative appraisal of an event (Clark, 1989; Wells, 1997). The therapist draws a circle and then asks the client to allocate a section of the pie to each of the alternative explanations/reasons. The client is asked to ascribe a probability rating in percentage terms for each of the alternatives, which is translated into a section of the pie. When the alternative explanations have been exhausted, typically there is very little room left for the original negative appraisal. This presents the client with a visual representation of alternative explanations.

IDENTIFYING AND LABELLING THINKING ERRORS

Beck (1976) proposed that people with emotional disorder tend to make systematic biases in their thinking. The initial goal of the therapist is to identify and note these systematic biases or thinking errors. Enabling the client to identify and label thinking errors in NATs aids the client in evaluating the validity of their NATs. Several types of thinking errors have been identified (cf. Burns, 1980; Beck, 1995) including:

- *catastrophizing*—dwelling on and exaggerating the probability that the worst will happen;
- *dichotomous thinking*—thinking in all-or-nothing terms;
- *mind reading*—making negative assumptions about how people feel about you in the absence of evidence;
- *selective abstraction*—focusing on the negative aspect of an event and discounting the positive elements;
- *personalization*—assuming negative external events are attributable to oneself, rather than looking for alternative explanations;
- *overgeneralization*—drawing all encompassing conclusions based on a single incident.

Clients are encouraged to ask themselves "what type of thinking error am I making?" For example, the NAT may be "everything I do turns out badly," this is an example of overgeneralization and labelling it is a step to making a rational response. In this instance, the rational response could be "I didn't do as well as I would have liked this time, but more often than not I do things well."

ADVANTAGES–DISADVANTAGES ANALYSIS

Sometimes it is useful to sidestep the question of how true a thought is and instead focus on the utility of the thought for the client (Beck, 1995). One method of doing this is to use an advantages–disadvantages analysis. This technique is particularly useful when the client continues to believe strongly in a NAT, despite verbal and behavioural reattribution and when it proves difficult to establish the extent to which a NAT is true.

In its most detailed form the advantages–disadvantages analysis consists of the following stages (Wells, 1997):

- select a NAT for discussion;
- draw a two-column table, with one column labelled "advantages," and the other labelled "disadvantages";
- work collaboratively to generate a list of advantages of holding the thought;
- repeat for disadvantages;
- assign weights (e.g., scores of between 1 and 10) to each of the items in the two lists;
- sum the weights separately for the advantages and disadvantages columns;
- use the results to discuss the usefulness of the thought.

DOUBLE STANDARD TECHNIQUE

The double standard technique (Burns, 1989) involves asking the client whether he or she would apply the same standard to another person as he or she is currently applying to him or herself. First the client is asked to imagine another person in the same situation. It is helpful to select a specific person, such as a family member or friend; otherwise, the client may be able to make general statements that support his or her view (Persons, 1989). Once the client has someone in mind, the therapist asks such questions as:

- "what would you say to that person?";
- "would you think the same way about that person as you do about yourself?"

Usually the client would not be so negative toward the other person as he or she is toward him or herself and the therapist can then point out the existence of a double standard. To generate a rational response, the client can be asked to apply what he or she would say to another person to him or herself.

REATTRIBUTION TRAINING

Abramson, Seligman, and Teasdale (1978) proposed that people who are depressed tend to have an attributional style in which negative events are attributed to internal (personal), stable (unchanging), and global causes (wide-ranging), whereas positive events are attributed to external, unstable, and specific causes. More recent formulations (e.g., Alloy, Abramson, Metalsky, & Hartlage, 1988) have emphasized the importance of the attributions for negative rather than positive events, because it is the attributions for these events that seem to correlate with depressed mood (Brewin, 1985). Reattribution training aims to help the client challenge these maladaptive causal attributions (Williams, 1992). If the therapist judges that a client's depressive thoughts are linked to this attributional style, then a number of reattributional training techniques could be used, such as the one discussed by Williams (1992), based on the work of Cleaver (1981).

First, it is necessary to introduce the client to the concept of attributions and to illustrate how attributions can influence mood. The client could be given the example of failing at a maths test and could then be asked how an internal, stable, and global attributional style would affect a person's mood. The therapist then discusses with the client a number of hypothetical and real situations, and the attributions the client makes are labelled and if necessary challenged. Examples of situations for discussion include a friend passing the client in the street and ignoring him/her, or writing a letter to a friend asking for a reply but not getting one. If an internal attribution is made, the client is asked to identify possible reasons for the situation to do with other people rather than him or herself. Stable attributions are addressed by asking the client to generate examples of how things could change. If the client makes a global attribution, he or she is asked to think of specific reasons for the event.

POINT AND COUNTERPOINT

Point and counterpoint strategies consist of a role play in which the therapist and client alternate in arguing for and against a thought (Wells, 1997). The therapist may begin by arguing for the thought, using the type of arguments or evidence that the client has already used. The client must act as therapist, using strategies picked up during therapy, such as looking for thinking errors. Roles are reversed once the client finds it difficult to challenge the thought. The roles can be reversed several times during the discussion.

CONTINUA WORK

Continua work is useful when the therapist identifies that the client is using dichotomous thinking (Beck, 1995). This technique consists of generating a

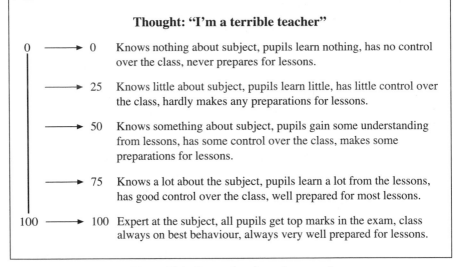

Figure 12.1. Example of continua work

continuum for a particular construct to help the client move from a dichot-omous view to one allowing shades of grey. The process of developing a continuum begins by asking the client to define the two poles of the construct and placing them on a continuum at 0 and 100. For example, a teacher who had the thought "I'm a terrible teacher" can be asked to define "terrible teacher" and "brilliant teacher." The client is then encouraged to define points along the continuum. This can be done by generating a list of character-istics, or by using people the client knows. Using these anchor points, the client is then asked to place him or herself on the continuum. An example of a completed continuum is given in Figure 12.1.

DYSFUNCTIONAL THOUGHT RECORD (DTR)

The DTR provides a useful structure for identifying and formally challenging NATs in session. The client can also use it between sessions to identify and challenge thoughts as they occur (Fennell, 1989) and in this way become their own cognitive therapist.

There are several versions of the DTR, each deriving from the Daily Record of Dsyfunctional Thoughts described in Beck et al. (1979). Figure 12.2 gives an example of a completed DTR. The first three columns record background information, such as the date, situation, and accompanying emotion, the severity of which is rated on a 0–100 scale. The fourth column asks the client to describe the thought he or she had and the extent to which he or she believes it (0–100%). The client challenges the thought in the fifth column

Date	Emotion What do you feel? How bad is it (0–100)?	Situation What were you doing or thinking about?	Thoughts What exactly were your thoughts? How far did you believe each of them (0–100%)?	Alternative responses What are you rational answers to the automatic thoughts? How far do you believe each of them (0–100%)?	Outcome 1. How far do you now believe the thoughts (0–100%)? 2. How do you feel (0–100)? 3. What can you do now?
3 March	Sad, upset (70)	In butchers. Butcher didn't speak to me much, even though last week I had a long conversation with him.	He doesn't like me. (80%)	He must see 100s of people every week. He might not have recognized me. (40%) When I spoke to him last week there was no-one in the shop, but this week there were four people waiting to be served. He might have been busy. (60%)	1. 40%. 2. Feel less sad. (40) 3. Remind myself not to jump to conclusions. See how he acts toward me the next time I see him.

Figure 12.2. Example of a Dysfunctional Thought Record (DTR)

by generating alternative or rational responses and then rates the extent to which he or she believes each of them (0–100%). The final column asks the client to rerate the thought and the emotion and what he or she can do now (i.e., how he or she could think or act differently).

BEHAVIOURAL REATTRIBUTION

Sometimes verbal strategies used alone can achieve a marked shift in the content of the client's depressive thoughts, but verbal reattribution strategies used alone often have a limited effect. One method of maximizing cognitive change is to use a behavioural experiment to test the validity of a specific thought (Beck et al., 1979).

The design of a behavioural experiment is similar to that of a scientific experiment (Fennell, 1989). Both involve developing and testing a hypothesis, recording the results, and making conclusions, one of which may be the need for further experimental work.

Wells (1997), in his discussion of the treatment of anxiety disorders, provides a useful framework for designing and implementing behavioural experiments. A modified version of this framework can be used in the treatment of depressive thinking.

STAGE 1: PREPARATION

(a) Elicit and challenge thought

The first stage involves identifying a key cognition and then carrying out preliminary verbal reattribution, as described above.

(b) Set up a testable hypothesis

In the design stage the therapist and client work collaboratively to design a way of testing the thought. The more the client is involved in the design of the experiment, the more compelling a successful result is likely to be for him or her. Therefore, at this stage it can be useful to ask the client such a question as "what could you do to find out whether that thought is true?" One method of generating an experiment is to discuss situations in which the thought occurs and then identify behaviours that may prevent disconfirmation of the thought. For example, one client reported she was finding it difficult to understand a night class she was taking in mathematics, and this had triggered the thought "I've fallen behind the rest of the class." She had avoided talking to her classmates or her teacher about this, which prevented her finding out whether the thought was true. In this situation the client could conduct a "minisurvey" to find out how many of the rest of the class were also having difficulties.

The design needs to include a testable prediction, meaning that if the thought is true one consequence will be observed, whereas if the thought is not true there will be another distinct consequence. The contents of the prediction should also be clearly operationalized, so that unambiguous disconfirmation can take place. In the example discussed above it would be necessary to specify what proportion of the class will need to say they do not find it difficult for this to be taken as evidence of falling behind. The therapist should also obtain a belief rating based on the testable prediction (e.g., 0–100% scale). Here the client could be asked, "How much do you believe that more than half of the people you talk to will say they have no problems understanding the class?" The therapist should also keep a written record of both the prediction and the belief rating. This can help avoid a retrospective bias in which the result of the experiment influences the client's perception of the probability of that result.

Even well-designed experiments often need to be refined and repeated, so it is useful to try and minimize avoidable repetition from the start. Once a preliminary design has been agreed upon, it is useful to ask the client whether he or she can identify any features of the design that may make the results unconvincing. If a confound is identified, the therapist and client should discuss how the design could be modified to address the difficulty.

(c) Provide and check rationale

The therapist should provide a rationale to the client for the experiment and then ensure that the client understands the rationale. Without this the client might not carry out the task, or the results may not be used to modify cognitions.

Once the therapist is happy that the client understands the reason for carrying out the experiment, it is useful to ask the client whether he or she is willing to carry it out. If difficulties are identified, then practical problem-solving or further verbal reattribution will be needed.

STAGE 2: CONDUCT EXPERIMENT AND RECORD RESULTS

The second stage involves the client carrying out the behavioural experiment and recording, as necessary, the results. The experiment can be carried out either within or between sessions (Beck, 1995). It is usually preferable to conduct the behavioural experiment in session because potential problems can be addressed immediately, rather than having to wait until the next session. However, an effective test of many types of depressive thought will inevitably require a between-session test.

STAGE 3: SUMMARIZE RESULTS

The third stage involves summarizing the results of the experiment (e.g., by asking the client what he or she has discovered). The therapist should also check with the client how much he or she now believes the thought, which will indicate whether a further behavioural experiment is needed. If the belief rating has not reduced, or has reduced but is still substantial, the therapist can ask such a question as, "what is keeping the belief at 35%?" This can lead to the refinement of the existing design or the development of a new experiment to challenge the residual belief.

SCHEMA WORK

When some symptom relief has been obtained using the techniques outlined above, the therapist may choose to focus on core beliefs and assumptions at the schema level. A number of techniques can be used to identify core beliefs and assumptions. One commonly used method is the downward arrow technique (Burns, 1980). This involves repeatedly asking about the meaning of a thought until an assumption or core belief is uncovered, using such a question as "if that were true, what would be so bad about that?" Other techniques include:

- looking for common themes in automatic thoughts (Fennell, 1989);
- examining times when the client felt extremely happy, because this might indicate the demands of an assumption have been met (Fennell, 1989);
- using questionnaires designed to measure core beliefs and assumptions, such as the Dysfunctional Attitudes Scale (Weissman & Beck, 1978).

The verbal reattribution and behavioural reattribution strategies described above can be profitably applied to work at the schema level. For example, the therapist can ask about the evidence for and against a particular assumption (e.g., "unless I am liked by everyone, I am a bad person") or a core belief (e.g., "I am unlovable"). Behavioural experiments are also important at this stage to examine the effects of new ways of behaving that run counter to an original belief or assumption. For example, one client had a conditional assumption that unless he always puts others' needs before his own he would be rejected. The behavioural experiment involved making his own needs known when out with his friends, to find out whether they would reject him. In addition to the methods already described, there are a number of additional strategies that can be used when working at the schema level.

EXAMINING THE EFFECT OF BELIEFS AND ASSUMPTIONS ON CURRENT DAY-TO-DAY LIFE

A useful starting point is to ask the client to consider how beliefs and assumptions are currently affecting day-to-day life (Williams, 1992). This requires the client to identify a recent situation in which a belief or assumption was activated; he or she then examines how it affected mood and behaviour. Standard verbal reattribution techniques are used to challenge the belief or assumption, with the aim of developing a more moderate or realistic one. The therapist then helps the client to consider how holding this new belief or assumption would alter his or her mood and behaviour.

EXAMINING THE ORIGIN OF BELIEFS AND ASSUMPTIONS

Once a core belief or assumption has been identified, the therapist can ask the client how he or she thinks the belief or assumption arose. Useful questions include "when do you first remember having that belief about yourself?" and "was there anything that happened around the same time that could explain why you developed this belief?" For example, a client with the belief that he is worthless may discuss an experience of being compared unfavourably with his two sisters. Examining the origin of core beliefs and assumptions can be a powerful strategy because it emphasizes to the client that these are learnt beliefs, rather than unquestionable truths (Persons, 1989).

EXAMINING THE MAINTENANCE OF BELIEFS AND ASSUMPTIONS OVER TIME

If a client accepts a belief or assumption as completely true, then over time the person may act in such a way as to confirm it, or at least prevent it being disconfirmed. For example, a client with the core belief that she was unlovable reported three instances over a five-year period in which she was asked out on a date, each time by a person she felt attracted to, but on each occasion she turned down the request. On discussion it turned out she had done this because of such thoughts as 'they feel sorry for me," "they are doing it for a bet," or "they will reject me as soon as they get to know what I'm really like." Examining how the belief has been maintained over time can help the client to realize what needs to be done to evaluate and change the belief.

CORE BELIEF WORKSHEET

Core beliefs and assumptions are often extreme in their nature, containing "shoulds," "musts," and "oughts." The aim of schema work is to develop more moderate and realistic assumptions and beliefs. The Core Belief Worksheet (Beck, 1995) provides a systematic structure for the client to practise

---

CORE BELIEF WORKSHEET

OLD BELIEF: *I'm powerless*

How much do you believe this belief right now? (0–100)   *50%*
What is the most you've believed it this week? (0–100)   *80%*
What is the least you've believed it this week? (0–100)   *25%*

NEW BELIEF: *I have power and control in many areas of my life*

How much do you believe the belief right now? (0–100)   *35%*

Evidence that contradicts old core belief and supports new belief	Evidence that supports old core belief with reframe
My friend asked me to babysit, but I had already arranged to do something else on that night. Rather than just giving in, I explained this to him and and said I wouldn't be able to babysit.	*Already snowed under at work, but given more tasks to do. Couldn't say no. However, it's a difficult time for the company at the moment, and everyone is working hard, not just me. At other times I've managed to say no.*
Made a suggestion at work about a change in my role, the managers agreed to this.	*Dad asked me to visit him. I didn't really want to go this week, but I went anyway. However, I don't give*
Made a suggestion to husband about where we could go on holiday this year. He agreed, and I booked it.	*in to Dad all the time. Giving in some times doesn't mean to say I've no control over my life.*

Figure 12.3. Example of a Core Belief Worksheet
From Beck (1995)

doing this, a completed example of which is given in Figure 12.3. The Work-sheet first asks the client to specify the old core belief and the new, more moderate alternative belief, along with belief ratings. Both within and between sessions the Worksheet is used to record evidence that does not support the old belief. The client also records evidence that does support the old belief, but this is accompanied by challenging that evidence, or reinterpret-ing it.

SUMMARY AND CONCLUSIONS

This chapter has summarized a number of the more commonly used strategies for challenging the content of depressive thoughts. Behavioural strategies, such as activity scheduling, can be used early on in therapy to challenge depressive thinking. However, the main body of therapy consists of eliciting and challenging cognitions using a combination of verbal reattribution and behavioural experiments. Later on in therapy, the therapist may focus on modifying beliefs and assumptions at the schema level.

Over the last 30 years CT has led to a paradigm shift in the way depression and other emotional disorders are conceptualized and treated. In the clinical theory developed by Beck, cognition is seen as having a central role in depression, and the aim of treatment is to modify these cognitions. In its original form, as outlined in this chapter, the content of cognitions is the focus of the intervention. This therapeutic strategy has proved to be an effective treatment in trials, but these trials have also identified high rates of relapse. Expanding the focus of CT for depression to include cognitive processes or thinking styles may be one method of improving treatment outcome. The next chapter, by Wells and Papageorgiou, discusses treatment strategies for doing this.

REFERENCES

Abramson, L. Y., Seligman, M. E. P., & Teasdale, J. (1978). Learned helplessness in humans: Critique and reformulation. *Journal of Abnormal Psychology*, **87**, 49–74.

Alloy, L. B., Abramson, L. Y., Metalsky, G. I., & Hartlage, S. (1988). The hopelessness theory of depression: Attributional aspects. *British Journal of Clinical Psychology*, **26**, 5–21.

Beck, A. T. (1967). *Depression: Clinical, Experiential and Theoretical Perspectives*. New York: Harper & Row.

Beck, A. T. (1976). *Cognitive Therapy and the Emotional Disorders*. New York: International Universities Press.

Beck, A. T., Rush, A. J., Shaw, B. F., & Emery, G. (1979). *Cognitive Therapy of Depression*. New York: Guilford Press.

Beck, J. S. (1995). *Cognitive Therapy: Basics and Beyond*. New York: Guilford Press.

Blackburn, I. M., Eunson, K. M., & Bishop, S. (1986). A two year naturalistic follow-up of depressed patients treated with cognitive therapy, pharmacotherapy and a combination of both. *Journal of Affective Disorders*, **10**, 65–75.

Brewin, C. R. (1985). Depression and causal attributions: What is their relation? *Psychological Bulletin*, **98**, 297–309.

Burns, D. D. (1980). *Feeling Good: The New Mood Therapy*. New York: New American Library.

Burns, D. D. (1989). *The Feeling Good Handbook*. New York: William Morrow.

Clark, D. A., Beck, A. T., & Alford, B. A. (1999). *Cognitive Theory and Therapy of Depression*. New York: John Wiley & Sons.

Clark, D. M. (1989). Anxiety states: Panic and generalised anxiety. In: K. Hawton, P. Salkovskis, J. Kirk, & D. M. Clark (eds), *Cognitive Behaviour Therapy for Psychiatric Problems: A Practical Guide*. Oxford, UK: Oxford Medical Publications.

Cleaver, S. (1981). Attributional modifications in the treatment of depression. Unpublished MSc dissertation, University of Newcastle-upon-Tyne, UK.

DeRubeis, R. J. & Crits-Christoph, P. (1998). Empirically supported individual and group psychological treatments for adult mental disorders. *Journal of Consulting and Clinical Psychology*, **66**(1), 37–52.

DeRubeis, R. J., Gelfand, L. A., Tang, T. Z., & Simons, A. D. (1999). Medications versus cognitive behaviour therapy for severely depressed outpatients: Mega-analysis of four randomized comparisions. *American Journal of Psychiatry*, **156**, 1007–1013.

Fennell, M. (1989). Depression. In: K. Hawton, P. Salkovskis, J. Kirk, & D. M. Clark (eds), *Cognitive Behaviour Therapy for Psychiatric Problems: A Practical Guide*. Oxford, UK: Oxford Medical Publications.

Leahy, R. (1996). *Cognitive Therapy: Basic Principles and Applications*. New Jersey: Aronson.

Nezu, A. M., Nezu, C. M., Trunzo, J. J., & McClure, K. S. (1998). Treatment maintenance for unipolar depression: Relevant issues, literature review, and recommendations for research and clinical practice. *Clinical Psychology: Science and Practice*, **5**, 496–512.

Papageorgiou, C. & Wells, A. (2001). Positive beliefs about depressive rumination: Development and preliminary validation of a self-report scale. *Behavior Therapy*, **32**, 13–26.

Persons, J. B. (1989). *Cognitive Therapy in Practice: A Case Formulation Approach*. New York: W. W. Norton.

Shea, M. T., Elkin, I., Imber, S. D., Sotsky, S. M., Watkins, J. T., Collins, J. F., Pilkonis, P. A., Beckham, E., Glass, D. R., Dolan, R. T., & Parloff, M. B. (1992). Course of depressive symptoms over follow-up: Findings from the NIMH [National Institute of Mental Health] treatment of depression collaborative research program. *Archives of General Psychiatry*, **49**, 782–787.

Weissman, A. N. & Beck, A. T. (1978). Development and validation of the Dysfunctional Attitude Scale: A preliminary investigation. Paper presented at *Annual Meeting of the American Educational Research Association, Toronto*.

Wells, A. (1997). *Cognitive Therapy of Anxiety Disorders: A Practice Manual and Conceptual Guide*. Chichester, UK: John Wiley & Sons.

Williams, J. M. G. (1992). *The Psychological Treatment of Depression: A Guide to the Theory and Practice of Cognitive Behaviour Therapy*. London: Routledge.

13 Metacognitive Therapy for Depressive Rumination

ADRIAN WELLS
Academic Division of Clinical Psychology, University of Manchester, UK

COSTAS PAPAGEORGIOU
Institute for Health Research, University of Lancaster, UK

Few treatments or techniques have been directly targeted at treating rumination in depression (for further details, see Chapter 11 in this book by Christine Purdon). This is most probably because ruminative styles of thinking have not been given prominence in cognitive–behavioural models of disorder. Guided chiefly by schema theory (Beck, 1967, 1976; Beck, Rush, Shaw, & Emery, 1979), cognitive treatments have focused on modifying the *content* of negative automatic thoughts and beliefs about the self, world, and future, and associated behaviours. While this approach has met with success and has had considerable impact on research and theory, a large proportion of depressed patients fail to respond fully or relapse following treatment (Roth & Fonagy, 1996).

Two lines of work suggest that it may be of advantage therapeutically to develop a treatment that specifically targets the *process* of rumination. First, theoretical developments have linked rumination to the development and persistence of depression (Nolen-Hoeksema, 1991; Teasdale & Barnard, 1993; Wells & Matthews, 1994). Second, empirical evidence has amply demonstrated that rumination is linked to emotional vulnerability (for further details, see Chapters 1–5 and 7 in this book). One theoretical approach in particular—the Self-Regulatory Executive Function model (S-REF: Wells & Matthews, 1994, 1996)—provides grounding for the development of a rumination-focused treatment. As described in Chapter 1 of this book, Papageorgiou and Wells (2003) have used it to construct a specific model of relationships between rumination, depression, and metacognition. This model has preliminary support from clinical and non-clinical data. Further foundations for developing a treatment of rumination can be obtained from the examination of the metacognitive treatment approach to generalized anxiety disorder (GAD) (Wells, 1997,

Depressive Rumination: Nature, Theory and Treatment
Edited by Costas Papageorgiou and Adrian Wells. © 2004 John Wiley & Sons Ltd

1999). The thinking style in generalized anxiety disorder is characterized by excessive and difficult-to-control worry, which overlaps considerably with rumination. While worry and rumination can be distinguished (Papageorgiou & Wells, 1999a, b; see also Chapter 1 of this book), these processes show much overlap, suggesting that similar interventions might be appropriate.

A BRIEF OVERVIEW OF THE S-REF MODEL

The S-REF model is a generic metacognitive framework for conceptualizing vulnerability to and the maintenance of emotional disorder. According to the S-REF model, emotional disorders are maintained by perseverative styles of thinking (worry/rumination), attentional strategies of threat monitoring, and behaviours that fail to modify dysfunctional self-beliefs. This array of factors constitutes a cognitive–attentional syndrome (CAS), a generic marker for which is heightened self-focused attention. Perseverative processing occurs in the form of worry and/or rumination that, along with threat monitoring, are viewed as maladaptive coping strategies. These strategies are derived from the individual's metacognitive knowledge, which is activated in problematic situations and drives processing. Two types of metacognitive knowledge are identified in the model: (1) propositional beliefs (e.g., "ruminating stops me forgetting what is important in life") and (2) programs or plans that guide processing and are not directly verbally accessible. Both types of knowledge are seen as separate from more general negative beliefs about the self and world and explain individual differences in response styles.

The model emphasizes dynamic factors in the initiation and maintenance of emotional disorder. It is not the activation of negative non-metacognitive beliefs or thoughts that is problematic, but the development of self-perpetuating processing configurations (the CAS) that lock the individual into a state of pathology or increase the risk of relapse. The CAS is problematic because coping strategies, such as rumination and threat monitoring, may increase the accessibility of negative information and negative thoughts. Coping by negative self-criticism or repeated analysis of the self can set up negative styles of person–environment interaction. Predominantly verbal ruminative activity may drain the cognitive resources needed for implementation of more adaptive and effortful appraisal and coping strategies. Worry and rumination may interfere with low-level reflexive adaptation processes, such as exposure to imagery, that are necessary for habituation and emotional processing following stress (Wells & Papageorgiou, 1995). Coping through avoidance of situations and reduced activity may impair person–environment interactions and fails to expose the individual to situations that can provide evidence that contradicts negative self-beliefs.

Even if the depressed person does encounter situations that contradict negative appraisals and beliefs, these may not be translated into stable changes in thinking style. The CAS may prevent the metacognitive operations necessary for transforming beliefs and knowledge. Two broad modes of processing are distinguished in the S-REF model: (1) *object mode* and (2) *metacognitive mode.* Object mode is the default mode of processing in which negative thoughts are accepted as accurate representations of reality and coping responses are mobilized to deal with the negative situation. In metacognitive mode, however, negative thoughts are seen merely as events in the mind that should be treated as objects, and efforts should be devoted to changing one's relationship with them. An example will serve to illustrate the difference in modes. Following criticism from the boss an individual thinks: "I'm a failure." In object mode, this thought is taken as a fact and guided by metacognitive beliefs, ruminative coping responses are geared toward dealing with the problem. This consists of ruminating on past examples of failures and criticism to try and work out the reason for the problem and ways to overcome it. In contrast, in metacognitive mode the individual views his or her thought as an event in the mind, the validity of which may be questioned. Responses are aimed at discontinuing further ruminative appraisals and efforts are mobilized to prevent criticism in the future. The development and strengthening of a metacognitive mode of processing that can be flexibly called is seen as a factor underlying therapeutic change processes.

CLINICAL IMPLICATIONS OF THE S-REF MODEL

The metacognitive approach has implications for the treatment of depression. It implies that it will be beneficial to treat rumination directly, not merely by targeting the content of rumination and reality testing that content but by modifying the underlying metacognitions that contribute to the ruminative style of coping.

The S-REF model views rumination as the online processing style that is linked to the individual's metacognitive schemas (plans and beliefs) that are represented separately from the more general dysfunctional beliefs of schema theory. In schema theory (Beck, 1976) general (non-metacognitive) beliefs about the self (e.g., "I'm a failure" or "I'm worthless") are not directly responsible for the style of processing and coping adopted by the individual. However, in the S-REF model transient mood disturbances associated with negative appraisals of life events are amplified into clinically depressive experiences because the individual employs ruminative coping, threat monitoring, and behaviours that lock him or her into an emotion-focused, self-perpetuating negative coping state. Over time, with repeated activation of such a configuration, there is an increased likelihood that the individual will develop a more stable negative response pattern. Thus, treatment should consist of attempts to bring rumination under executive control, challenge maladaptive metacognitive beliefs, and provide greater flexibility in modes of processing.

An implication of the metacognitive approach is that relapse following the treatment of depression may be linked to the readiness with which individuals activate the CAS in future encounters with loss and personal challenges. Because the metacognitive schema is seen as separate from the general negative self-schema and standard CBT (cognitive–behavioural therapy) focuses on modifying the content of non-metacognitive schemas, vulnerability to relapse is likely to remain high. Direct modification of the ruminative style and the metacognitions that underlie the propensity with which it is activated could confer greater resistance to relapse.

AN OUTLINE OF METACOGNITIVE THERAPY FOR DEPRESSIVE RUMINATION

Assessment of the nature of rumination, its base rate, and the metacognitive beliefs supporting it is the first objective of treatment. Analysis of the nature of rumination consists of exploring its controllability and the goals of the activity. The frequency and duration of rumination should be monitored using diary or rating scale methods, and this can be augmented by the use of standardized instruments, such as the Ruminative Responses Scale (RRS: Nolen-Hoeksema & Morrow, 1991) and the Rumination on Sadness Scale (RSS: Conway, Csank, Holm, & Blake, 2000).

Metacognitive beliefs about rumination may be assessed on a self-report level by the Negative Beliefs about Rumination Scale (NBRS: Papageorgiou, Wells, & Meina, in preparation) and the Positive Beliefs about Rumination Scale (PBRS: Papageorgiou & Wells, 2001a). Interview methods of reviewing the advantages and disadvantages of rumination are also useful for determining metacognitive beliefs about the activity. Hypothetical questions, such as asking about the consequences of not being able to ruminate about a situation, can also be used to elicit beliefs about the activity.

Initially, patients believe that rumination is uncontrollable and in some cases are not motivated to fully interrupt the activity, at least initially. Several factors contribute to reluctance to or apparent difficulty in controlling rumination. First, patients may have a lack of awareness of the pervasiveness of the activity, and so they have to be trained in recognizing the onset of rumination. Second, patients believe erroneously that rumination is uncontrollable, and this erroneous belief should be corrected through verbal and behavioural reattribution strategies. Third, there is reluctance to fully abandon rumination as the activity is seen as advantageous. More specifically, positive beliefs about rumination as an effective strategy support its continued usage. Fourth, some patients may actually lack the flexible metacognitive control necessary to disengage processing resources from self-focused ruminative activity. This diminished executive control may be apparent or real and is likely to be influenced by erroneous beliefs concerning the uncontrollability of thoughts, impediments to executive control resulting from deepening depression, and/or the development of strong reflexive initiation of rumination due to repeated practice. In each case, strategies are available that deal with these issues and target the metacognitive mechanisms involved in the problem.

The goals of metacognitive therapy are: (1) socialize patients to the idea that ruminative styles of thinking and attentional monitoring for threat (e.g., excessive self-focus on symptoms) are a source of the problem; (2a) facilitate abandonment of ruminative thinking and (2b) enhance flexible control over cognition; (3) challenge metacognitive beliefs; and (4) modify negative beliefs about emotion that contribute to self-preoccupation and fear of relapse.

SPECIFIC TECHNIQUES

(1) SOCIALIZATION

In the first treatment session, the therapist reviews with the patient the thinking and behavioural style that is associated with the triggering of depression and its persistence. The aim is to show how ruminative thinking is activated during depression. This can be achieved in several ways. Discussion can focus on how thinking style changed as a consequence of becoming depressed. When there have been multiple episodes of depression the therapist asks about each episode to raise awareness of consistency in the change in thinking styles that occurs across episodes. The therapist also enquires whether behaviour has changed following the onset of depression. This process is used to show how reductions in behavioural activity do not lead to the effective resolution of problems and contributes to an inward-focused, negative and repetitive thinking style.

The intermeshed role of behaviour and rumination in maintaining depression is illustrated by asking about times that the patient has felt depressed and identifying occasions when low levels of activity or rumination have been interrupted by the necessity to engage in behaviours, or by external distractors. Such episodes are used as examples of how ruminative thinking leads to persistence of mood disturbances. Behavioural experiments involving activity scheduling can be used to illustrate how by engaging in activities that displace rumination mood can improve. Thus, activity scheduling is used to help interrupt rumination early on and as a socialization technique to illustrate the role of rumination and behaviour in problem maintenance.

(2a) FACILITATING ABANDONMENT OF RUMINATION

Advantages/Disadvantages analysis

Next, the therapist helps the patient identify problems associated with rumination and the beliefs about rumination that can make it difficult to relinquish the activity. The advantages/disadvantages analysis provides a means of showing how rumination is problematic, of eliciting positive and negative metacognitive beliefs about rumination, and of strengthening the perceived disadvantages so that the patient is more motivated to interrupt the activity. The advantages are identified by asking the question: "what are the benefits or advantages of rumination and dwelling on the way you feel when you are depressed?" Once the advantages have been identified (which relate closely to positive metacognitive beliefs), the therapist continues to elicit the disadvantages ("what are the disadvantages or problems associated with rumination and dwelling on your feelings?"). In each case, it is often helpful to provide examples of the advantages or disadvantages, and scales such as the NBRS and PBRS can be used to provide a basis for exploring specific beliefs. The therapist can potentiate this process by asking about specific advantages, which includes: rumination helps to find ways to deal with problems; helps to cope with depression in the future; helps the patient discover what is wrong with him or her; prevents the patient forgetting important people or events; means that he or she is in touch with reality; and guards against the dangers of thinking too positively (i.e., prevents disappointment, does not tempt fate, etc.). The therapist should especially assist the patient in identifying disadvantages of rumination since these should be reinforced so that they outweigh the advantages. Examples of disadvantages include: rumination is biased and focuses predominantly on negatives; does not often lead to solutions; intensifies negative mood; focuses the individual on wider negative aspects of the self; interferes with focusing on outward tasks; makes the individual appear withdrawn; can have a negative social impact on others; is not productive; impairs concentration; interferes with sleep; and increases a negative outlook.

(2b) ENHANCING FLEXIBLE CONTROL OVER COGNITION

Attention training

As the S-REF model predicts that patients have difficulty interrupting self-focused rumination, training in executive control skills that directly disrupt the CAS is likely to be beneficial. Attention training treatment (ATT: Wells, 1990) was developed for this purpose, as a means of counteracting adhesive self-focus and preoccupation and of enhancing flexible control over processing. The procedure consists of attending flexibly to a range of different external auditory stimuli. The procedure has three phases—selective attention, rapid attention switching, and divided attention—which together constitute a single session of ATT practice.

ATT as a sole treatment strategy appears to be effective in single-case evaluations across a range of disorders (Papageorgiou & Wells, 1998, 2000; Wells, 1990; Wells, White, & Carter, 1997), and in a recent controlled trial ATT was shown to be an effective treatment for hypochondriasis (Cavanagh & Franklin, 2001). Cavanagh and Franklin (2001) showed that ATT reduced the amount of time individuals with hypochondriasis spent worrying about their health. In a preliminary study of four patients with recurrent major depression treated with ATT, Papageorgiou and Wells (2000) showed that the procedure appeared effective in reducing depression and anxiety and gains were maintained at six-month follow-up after withdrawal of the procedure. Moreover, the results showed that ATT reduced rumination and metacognitive beliefs in the patients treated.

The therapist introduces ATT in the treatment of depression using a rationale that emphasizes interrupting unhelpful thinking styles. A typical rationale is as follows:

We have seen how when you become depressed your thinking pattern changes and you begin to focus your attention on your feelings and brood on negative thoughts concerning past, present, or future. This form of preoccupation or rumination is a problem because it keeps depression going. You might be able to see this effect when you think about your own experiences. When you dwell on your negative thoughts and feelings this does not help you to feel better, and when something happens to interrupt this activity you can feel better even if only for a short time. Unfortunately, it probably isn't long before your rumination starts again. In order to make more stable improvements in your mood it is helpful to practise a technique called attention training, which will allow you to reduce your unhelpful patterns of rumination and attention that keep your problem going.

Once the rationale for ATT has been presented, the therapist checks for credibility by asking: "How helpful do you think this procedure will be in overcoming your problems. Please give me a rating on a scale from 0 (not at all helpful) to 100 (very helpful)." When ratings of credibility are low (below 50), the therapist examines the reasons for such judgements and attempts are made to enhance credibility by providing further socialization examples. This can include brief in-session practice of controlled negative rumination and self-focusing to illustrate their effects on the intensification of symptoms, and/or external focusing procedures (e.g., describing in detail a picture on the wall) to illustrate how reducing self-attention and rumination can temporarily alleviate symptoms.

After presentation of the rationale, the therapist asks the patient to make a self-focused attention intensity rating on a scale ranging from -3 (entirely externally focused) to $+3$ (entirely self-focused). Self-focus ratings are administered before and after in-session practice of ATT. Failure to produce a reduction in self-focus following the procedure should be explored. It is typical for reductions of at least 2 points to be achieved following the first session of ATT practice.

Basic ATT instructions

The therapist presents ATT in a slow, consistent tone of voice. At least three competing sounds are introduced into the consulting room (one is the therapist's voice, others can include tapping on a book, a clock, a radio, etc.). Four to six further sounds should exist outside the practice room. If naturally occurring sounds cannot be heard, an alternative strategy is to introduce further sounds into the practice room, locating each at different positions and at different volume levels. The selective attention and attention switching phases of the procedure take up most of a 15-minute ATT practice period, with approximately 3 minutes devoted to divided attention.

Therapist dialogue

An example of the dialogue used by the therapist is given below. This is adapted from Wells (2000, pp. 145–146):

> I am going to ask you to focus your gaze on a dot marked on the wall. I will sit slightly behind you so that I do not interfere with your fixed gaze. I would like you to keep your eyes open throughout the procedure. You may experience distracting thoughts or feelings during the exercise, but that doesn't matter—the aim is to practise focusing your attention in a particular way.
>
> I will begin by asking you to focus on the sound of my voice (S1). Pay close attention to that sound, for no other sound matters. Try to give all of your attention to the sound of my voice. Ignore all the other sounds around you. Focus only on the sound of my voice. No other sound matters, focus only on the sound of my voice.
>
> Now focus on the tapping sound (S2), the sound that I make as I tap on the table. Focus only on the tapping sound, no other sound matters [Pause]. Closely monitor the tapping sound [Pause]. If your attention begins to stray or is captured by any other sounds, refocus all of your attention on this one sound [Pause]. Give all of your attention to that sound [Pause]. Focus on the tapping sound and monitor that sound closely, filter out all of the competing sounds, for they are not significant [Pause]. Continue to monitor the tapping sound [Pause]. Focus all of your attention on that sound. Try not to be distracted [Pause].
>
> Now focus on the sound of (S3) (e.g., a clock in the room), focus all of your attention on that sound [Pause]. The other sounds do not matter. Focus on that sound, paying close attention to it and not allowing yourself to be distracted [Pause]. This is the most important sound and no other sounds matter [Pause]. Give all of your attention to that sound. If your attention strays, refocus on the sound of (S3) [Pause]. Focus only on the sound of (S3). Give all of your attention to that sound [Pause]. Continue to monitor that sound closely, pay full attention to that sound [Pause]. Try not to be distracted.

The above instructions should be repeated for the other sounds (S4–S6 and S9), and after this stage the therapist moves on to stage 2:

Now that you have identified and focused on different sounds I would like you to rapidly shift your attention between the different sounds as I call them out [Pause]. First focus on the tapping sound, no other sound matters, give all of your attention to that sound [Pause]. Now switch your attention and focus on the sound of (S8) outside of this room, focus only on that sound, no other sound matters [Pause]. Now switch your attention to the tapping sound [Pause]. Refocus on the sound of (S3) [Pause]. Now back to the tapping sound (S1). Now the sound in the far distance (S9). Focus back again on the sound of (S3) [Pause] (continue with S4 ... S8 ... S3 ..., etc.).

Following this phase the exercise concludes with a brief divided attention instruction:

Finally, expand your attention, make it as broad and deep as possible and try to absorb all of the sounds simultaneously. Try to focus on and be aware of all of the sounds both within and outside of this room at the same time [Pause]. Mentally count the number of sounds that you can hear at the same time [Pause]. Try to hear all of the sounds simultaneously. Count the number of sounds you can hear at the same time.

This concludes the exercise.

How many sounds were you aware of at the same time?

Homework practice of ATT

Patients are asked to practise ATT twice a day for homework. Each practice session should be for a period of 10–15 minutes. To facilitate compliance the therapist reviews with the patient the types of auditory stimuli that will be acquired/used in the home practice environment. Tape versions of ATT have been used in some interventions, but care must be exercised that task difficulty is not compromised due to repeated practice and familiarity with the same tape. It is important that the exercise loads attention when practised.

A small number of patients treat ATT practice as a nuisance that needs to be completed quickly so that they can return to the activity of rumination. Normally, a ban on rumination is introduced in conjunction with ATT practice (see p. 268).

Attentional coping responses can interfere with the effects of ATT. Some patients report frequent self-monitoring for mood and symptom changes as a means of judging their psychological status. It is useful to use the analogy of a "mood radar" when exploring whether the patient has developed unhelpful self-monitoring strategies as a means of making decisions. For example, a patient reported checking his level of alertness first thing in the morning and several times during the day to determine if he was functioning normally or whether his depression was going to become a problem. Checking of this kind should be identified as problematic and as part of the rumination response, it can then be dealt with in the same way as rumination (see p. 268).

Prescribed rumination ban

In conjunction with ATT, patients are asked to notice early signs of rumination and ban the activity. Rumination is broadly described as dwelling on your feelings and negative thoughts in an attempt to understand or cope with negative situations and feelings.

Motivation to attempt the rumination ban is usually increased following the advantages/disadvantages analysis previously undertaken. Obstacles to the effective implementation of this strategy are typically: (1) failure by the patient to be aware of the pervasiveness of rumination; (2) the erroneous metacognitive belief that the activity is uncontrollable (e.g., "I can't stop it" or "I have no control"); and (3) metacognitive belief in the need to continue rumination because it is helpful.

The therapist should repeatedly identify patient examples of rumination in the first few sessions in order to raise patient awareness of the breadth of the activity so that the rumination ban can be applied to most episodes. Self-monitoring can be used to enhance awareness of rumination by asking the patient to make a note in a daily diary each time a period of rumination is identified. This is used as the signal to ban continued engagement in the activity. The process of banning rumination becomes easier with practice and is facilitated by the training of executive control skills provided by ATT.

Detached mindfulness

A further strategy that facilitates the interruption of ruminative thinking is "detached mindfulness" (Wells & Matthews, 1994, 1996). Rather than using conscious processing to challenge the validity of individual negative thoughts, the S-REF model advocates the development of a detachment from thoughts that trigger rumination while maintaining objective awareness of them. Essentially, this is a strategy of learning not to actively engage with thoughts, but to maintain awareness of them as a passive observer. According to Wells and Matthews (1994), "The initial aim of treatment based on the S-REF model is the development by the patient of a higher meta-cognitive awareness at which level the individual is encouraged to 'reside', rather than residing at the level of negative S-REF appraisals themselves. This type of detached processing may be useful in preventing full S-REF activation and may be developed as an adaptive coping strategy which facilitates cognitive control and disconfirmatory processing" (p. 306).

Detached mindfulness is introduced by asking patients if they have ever watched their thoughts in a detached way without controlling them or engaging in further analytical thinking. A number of strategies can be used to illustrate the principle and provide the setting conditions for developing the ability. Prescriptive "mind wandering" can be introduced as a means of familiarizing oneself with this procedure. The therapist asks the patient to have a thought, such as the image of a tree, and to watch the tree without influencing it in any way. The patient is instructed that it is fine if their attention strays away from the tree, or if the image changes, and they should merely be aware of the changing content of their attention without influencing the nature of that content in any way. Passive free association effects are also useful as a means of illustrating a detached relationship with thoughts. The therapist reads out a series of words (e.g., apple, bicycle, chocolate) and asks the patient to allow his or her thoughts to roam freely in response. Once the concept of not engaging with thoughts is grasped, the patient is asked to disengage from negative thoughts that trigger rumination each time they occur. This can be facilitated by asking patients to use imagery exercises, such as hanging the negative thought on the tree and leaving it there rather than responding to it with continued rumination or unhelpful behaviours.

(3) MODIFYING NEGATIVE AND POSITIVE METACOGNITIVE BELIEFS

Negative metacognitive beliefs concern the uncontrollability of rumination and the consequences of affective symptoms. Erroneous beliefs about uncontrollability are tested with implementation of the rumination ban as discussed previously or with postponed rumination experiments. In the latter, patients are asked to notice rumination and to interrupt the activity and postpone the process until a specified time later in the day. At that time, they can choose to activate a brief (10-minute) rumination period. Many patients forget to use the specified rumination time, but even if they do use it the fact that they have been successful in interrupting the process is used as evidence of the controllability of the process.

Negative beliefs concerning the meaning of affective symptoms and rumination centre on themes of mental breakdown, ineffectiveness, inferiority, and vulnerability to psychological disorder (see Papageorgiou & Wells, 2001b). Such beliefs underlie a tendency to catastrophize minor symptom experiences and, for example, interpret them as a sign of relapse or of being vulnerable to psychological illness. In these instances, symptom experiences and changes in affect are normalized by the therapist and minisurveys can be used to demonstrate how other people also experience fluctuations in mood, energy levels, optimism, fatigue, and so on. The occurrence of symptoms can be reframed as an opportunity to practise alternative thinking strategies and an opportunity to refocus attention onto external activities and tasks rather than activating self-focused rumination.

Positive beliefs about rumination centre on the usefulness of the strategy as a means of coping, finding solutions, and understanding problems. To challenge these beliefs the therapist uses verbal reattribution strategies of questioning how long the patient has been ruminating to determine if solutions to the depression problem have been achieved. This is followed by exploring evidence

supporting the belief that rumination is an effective strategy, and then exploring the counterevidence. The co-occurrence of both positive and negative
beliefs about rumination should be highlighted and the patient asked how
rumination can both assist in coping and yet also be problematic (e.g., intensify
depression). The strengthening of dissonance increases the likelihood that one
of the beliefs will be weakened.

Often patients equate the act of ruminating with planning ahead, which they
view as a helpful strategy. However, these mental activities are not equivalent
and the therapist should help the patient to differentiate between them.
Planning ahead involves thinking about the future and what one will do.
Rumination, in contrast, involves focusing on one's negative feelings and
performance. Once this distinction is made, the therapist can ask how dwelling
on negative feelings and negative aspects of the self can be an effective means of
planning a positive future. The necessity to engage in forward planning should
itself be challenged as this may lead to the persistence of ruminative styles of
thinking even if the content is changed.

A variant of the worry modulation experiment used to modify positive
beliefs about worry in GAD (Wells, 1997) can be used to challenge positive
beliefs about rumination. Here the patient is asked to deliberately ruminate for
a specified period of time (e.g., 10 minutes) at the beginning of a day and the
following day to ban such activity. The effect of rumination on coping
and daily outcomes can be compared, to show that rumination confers no
advantage.

(4) DECATASTROPHIZING EMOTION

Emotional disorder is associated with negative beliefs about emotion. Panic
and agoraphobia are linked to fear of fear (e.g., Goldstein & Chambless, 1978)
and negative misinterpretation of emotional symptoms (Clark, 1986). Teasdale
(1983) suggests that depression may be compounded by depression about
depression, and generalized anxiety is associated with worry about worry
(Wells, 1994). In the S-REF model, these responses have been termed
"secondary emotion" (Wells & Matthews, 1994, 1996), but might be more
accurately labelled as metaemotional responses. In the context of depression,
individuals have negative beliefs about the consequences of rumination and
depression that pertain to themes of danger. Thus, fear of depression and fear
of recurrence is a factor that contributes to emotional disturbance. Depression-
prone individuals are often oversensitive to early signs and symptoms of
depression and tend to interpret such symptoms negatively as a sign of
relapse or ongoing "abnormality." Such a tendency can reactivate patterns
of rumination, self-monitoring, and avoidance as maladaptive coping strategies, thereby feeding the CAS and contributing to depression and anxiety.

To reduce the risk of this response pattern, metacognitive treatment assesses
the presence of metaemotion and focuses on challenging negative beliefs about

symptom experiences. The first step is to normalize the experience of mood fluctuations. The therapist helps the patient to see how most people experience fluctuations in negative symptoms (energy levels, motivation, fatigue, sadness, pessimism) on a daily basis and how the patient is attributing special and unnecessary significance to these experiences. Teaching reasoning errors, such as catastrophizing (e.g., "I feel tired therefore I must be getting ill"), provides a shorthand means for patients to distance themselves from negative thoughts of this kind. The aim is to enable patients to experience different feelings without the need to act on them or evaluate them in any detailed way. The latter type of response is a pathway into rumination.

SUMMARY AND CONCLUSIONS

This chapter has briefly described some of the basic treatment implications of a metacognitive approach to rumination and depression. The S-REF model implies that it is possible and desirable to treat directly the CAS that contributes to emotional disturbance. A significant component of this syndrome is the tendency to engage in ruminative thoughts and self-focused processing as coping strategies. The direct treatment of the ruminative style provides an adjunct to traditional cognitive therapy approaches, which focus chiefly on modifying the content of non-metacognitive thoughts and beliefs. Metacognitive treatment may be effective as a sole treatment of depression in some cases. There is some very preliminary evidence that ATT alone may be effective as a treatment (Papageorgiou & Wells, 2000). However, the approach remains to be tested on larger and more heterogeneous samples of patients in controlled evaluations.

The treatment approach described briefly here is based on implications of the S-REF model and treatment techniques developed for the treatment of chronic worry in GAD (Wells, 1997). From this perspective, treatment consists of disengaging the ruminative thinking style as a prerequisite to standard cognitive therapy or as a predominant treatment strategy, and the modification of metacognitive beliefs. A range of metacognitive therapy strategies was described. Executive control and interruption of the CAS is facilitated by training in executive control by ATT, and the modification of metacognitive beliefs focuses on positive and negative beliefs about rumination and unhelpful cognitions underlying metaemotional responses.

Metacognitive therapy is one of a number of recent approaches to psychological treatment that emphasize modifying the control of thinking and the relationship that the individual has with thought processes. Teasdale et al. (2000) have evaluated the positive impact of mindfulness meditation techniques as a relapse prevention approach in depression. Here also, patients are instructed to experience thoughts as events in the mind, but focusing attention on breathing is used as an anchor to bring attention back to present moment experiences. This is of course a metacognitive-focused approach, the effects of which can be interpreted within the S-REF model. From this perspective, mindfulness meditation is training patients to interrupt ruminative processing and is strengthening the metacognitive skill of distancing oneself from thoughts. That is, it enables patients to shift from an object mode to a meta-mode of processing. This is likely to be a valuable skill that can be used to interrupt or attenuate the effects of depressive thinking patterns. However, if the metacognitive beliefs that drive ruminative styles remain unmodified, this may still contribute a significant risk factor. We suggest the development of a broad-based metacognitive treatment of rumination in depression. Guided by the S-REF analysis, this approach consists of training in flexible executive control, establishing a metacognitive mode, detached mindfulness, suspending rumination, modifying erroneous positive and negative beliefs about rumination, and challenging negative beliefs about emotions.

REFERENCES

Beck, A. T. (1967). *Depression: Clinical, Experimental, and Theoretical Aspects*. New York: Harper & Row.

Beck, A. T. (1976). *Cognitive Therapy and the Emotional Disorders*. New York: International Universities Press.

Beck, A. T., Rush, A. J., Shaw, B. F., & Emery, G. (1979). *Cognitive Therapy of Depression*. New York: Guilford Press.

Cavanagh, M. J. & Franklin, J. (2001). Attention training and hypochondriasis: Preliminary results of a controlled treatment trial. Paper presented at the *World Congress of Behavioral and Cognitive Therapies, Vancouver*.

Clark, D. M. (1986). A cognitive model of panic. *Behaviour Research and Therapy*, **24**, 461–470.

Conway, M., Csank, P. A. R., Holm, S. L., & Blake, C. K. (2000). On assessing individual differences in rumination on sadness. *Journal of Personality Assessment*, **75**, 404–425.

Goldstein, A. J. & Chambless, D. L. (1978). A re-analysis of agoraphobia. *Behavior Therapy*, **9**, 47–59.

Nolen-Hoeksema, S. (1991). Responses to depression and their effects on the duration of depressive episodes. *Journal of Abnormal Psychology*, **100**, 569–582.

Nolen-Hoeksema, S. & Morrow, J. (1991). A prospective study of depression and posttraumatic stress symptoms after a natural disaster: The 1989 Loma Prieta earthquake. *Journal of Personality and Social Psychology*, **61**, 115–121.

Papageorgiou, C. & Wells, A. (1998). Effects of attention training on hypochondriasis: A brief case series. *Psychological Medicine*, **28**, 193–200.

Papageorgiou, C. & Wells, A. (1999a). Process and metacognitive dimensions of depressive and anxious thoughts and relationships with emotional intensity. *Clinical Psychology and Psychotherapy*, **6**, 156–162.

Papageorgiou, C. & Wells, A. (1999b). Dimensions of depressive rumination and anxious worry: A comparative study. Paper presented at the *33rd Annual Convention of the Association for Advancement of Behavior Therapy*, Toronto.

Papageorgiou, C. & Wells, A. (2000). Treatment of recurrent major depression with attention training. *Cognitive and Behavioral Practice*, **7**, 407–413.

Papageorgiou, C. & Wells, A. (2001a). Positive beliefs about depressive rumination: Development and preliminary validation of a self-report scale. *Behavior Therapy*, **32**, 13–26.

Papageorgiou, C. & Wells, A. (2001b). Metacognitive beliefs about rumination in recurrent major depression. *Cognitive and Behavioral Practice*, **8**, 160–164.

Papageorgiou, C. & Wells, A. (2003). An empirical test of a clinical metacognitive model of rumination and depression. *Cognitive Therapy and Research*, **27**, 261–273.

Papageorgiou, C., Wells, A., & Meina, L. J. *Development and preliminary validation of the Negative Beliefs about Rumination Scale*. Manuscript in preparation.

Roth, A. & Fonagy, P. (1996). *What Works for Whom? A Critical Review of Psychotherapy Research*. New York: Guilford Press.

Teasdale, J. (1983). Negative thinking in depression: Cause, effect or reciprocal relationship? *Advances in Behaviour Research and Therapy*, **5**, 3–25.

Teasdale, J. D. & Barnard, P. J. (1993). *Affect, Cognition and Change: Re-modelling Depressive Thought*. Hove, UK: Lawrence Erlbaum.

Teasdale, J. D., Segal, Z. V., Williams, J. M. G., Ridgeway, V. A., Soulsby, J. M., & Lau, M. A. (2000). Prevention of relapse/recurrence in major depression by mindfulness-based cognitive therapy. *Journal of Consulting and Clinical Psychology*, **68**, 615–623.

Wells, A. (1990). Panic disorder in association with relaxation induced anxiety: An attentional training approach to treatment. *Behavior Therapy*, **21**, 273–280.

Wells, A. (1994). Attention and the control of worry. In: G. C. L. Davey & F. Tallis (eds), *Worrying: Perspectives on Theory, Assessment, and Treatment*. Chichester, UK: John Wiley & Sons.

Wells, A. (1997). *Cognitive Therapy of Anxiety Disorders: A Practice Manual and Conceptual Guide*. Chichester, UK: John Wiley & Sons.

Wells, A. (1999). A metacognitive model and therapy for generalised anxiety disorder. *Clinical Psychology and Psychotherapy*, **6**, 86–95.

Wells, A. (2000). *Emotional Disorders and Metacognition: Innovative Cognitive Therapy*. Chichester, UK: John Wiley & Sons.

Wells, A. & Matthews, G. (1994). *Attention and Emotion: A Clinical Perspective*. Hove, UK: Lawrence Erlbaum.

Wells, A. & Matthews, G. (1996). Modelling cognition in emotional disorders: The S-REF model. *Behaviour Research and Therapy*, **34**, 881–888.

Wells, A. & Papageorgiou, C. (1995). Worry and the incubation of intrusive images following stress. *Behaviour Research and Therapy*, **33**, 579–583.

Wells, A., White, J., & Carter, K. (1997). Attention training effects on anxiety and beliefs in panic and social phobia. *Clinical Psychology and Psychotherapy*, **4**, 226–232.

Index